KEY to LOCATIONS

NORTH ISLAND

1. Sweetwater
2. Motukiore
3. Waitangi
4. Ngararatuna
5. Whangarei
6. Marsden Bay
7. Puhoi
8. Waitemata City
9. Auckland
10. Taumaranui
11. Turangi
12. Jerusalem
13. Patea
14. Kai Iwi Beach
15. Wanganui
16. Takapau
17. Kopua
18. Foxton
19. Akitio
20. Lower Hutt
21. Petone
22. Wellington

SOUTH ISLAND

1. Rocklands
2. Christchurch
3. Ripa or Ripapa Island
4. Mt Somers
5. Mt Cook
6. Ball Glacier
7. Tasman Glacier
8. Mt Aspiring
9. Matukituki Valley
10. Wanaka & Mt Iron
11. Luggate
12. Queenstown
13. Dunstan now Clyde
14. Alexandra
15. Blackstone Hill
16. Naseby
17. Maniatoto Plains
18. Hyde
19. Rock and Pillar Range
20. Paerau
21. Middlemarch
22. Gladbrook
23. Shannon
24. Mosgiel
25. Dunedin
26. Purakanui
27. Scroggs Hill
28. Brighton
29. Gabriel's Gully
30. Kaitangata
31. Winton
32. Virginia Lake

SOUTH ISLAND

W9-BGN-904

Cape Farewell

Tasman Bay

Golden Bay

NELSON

Wairau R
Blenheim

Westport
Cape Foulwind

Buller R

Grey R
Greymouth
Taramakau R
Hokitika

Hurunui R

Waimakareri R

BANKS PENINSULA

3764
Rakaia R
Ashburton
Ashburton R

L Tekapo

L Pukaki

TIMARU

L Ohau
L Benmore

2885

L Hawea

Waitaki R

L Wanaka

Oamaru

L Wakatipu

L Te Anau

Taieri R

Otago Peninsula

Oreti R

Manapouri

Balclutha
Clutha R

Waiau R

INVERCARGILL

FOVEAUX STRAIT

STEWART ISLAND

SOUTH PACIFIC OCEAN

SOUTHERN ALPS

FIORDLAND

100 KILOMETRES

The Life of
James K. Baxter

The Life of
James K. Baxter

Frank McKay

Auckland
OXFORD UNIVERSITY PRESS
Melbourne   Oxford   New York

Oxford University Press

Oxford University Press, Walton Street, Oxford OX2 6DP

OXFORD   NEW YORK   TORONTO
DELHI   BOMBAY   CALCUTTA   MADRAS   KARACHI
PETALING JAYA   SINGAPORE   HONG KONG   TOKYO
NAIROBI   DAR ES SALAAM   CAPE TOWN
MELBOURNE   AUCKLAND
and associated companies in
BERLIN   IBADAN

Oxford is a trade mark of Oxford University Press

First published 1990
© Oxford University Press 1990

Published with the assistance of the Literary Fund
of the Queen Elizabeth II Arts Council
of New Zealand

ISBN 0 19 558134 2

Cover illustrated and designed by Hilary Ravenscroft
Photoset in Bembo by Rennies Illustrations Ltd.,
Printed by Griffin Press Limited, South Australia
Published by Oxford University Press
1A Matai Road, Greenlane, Auckland 3, New Zealand

Contents

To Dorothy and Michael
with gratitude

Preface

James Keir Baxter was born at 97 Elm Row, Dunedin on 29 June 1926 of parents from very different backgrounds. His mother, Millicent Baxter, was the highly educated daughter of a foundation professor at Canterbury University College. His father, Archibald Baxter, from the tiny village of Brighton in Otago, made a modest living as a small farmer, rabbiter, and labourer. A good deal is known about both parents from their autobiographies. Millicent published her *Memoirs* and Archibald, a personal testament, *We Will Not Cease*. Both books illumine some of the most important formative influences on their famous son, though his mother's view, which is in danger of becoming the official version, needs considerable modification. James would die at the tragically early age of forty-six.

In so short a life he became New Zealand's most widely read and admired poet, a pioneering dramatist, a literary critic, an essayist, and a lecturer with genuine charisma. His reputation rests securely on his writings, above all on the poetry which he wrote so prolifically. But beyond that, more than any other New Zealand writer, he became a national figure. A social prophet; a conspicuous irritant to established society (an academic critic called him 'a hairy nuisance'); a cult leader and founder of a commune at Jerusalem; he was known by name to most New Zealanders through the press, the radio, and television.

All his life he was a man on the move. In cities like Dunedin, Christchurch, Wellington, and Auckland, he became as familiar as a landmark. In his final years his long hair and beard, his bare feet and general messianic appearance could not fail to attract attention. Once, a woman entering St Mary of the Angels church in Wellington tripped in the semi-gloom over a shaggy, roughly dressed man kneeling at the back of the church. It was James K. Baxter. Many people tripped over him at various phases of his life, but very few knew him over the whole course of it.

Today Baxter remains a challenging figure, complicated by contradictions and frequently misrepresented. He has always generated a certain amount of hostility, compounded at times by frustration at the inability to dislodge him from the central position he occupies in our literature. His colourful story must be told in its entirety if he is to be understood. He told part of it himself in an autobiographical essay, 'Notes on the Education of a New Zealand Poet', in many articles and lectures, and in his poetry. But there is a big difference between what poetry and biography make of the material. And biography can be written in a variety of ways. At the beginning of his great biography of Samuel Johnson, Boswell thought that one of the merits of his work would be 'literary and characteristical anecdotes . . . told with authenticity and in a lively manner'.

Baxter's life must be placed in a historical context. He belongs to an era that included the last troubled years of the Depression, the Second World War, the Vietnam war, the optimistic decade of the sixties, and the first years of the disillusionment that followed. It is a fascinating period in our history and James K. Baxter played a prominent part in many of the events that made it significant.

I first met James K. Baxter in 1950. Gradually, over the years, I came to know him well and to feel a great affection for him. Occasionally I took notes of our conversations, but it never occurred to me that one day I would write his biography. Although I had a camera, I never photographed him. It was not until about 1978 that with the warm encouragement of his widow and literary executor, Jacquie Baxter, I embarked on the present work. Since then it has never been far from my consciousness. I worked on it on and off as I collected material. In recent years it became a major activity as relative freedom from other demanding matters allowed more sustained application.

I have drawn on my own memories of Baxter and on our correspondence. I have tried to read everything written by so prolific a writer, published and unpublished. Dozens of his letters were also made available to me. For almost every phase of his life I have been fortunate to find people who were closely associated with him. With some of them I had many conversations and the dialogue at times carried on over several years. I have tried to make sense of this abundant and occasionally conflicting testimony. The aim was always to present the life as lived despite all the shifting lights that play over such an undertaking. I have also tried to steer between the twin perils of hagiography and the more fashionable inverse hagiography. This biography is very much Baxter as his contemporaries saw him. That cannot be done again for the simple reason that some of the key witnesses, with whom I spent many hours, are now dead. Since place was so important in Baxter's writings, I have traced his footsteps from Brighton to Sibford to Jerusalem. Some places I visited a number of times.

There is a time for a moratorium on biographies of Baxter and there will be a time for a new biography. The materials I collected, some of which would otherwise have been lost, will be deposited in a New Zealand library.

Like all biographies, indeed like all lives, this biography is provisional. It is what one person made of what he was given. I have added my own perceptions since that is part of a biographer's task, but I have tried to give due weight to Baxter's viewpoint whether or not it was different from my own. Throughout I have offered the elements that seem to me necessary in any judgement a reader chooses to make.

There is only a select bibliography. A full one has already been compiled with great thoroughness by John Weir and Barbara Lyons; John Thomson will provide an updated bibliography in the forthcoming *The Oxford History of New Zealand Literature*.

When this biography was well advanced, Bridget Williams of the Port Nicholson Press brought out W. H. Oliver's *James K. Baxter: A Portrait*. The heavy culling of the Baxter photographic archive necessary for their work has meant some duplication here. It has still been possible to find some photos that will be new to most readers. It was an unexpected stroke of luck to find one of Baxter the day he died.

Frank McKay
Wellington 1989

Acknowledgements

The Dominican writer, Vincent McNabb, once dedicated a book 'To all the friends God gave me, everyone I have ever known'. In a country where everyone seems to have known Baxter, my acknowledgements need to be almost as comprehensive. The impossibility of writing this biography without the help of many people is clear in every chapter.

My first debt is to the Baxter family, above all Jacquie Baxter, the poet's widow and literary executor, who has encouraged and supported me from the beginning. I should also like to acknowledge the help of the late Millicent Baxter, from the time I first met her in the seventies, until shortly before her death. I thank Hilary and John Baxter, James's brother Terence, Mrs Lenore Baxter, Jack Baxter, and the Baxter clan at Brighton. With them I associate their lifelong friend, Mrs Patricia Lawson, and her husband, Don, and I thank them for their hospitality at Trevose and for the immense help they gave me on my visits to Brighton and in our correspondence.

One of my greatest debts is to James Bertram, with his unrivalled knowledge of the history of our literature and his meticulous scholarship. Without John Weir's major contribution to Baxter scholarship, his edition of the poems, his bibliography, his papers, my task would have been even more protracted. I have greatly benefited from John's conversation over the years.

I am indebted, too, to my students in the New Zealand Literature courses at Victoria, and to my university colleagues, especially Roger Robinson, Don McKenzie, Vincent O'Sullivan, Harry Orsman, David Norton, Bill Manhire, John Thomson and Jo McComish. With them I associate Lauris Edmond and Gill Boddy.

The leave committee at Victoria granted me four months special leave to draft the early chapters, and the Research Committee helped with funds for travel and research assistants. I thank especially Margot Schwass, who brought order to a great mass of material; Damien Wikins, who once put on the trail could find almost anything, and Sophie Tomlinson. The Computer Studies Department was unfailingly helpful. Through them, and with Irene Pearson, David Norton, and Harry Orsman as patient mentors, the computer became a dependable ally. To John Casey and his colleagues in the Photography Department, to whom nothing was a trouble, I am also grateful.

I should like to thank the Librarians of the chief New Zealand libraries, the Hocken (especially Michael Hitchings and his successor, Jonathan Miller), the National Archives (especially Ray Grover), the Alexander Turnbull Library (especially J. E. Traue), Victoria University (especially the Beaglehole librarian, Katherine Coleridge), Canterbury University (especially Robin Irwin), the Department of Education and the Wellington Teachers' College for the use of their records. To the Hocken Library, holder of the main Baxter archive and of the Brasch Papers, I owe a special debt for their courtesy and prompt attention. Of the many research libraries I have used in both hemispheres, the Hocken offered the speediest service.

To the Provincial of the Society of Mary for deferring another appointment until this task was completed, to Fathers Jim Beban, Brian O'Connell, John Walls, and George McHardy, who all knew Baxter well, I am also grateful.

Among the many people who helped me in a variety of ways, interviews, the loan of letters, unpublished poems and photographs, or simply with their memories, I wish to thank especially the following, some of whom made substantial contributions: Grace Adams, Fleur Adcock, Peter Alcock, Antony Alpers, John Ashton, C. E. Beeby, Peter Bland, Jenny Blumsky, John Brown, Alistair Campbell, Anna Campion, Richard Campion, Patric Carey, Rosalie Carey, Bob Craigie, Ian Cross, Allen Curnow, John Davidson, Father Al Dianni, Terry Dibble, Basil Dowling, Colin Durning, Jim Erikson, Roderick Finlayson, Phyllis Gant, John Garrett, Noel Ginn, I. A. Gordon, Bob Gormack, Cherry Hankin, Margaret Hargreave, Kathy Hohoia, George Hughes, Hank Huber, Kevin Ireland, Lawrence Jones, Marion Jones, Bernard Kearns, Doreen Kendall, Rodney Kennedy, Michael King, Judi Lowry, Vanya Lowry, Doris Lusk, Patrick Macaskill, Johann McComish, Fraser McDonald, Howard McNaughton, Keith Maslen, Frances Mulrennan, Rae Munro, Barrie Naylor, Els Noordhof, Philip O'Sullivan, Betty O'Dowd, Cliff O'Malley, Richard Oliver, W. H. Oliver, Bill Pearson, Hugh Price, Jeff Pratley, Hilary Proctor, Harold Pugmire, Kenneth Quinn, Bill Renwick, Keith Russell, Stuart Sellar, Anthony Scott, Margaret Scott, Gill Shadbolt, Maurice Shadbolt, Tim Shadbolt, Keith Sinclair, Hal Smith, Kendrick Smithyman, C. K. Stead, Margaret Still, John Summers, Peter Sutton, Jean Tuwhare, Gwen Wales, J. C. Ward, and Ray Watchman.

Finally I wish to thank my editors at Oxford, the chief editor Anne French, for many helpful criticisms and suggestions, to Frances Whistler of the Clarendon Press during her brief stay in New Zealand, and to Jill Rawnsley who brought reinforcements at the eleventh hour.

While I was engaged on this biography, some of those who gave indispensable help have died. I think of Denis Glover, Louis Johnson, Lawrence Baigent, Michael Illingworth, W. J. Scott, Anton Vogt, Leo

Bensemann, Colin McCahon, Evelyn Page, Winston Rhodes, and Pamela Tomlinson.

I thank the literary executor of the Frank Sargeson estate for permission to quote from a Sargeson letter, and Price Milburn for the use of a complete Jerusalem sonnet and one other from *Autumn Testament*. I am also grateful to Heinemann Publishers to be able to adapt material from my preface to *James K. Baxter as Critic*, and to the editors of *Landfall* for a revised version of part of an article I first published in its pages. To anyone else who helped me in any way, and who has inadvertently been omitted, I am also grateful.

I
The Ancestral Face

The strings' excitement, the applauding drum
Are but the initiating ceremony
That out of cloud the ancestral face may come.[1]

Baxter was more conscious than most of his ancestors. Even six years before his death he claimed that the only tribe he knew was that of his 'first ancestors in this country, those Gaelic-speaking men and women, descending with their bullock drays and baggage to cross the mouth of what is now the Brighton river; near to sunset, when the black and red of the sky intimated a new thing, a radical loss and a radical beginning; and the earth lay before them, for that one moment of history, as a primitive and sacred Bride, unentered and unexploited.'[2] And he felt the need to celebrate them:

> I would glorify
> Innumerable men in whose breasts my heart once beat,
> Is beating.
>
> (CP 31)*

The forebears who most stirred his imagination came from the Scottish Highlands, which became for him a place of disinheritance and a spiritual home. His lifelong preoccupation with origins is largely explained by the influence of a family for whom Scottish history was part of themselves, and the ancestors living presences. Since the ancestors came from a far country, outside Baxter's own historical time, they readily assumed for this most mythopoeic of our poets the dimensions of myth. And he had the strength of imagination to acclimatize the myth in his own region of Otago: 'The peasant clansmen of the Western Highlands of Scotland became the clannish farmers of Otago. The Otago hills and sea-coast are not unlike the hills and sea coast of Argyllshire. So I have been fortunate enough to find the ready-made myth of longbearded Gaelic-speaking giants distilling whisky among the flax from time immemorial. The ancestral face is very familiar to me.'[3]

John Baxter came from Rothesay on the isle of Bute in the Western Highlands. With his wife, Mary, sons Archibald and John, and daughter Isabel, he left Greenock aboard the s. s. *Lady Egidia* bound for Dunedin, in New Zealand, in the autumn of 1860. There were enough Gaelic speakers on board to warrant special religious services in Gaelic. A quarter of the

*All page references are to Baxter's *Collected Poems*, John Weir (ed.), OUP, 1980.

1

passengers were under the age of twelve and they found the conditions rigorous. Thirty children and two adults died.[4] After a journey of 104 days to the Otago heads the s. s. *Lady Egidia* arrived at Port Chalmers on 28 January 1861 bringing the largest number of passengers ever landed in Otago by one vessel.[5]

The Otago settlement had been established by the Free Church of Scotland to reflect the Church's Presbyterian doctrine, policy and discipline. It was a patriarchal Christianity whose reliance on the Word of God was symbolized by the Bible's taking pride of place in every kirk. Its ministers sternly admonished their congregations on the importance of family unity and righteous behaviour. The hearers for their part felt confident they were among the elect. And they were encouraged by the assurance that Jehovah rewarded the virtuous even in this life. For most of the early Scottish settlers the Kirk 'provided moral leadership, a link with their ancestral homeland, and a social centre'.[6]

One reason for John Baxter's decision to look for a new and better life in New Zealand was the prospect of steady employment and good wages. His hopes were fulfilled. The year before John arrived, the ever-sanguine James Macandrew, Superintendent of the Province, had announced an ambitious, labour-intensive programme of public works, which included as a high priority the building of roads. Baxter and his fellow immigrants also had the good fortune to arrive in time for the harvest in a province that was already exporting wheat to the profitable Sydney market. The new immigrants could begin work as soon as they were ready. Their first decade in New Zealand was one of extraordinary prosperity, following the discovery of rich and extensive goldfields in Otago. Dunedin became the first city in the colony industrially and commercially, and the population of Otago grew to almost six times what it had been at the start of the decade.

Along the beach at Dunedin were the 'immigrant barracks', roughly constructed communal shelters, offering new arrivals room for their belongings and bare necessities such as sleeping berths and an open fireplace, but no cooking facilities.[7] John Baxter and his family stayed there briefly before moving to Brighton, a small seaside village between Dunedin and the mouth of the Taieri River. Its first settlers, who lived in wattle and daub houses, were mainly farmers, whose needs were met by the support services which were quickly provided. There was plenty of seasonal work and the area had good resources of coal and flax. John, a solidly built man with great physical strength, was a tireless worker. Not having enough capital to buy a farm, he worked as a cook. He had a keen eye for business, and at a time when there were no proper roads in the interior of the province and supplies had to be brought in by pack-horse, he set up a very profitable cook-house at Harper's Pass to cater for the diggers pouring into the West Coast goldfields in the Taramakau Valley. He had prospected without success at Gabriel's Gully, where some had made a fortune, but he struck gold at the Dunstan. Bringing it out safely could be hazardous as many a miner in late nineteenth century Otago found. Once on the way back to Dunedin, John was following the old Dunstan track from Paerau to Rocklands. In the distance, where the road climbs over the Rock and Pillar range, he noticed some men come out from behind a large rock. When he reached the spot they surrounded him, but with the aid of a certain natural shrewdness and a gift with words, he spun the tale of a miner down on his luck and got free. He always believed the men were Burgess, Kelly, Sullivan, and Levy, a notorious gang of cut-throats, who murdered travellers for their gold.

Always on the look-out for an opportunity to improve his situation, John Baxter returned to Glasgow with the money he had made, and invested in a line of small steamers on the Clyde. But the pull of his adopted country was too strong, and he returned to New Zealand. He was considered an austere man, but he amused himself by playing the bagpipes and by going swimming. Until the year before his death at the age of ninety-four, he took a daily dip at a little bay just north of the big rock at Brighton, even during the intense cold of an Otago winter. This was one manifestation of his obsession with personal cleanliness. Little is known of his wife and their life together. The silences in the early family history reflect the patriarchal society to which Baxter's ancestors belonged.

On his maternal grandfather's side, James K. Baxter was descended from another family of Highlanders, the McColls of Appin. They were from Ballachulish on the shores of Loch Leven, in the West Highlands. Baxter's great-grandfather, Archibald McColl from Glencrevan, with his wife Margaret, five sons and two daughters, arrived in Port Chalmers 'Intermediate and Steerage' on the *Alpine*, 12 September 1859. They had left Glasgow on 10 June and arrived after a passage of ninety-three days. Eight children died on the voyage but Mary McColl, who was still a baby, survived. She was to become James K. Baxter's grandmother. In his diary of the voyage, Alexander Campbell Begg, one of the two chaplains on board, recorded that a number of the Highlanders could not speak English and that family worship was conducted among them in Gaelic.[8] Archibald McColl presumably attended because his mother tongue was Gaelic and he never learnt to speak English perfectly.

The family emigrated for the usual economic reasons, and because one of the sons, John, was a keen poacher and a violent man. It was feared he might shoot a keeper and be transported or hanged. In Brighton the ex-poacher took up farming, and those who knew him well could not believe that so gentle a man deserved his earlier reputation. In James's mythology he became the type of an ancestor deprived of legitimate hunting rights by the

3

land-owning gentry. He symbolized the difference between legality and morality.

After the usual spell in the immigrant barracks, the McColls moved to Brighton. Archibald, called 'Little Archie', began to farm a property at Creamery Road. He became well known as a friendly and kindly Highlander. He wrote home to his brother Duncan in Ballachulish: 'Come out, you'll enjoy it.' Duncan replied, 'Our father is eighty-six and I can't leave him.' The old man, another Duncan, said to his son: 'Don't be absurd. I'll come out with you.' The pair arrived a year after Archibald and his family and Duncan bought a farm above the Black Bridge at Brighton. His house at the top of the hill was the one James had in mind in his poem 'The Fallen House'. Duncan's father was so sturdy and self-reliant that everyone thought he would live to be a hundred. But at the age of ninety-four he fell into a ditch and lay there for several hours before he was found. He caught a chill and died. During his six years in Brighton his family and friends came to appreciate this hard-drinking old man.

While Archibald and his brother Duncan farmed, the other McColl men worked on the public works schemes launched by the Provincial Government. One of their jobs was helping with the construction of the road that runs from Dunedin to Taieri. They brought with them unusually rich family traditions. Their forebears had fought in the battle of Culloden in 1746 when the Highland clans, making their last stand against the English forces under the Duke of Cumberland, were butchered by superior artillery. Among the relics of the battle preserved in Edinburgh Castle is a flag of the Stewarts of Appin 'stained with blood, much of it McColl, as eight of them were killed defending it'.[9]

The McColls were also involved in one of the most famous of Scottish murder mysteries. In 1752 Colin Campbell of Glenure, nicknamed 'The Red Fox', came to their region as King's factor. His task was to evict from their estates tenants such as the McColls who had been involved in the Jacobite rising six years earlier. On the property of Charles Stewart of Ardshiel he was shot in the back as he rode through a wood. A certain Alan Breck Stewart agreed to take the blame for the murder and fled to France. But the authorities, greatly incensed by the death of Campbell, were determined to have a victim. They arrested James Stewart and hanged him as an accessory. From the time of his arrest his friends and relatives have maintained his innocence.[10]

Another traditional family tale, which as we shall see could have been re-enacted in Millicent's case, was that of an English baronet, Mark Learmond, who married a commoner, Janet McIntosh, and was disinherited by his family. He died shortly afterwards, but the McColls believed that had he lived he would have been re-instated in his baronetcy. His daughter from the marriage, Margaret Learmond, married Archibald McColl and emigrated to New Zealand with him in 1859.

Her daughter, who was called Mary McColl, married John Baxter before the registrar at Winton on 16 August 1879. John was twenty-eight, Mary twenty-one. She had been born at Glencrevan, Ballachulish in 1858. When John, who was a heavy drinker, asked for her hand in marriage her father replied: 'I've got nothing against you personally but the drink. If you can keep off that for six months you can marry my daughter'. That was beyond him, but they were married all the same. After their marriage and the birth of their first son John, they returned to Brighton. Their second son, Archibald McColl Learmond Baxter, the poet's father, was born on 13 December 1881 in his McColl grandfather's sod cottage on the Creamery Road farm. Six more children followed, five sons: Mark, Hugh, Billie, Donald, Sandy, and one daughter, Margaret.

Mary Baxter was a short woman, very feminine in appearance, and sturdy. She needed to be to cope with an erratic husband and the bringing up of eight children with little money coming in. He expected her to make the decisions and to run the house. She could turn her hand to anything and did more than her share of the domestic chores.

> She carried a sack of oatmeal on her back
> Twelve miles, walking beside the breakers
> From the town to her own gate.
> (CP 389-90)

The distance from Dunedin to Brighton is twelve miles. In such a demanding life, Mary could not have had much leisure, yet she found time for taxidermy, and for painting in both oils and water-colours. She was a warm person with a great sense of fun and was equal to most occasions. Once, when she was bringing a large white ferret from Brighton to Middlemarch by train, it escaped from its cardboard box on the luggage rack. She calmly lifted it down and held it on her lap for the rest of the journey, explaining to her alarmed fellow passengers that it was harmless. When she was met at the station she handed it over to a nephew, saying, 'Hold that, will you.'

From all accounts her husband John was an excellent worker, but he could not hold down a job. He took casual employment on farms, or seasonal work such as shearing. Money ran through his fingers like water, and the fact that such a hardened drinker often became intoxicated after only a few drinks suggests that he may have been an alcoholic. When he was drinking in the house with his bagpipe-playing friends, Mary did not hesitate to throw them out when she felt she had stood enough.

John Baxter was a religious man. In the Taieri and in the Otago block generally the Presbyterians had come to dominate social and moral life. When Plymouth Brethren preachers came to Brighton, however, John Baxter was independent enough to go to hear them. He was powerfully affected and gave up alcohol for thirteen years. His drinking was cured but not his extravagance, and the large family lived from hand to mouth. Since his father could not provide adequately for the family, Archie had to leave school before his teens and go out to work. Within a few years he was able to buy his mother a cow, which proved a real godsend for a big family. From then on they had plenty of milk and cream, and Mary was able to make her own butter.

As the sons grew into manhood they went up country for casual labour on farms, or rabbiting, shearing, or fencing. Such was Archie's skill with horses that he eventually became head ploughman at Sir John Robert's station at Gladbrook, some sixty miles from Brighton. The sons always returned to their parents' home, which became a popular meeting-place for the Baxter and McColl families. Mary was especially skilful at entertaining and keeping the clan united. The daughter Margaret, known in the family as Peggy, was very attractive and a great help to her mother. They all led strenuous lives. Mary's brother, called Black Archie, was the

> One who drove a bullock team
> In the gold-rush on an upland track.
> (CP 31)

to bring in supplies for the miners.

John always felt that if only he had a farm of his own his problems would be solved. As it happened some of the big runs were being cut up into small parcels of land, and lotteries were held to distribute them equitably. Archie was in luck and won a small farm on Scroggs Hill, Brighton. He stocked it with cattle, sheep, pigs, and fowls and handed it over to his father. But John was no manager and he was soon heavily in debt. Bailiffs were brought in and the whole place sold up. When the news reached Archie in Central Otago, where he was rabbiting, he came home, bought back the farm and began to work it himself. It soon became profitable; of the whole Baxter-McColl clan, Archie was the most successful with money.

John Baxter would hit the drink hard and then go on the wagon for a few months, or even for that long stretch of thirteen years. As an aid to keep him on the straight and narrow he used to hang biblical texts around his house. He was an emotional man. Once when he was being driven back to Brighton, the sight of Saddle Hill, near where he had once had his farm, caused him to burst into tears. He greatly enjoyed playing the bagpipes and he liked nothing better than going to a country show, where there would be piping competitions. On the actual day he became so excited that he would rise about three or four in the morning to get himself ready. As a man, he was absolutely fearless. Archie observed that his father was the last person in the world to be silenced by threats.

With the characteristic longevity of these early Baxters, John lived until he was eighty-six. His wife Mary had died in 1932, seven years earlier. While he was lying in hospital, unconscious after heavy strokes, his eldest sons Jack and Archie visited him. Just before his father died, Archie believed he saw lying down beside him on the bed the figure of an old man, whom he took to be one of the ancestors come to help his father over.[11]

Though their economic circumstances meant that the Baxter brothers had had to go to work before they had received much formal education, they were all fond of reading. With his excellent memory, Archie enlivened many a gathering of family and friends with poetry delivered in a soft West Highlands voice. He also wrote the verse which is preserved in the Hocken Library. It is mostly derivative nature verse in the Romantic tradition, but there are also a couple of lively squibs, one directed at the Taieri County Council. There was also an unpublished novel which survives in the Hocken.[12] It is a fictionalized account of Archie's Gaelic-speaking ancestors after their arrival from Scotland, and of their adventures at Gabriel's Gully, the Dunstan, and the early Brighton region. In his perception of life Archie was undoubtedly a poet and visionary. Today it is often implied that the distinguishing mark of a poet is technical accomplishment. Vision is correspondingly undervalued. Archie, in his life, is an instance of the observable phenomenon that many people who do not write verse, or who do not write it well, have deeper and more delicate insights into what is central in human experience than many of those who do.

Archie was respected in the district as a quietly dignified man, who never expressed violent opinions. He was a natural leader, whose counsel was greatly valued inside and outside the family. But he had been born into a barbarous age and would fall its victim. In 1914 the First World War broke out, and his views brought him into direct confrontation with the Government. Already he had come to believe that all war was 'wrong, futile and destructive alike to victor and vanquished'.[13] His belief was not based on religious grounds, since he belonged to no organized religion, but on his own understanding of Christ's command, 'Thou shalt love thy neighbour as thyself.'

In New Zealand the National Council of Women, established in 1897, had spoken out against the Boer War, and in 1902 a Peace and Humanity Society was founded in Wellington. Though it soon folded, it was the forerunner of many peace groups, religious and political. In 1909 the Defence Act introduced compulsory military training for young men between the ages of fourteen and twenty. They formed the reserve force called the Territorials. There was considerable opposition in many parts of the country, and the Draft Resisters' Union and the Peace Council were formed. Many defaulters were sentenced for refusing to serve. The most celebrated were the thirteen young men between the ages of sixteen and twenty-two who were imprisoned on Ripa Island in Lyttelton harbour, and became known as 'the martyrs of Ripa'. The anti-militarists received strong support from the growing Labour Party with its ideal of universal brotherhood and peace.[14] But in Brighton Archie felt he stood alone, both in his pacifism and in the 'socialism which I looked on as a necessary part of it'.[15] For socialists war was merely a device for capitalists to secure economic advantages. War was not caused by the workers, nor was it in their interest. Since this was true in all countries, workers should not fight against each other. It is surprising that Archie should have felt isolated as a socialist in the years before the First World War. There was certainly plenty of socialism in Dunedin by then. Perhaps he meant his own brand of it, the kind represented by the Scottish Labour leader Keir Hardie, whom he greatly admired. Gradually his family came to share Archie's pacifist views and the notoriety they inevitably attracted.

In 1915 a national register of men of military age was drawn up and about one-sixth said they would not undertake war service either at home or abroad. Compulsory military service was mooted but there was widespread opposition. A Conscription Bill (called the Military Service Bill) was none the less passed on 31 May 1916 with little resistance apart from the protest made by the Labour Party. Several of its leaders, among them Bob Semple, Paddy Webb, M.P. for Grey, and Peter Fraser, the secretary of the Anti-Conscription Conference, were to be imprisoned in the course of the war.

Archie's farm had prospered, but he realized that with the coming of conscription he would no longer be allowed to work it. In the summer of 1916-1917 he took a hard season's shearing so as to leave behind as large a cheque as possible. Though he knew he would be arrested sooner or later, he expected to have a few weeks to settle his affairs. But he was hardly back in his parents' house, and had not even received official notice to serve in the army, when the local constable called under the pretence of discussing some farm statistics. He and Archie had walked a short distance from the house when another policeman sprang out from behind a hedge and Archie was arrested. He was not even allowed to get his personal things. His two brothers were apprehended in the same clumsy fashion. With Archie's arrest a long process of cruelty, bullying, and the flouting of ordinary human decencies began.

After being confined in the Terrace jail, Wellington, alongside common criminals, Archie, Jack and Sandy Baxter, together with eleven other conscientious objectors, were forcibly placed aboard the *Waitemata*, which sailed from Wellington for England on 14 July 1917.[17] Two others who were shanghaied were the prominent pacifists L. J. Kirwan and Mark Briggs. There were huge meetings in Wellington and other centres, and demands for the return of the deported men, but all was to no avail.[18] Meantime at home in Brighton, even people who had once been sympathetic to Archie's opinions now adopted the prevailing view that the war was justified. Those who shared Archie's convictions were often insulted. Peggy especially suffered from the general opprobrium. Young men who had once vied with each other to go out with her now wanted nothing to do with the sister of 'those terrible Baxters'. At this period she contracted the tuberculosis which was later to kill her.

As the *Waitemata* approached the Cape of Good Hope there was an outbreak of measles, so the passengers had to be put ashore to recuperate. They were allowed considerable freedom and made many excursions into the surrounding countryside. They were warned, however, that 'to be on friendly terms with a coloured person, or even to be seen talking with one in a social way, is a crime'.[19] Archie observed that such an approach could not prove right in the long run.

Towards the end of November 1917, after about three and a half months in South Africa, the conscientious objectors were put on board the *Llanstephan Castle*, which reached Plymouth on Boxing Day. From there Archie was taken to Sling Camp on the Salisbury Plains, and about a month later shipped over to Boulogne in north-west France. From the time of his first arrest in New Zealand he was forcibly dressed in military uniform several times, but each time he tore it off, and he continued to refuse war service of any kind. For the voyage to France he was saddled with a full pack and handcuffed so that he could not throw it off.[20] After a brief stay in Boulogne, Archie was taken to Etaples, which was then the British base camp, and then to the village of Abeele in Belgium. From then on, that is from about the end of January 1918 until August of that year, Archie's life was a virtual hell. British officers thought they could break his resolution by sentencing him to twenty-eight days of No. 1 Field Punishment. Before the ordeal the examining doctor said: 'I don't believe you are fit, but I am going to pass you as fit. You're such a damned fool you deserve all you get.'[21]

Archie was taken to a compound known as Mud Farm, not far from Dikkebus in Belgium, where a lieutenant of the Imperial Army and a New Zealand sergeant were in charge. Mark Briggs and L. J. Kirwan were already there and had undergone No. 1 Field Punishment. Kirwan had just been sentenced to another dose of twenty-eight days. By the roadside, in full view of passers-by, there were two willow poles six to eight inches in diameter and twice the height of a man. One of them was inclined out of perpendicular. Archie was placed against it, then tied by the ankles, knees and wrists. Of his torturer he said:

> He was an expert at the job, and he knew how to pull and strain at the ropes till they cut into the flesh and completely stopped the circulation. When I was taken off my hands were always black with congested blood. My hands were taken round behind the pole, tied together and pulled well up it, straining and cramping the muscles and forcing them into an unnatural position . . . The slope of the post brought me into a hanging position, causing a large part of my weight to come on my arms, and I could get no proper grip with my feet on the ground, as it was worn away round the pole and my toes were consequently much lower than my heels. I was strained so tightly up against the post that I was unable to move body or limbs a fraction of an inch.[22]

However, No. 1 Field Punishment failed to break Archie's spirit. He was sent up to the front lines of the Ypres front and stationed by an ammunition dump, which had come within range of German artillery:

> I was in the midst of a storm of spouting, belching mud and fire and flying fragments. The shells seemed to strike everywhere but where I was. I believe that if I had moved at all from where I stood, I should inevitably have been killed. If the dump had gone up I should have gone with it. I stood and waited for what seemed inevitable death.[23]

Finding Archie indomitable, the authorities confined him to a mental hospital at Boulogne. Their concern was not for his sanity. It was a fresh tactic to put pressure on him. As the story was later told by Millicent, the family firmly believed that what the New Zealand Government really wanted was to have him shot. If that was the intention, the plan was thwarted by a British doctor, who certified Archie as insane. It appears he did it to protect him, and it may well have been the only way. Certainly there is no evidence to suggest Archie was ever mentally deranged.

After a few months in another hospital, this time in England, Archie was sent back to New Zealand. He travelled from Southampton to Le Havre and from there took a train to Marseilles, where he embarked for New Zealand on the *Marama*. By September 1918 he was back in Wellington. His case was well known through the press, particularly the New Zealand *Truth*, which in those days was sympathetic towards pacifists. To silence public criticism, the Minister of Defence, Sir James Allen, issued a document in October containing 'official statements' on the fourteen who had been deported to Europe during the war. After referring disparagingly to Archie he stated: 'The medical examiners found that he was not insane, and that he did not require to be sent to a hospital, mental or otherwise.'[24]

The war was over, but the Government had no intention of allowing the conscientious objectors, who had defied them, to return quietly to civilian life. A bill was passed in December depriving all military defaulters of civil rights, including the franchise, for ten years from the passing of the Act. It was argued: 'If a man would not fight for his country he should not be accorded citizen rights in that country.'[25] On 24 October 1918, a month after Archie's return to New Zealand, an article appeared in *The Otago Daily Times:* 'Baxter Case: The Conscientious Objector'. It was a statement issued by Sir James Allen to discredit Archie. Allen took little account of the indignities to which Archie had been subjected. He blandly asserted that arrogance was the cause of all his misfortunes because he had consistently opposed his will to that of the community. Archie's reply, which reached only a handful of readers, was published in *Armageddon or Calvary:* ' . . . it was not a matter of setting up my will against the public, but of doing what I believed to be right, and refusing to do what I believed to be wrong; and I do not believe that all that was done to me and to other Objectors was done by the will of the community.'[26] In the euphoria that followed the war the dominant mood of the public was jingoistic and assertive. The new heroes were the returning troops whose courage and sacrifice had won victory. With his brand of heroism dismissed, and his case misrepresented in the most widely read newspaper in his area, Archie could never again enjoy the standing he once had in Brighton. The contemptuous attitude of the Minister of Defence had indicated what was to be thought of him.

In the years following the war the Baxter brothers still met a good deal of hostility. Besides their unacceptable views on war, they were politically non-conformist. They could be described as radical independents. And their attitude to work was different from that of most others in Brighton. They were seasonal workers who took on hard manual work like shearing, fencing, and road-making. They were happy-go-lucky and not interested in acquiring property or amassing wealth. When the fish were running in Brighton Bay they would down tools smartly, and if a chance to go hunting came up, off they went. After a stint of work like shearing, they would take several weeks or even months off until the money ran out. In reaction to the example of their hard-drinking father, they were wary of alcohol. But, with the exception of Archie, they all liked a flutter on the horses and were keen racegoers. None of them went to church and Archie was a humanist, though he believed in God and prayed to Him.

The Baxters' free-flowing mode of living protected them from constant niggling and by-passed the preference the law gave to servicemen in most of the best jobs. After their years of confinement they greatly relished the open country of Central Otago and the freedom to please themselves. Since, unlike almost everyone else, they had not settled down to steady jobs with all their constraints, they provoked some resentment and were labelled a shiftless breed. Archie, of course, belied the allegation. He was quite capable of settling down if he wished, as his earlier record in farming showed. But he had to make up for the lost years of the war and build up badly needed capital. Rabbiting in Otago offered quick returns.

On his father's side, James K. Baxter's immediate antecedents were pioneering stock, who took their chance by migrating to the uncertain world of the Otago settlement. Without economic, social, or educational advantages, they established themselves by dint of hard physical labour. But the ancestors on his mother's side, the Macmillan Browns, could hardly have been more different. Prosperous, well-heeled and conventionally educated, they were much less colourful. Their branch of the Macmillans had been a prophesying clan whose chief burden had been woe to the Campbells, a powerful rival clan who had driven them from their ancestral lands. But that was long ago. Baxter's Macmillan Brown great-grandfather was a sea-captain and merchant who owned his ship. Often he was away for long periods trading in the South Seas, China, or the West Coast of America. His return was an event in the family since he brought home great jars of tamarind and ginger, baskets of dried litchi and persimmons from China, candied seaweed from Japan, bird of paradise feathers, and carved ivory.

The shipmaster had several children, one of whom, John Macmillan Brown, has an important place in this biography. He was born at Irvine in Ayrshire in 1846.[27] Young John's early life was strongly affected by the evangelical tradition of his Calvinist family. His first ambition was to become a Presbyterian preacher and that was what his early companions expected he would be. Just as he was about to enter university, his father, who was not insured, lost his ship and cargo in Belfast Lough. Financial support from his parents was now out of the question. John would have to make his way by intelligence and industry. He went off to Edinburgh University and supported himself by giving private lessons.

Thomas Carlyle, the idiosyncratic Victorian moralist and historian, had just been elected Lord Rector by the vote of the students. He was then an old man whose books were well known and Macmillan Brown, who was steeped in his teachings, idolized him. Carlyle's inaugural address was a memorable occasion, not because of what he said, since only those in the first few rows could hear him, but because of his aura of Victorian sage. Macmillan Brown remembered seeing three of the greatest scientists of the day during the lecture, Louis Pasteur, Thomas Huxley, and John Tyndall. When the address was over, Macmillan Brown, with other students, followed Carlyle down the street applauding him. He remembered too the disappointing farewell address of William Ewart Gladstone, the English statesman who was Carlyle's predecessor as Rector.

In 1865 Macmillan Brown returned to Glasgow University and in 1869 was awarded First Class Honours in Mental Science, which comprised philosophy and psychology. He also won the coveted Snell Exhibition for Classics and Philosophy which allowed him to go on to Balliol College, Oxford, for five years. He went up in 1869 and soon became the friend and protégé of Benjamin Jowett, who was elected Master of the College in 1870. Jowett's lodgings became one of the most celebrated of Victorian salons and Macmillan Brown was often invited there. There he met poets like Matthew Arnold and Algernon Swinburne, as well as titled nonentities. One of his disappointments was to have been out of Oxford the night George Eliot visited, since she was 'the literary person of the age that I should have most desired to meet, so great an impression had her novels made upon me.'[28] By the time he left Oxford, Macmillan Brown had met or listened to some of the most eminent of the Victorians. During this period his earlier religious beliefs faded. He became a rationalist and lost faith in an afterlife. Ill health prevented him from finishing his course, but he had acquired some powerful patrons. Ahead of him lay a distinguished academic career.

In New Zealand the founding fathers of the Canterbury Settlement planned a university 'as nearly similar as possible to Colleges in Oxford and Cambridge'. In 1873 the Provincial Government decided to act, and the following year the first professor arrived from England to take up the chair of chemistry in the yet unbuilt college. Chemistry was chosen as the first chair in the hope that the new professor would make a major contribution in the application of science to agriculture, so important to the province. Governments then and now like universities to be useful. Professor Bickerton's inaugural lecture was printed in the *Lyttelton Times*, filling three columns in a paper of four pages.[29] It is not surprising that the early professors in the new university formed an elevated notion of their importance.

When the Chair of Classics and English at the newly constituted Canterbury University College came up in 1874, the committee of appointment included Jowett, and Macmillan Brown's former Classics Professor at Edinburgh. Macmillan Brown was appointed. Hardly had he arrived in Christchurch when he received a letter from the mother of a fifteen-year-old girl asking if he intended to admit women students to his classes. He replied cautiously: 'That is not a matter for me but for the University of New Zealand. But bring your daughter to see me.' The girl was Helen Connon. Born in Melbourne in 1860, she had come to New Zealand at the age of five. All her early teachers, one of whom was the future Chief Justice of New Zealand, Sir Robert Stout, had remarked on her precocity. She made an immediate impression on the young professor, and after completing some preliminary studies was duly enrolled as the first woman student at Canterbury College, matriculating in 1876. Three years later, when she was nineteen, they became engaged.

Macmillan Brown quickly became celebrated as a lecturer, drawing large classes in days when student fees went to the professor. The fees from Classics alone had become almost equal to his fixed salary of six hundred pounds, so his financial position improved rapidly. But he was overworked, and could not cope with the growing number of students. In 1880 Classics became a separate department with its own professor, who was an Englishman. His emphasis was on style and elegance, and he disapproved of his blunt, hard-driving predecessor, who was a Scot into the bargain. The two became lifelong enemies. Macmillan Brown had relinquished Classics, but he retained English, History, and Political Economy, a wide enough empire for any antipodean Colossus to straddle.

In 1881 Helen Connon took First Class Honours in Latin and English, and became the first woman to graduate with Honours from a British University. The same year, before the Students' Dialectic Society, she had supported the motion that women should be given the opportunity for higher education. The motion was lost. She knew the arguments, but she was no feminist in the modern sense. Helen was remembered at Canterbury as a beautiful girl with a shapely figure. A contemporary described her in rather Yeatsian terms as 'a sedate beauty . . . touched with the spirit of ancient Greece.'

In 1882, at the age of twenty-three, she became Principal of Christchurch Girls' High School. On his occasional visits to the school, Macmillan Brown admired her serenity and the easy control she exercised over her pupils. They seemed to worship her and she never needed to raise her voice. Her academic standards were high. She encouraged the girls to go on to university and they arrived well prepared. The curriculum and teaching methods she introduced made the school famous, and affected secondary education throughout the colony. The public began to look more favourably on the higher education of women.

After a seven year engagement, Helen Connon and Macmillan Brown were married in a simple ceremony in 1886. The delay was long because Helen felt obliged to help with the education of her two sisters, who were much younger. Then she was determined to make Christchurch Girls' the kind of place she wanted. Helen had been much sought after by other men and Macmillan Brown was delighted at succeeding against many rivals. Among their wedding presents was a mahogany desk from his students. The couple went to live in a fine house at Holmbank in Wairarapa Terrace. It was secluded and not far from Canterbury College. There was a spacious garden and a boat-house on the Avon. Helen's salary paid for most of the household expenses, allowing Macmillan Brown to put money by for investment so as to make their future financially secure.

Their first daughter, Millicent Amiel (Amiel after a nineteenth century French essayist they both admired), was born at Holmbank on 8 January 1888. A second pregnancy was aborted because the doctor considered Helen's life to be endangered.[30] The experience affected her health and her husband urged her to resign from Christchurch Girls', but she did not wish to do so. Macmillan Brown himself was being plagued by insomnia and severe headaches. For the sake of their health they decided to visit Europe in 1892. They stayed with Jowett in the Master's Lodge at Balliol, and Macmillan Brown noticed that his old mentor, a man rarely impressed by women, made more fuss of Helen than of himself. He even gave her his ticket to a prestigious Oxford lecture. Jowett strongly advised Helen to retain her position at Christchurch Girls'. However, partly for health reasons (like her husband, she had become a chronic insomniac) and partly to give more time to him and to her six-year-old daughter, she resigned in 1894.

She was married to a man whose life was consumed by his professional duties and who drove himself hard. He would put in a sixteen-hour day, even in vacations, for then he was busy examining University Entrance, Junior Scholarship, and Teacher's Certificate. He was a demanding teacher, who lived up to his own exacting standards. In these days of narrower specialization the range of his teaching appears astonishing. Yet when he marked the great piles of student essays, he corrected every fault, rewrote defective sentences and phrases, and after comparing each essay with the student's previous efforts, wrote a full criticism. Parts of the essays which he considered well written were read out in lectures and their authors named.

He disagreed with those who claimed that examinations develop only the memory, and argued that if they were properly conducted they trained people to organize their thoughts quickly, and invigorated their knowledge. On one occasion, he affirmed before the Senate of the University of New Zealand 'the fact, acknowledged by all teachers from Socrates downwards, that the heart and soul of teaching is examination, and that the most trustworthy test of teaching is the external examination.'[31] Macmillan Brown took his position as a university professor very seriously. He considered it his duty not only to stimulate the thought of his students but to influence their character.[32] And he mixed freely among them. He was undoubtedly autocratic, and despite his talk of stimulating thought, my impression is that he saw his role as that of dispensing undisputed knowledge rather than the discovery of truth through dialectic.

It is clear that he was devoted to his students and generous in promoting

15

their interests. Though he had the reputation of being tight-fisted, he would spend as much as half his salary on buying books that would be useful to them. He did not, however, give them the books to keep. After they were returned, he added them to his rapidly expanding private library. He encouraged his students to make money by selling copies of the notes taken in his lectures. They became widely used from Whangarei to Invercargill. In his *Memoirs*, Macmillan Brown said that Justice Alpers (father of the future biographer of Katherine Mansfield) and his partner W. H. Ward between them regularly made six hundred pounds a year in this way. When customers complained of the calligraphy of the scribes, Macmillan Brown commissioned Whitcombe and Tombs to publish the lectures. The quality of his teaching and the personal interest he took in his students account for their extraordinary success in the final examinations, conducted at that time from the United Kingdom. They won many scholarships and helped to build up a very high reputation for Canterbury University College. Macmillan Brown himself became well known abroad. In the course of his career he turned down two chairs, one at Melbourne University, and later one at Merton College, Oxford. Both times he told his backers that with his salary and the fees from students he stood to make more at Canterbury than the other universities were offering.

Besides his teaching duties, Macmillan Brown was prominent in the administration of the University of New Zealand. At the end of 1876 he had been appointed a Fellow of the Senate, and he kept on being elected by the Court of Convocation. In all he was to serve on the Senate for fifty-eight years.

Neither in his own *Memoirs* nor in the accounts we have of him is there much mention of recreation. He came to feel, none the less, that he needed a sea trip each year, either around the New Zealand coast or overseas. This son of a sea captain had inherited sea fever, and was an excellent sailor.

His daughter Millicent did not go to school until she was twelve, but was taught at home. Her reading was precocious. By the time she was seven she had read widely in fairy tales, both classical and Scandinavian, and was tackling what she called in her old age 'grown-up novels'. What they were we do not know, but they must surely have included *Silas Marner* and *Adam Bede*, which had made a deep impression on her father when he was young. Helen gave most of the tuition, though she received some help from her husband and from outside tutors. She tried to teach her daughter music, but finding that she was quite unmusical, gave up in irritation. Macmillan Brown's health had not improved, and his headaches and eye strain had become so severe that in 1895 he resigned from the chair of English, which he had held for sixteen years.

The following year the family again visited Europe. After their return a second daughter, Viola Helen Lockhart, was born on 16 November 1897. This time there were no complications, and both parents were grateful for the advice they had been given by a leading Edinburgh obstetrician. In 1900 the family once more set out for Europe. There was some talk of settling in England, but nothing came of it. When they were in Switzerland, Millicent, who was now twelve, was enrolled in the local High School at Montreux at the eastern end of Lake Geneva. She had to speak French throughout the day, so laying the foundation for that grasp of the language she kept all her life. She was there about six months. An assured child, she did not hesitate to challenge in class the teacher's exposition of Pacific history.

Towards the end of their time in Montreux, Helen had a miscarriage and became very ill. When she was sufficiently recovered, they returned to New Zealand after an absence of two years. But Helen's health never really picked up. She developed ulcers in the mouth, which she left untreated, perhaps fearing her husband's impatience with illness. During a family trip to the North Island the ulcers spread to her throat. She could hardly swallow and was taken to hospital. Her illness was diagnosed as diphtheria, although there was some doubt about its true nature. She died on 27 February 1903, at the age of forty-three, and was buried in Rotorua, where a broken column marks her grave. Millicent was then aged fifteen, Viola five.

Macmillan Brown was heartbroken. From all accounts Helen had inspired in him a deep and lasting affection, and she had been a good mother. She tolerated her children's faults, and with the commonsense of a school teacher had kept their problems in perspective – something her husband could not always manage.[33] But even with her children she maintained a formality associated with the Victorians. Millicent, in a rare moment of personal revelation, admitted that she had received little emotional warmth from her mother and regretted it.[34] In her *Memoirs* she would write: 'I had been very attached to my mother, not nearly so much to my father,'[35] and remarked that had her mother lived longer, their lives might have been different. In 1918 the Board of Canterbury College opened the first Women Students' Hall of Residence and called it Helen Connon Hall. Her name is also preserved in the Helen Macmillan Brown bursaries established by her husband.

With his wife's death, Macmillan Brown decided to take Millicent's education in hand. He coached her intensively for the New Zealand Junior Scholarship examination and also for the Sydney Senior. As a tutor he was not a success. He was demanding and irritable, and he overestimated his daughter's ability. She was intelligent but not brilliant, and she became very resentful. The work was beyond her and she failed both examinations. With no mother and a father who was a martinet, she was deprived at a crucial period in her development of the emotional warmth and encouragement adolescents need. Without doubt her early history accounts for that reserve in expressing affection, of which her son James would one day complain. With Viola, who was only a child, Macmillan Brown was different. In her he saw a beautiful little replica (his words) of his wife.[36] Every night he was home, over a period of ten years, he made up bedtime stories to tell her. She found them so good she told him to write them out so other children could enjoy them too. The sisters got on well, and there is no evidence that Millicent felt any jealousy.

Millicent attended Presbyterian Ladies' College in Croydon, Sydney, for one year in 1905, where she did better. The following year she went on to Sydney University to study Arts. It was chosen over Canterbury College because her father did not believe that his old adversary, the professor of Classics, would treat his daughter fairly. In her final year, 1908, she passed Latin III, German III, and French III. In her best subject, French, she was awarded Third Class Honours.

After Millicent had graduated BA from Sydney, her father put up the money to send her to Newnham College, Cambridge. In 1909 she enrolled in the French and Old French section of the Modern and Mediaeval Languages Tripos. Her tutor in French was the sister of the biographer, Lytton Strachey. An austere, reserved figure, she wore pince-nez and always signed herself J. P. Strachey. Her speciality was Old French, and though she stimulated a lively interest in her pupil, she could not persuade her to apply herself. Macmillan Brown had been hard up while he was at Oxford and he expected his daughter to be canny at Cambridge. She had to account for every penny. If she spoke in a letter of going somewhere in London by taxi he would write and ask 'Why didn't you go by tube?' And he was very conscious of how fortunate his daughter was to be getting an Oxbridge education. That was still a rare enough opportunity for women. In 1911 Millicent passed Part I of the Tripos and in 1912 Part II, with Second Class Honours in both divisions. She could not take a degree since it was not until 1921 that the University granted degrees to women. Her teachers were disappointed in her results and told her she was capable of a First. Either they were polite or unduly sanguine. Her previous record suggests a First was beyond her powers. She knew that her father would be disappointed, but she was not in the least put out, and simply said: 'I was born lazy'. In 1913 she went to Halle University in Germany to do a Ph.D. Halle was chosen because Old French was one of its special strengths. Her limited German proved too serious a handicap and after eighteen months she left without completing the degree.

She was 'brought back', as she put it, by her father to be his hostess at Holmbank, where there were many visitors. I have no impression, however, that his house was a meeting-place for artists and writers, nor any kind of salon. His preference was for academics. Millicent fulfilled the role of hostess without any panache. She was too insecure and never knew what to say. Her European education had strengthened her natural independence and she did not get on well with her father. They were too much alike and both were very strong-willed. But she and her sister Viola, who was now seventeen, became very close. Millicent's duties were light and she had plenty of time on her hands. She took on the task of cataloguing her father's vast library, and when she became bored read her way through whole sections. Biography especially fascinated her and became a lifelong passion. The more personal detail there was the better, and she disliked any bowdlerizing. For her the fine print best revealed the true life.[37] The attraction to biography highlighted one of her characteristics. She was much more interested in people than in ideas.

During Otago University's jubilee celebrations in February 1920, Professor Gilroy, the Professor of English, was reading the second lesson at the University service in Dunedin's First Church. Suddenly he collapsed and fell forward dead, carrying the lectern with him.[38] With a new session about to begin, the university had some difficulty in finding a replacement. Macmillan Brown, who was then Vice-Chancellor of the University of New Zealand, generously offered his services without emolument until a successor could be found. Millicent felt that the University Council did not really want a man of seventy-four, especially one with such a formidable reputation, but they were reluctant to turn him down. The students were less inhibited and gave him a rowdy reception. There was pandemonium as he climbed on to the rostrum for his first lecture. But the seasoned campaigner kept his good humour and gradually won them over. From then on he had complete control and was soon going full blast. The moderate south was astounded by his stamina. He lectured continuously all Saturday morning and appeared not to notice the students who left to prepare for the afternoon's rugby. His capacity for sustained eloquence was part of the legacy he left to his descendants.

At her father's insistence, Millicent had accompanied him to Dunedin. They lived in a boarding-house at St Kilda and Millicent had plenty of time on her hands. She continued to read widely and she learnt to type.[39] The move to Dunedin also gave her the chance to see a person she had wanted to meet for a long time.

II
The Colour of Identity

Here, where only the wind moves,
I and my crooked shadow
Bring with us briefly the colour of identity and death.
(CP 415)

On 5 March 1918 Archibald Baxter had written a letter 'from somewhere in France' to prepare his parents for what looked to be his certain death. A copy made by the New Zealand poet Blanche Baughan had been given to a friend of Millicent's, who showed it to her. It read:

> I have just time to send you this brief note. I am being sent up the lines tomorrow. I have not heard where Jack and Sandy are. As far as military service goes, I am of the same mind as ever. It is impossible for me to serve in the army. I would a thousand times rather be put to death, and I am sure that you all believe the stand I take is right. I have never told you since I left NZ of things I have passed through, for I know how it would hurt you. I only tell you now, so that, if anything happens to me, you will know. I have suffered to the limit of my endurance, but I will never in my sane senses surrender to the evil power that has fixed its roots like cancer on the world. I have been treated as a soldier who disobeys (No. 1 Field Punishment). That is hard enough at this time of year, but what made it worse for me was that I was bound to refuse to do military work, even as a prisoner. It is not possible for me to tell in words what I have suffered. But you will be glad to know that I have met with a great many men who have shown me the greatest kindness. I know that your prayers for me are not in vain. I will pray for you all to the last; it is all I can do for you now. If you hear that I have served in the Army or that I have taken my own life, do not believe that I did it in my sound mind. I never will.[1]

The letter changed Millicent's life. Having been active in the Red Cross and holding conventional attitudes to the war, she now became strongly pacifist. Her change of views made her feel guilty because it seemed disloyal to her father. Yet at the first chance she got, she went out to Brighton to meet Archie, whose letter she carried everywhere in her handbag. He was away, but his family received her well.

Her cultivated speaking voice with its English accent, her blue eyes and complexion still in its first bloom, made quite a stir. Later she was delighted to hear that Archie's friends had remarked that her beauty was genuine and not out of a bottle. She went out to Brighton several times before she and Archie met at last. His appearance was disappointing, for he was not at all

▲ Brighton in 1876, by George O'Brien. *Otago Early Settlers' Museum*

Rattray Street, Dunedin 1862, as Baxter's ancestors saw it on arrival. *Otago Early Settlers' Museum* ▼

▼ Archibald and Margaret McColl (James's great-grandparents), who emigrated to New Zealand in 1859. *Private Collection*

▲ John and Mary Baxter (James's grandparents) at the Creamery Road farm, Ocean View, near Brighton in the 1920s. *Private Collection*

John Baxter and bagpipes, Bath Street in Brighton, *c.* 1921. *Private Collection* ▲

▲ John Macmillan Brown, 1918.
Canterbury Museum

▲ Helen Connon, *c.* 1881.
Canterbury University

▼ Macmillan Brown family at Holmbank on Wairarapa Terrace, Christchurch, *c.* 1898. From left:
Millicent (sitting on ground), Helen, John holding Viola. *Canterbury University*

Viola Macmillan Brown and Angelo Notariello
on their wedding day, 1936. *Private Collection* ▶

▲ Archibald Baxter, 1921. *Private Collection*

▲ Millicent Macmillan Brown at the time she met Archibald Baxter, 1920. *Private Collection*

View of the site of the Kuri Bush farmhouse, bought by Millicent and Archibald Baxter in 1921. ▼
Private Collection

▲ Millicent and James (aged 15 months), 1927.
Hocken

James, aged 3. *Private Collection* ▶

▲ Millicent and James (aged 6) beside the Brighton River, 1932. *Private Collection*

Terence, Archibald, and James, camping. *Hocken* ▼

▲ Archibald and James.
Private Collection

▲ James and Margaret Herbert at Sibford School, 1937. *Private Collection*

good-looking. Nevertheless she realized almost immediately that this was the man she wanted to marry. His whole personality and manner matched the impression she had formed from his letter and what she knew of his history. Set beside that, his socio-economic circumstances were of no account. Archie felt the same way towards her. He liked her common sense and idealism. Later, he believed Millicent was the only person he would ever have married.

Neither family was pleased with the proposed marriage. Professor Macmillan Brown was disappointed. This was not at all the brilliant match he had hoped for his highly educated daughter. He remonstrated with Archie that their backgrounds were too different, and that with such limited financial resources he would never be able to give Millicent the opportunities nor the comfortable life to which she was accustomed. To his daughter he said: 'You will regret it; it's most unwise. This is a physical passion which will pass. Then it will be tragedy.' He was to be proved wrong in the event. Recounting his objections much later, Millicent told a friend: 'With me the physical passion came later.' It should be added that no one who knew her well ever thought of her as a passionate woman. That was something Archie missed in her. But theirs was a meeting of true minds.

Since neither she nor Archie belonged to any religious denomination, they were married in the registrar's office on 2 February 1921. Millicent was thirty-three, Archie was thirty-nine. By marrying outside her educational and social background in the face of conventional expectations, Millicent demonstrated that she had the same independence as her husband had displayed.

Archie and Millicent did not bother with a wedding breakfast. They spent their marriage day at the Ross Creek reservoir, and the next week going for picnics on the Brighton River. Then Archie was off rabbiting, first at Middlemarch and then on the farm of a family called Kenny at Hyde. The hut he used beside the Taieri River is still standing. He had great success with what was then the new technique of strychnine poisoning, which he and his brother had mastered.

In the early spring of 1921, Archie had enough money to buy a small farm at Kuri Bush, just south of Brighton. The water supply for the little four-roomed cottage came from outside tanks. Millicent cooked on a stove with Archie keeping her well supplied with wood from the bush at the back of the property. She did the washing in zinc tubs on an outside bench, using water heated on the stove. There were brass kerosene lamps for lighting and an earth closet. Later in life she recalled that people would say, 'Look what he's brought her to', and with a twinkle in her eye she drew out the long vowel in 'brought'. 'If only they had known how happy I was.'

The Kuri Bush farm was a couple of hundred yards from the sea, and the sandy soil was far from ideal for crops. The farm was run down when Archie bought it. He stocked it with cattle, sheep, and pigs, and kept a few horses for ploughing. Inevitably he ran fowls. He was still being harassed because of his stand in the war. Though he had less gorse on his property than most of the coastal farmers, he was always getting notices to remove it, and he was often fined for breaking laws he knew nothing about. Regulations concerning animals were rigidly enforced. Whenever Archie sent sheep to the Burnside freezing works, objections were bound to be raised. They were said to have lice, or some other pretext was found. His fences were broken down by persons unknown, and stock was let out of the paddocks. An attempt was even made to frame him for receiving stolen goods. Two strangers drove up and offered him a bolt of cloth for a song, but he was too honest and too experienced to fall into the trap. Yet not all the neighbours were unfriendly. When it came to leading in, harvesting, and chaff-cutting, everyone mucked in and sometimes as many as ten farmers sat down to dinner at the Baxters' table.[2]

The first son of the marriage was born on 23 May 1922 and named Terence after

> MacSweeney the Lord Mayor of Cork
> Who died on hunger strike.
> (CP 267)[3]

Millicent embraced her new role of mother enthusiastically. She and Archie reared the baby carefully, poring over the Plunket Book as an authoritative guide. Terence grew up a contented child. Whenever he referred in later years to his time on the farm before he started school, he spoke like 'one cast out of Eden'.[4] His secure and happy existence was broken only when his parents went to town and he was left at Brighton with Archie's brother, Mark, whose five little boys welcomed him as a windfall. They mimicked the way he spoke – he said 'cows' instead of 'keows' – and they bullied him mercilessly. This first encounter with other children was unpleasant, but his second, with the tribe of country kids who went to the same school at Kuri Bush, was much worse. He was roughly initiated into the facts of life.

His parents very much wanted another child, and after several miscarriages early in pregnancy, Millicent conceived again. She nearly lost the baby and had to be very careful. Her doctor was not sure whether to induce labour or let the pregnancy go the full term. The baby made his own decision and arrived five weeks early on 29 June 1926. As his mother remarked: 'He could not wait to come into the world.' He was born in Dunedin at Nurse Ross's maternity home, La Rochelle, on the corner of Elm Row and Arthur Street. The birth was easy and Millicent regarded it as quite remarkable. In her old age, she recalled feeling that she had been caught up in some great cosmic experience. The baby weighed only five pounds four ounces, and was ironically called Jumbo the elephant, and 'Jum' remained the name used by relatives and close friends. He was not christened, but his family called him James Keir after the Scottish socialist Keir Hardie, a founder of the British Labour Party.[5]

In contradiction to the prevailing belief that premature children did not live long, James thrived. After six months he weighed eighteen pounds. At first Terence resented his arrival. He even crept up on him in his pram and prodded him with a straw broom, breaking the skin. His parents took a tolerant view and little by little Terence came to accept his brother. James contracted the usual childhood diseases. During an attack of whooping cough when he was about three, his mother moved him into her bedroom so that when a fit came on he could be lifted as he struggled for breath. On one such occasion he looked over to the bed where his father was sound asleep and observed in a very superior manner: 'Dear me, doesn't he sleep soundly.' He never slept like that himself.

Gradually the farm at Kuri Bush became more productive. Despite their rudimentary living conditions the family was happy, and Millicent revelled in the life. When she was first married, she could cook only scrambled eggs and shortbread but now she had a chance to use the recipe books she had collected on her European travels. She became an excellent cook. Though she never learnt to use a sewing-machine she could sew, and until the boys were seven she made their shirts out of old clothes.

The farm was exposed to a biting sea wind that blighted the wheat. The location did not suit Archie's health, and his rheumatism began to play up. In 1931, after the family had been at Kuri Bush for nine years, the farm was sold, and they moved up the coast to Brighton. There they bought a small four-roomed cottage at 13 Bedford Parade, a street that runs parallel to the sea.[6] In those days Brighton, with a population of some three hundred, was a small, close-knit community. People always knew what their neighbours were up to. Local characters included McLeod the butcher, who was also a Presbyterian elder, Murdoch the grocer, and Coutts, a boat-builder who hired out boats for the Brighton River from his shed below the main road bridge. Only twelve miles away from Dunedin, where temperatures of five degrees Celsius are not unknown even in January, the picturesque cove was deemed a good swimming beach by the hardy residents of Dunedin. Some built weekend baches there. During summer, in the long southern twilight, the beach and sandhills, with their lupins and marram grass, were often crowded well into the evening.

The tempo of life at 13 Bedford Parade was unhurried, and visitors noticed the general atmosphere of domestic harmony. Archie and Millicent greatly enjoyed each other's company and had a similar sense of humour. And there was much good talk. A frequent visitor said she never heard music in the Baxter house. At night they sat by the fire and read. English and Scottish history became a veritable passion, and surprisingly, Millicent took a greater interest in Archie's family tree than in her own. What we know about his ancestors is mainly through her.

Millicent, who must have picked up something from watching her father's gardeners, enjoyed spending a good deal of time in her garden. The house itself was untidy. Books and papers lay everywhere. The general disorder was a great trial to Archie, who was a neat and orderly person, but his protests grew fainter and fainter. His wife was generally regarded as a learned woman but no housekeeper, and she had no sense of time. The family never knew when meals would be ready. When they did arrive they were ample and well-prepared. They were taken in comparative silence, since the family read books as they ate. Sometimes the dishes were not cleared away for some time and attracted flies.

Despite this domestic disorder, the whole household depended on Millicent's good sense and assurance, a necessary complement to Archie's anxious approach. She made the decisions, and made them firmly and sensibly. She never mislaid anything important and could always find accounts and receipts. She was frugal and could manage on whatever they had. All the Baxter men cast their wives in a similar role to that of Millicent. Even her qualities did not prevent Archie from falling in, however mildly, with the usual Baxter pattern of considering himself dominated by a woman and grizzling about how he had to humour his wife.

Archie did not have the domestic skills to restore order to the house, but he came into his own in the garden, supplying enough vegetables and fruit to meet the family's needs, and he grew roses as well. His was a strong, dependable presence, gentle and unassuming, but his passion for justice, usually on behalf of someone else, could flash out unexpectedly in anger. Like his wife he had admirable manners. A great talker, he had a reputation as a raconteur. With his outstanding probity, and the wisdom that sometimes comes from suffering, Archie was in great demand as a counsellor. He was a warm person who touched people easily and was comfortable with embracing. Millicent hated to be touched and this caused some friction between them.

When visitors came, they always spoke to James and often took time to read to him. He was a serious little boy with straight golden hair and very blue eyes. His disposition was cheerful and happy and he was open and direct – a true extrovert. Both he and his brother were contented children who got on well together. But James could be a little devil and often provoked

24

Terence, who was much more dutiful, and had a natural sense of propriety that his brother lacked.

Archie had been politically active in the early, more radical days of the Labour Party. Its object, as stated on his membership card, was 'the socialization of the means of Production, Distribution and Exchange'. Even after the birth of Terence, Archie used to go to Labour Party conferences. Now he entered local politics and became chairman of the school committee. He stood for the Taieri County Council but was not elected. A local doctor told Millicent he voted for her husband because 'I'm not going to have my voting dictated to me by anyone'.[7] It was found that opposition to Archie had been orchestrated from Dunedin. His war record had not been forgotten. But he remained unrepentant. He and his wife campaigned against compulsory military training in schools – schoolboy conscription, they called it – and they founded the Dunedin branch of the No More War movement. Millicent was politically-minded enough to become president for a time of the local branch of the Women's Movement.

These were the years of the Depression, and Brighton felt its effects. Two of Archie's brothers, who were in poor health, were on the dole. Millicent helped, with clothes and blankets, many a family whose bread-winner was out of a job, and she did it without any fuss. Concern for the down-and-out was considered by many who knew the Baxters to be a characteristic of all of them. The wartime experience enabled them to empathize with the sufferings of the unemployed, indeed with all outcasts of society. The neighbours were curious about how Archie's family managed to support itself. He was retired and his time seemed to be taken up with odd jobs, such as cutting firewood. They thought Millicent must have received money from her father. But there is no evidence that they received any allowance at this time. Between them they must have had enough salted away.

At the age of five, James went to the Brighton primary school, where the headmaster and his assistant taught fifty pupils between them, in two classrooms. To prepare the little boy for this new phase of his life, his mother proposed to teach him the basic facts of sex. Nine-year-old Terence remonstrated: 'Oh mother, if you tell Jum he'll tell the whole school.'[8] Consequently, his knowledge was picked up from playground gossip.

His academic education began badly: 'On that first grim day I sidled into the room and went straight to the fat black stove and put my hand on it. It was hot: not red hot, but black hot. So I hid behind the teacher's dress. She probably comforted me. I remember her as a vague, kind middle-aged woman. Some time later, when I stole her strap and took it home and hid it in a rusty can under a macrocarpa tree, she did not punish me for this infantile protest.'[9] Before that first day at school he could already read. This made him lazy because he could do what he was asked without effort. He took little interest in what was taught and scored among the lowest marks in the class. The headmaster did not relate well to him and interpreted his frequent lack of attention as a sign of low intelligence. James took part in school plays such as *Sleepytown Express*, and performed charmingly as the baby bear in *The Three Bears*. The infant mistress at Brighton Primary did not always teach poetry in a way that satisfied this son of a professor's daughter. One night he recounted indignantly how 'Brown Mouse' had been read at school and then gave his own virtuoso performance. He lacked the physical co-ordination to do well in school sports such as rugby, soccer, and hockey, and in any case he found them boring. His interests were less organized and allowed for maximum freedom.

Long before James went to school Archie used to sit him on his knee and read him Burns, whose poems were almost his Bible, and English romantic poets, Keats, Shelley, and Byron. This substitute for nursery rhymes made him precocious. And the little boy's first experience of poetry was of something eloquent, and capable of powerful effects through rhyme.

With Archie's encouragement both boys began to write verse. James's motivation in writing poetry was to win his father's approval. His first poem was written at the age of seven.

> I climbed up to a hole in a bank in a hill above the sea, and there fell into the attitude of *listening* out of which poems may rise – not to the sound of the sea, but to the unheard sound of which poems are translations – it was then that I first endured that intense effort of *listening*, like a man chained to the ground trying to stand upright and walk – and from this intensity of *listening* the words emerged –
>
> > O Ocean, in thy rocky bed
> > The starry fishes swim about –
> > There coral rocks are strewn around
> > Like some great temple on the ground . . .[10]

From this time he carried a notebook and pencil with him and there were always bits of paper in his pockets. A good deal of his writing was done immediately the impulse took him. He would just leave whoever he was with and go off to a quiet place.

Millicent had retained from her own childhood a great number of books of legends which her son read avidly. He became steeped in classical myths and in those of Ireland and Scandinavia. Later he wrote: 'I became the companion of Odin and Thor and Jason and Ulysses. That was an indispensable education.'[11] Throughout his childhood he was devoted to the classical fairy tales of Andrew Lang – the *Yellow*, the *Blue*, and the *Green* books. Scandinavian legends especially appealed to him, perhaps because they were nearer to his Highland background. When he was a little older, the family was discussing why some relatives had called their daughter Gaynor. Someone remarked, 'That's an ugly name.' James replied, 'Oh, that's the goddess who lies right around the world.' To him myth seemed to be the obvious explanation.

At Christmas and Easter, Millicent would read the boys passages from the Bible, thus familiarizing James with its rhythms and enriching his memory with images and stories. Even as an adult he could remember her reading them St Luke's tale of the nativity, and German stories of the Christ child. Terence said that in earlier years his mother would also sing them hymns, one of which was 'Mothers of Salem'.[12] As the boys grew older they readily committed whole poems to memory, as well as passages from the family Bible.

Terence and James got on well. Millicent thought that there was some jealousy between them. It should not be overlooked that when they were young James was much more trouble to his parents, and it did not look as though he would fulfil their expectations. He himself told an in-law that Terence was the favourite in the family, especially with his mother.

It is easy to suppose that Terence was a pragmatic, outgoing young Kiwi, and James his sensitive younger brother. This was not the case. Terence confirmed the stereotype of the sensitive, introspective first child, which some psychologists have presented, and James that of the relaxed, more outgoing younger brother. They were very different physically. Terence was rather tense and tended to be moody. James was thickset, and used to lumber along. He was easygoing and for the most part good-tempered.

Other children saw Baxter as very different, but accepted him. His manner was somewhat distant, and those who spoke to him might not get a reply. He simply did not hear because his thoughts were elsewhere. Some Saturday afternoons, a childhood companion used to go with him to the pictures at Green Island. He remembered James turning up at the bus-stop wearing a suit and tie but no shoes. He assumed it was because he had not noticed. And his enthusiasms were different from those of other children. At the age of about eight he knocked on a neighbour's door before breakfast to announce excitedly: 'The crocuses are out this morning.'

At school he could be hot-tempered and aggressive, and was inclined to hit anyone who molested him. Unlike Terence, he was quite prepared to take part in playground fighting: 'I was a slow lad and physically timid, but I had the advantage of weight. If I could get a headlock on my opponent, and drag him down and sit on him, the battle was mine. But the time would come when I had to let him up again – and on his feet he would be quicker than me, and angrier, and I would usually end up with a bloody nose.'[13] His opponents must have been small boys, because though he was healthy, he was not muscular, and he soon realized his limitations. 'Once, inspired by boredom, when the class had been set to cut up sheets of coloured paper, I clipped a stronger boy's nose with the scissors – unwisely, for he jumped on me from a high bank as I dawdled home after school, and punched my face while the back of my head rested on the ground. It taught me to find other ways of countering boredom.'[14] He first witnessed adult cruelty in the form of corporal punishment at Brighton Primary, a way of enforcing discipline then widely practised. It was administered in Baxter's class by:

> a young tough lass with a black moustache, who decided to give one cut for each spelling mistake over two in the morning test. I did all right there, because my home was full of books, and my reading was well ahead of anything I learnt at school. But the farm boys, who had no books in their houses, and had to milk the cows before they left home in the morning, came off badly. I remember one big mother's boy with a running nose going up for his dose of leather morning after morning. The question was *Would he howl or wouldn't he?* Sometimes he did; sometimes he didn't. This early initiation into the rites of sadism gave me an insight into myself and others. The audience were always fully awake – on their toes, you might say.[15]

Baxter's home experience was different. His mother rarely smacked her children, believing that what they needed was '*loving discipline* and guidance'.[16]

The formal side of his primary education at Brighton does not seem to have had much effect on him. It was just something he had to go through. It was too English to help him find his bearings as a young New Zealander: 'When I was at primary school the classroom murals represented the English seasons, with lambs and green fields in April, and the verse used most was not even Australian ballad poetry, but that of Walter de la Mare.'[17] Later Baxter explained his passive resistance at Brighton Primary as an instinctive protection of the precious resources needed if he was to become a poet. 'I was already unconsciously erecting my defences around that core of primitive experience, that ineducable self which I like to call a dinosaur's egg. Unfortunately the abstract analytical processes which the schools were able to offer me – and ram down my throat, if necessary – have the side-effect of neutralizing this kind of experience and making it inaccessible to the conscious mind.'[18] The threat to creativity posed by formal education was to become a lifelong obsession.

Mercifully, the life of primary schoolchildren is not confined to the class-room. In Brighton the great playground was the sandy beach where they flocked after school. With its prominent rocks – Parson's Rock, Middle Rock, Barney's Island, the rock pools and kelp beds – it was the never-failing source of excitement that similar beaches have been to generations of New Zealand children. James spent many hours there and made:

> My own mythology of weeds and shells
> And dreamed I heard from the green water shade
> The pealing of sea drowned cathedral bells.
>
> (CP 72)

He went exploring, gathering mussels from the rocks, and fishing for red cod and green-bone.

Bob Craigie, a boy of the same age as James, lived in his street and sat beside him in class. He had known him from the age of five and was his closest friend in those days. In 1845 the Craigies had emigrated from the Orkneys and settled on the Taieri River. The Highland background they shared with the Baxters drew the families together, and the two small boys were inseparable. They were sturdy and had great reserves of energy. Bob said 'I reckon Jim and I knew every hollow, every swamp within twenty miles of Brighton. We had been over it time and again.'[19] Both families were poor and the boys did not even have a push-bike between them. They walked everywhere.

Sometimes their expeditions took hours. When it got late and they were still not back, their parents worried, but Bob could always blame his companion because everybody knew he had no idea of time. James was fascinated by the features of the district. He knew all the existing names and invented others. He had names for the principal rocks along the coast: the Black Rock, the Big Rock, the Phoenix Head, the Lion Rock ('a hump-backed jut of reef'); and for every part of the river and its banks: the Devil's Elbow, and the Giant's Grave. The boys never referred to a place in general terms but said 'above the Black Bridge', 'near Duffy's Orchard'. James also loved to play on the Brighton River, which he invested with legends. A deep part of the river, two hundred yards down from his home, became 'A black bottomless hole', and when he and his brother Terence went canoeing they would paddle very slowly over it.

As the road from Ocean View approaches Brighton, the site of the McColls' farm is on the right at the bottom of Saddle Hill. Behind a low ridge of hills there is a valley with limestone caves, where the two boys searched for fossils. Baxter was quite knowledgeable and even as a primary school boy knew the names of the geological periods. On the McColls' property there was a disused coal-mine which the boys used to go down. James had a real fascination for entering caves and holes in the ground. Later he would draw on this childhood experience for his poem 'The Cave'. Sometimes these amateur speleologists took foolish risks, and they had a few narrow squeaks – but James was always incautious. His mother recalled that even when he was quite small he would leap off the top of the sofa for the experience – something that Terence would never do. And he was always ready to accept a dare, he would rush into things without thinking.

The local identities intrigued James and Bob. Donald McKenzie, an old fisherman of about seventy and a son of first generation Highland immigrants, lived up the Brighton River. Though he was a bit strange he liked children, and the boys often visited his shack. As they sat on the small verandah, he told them stories about the early settlers in the district and their difficult lives. James was fascinated. He knew a good deal already about the history of his own family and that of other Highland descendants in the area right down to Taieri mouth. To find out a new fact about them or the privations they endured delighted him. McKenzie explained the old course of the river, how clear it was before the weed spread and how trout were introduced near the Black Bridge. He used to row Bob out to Green Island, a distance of about three miles, to catch groper and blue cod, but James never went. Another strange fellow was old Duffy, who owned an orchard up past the Black Bridge. It was hard to reach because it was set in a valley surrounded by thick scrub. His wife, who was also somewhat odd, died 'like a bird in the frost', as her husband expressed it. These Brighton identities would one day enter Baxter's poems. In 'The Waves', for example, McKenzie was the half-crazed fisherman who blasted a channel in the rock between Barney's Island and the shore, to allow his boat to go in and out behind the long line of breakers in Brighton Bay.

Bob and James used to go eeling down by 'a narrow tumulus', the Giant's Grave, attaching their lines to an overhanging tree. Behind was a steepish hill. They would cut the top out of a cabbage-tree, put it between their legs and slide down. James was also much given to lighting fires in gorse hedges. Sometimes they flared up more than he expected and he grew alarmed. His mother described him as a born pyromaniac. He was also a great innovator. The inside fibre of dead cabbage trees looks like tobacco, but Bob, who was urged to try it, found it a wicked brand. Forty years later, Bob read Baxter's poems for the first time. He was amazed at how vividly the poetry brought back the places they had explored as children.

Every summer, up to 1935, the Baxters went to the mountains in their little two-seater Ford car for three weeks. On their first trip they took the Niger hut at the head of the Matukituki valley where the river divides into its East and West branches. But they found the mountains so oppressive that they left and went down to Lake Wanaka, camping by the shore.[20] The mountains over the Matukituki were the first mountains young James knew. One day he would celebrate the area magnificently in 'Poem in the Matukituki Valley'. The family camped where they liked, by lake or river, and Archie did the cooking over a big fire 'in billies slung on an iron bar, fitting into forked sticks at either end'.[21] In fact, he did almost everything. Millicent's only chore was to keep the tent tidy.[22] At Christmas 1931, the family went to Stavely near Mt. Somers and from there to Mt. Cook, camping on the way by Lake Tekapo. They visited several glaciers, including the Tasman and the Ball. On a trip to Lake Ohau, their favourite spot, they camped in perfect weather for three weeks, delighting in walks through the valleys and in the changing moods of the weather over the lake.

Every year Millicent and the children used to take the train to Christchurch to see her father and her sister Viola. The three-storeyed house in Macmillan Avenue, with its spacious gardens tended by full-time gardeners, was a far cry from her home at Kuri Bush or even at Bedford Parade. But she had no regrets. Macmillan Brown had gradually come to accept her marriage because he could see it was working. By now, he appreciated Archie's qualities. And he greatly enjoyed the company of his grandchildren. He was very reserved, however, and never took them on his knee nor cuddled them, and when he was reading in his library he did not like to be disturbed. When he grew up, James recorded his childhood memory of 'a white-haired elderly man in a black coat who inhabited a vast private library, which one entered by a varnished staircase – a benign figure who patted me on the head when I showed him my Christmas presents.'[23]

Viola helped her father in much the same way as Millicent had done, but they got on better. She understood him and accepted his own valuation that his character had two sides, 'one inherited from his puritan and anxious mother, the other from his gay and companionable father.'[24] He was much less testy with her than he had been with Millicent and she was devoted to him. Terence remembered his aunt as being very pretty – prettier than his mother. She was always on the phone talking to her women friends and she was very popular with men. He recalled the sports cars arriving with suitors anxious to take her out. She was fond of skiing and climbing, whereas Millicent's interest in mountains was in their beauty. Viola also drove a car, something not very common in the mid 1920s. She trained at the Slade School of Art and became a painter. Evelyn Page regarded her work as very refined and reticent. But painting remained only a small part of her life. Millicent, in contrast, was never really interested in the visual arts.

A very good Italian opera company toured New Zealand in the twenties and performed most of Verdi's operas. When someone in the management absconded with the funds, the artists were stranded in New Zealand. Professor James Hight of Canterbury University College arranged for some of them to make a little money by giving singing lessons. One who took up the offer was Angelo Notariello, the lead tenor, who had once sung with Melba. New Zealand became his base for the next six years. Viola had a great admiration for Italy, where she had already been several times. Her weak chest made it desirable to escape the rigours of a Christchurch winter, and her father could well afford the cost. She wanted to improve her Italian and in 1924 Hight's daughter arranged for Angelo to give her lessons. They soon fell in love. Viola knew it would be fruitless for an opera singer to ask her father for her hand. He expected a much more substantial man financially as a son-in-law. One maverick marriage was enough. The courtship had to be carried on secretly, and when Angelo left New Zealand in 1927 he and Viola corresponded for nearly nine years. It was only after Macmillan Brown's death that they married at Bournemouth in England in 1936. They had two daughters.[25]

The stress of Millicent's marriage did not prevent her father from continuing to play an active part in university administration. In 1921 he was Vice-Chancellor of the University of New Zealand, and two years later he was elected Chancellor in succession to Sir Robert Stout. He retained the office until 1935. In his later years, Pacific anthropology became a consuming interest. He had the health and stamina to travel widely, observing native customs and artefacts. His findings were published in three books. Not surprisingly, they do not stand up to the scrutiny of so specialized and fast-changing a discipline as modern anthropology. Lesser men have sometimes been knighted, but when his case was discussed, the Governor-General, Lord Bledisloe, is reported to have said that he would not give a knighthood to a man who had made money out of education.

Macmillan Brown died in Christchurch in 1935 at the age of eighty-nine. In his will he left Millicent four hundred pounds a year for life, a considerable sum at that time. The will also provided that in the event of her death, the trustees should apply as much of the income as was necessary 'for the maintenance, education and advancement in life of her children, until the youngest reached the age of twenty one'.[26]

James always felt closer to the rugged, uneducated, working-class Baxters. Macmillan Brown represented for him a system of education, a puritan devotion to hard work and material advancement, conformity, and respectability. Against these he was increasingly to rebel. From an early age he resisted the suggestion that as the grandson of a distinguished academic he should make a career in the university.[27]

James was nine when his grandfather died, and that year the family shifted north to Wanganui. Archie's health had not been good, and it was felt that a milder climate might suit him better. They rented a house on fashionable St John's Hill, with its well laid out gardens and scarlet flowering gums. James was enrolled in the nearby Friends' School, chosen because of its avoidance of doctrinal teaching, and because of the Quakers' stand for peace during the war. Their readiness to accept children of parents belonging to no denomination also suited the Baxters. Terence was already a pupil. His parents had removed him from Brighton Primary because, in Millicent's account, a rather excitable teacher had thrashed him for mistakes in his arithmetic examination. What she did not know was that the teacher was much incensed by a relationship Terence, then thirteen, had been having with a sixteen-year-old girl.

At the Friends' School:

. . . they used to sing Blake's *Jerusalem* in the morning assembly, and this gave me a strong sense of religious joy; though in the Scripture tests I got full marks for the theory that Jesus was the son of Joseph, but a good man nevertheless. There was a gully below our house where bushes made a thick roof above a small creek. There my personal education went on at its own pace; and also at Virginia Lake and Kai Iwi beach –

> And by the bay itself were cliffs with carved names
> And a hut on the shore beside the Maori ovens.
>   We raced boats from the banks of the pumice
> creek
> Or swam in those autumnal shallows
> Growing cold in amber water, riding the logs
> Upstream, and waiting for the taniwha.
>
> (CP 45)

At this school they had an interesting system of discipline. Each child carried a penny notebook on its person, in which a teacher would set down a black mark, the nature of the child's offence, and his (the teacher's) initials. Thus each pupil had his or her own criminal file to look at. At the end of the week one took the notebook to the headmaster's study, and there was a close examination of motives and causes, and penalties assigned if one had more than three black marks. Some stainless individuals acquired no black marks at all. The system induced in me a curious reaction. After I had acquired two or three black marks, a kind of impenitent despair would take charge of me, and I would acquire in rapid succession fifteen or twenty of them. As a result I found myself more or less permanently deprived of privileges and confined to the dungeons.[28]

The family enjoyed its time in the North Island, finding the climate agreeable, if a trifle damp, but they felt that Archie especially needed a change. He was a chronic worrier and subject to deep bouts of melancholy. They decided to visit Europe with funds from the sale of a small cottage Archie had built in Brighton, and from the sale of shares. When they moved from their Wanganui home, Terence worked like a grown man, though James, at ten, was not much use. Early in 1937 they sailed from Wellington on board the *Wanganella*.

After some time in Sydney they embarked on the *Ormonde*, which called at Hobart, Adelaide, and Perth. Suez fascinated the boys. So did Crete, where the captain brought his ship in close and explained the history of the fabled island. He would never know how deeply he impressed the ten-year-old boy, who would one day exploit so memorably the legend of the minotaur. Visits to Naples, Pompeii, and the South of France followed. Then it was England 'and Plymouth bitter with snow'.

Archie and Millicent settled in Salisbury in a well appointed house, and Archie's uncertain health began to improve. They were not far from the deserted site of Sling Camp. A visit prompted Archie to begin his memoir of his war experiences, *We Will Not Cease*. Its composition was therapeutic, liberating him from the lingering effects of his ordeal. His dictation to Millicent was laconic and she kept urging him to put some flesh on the bare bones. With patience and understanding she supported him through the painful reconstruction of the attempt to destroy him as a man. It was James's first experience of being close to the making of a book, and of following its fortunes up to publication. A publisher was difficult to find. The reader for the firm of Michael Joseph said: 'Who would be interested in the experiences of a New Zealand farmer?', a comment which shows how New Zealand was regarded in England in the thirties. *We Will Not Cease* appeared eventually in Gollancz's Left Book Club list for 1939, and was favourably reviewed in the *New Statesman and Nation*. Mark Briggs, who had suffered with Archie in France, received a copy inscribed: 'In memory of days that we can't yet afford to forget.' What is remarkable about *We Will Not Cease* is that a man subjected to so many injustices could write without any sense of bitterness or self-pity.[29]

The story of his father's wartime experience and of the strongly pacifist views his parents shared with many of their friends was familiar to James. The book became a kind of family Bible and kept fresh his earlier recollections. One day he would write: 'the Pacifist Church had its confessors and martyrs – my father had been one of the greatest.'[30] In her *Memoirs*, Millicent said that James was deeply affected by his father's experience, and this is borne out by his writings. To the strong sense of clan was added an awareness of common peril. In the example of an admired father, James found a model who was at once victim and hero. His history brought home to him at an impressionable age just how far public authority in New Zealand could go, through its instruments, the army and the police. It was clearly prepared to flout the rights of anyone who refused to conform. A deep distrust of authority was part of the inheritance he would carry with him from childhood. The effect of the wholesale slaughter of the First World War and his father's escape from death was profound on the imagination of the sensitive young boy. It initiated that preoccupation with death which was to become so much a part of his consciousness.

In England the boys were enrolled at Sibford School, a coeducational

Quaker boarding school in Sibford Ferris, a small Oxfordshire village on the edge of the Cotswolds and seven miles west of Banbury. At the time it had a roll of one hundred and eighty pupils between the ages of ten and sixteen years. It had been chosen for much the same reasons as the Friends' School in Wanganui, and it was not as expensive as some of the other Friends' schools. School life was spartan. The dormitories were unheated and supper before bed consisted of dry bread and cocoa. Although about one third of the pupils were not from Quaker families, Sibford reflected the Quaker view that war is irreconcilable with Christianity. One period a week was devoted to religious instruction, which included a study of the Bible in the Authorized Version. Each morning after breakfast, staff and pupils would assemble for a hymn, a reading, and a short period of meditation. Worship on Sundays at the nearby Quaker meeting-house lasted for an hour and was held in silence, broken only when someone felt moved to speak.

James's English teacher, Mr Barrie Naylor, remembered him clearly: 'When he came to Sibford in 1937, [he] was a very small boy – with prominent ears! He was reserved, but not anti-social, friendly, but not gregarious . . . The staff liked him (as did his peers) and I was particularly fond of him because behind his shyness there was such a likeable and sensitive nature.' In a postscript he added: 'James had a puckish sense of humour!'[31] This estimate was confirmed by one of Baxter's class-mates, who described him as slightly unkempt, idealistic, always full of impish fun, but able to become serious very quickly. Baxter was very much at home in the school. He liked the district and the farms where boys could 'escape at times to disturb the tribes of rooks in the high trees and steal eggs from the farmers' chicken sheds . . .'[32] The boys had a fair amount of free time. Wednesday afternoon was free, and often the whole of Saturday.

In July 1937, at the end of the first term, the family set out for Denmark to attend the War Resisters' Conference in Copenhagen. At Liverpool Street Station they found themselves in the same carriage as other pacifists, including a certain Lord Ponsonby. Partly because of a superior attitude towards 'colonials', he ignored the Baxters. His pacifist sympathies were too academic to appreciate the veritable John Hampden who was in the party. Terence and James were the only children at the conference and they were very lively. At the Hotel King of Denmark they ran pencils endlessly down the grooved bannister and kept racing up the down escalator. They even persuaded the lift-man to let them take the lift up and down. James charmed the women. At one function a lady sent him a note across the room, 'To the best-behaved boy I have ever met'.[33] His mother thought that was going a bit far.

After the conference, the family travelled through Germany along the Rhine and through the Thuringia forest to Berlin. They followed the upper reaches of the Danube, beneath steep cliffs crowned with castles, and crossed the Black Forest. Then it was Switzerland and France, where they stayed for six weeks at Serrières beside the blue water of the Rhône. Millicent found it very pleasant travelling with Archie. Both had much to remember. She was amused at the number of women who approached him, and wryly observed that no one ever approached her.

With the onset of puberty, James had begun to masturbate and to grow curious about women's bodies. In 'At Serrières' he later wrote of that period:

> The new guitar of sex I kept on twanging
> Inside the iron virgin
> Of the little smelly dyke, or that Easter Sunday,
> Through a chink in the bedclothes, watching my mother dressing:
> The heavy thighs, the black bush of hair.
>
> (CP 250)

But there is none of this in the poem on Serrières he wrote at the time. He was writing poems on nature themes, or as the mature poet put it, 'on clouds and comets'. And they were based on what he had read, not on what he had observed. Abroad, James showed no facility with languages, though he could speak a few words of French.

Early in 1938 they crossed the English Channel and the boys returned to Sibford. Their spring holidays that year were spent at Bournemouth, where the woods were full of 'primroses, wood anemones and the May lily . . . and the fields were bright with campion and orchids.'[34] At Sibford Mr Naylor encouraged his pupils to write verse, and some of them became enthusiastic. He considered James's work easily the best and that he had the makings of a poet. Among his compositions, written by the time he was twelve, was 'The Curse of War':

> Why should Man his brother's life,
> Heedless of Religion, take!
> Should the cannonades of Strife,
> Many homeless orphans make?
>
> All the armaments of Man,
> In carnage and Destruction seen,
> Since the human race began
> Accursed to the world have been.
>
> Haul down the bloodstained banner,
> Hoist better in its place,
> And let the pilgrims enter,
> Who battle now for Peace.

▲ The Brighton Boat House. *Lloyd Godman*

▲ Archibald Baxter, *c.* 1940.
*A. C. Barrington,
Alexander Turnbull Library*

▲ 15 Bedford Parade,
Brighton. *Lloyd Godman*

▲ Millicent, Archibald, and James on an excursion in the 1940s. *Hocken*

The Highland Dancer, 1943. *Private Collection*

▲ James at King's High School, 1943. *Private Collection*

▲ 'A Family Portrait' — James, Archibald, and Millicent. *Hocken*

▼ Interior of James's bedroom at 15 Bedford Parade, Brighton. *Lloyd Godman*

▼ Handwritten copy of 'Beyond the Palisade', written in 1942 and sent to Margaret Hargreave (née Herbert). *Private Collection*

Jane Aylmer at the time she met James, 1945. ▲
Private Collection

Noel Ginn, *c.* 1937. *Private Collection* ▶

▲ James (aged 18) at time of publication of 'Beyond the Palisade'. *Otago Daily Times*

▲ Jacqueline Sturm and James Baxter in Hagley Park after their engagement, Christmas 1948. *Private Collection*

◀ Baxter on his wedding day,
outside St John's Cathedral in Napier, 1948. *Hocken*

Baxter at Mt. Aspiring, near Wanaka
— working on the script for 'The Ascent of Mt. Aspiring'
January 1950. *National Publicity Studios Collection,
Alexander Turnbull Library*
▼

'The Turncoat'.   ▲
Baxter at Canterbury University
College in 1948. *Private Collection*

The poem was written against the background of the Spanish Civil War, fought between 1936 and 1939, and the growing rumours of the fast-approaching Second World War. Baxter's closest friend at Sibford, Harold Pugmire, wrote that 'The Curse of War' expressed what many of them were feeling. He knew Archie's wartime experiences well, since Baxter had often spoken about them. They were the more pertinent since his own father had been one of the first conscientious objectors in England during the First World War and had been detained for some five years. The Sibford boys and girls held long discussions on pacifism, war, and politics.[35]

Baxter was writing a good deal of juvenile verse and had already acquired something of a reputation as a poet: 'An older boy asked me to write a poem for him to give, as his own, to a fair-headed lass in the Upper School whom he was courting.' The young laureate obliged, but after a conventional reference to her hair, eyes, and teeth, was defeated by his ignorance of anatomy.[36] His knowledge was advanced the day he saw one of the senior boys 'making the two-backed beast' (CP 118) with the school beauty in long grass. Much later he said that from that time he could not believe there was anything wrong in what they were doing. Another poem he wrote in this period was a close imitation of lines from Tennyson's 'The Brook', which he called 'The River Spirit'. The poem is one of several with a title that reflects the animism that would appear in his early volumes:[37]

> Far up in the wild, cold moorland hills
> My rushing stream has birth.
> And I tumble down past vale and town
> To join the rocky Firth –
> I fall from a ledge to marshy sedge,
> Wind through a rushy glen,
> Then forth I sally down the valley,
> On to the haunts of men.
> Past cobbled streets I softly flow
> And bubble under bridges,
> Then onward rush past bank and bush,
> To tumble o'er the ridges –
> Through all the smoke of busy towns,
> By sewer, wall and quay,
> I reach the sandy river-mouth
> And plunge into the sea.

The verse keeps closely to Tennyson's rhythms, and apart from 'sewer', to his language.

Baxter's school report for the summer term of 1938 records his best subject as English, which was 'outstandingly good', and his teacher added 'I wish especially to mention James' really promising work in poetry

37

composition.'[38] The Art and Modelling master was critical: 'Has good ideas, but until he's more attentive will not be able to carry them out well.' He was described in the same report as 'showing an interest in his garden' and as 'a keen and good swimmer'.[39] According to one of his teachers he tolerated Physical Training and played soccer, 'but not with relish'. Pocket money for the children was sent directly to the Headmaster, who returned what was unspent at the end of the term. Once James was refunded a halfpenny, a way of teaching that if you look after the pennies the pounds will look after themselves. It was a lesson he had already learnt at home in Brighton. Among her family and friends Millicent was well known for her frugality. Overseas travel and the purchase of books were possible because of the care with which she handled money, but she believed money was to be used rather than merely accumulated. And she was quite capable of going without if she was saving for something.

At Sibford James was also developing socially: 'The daughter of the wood-work master, used to meet me secretly in the lane beside the school and give me pies that she had made in the home cooking class. She was a large, square-built Circe. The attachment on my side was wholly gastronomic; on her side, maternal and romantic.'[40] To move the myth nearer to reality it should be added that the girl also washed his knees when he got them dirty and looked after his chilblains.[41] Millicent found it a strange relationship: he was a small boy, the girl was a big buxom lass several years his senior. The girl was Margaret Herbert, later to become Mrs Hargreave, who gave me her side of the story: 'I remember Jim as a small, slightly scruffy schoolboy, who liked to button his jacket although it was a bit tight . . . My father passed on many years ago, but I suspect his chief memory would be of Jim wandering into class late saying "No excuse, sir." In fact, he spent some time practically every Saturday afternoon in detention for this "offence". I used to buy him sweets from the village shop because school-shop was only open while he was "C.B." (confined to barracks).'[42]

Like many other girls, she was more attracted to Terence, who was in her class. Of his brother she said: 'I think in many ways I was "mothering" Jim.' She did not remember other boys being unkind to him, 'but I think they were puzzled by him.'[43] James and Margaret kept up a correspondence for many years. Even after her marriage she wrote giving details of her life and of the birth of her first baby. In his letters to her he enclosed a number of poems, including 'Beyond the Palisade', sent on 1 August 1942, and 'Haast Pass' sent on 18 February 1944.

In his final term at Sibford, the summer term of 1938, James had worked well and made progress. The housemaster, F. Parkin, commented on his report: 'His conduct is pleasing and we are very sorry indeed he is leaving.

He has our best wishes for the future.'[44] James marked the occasion with a poem, 'Farewell to Sibford':

> Farewell to all the beauty,
> That round old Sibford lies,
> The daily round of duty:
> The play 'neath sun and skies.
>
> God give me strength and courage
> To shape my destiny,
> On Christ, the perfect image,
> Of pure simplicity.[45]

The public life of the school was one thing. What lay behind it was another. The grown man wrote:

> This was a period of undesired sexual enlightenment for me. No doubt some turmoil at puberty is inevitable. But I think my own transition from childhood to manhood would have been less gruelling under different conditions – in a Maori pa, let us say. I remember the barbarities of the dormitory as the beginning of adult life. One could see clearly the irrelevance of any external authority in that world of violence and wry self-knowledge.
>
> I remember one night in winter when the strong men of the dormitory were engaged in beating up a homesick German lad. One at a time they moved over to his bed in the dark and punched him. I had a choice to make – for I too was a foreigner, and the gang initiative could easily swing in my direction. So I put on my slippers and moved over and got in a few hard punches. I knew somebody was being betrayed. And I knew too that this was the underlying process of the world in which I had to live from then on – either to betray, or else to be at the receiving end of group violence, either verbal or physical –[46]

The small world of the dormitory where this drama unfolded housed some twelve to fifteen boys about James's age. A motherly woman, who was ostensibly in charge, slept at the end of the corridor. When she tucked James in at night he would sometimes pretend to be a petulant child while he kept an eye on his delighted audience. The showmanship, which was to become characteristic, was there from an early age.

Terence did not see much of James at Sibford because he was in a different part of the school. He knew his brother used to get into scrapes because of his inability to react to normal social situations in the expected way. His clowning also confused his peers. They responded by taking it out on him. Terence was aware that bullying was going on. He recalled that one way the school got its own back on a boy was by making him run the gauntlet. The rest would form two lines and make him dash through them. As he ran he would be struck with belts, shoes, or anything to hand. James got himself into some sticky situations, yet in his own way he could look after himself and he was very plucky. Usually he could avoid coming to blows by talking his tormentors around. If there was no other resort, he was quite prepared to fight his way out. The violence and the 'undesired sexual enlightenment' were topics to which he often returned. The fullest comment is in 'School Days':

> I touch them with a word, so close they stand
> After a thousand hours and days,
> Older than Cocteau, in the dream museum
> Of corridors and changing rooms:
> A palace, jail and maze.
>
> There I imbibed, as at a breast, truth
> Beside the simple streams and elms;
> England, my wet nurse, with her bitter milk.
> So from sugared childhood came
> On to the watershed of tears
> With those small angular companions,
> Handlers of the penis and the pen.
>
> Hard to forgive them even now,
> Precursors of the adult nightmare –
> Franey, Nero of the dormitory,
> Holmes, with the habits of a jaguar
> And the sleek animal hide,
> Waiting in a bend of the high stone stair.
>
> Plunged early into the abyss of life
> Where the tormentors move,
> At war with God, the terrible Watcher,
> An octopus behind a round glass window
> With knives and justice, but no love.
>
> That guilt grew wrongly, driven underground
> With the first prickings of raw sense.
> Yet there was friendship, comics, dominoes,
> A dried newt like a bootsole in a drain,
> New conkers like peeled testicles,
> Sharing of exile, and the habit, pain.
>
> The village like a mother stayed outside
> With wells and horses, till the coat
> Of manhood could be stitched and worn –
> And the green mandrake Poetry
> Born whole and shrieking one bleak night
> Under stiff sheets and wincing at the dawn.
>
> (CP 194-5)

'Sharing of exile' in its literal sense refers to the Jewish boys who had already fled with their parents from Hitler's Germany. The guilt is clearly associated with the sexual experimentation that sometimes takes place in boarding schools. The youthful image of God is an Old Testament image of God as avenger. Sibford was clearly a crucial phase in James's development. According to his mother, Terence loved the place, James disliked it.

Looking back he wrote:

> And so those various negative violent occasions forced me to begin to grow up. Those from whom I stood in most danger were not my jungle companions, sad recent exiles from childhood, yarn-spinners, players of dominoes, amateur sadists and sodomites, but more likely the ones who lived in the upper branches of the tree of knowledge – harsh or kingly pedagogues who would muddle my mind if they could, or even the matron-housekeeper, the old lady at the end of the corridor, who often called me in to her room and called me a bad boy and stroked my hair, and gave me a cup of wrinkled warm milk before I went to bed. Before I left the school she gave me a copy of Wordsworth's shorter poems. This pillow-breasted mother-substitute was waving me back to the pastoral Muse and to childhood again. A journey that invariably kills the intellect. But I remember her good intentions.[47]

Before the term ended Archie and Millicent were already in Scotland. They sent Terence and James tickets and money for the taxi from Paddington to Kings Cross and for lunch on the train. The boys were too shy to go to the dining-car, and spent the money on chocolate and apples to sustain them between London and Edinburgh. In Scotland, the family visited many places associated with Robert Burns. Archie provided a commentary and quoted the poetry. They saw the cottage in Ayr where Burns was born, Kirk Alloway, celebrated in *Tam O'Shanter*, and Wanlochhead, the highest village in Scotland, where Burns had his horse shod with 'frosty caulkers' for the wintry roads. The bus driver was also well versed in Burns's legend and quoted whole poems on the tour. Burns was confirmed as central to Baxter's Scottish inheritance. Another pilgrimage was to Braemar where R. L. Stevenson wrote *Treasure Island*. One object of the visit to Scotland was to find places associated with their ancestors, and young James entered enthusiastically into the search. At Rothesay, in the Isle of Bute, they found the Chapel Hill Dam site where Archie's father, John Baxter, had been born. In Ballachulish they discovered the house which was the birthplace of his mother, Mary McColl, and where his grandfather, another Archibald, had lived. Millicent became caught up in the heated arguments that still raged over the hanging of James Stewart in the eighteenth century. Archie and James were interested, but Terence was bored.

On 15 September 1938, after nearly two years in Europe, the family embarked on the *Rangitiki*, bound for New Zealand via Panama. Basil Franey, who was older than James (and who was sweet on Margaret

Herbert's sister), went down to London Docks to see them off. The Europe they left behind was moving inexorably into war. Somewhere in the South Pacific, word of Neville Chamberlain's illusory peace at Munich reached them. So did the news that the New Zealand Labour Party had been returned to the treasury benches with a reduced majority. Since the passengers on the *Rangitiki* had voted at sea, the boys saw the democratic process in action. Another excitement was a visit to Pitcairn Island, which was then a regular stopping place. Years later, James wrote: 'I remember Pitcairn on a grey morning, when the ship anchored, and the islanders came out in their boats to exchange fruit and carved walking-sticks for old clothes or money. The payment seemed less than the value of what they brought.'[48]

On their return to Brighton their house in Bedford Parade was still let, so they rented a crib, or holiday house, on the main road which runs along the sea front. James put in the last few weeks of the final term in 1938 at Brighton Primary. One day he saw through the window of his home a boy bashing a hedgehog with a tennis racquet. He rushed out in fury and made him stop. Any form of cruelty enraged him. Both boys were very fond of animals and liked to have cats about the house. His mother remembered that on one of those early holidays at Lake Ohau, James came back to camp carrying a stoat in his arms. He had covered its head with a handkerchief so it would not be alarmed by his parents. Strangely the animal was not at all frightened of the child.

In 1939, at the age of twelve, he returned to the Friends' School in Wanganui, this time as a boarder. Twenty years later he wrote: 'Though I must have done the minimum work to avoid penalties, I can't remember any of the actual instruction I received there.'[49] His school reports fill out what he had forgotten. The music teacher lamented, 'unfortunate for a poet to lack music though he has a good sense of rhythm.'[50] He could also distinguish tunes – unlike another skilful versifier, W. S. Gilbert, who said he knew only two tunes: 'One was God Save the Queen and one wasn't.' The music teacher's comment was tolerant. Since James was tone deaf he took little interest in the lessons and used 'to sit in a corner of the room making farting noises with my hand under my armpit while the class was being instructed in *Doh Re Mi*. The relief of being regularly expelled from the class was countered by the fact that I had to visit the headmaster each time.'[51] In Scripture he was described as having 'outstanding knowledge and insight'. For the intriguing subject 'Public Work' he was censured as 'not interested in community needs', an umbrella expression covering chores like keeping the grounds tidy.[52] In French, his best subject, he showed the benefit of his time in France and scored 48 out of 50. Since he was no good at games, he was put on 'Sports Training'.

He had several outings from the school to family friends like the Hunters at Patea. He records with a small boy's passion for accuracy that on a whitebaiting expedition he caught two to Brian Hunter's thirty-four. And he learnt to ride a bicycle; 'It is a man's bicycle too.' But he assured his parents he was not going to ride fast, or go near traffic; and 'I promise not to ride on bad roads. I took great care not to damage it or get dirty.'[53] He continued to write verse and told his parents of the pains of composition: 'I often make up beautiful poems at night, which in the hard morning light seem senseless and meaningless.'[54] He was learning the difference between the dream-world of poetry, into which he liked to escape, and the workaday world.

Yet he seems to have been reasonably happy. He wrote to his parents: 'Every evening I go in for a bathe with the other boys and can live quite well now. I am not getting on badly at work and I really like everything quite well. Pugmire, a boy who was at Sibford, wrote to me and asked me to send him any poems I made up. Last night we had tea outside in the canoe encampment ground and later we had folk-dancing. Every evening Mr. Doyle reads us a story.'[55] This master had a good reading voice and gave himself to the boys and to the books he read. Baxter must have greatly improved his sense of language, his vocabulary, and feeling for verbal rhythms by hearing well-read stories before going to bed. The reference to his Sibford friend Pugmire shows he had not forgotten his English school. On 23 March 1939 he wrote to Margaret Herbert: 'I wish I was at Sibford, and often think about it.'

Baxter said nothing to his parents about something else which happened at the school in Wanganui. He kept it for 'Notes on the Education of a New Zealand Poet': 'But a difficult guerilla warfare developed between me and the headmaster. With the negative sexual obsession which is characteristic of a certain kind of pedagogue, he had intercepted letters written to me by the pie-cooking English girl, and had inevitably concluded that these were evidence of a precocious sexual liaison. My encounters with him were marked by avoidance on my side and a dour dislike on his.'[56] In response to a dare from the headmaster's son, James and another boy went one night to a place among the sandhills where some bulldozers had been working. There they

> . . . leapt and slid among the sandhills in the moonlight. There was a strong sense of the jailbreak about it – the wild mottled globe of the moon overhead; the feel of the wind on our faces; the noises of trains from the town in the distance. Trains have always struck me as being symbols of adventure and liberation. On our way back up the road we were met by a procession of torch-bearing staff members. There were hushed and lengthy investigations. There was talk of expulsion; for the headmaster could conceive of only one reason for two boys being out together at night; though in fact the only practising sodomite

in the school was a cautious immigrant lad whom the headmaster regarded as a potential saint. My own concern was mainly to conceal from him that his son had suggested the expedition. In this I was successful, and fortunately managed to avoid betraying anyone.[57]

When Harold Pugmire visited New Zealand in the autumn of 1969, Baxter walked across country to meet him. They spent three days talking over the old days and the way their lives had gone. Pugmire found him 'the same old Jimmie'. They visited the Friends' School at Wanganui and his friend was amazed at how vehemently Baxter resented the education he had received there. He contrasted its 'colonial conventionality' with the more spacious ways of Sibford.[58]

By the end of 1939 the Baxters were back in their cottage at 13 Bedford Parade, and James was looking forward to coming home. Archie was again active in local body affairs, and became Chairman of the Brighton Ratepayers' Association.[59] In 1940 they bought the big house next door, No. 15. Archie's brother Donald moved into the cottage. No. 15 had three bedrooms and an upstairs room with windows on all sides. The seats below them were always piled with books. James could see 'white ocean lashing/ Upon black coasts'.[60] At Brighton he had always lived within sound of the sea. Its appearance and rhythm were part of his growing consciousness. Away to the left is Black Rock and a fairish distance off shore, Green Island. To the right, a bare coast runs south to Taieri mouth, and beyond, in the far distance, is the headland called Quoin Point. The rear windows of the house looked out over the upper reaches of the Brighton River, farmland, and hills of which the most prominent are Saddle Hill and Scroggs Hill with their rich Baxter family associations. Downstairs there was a glassed-in verandah where even on a cold day you could catch some sun and settle down with a book.

Objectively, James's childhood was happy. In a closely united family he was loved and well looked after. But it must be remembered that his parents were older than most. By the time he was two and Terence six, his mother was forty and his father forty-seven. Older parents are often less adaptable, more cautious and anxious than those who are young. If they are intellectual as well, they tend to take a more serious view of the world. James told his sister-in-law: 'there was never any NONSENSE in our house – even the jokes were serious ones! And so many things were never mentioned (every thing was in such good taste, tempers were rarely lost and vulgarity rarely intruded) – yet you had this sense of all hell breaking loose over the garden fence – but never to be talked about.'[61] Millicent was better educated than her husband and from a different social class; she was also strong-willed. In the house, hers was the dominant personality and she took charge of the education of the boys. She maintained the standards and manners she had learnt as the elder daughter of the conventional Victorian home of Macmillan Brown. She said herself: 'I taught my boys excellent manners' – and she did.

Much of James's life was lived in reaction to the strict regime of his childhood and to the strong personality of his mother. He was always conscious of how different she was from his father and his Baxter relatives. She fitted in and made friends, but she could never become working-class. What saved her from any awareness of how far she was from being regarded by her sister-in-law and local women as one of themselves was her complete ignorance of how their networks operated. She was a constant reminder of a different way of life and of different standards. James's preference was for the attitudes and style of the Baxters. But he could not disown altogether, much less reconcile, the contrasting sides of his inheritance. As he wrote much later, 'In contradiction . . . I was born,' (CP 255). The result, from childhood, was a divided self and a perennial inner conflict.

His mother engendered in him the rebelliousness people like his Wanganui headmaster helped to foster. Without doubt she helped her son to develop his linguistic gifts and to establish an appropriate tone for his poetry. But his literary talent did not come from his mother's side, although she spoke excellent English and articulated her views with some authority. Neither her writing nor that of her father suggests that they had the least smack of creativity. James's vision and passion came from the Baxters.

With a diversity of schools and a spell in Europe, Baxter had a more varied and interesting childhood than most New Zealand schoolchildren. But shifting around between three different schools must have been unsettling, and he felt sharply the unhappiness that seems part of many people's schooldays: 'Objectively I remember my childhood as a happy time. My health was good. There were plenty of things to do. My parents, my schoolteachers and my companions treated me well enough. Yet a sense of grief has attached itself to my early life, like a tapeworm in the stomach of a polar bear. I would not like to turn it into a sense of grievance . . . Yet the sense of having been pounded all over with a club by invisible adversaries is generally with me, and has been with me as long as I can remember . . .'[62] His feeling at five or six was of 'a young calf being trodden underfoot in the infant school stockyard.'[63]

In retrospect he considered his education at Brighton Primary was so rooted in English culture that it created a barrier between him and his New Zealand situation. His English boarding school increased the sense of dislocation: 'I think the sense of a gap between myself and other people was increased considerably by the fact that I was born in New Zealand, and grew up there till I was nine [sic], and then attended an English boarding school for a couple of years, and came back to New Zealand at thirteen, in the first flush of puberty, quite out of touch with my childhood companions and uncertain whether I was an Englishman or a New Zealander. This experience too, though very painful, was beneficial; for I fell into the habit of poem-writing with a vengeance and counted it a poor week when I had not written four or five pieces of verse.'[64]

It was part of the myth of the outsider alienated from his environment, of the Shelleyan mood of 'I fall upon the thorns of life, I bleed'. It developed by exaggeration, by placing the emphasis on selected details, and by a fondness for striking imagery even if it distorted the reality. Nevertheless, there is plenty of evidence for the agonies his mother dismissed as invention. As the child of socialist-pacifist parents who had suffered publicly for beliefs they knew were still unpopular, he shared their sense of menace. There was the experience at Sibford: 'misery at midnight in the murderous dormitory', which clearly affected his outlook and development. Then a fair portion of his primary schooldays was spent in boarding schools, and sensitive youngsters like Baxter often experience that peculiar feeling of melancholy such institutions seem to generate. Beyond all this, the sense of grief came from the mysterious depths of the human person of which we are hardly conscious. At that level pressures and influences swirl like subterranean waters. A person as deep as Baxter tapped them for poetry more successfully than most. But like Baudelaire, when he looked into the depths of his own being, he saw the crocodiles. In his own analysis, the general sense of sadness came from an early experience of grief that rose ultimately from the loss of Eden. It is interesting that he believed the feeling of dislocation and the sense of grief helped him to write poems and accounted for their 'rather gloomy tone'. 'In a way the poems sprang out of a quarrel with the status quo. It could be that the root of it all was no more than an early perception of the state that theologians call Original Sin.'[65]

No region provided more grist to his mythopoeic imagination than Brighton: 'Waves, rocks, beaches, flax bushes, rivers, cattle flats, hawks, rabbits, eels, old man manuka trees' offered 'a great store of images that could later enter my poems.'[66] In fact: 'More than half of the images that recur in my poems are connected with early memories of the Brighton township, river, hills and sea-coast – especially the sea-coast.'[67] Brighton was to be the centre of James's life until he left secondary school. And it remained for him 'the home each sailor loves and runs away from' (CP 131).

Baxter's childhood was to be of lifelong significance for himself and for his writing. It was spent not among urban realities, but close to the natural world, which powerfully modified his sensibility. What was virtually a country childhood fostered in him the idea of the 'natural man' living close to nature. Since the person who affected him most was his revered father, it was to be expected that he would become a romantic poet. And he carried with him from childhood the memory of the Baxter clan, men who worked with their hands, and whose natural instincts, unlike those of the Macmillan Browns, were not 'overlaid with concern for social acceptability, material possessions and their own importance in the world.'[68]

III

King's High School 1940-1943

Baxter's home life at this period was evoked 'more objectively than I could see it at the time',[1] in 'A Family Photograph 1939', a poem written in the sixties:

> Waves bluster up the bay and through the throat
> Of the one-span bridge. My brother shoots
> The gap alone
> Like Charon sculling in his boat
> Above the squids and flounders. With the jawbone
> Of a sperm whale he fights the town,
> Dances on Fridays to the cello
> With black-haired sluts. My father in his gumboots
> Is up a ladder plucking down
> The mottled autumn-yellow
> Dangling torpedo clusters
> Of passion fruit for home-made wine.
> My mother in the kitchen sunshine
> Tightens her dressing gown,
> Chops up carrots, onions, leeks,
> For thick hot winter soup. No broom or duster
> Will shift the English papers piled on chairs
> And left for weeks.

Terence was good-looking, sociable, and popular with girls. James said of him: 'with his natural charm, no one could be unfriendly to Terence'.[2] He enjoyed dancing and was knowledgeable about boats. Baxter described himself:

> I, in my fuggy room at the top of the stairs,
> A thirteen-year-old schizophrene,
> Write poems, wish to die,
> And watch the long neat mason-fly
> Malignantly serene
> Arrive with spiders dopier than my mind
> And build his clay dungeons inside the roller blind.
>
> (CP 237-8)

With her usual common sense, his mother would remark: 'He had only to open the window.' But the world he wished to inhabit took no account of banalities such as opening windows. He was immersed in his books. By the age of thirteen he had ploughed through most of Walter Scott's novels, discovered with real pleasure those of H. Rider Haggard, and reduced himself to a nervous wreck through a surfeit of ghost stories. Now new demands were to be made on his time.

After a primary education spent mainly in small private schools, Baxter entered the hurly-burly of King's High School in Bay View Road, South Dunedin. He enrolled in a professional course on 5 February 1940 and gave law as his chosen career. His new school had been opened in 1936 to relieve the pressure on Otago Boys' High, which already had a roll touching a thousand. There had been talk of a school in the south of the city for a long time and land had been set aside for it. From the beginning, support for the new venture exceeded expectations. The foundation third form recruited five boys who had been top of their primary schools, and when Baxter arrived, King's had just over three hundred boys. The first rector, Dudley Chisholm, was an able man who had been a Staff-Captain in the First World War. He was a protégé of Frank Milner, the famous rector of Waitaki Boys' High who had acclimatized English public school traditions to New Zealand. In Milner's system of education the British Empire was God's gift for the advance of civilization.[3]

Chisholm was committed to excellence. He was determined to make his school the equal of the older established schools north and south of the city. Like most boys' schools of the period, King's was conventional, with a strict code of discipline and an emphasis on uniforms – socks up, caps on, shirts tucked in and buttoned up. Competitive sport was of major importance. In a small school especially, a high level of achievement was possible only if everyone pitched in. Dedicated training in all weathers, with the sacrifices that demanded, was deemed to develop character. School sport brought the boys together to face common challenges and to display their skills in a public arena. When success came, it gave the players status among their peers, and the whole school grew in confidence. It felt itself to be on an equal footing with other schools.

Every morning at a quarter to eight, with some half-dozen boys from Brighton, Baxter caught one of Hobbs' Motors' ageing Greyhound buses. On the strength of some obscure link with the famous American company, old Charlie Hobbs had painted a greyhound along the side of his vehicles. At Green Island a few more boys got on the bus, and the group was known to the school as 'the bus boys'. Baxter showed none of the high spirits of schoolboys travelling to and from school. He would have his nose stuck in a book, or be making up crossword puzzles or word-games. Occasionally he would jot down ideas on bits of paper. Observing him lost in his own thoughts, an adult enquired: 'What's wrong with that boy?' She was told with a smile, 'He's a poet.'

When the boys got off the bus they had a ten minute walk through Bathgate Park, down past the rope-works into the back entrance of King's. One of the bus boys recalled that when most of the others had arrived, Baxter and his friend Craigie had covered only a quarter of the distance. From Bob Craigie's account Baxter was a great talker from the time he knew him. He would hold forth on this or that, and stop to observe birds, grasses or flowers. In springtime there was more to be seen, so progress was even more leisurely. Naturally, the boys were often late for assembly. Bob Craigie's mother considered that Baxter lived in a day-dream. She had often seen him walking along with his head in the air, not seeing where he was going, looking at the stars, the sun, the sky, the movement of the clouds.

Baxter's third form report described him as 'logical and widely read'. Academically he scored one for initiative, which was the highest rating, two for intelligence and application, but for leadership and initiative in games, the low mark of four. He scored two for 'manners' and the mark of three for appearance was predictable. His hair was rarely combed ('He wouldn't know what a comb was,' recalled a companion); he merely wet his hair and plastered it back. A sloppy dresser, with baggy trousers below his knees, unbuttoned shirt often hanging out, and socks around his ankles, he did not respond to his mother's urgings to smarten himself up. The elbows were often out of his jerseys. To go barefoot, even in the warmest weather, was not then fashionable, but although there was sometimes snow in winter, he often wore no shoes. At times his legs and feet were blue with the cold. Several times he was reprimanded in assembly. Since he did not relate well to his peers he coped by adopting the role of 'character'. In his general appearance and behaviour he had no instinct for the protective coloration that affords many a schoolboy anonymity.

In his fourth form year he received as a Burn prize for written and spoken English, *Dr Jekyll and Mr Hyde* and *The Jungle Book*[4]. Before school, Baxter often sat on a bench and did the homework he should have done the night before. It surprised classmates that his handwriting and setting-out were so tidy. Already he was pondering philosophical and scientific questions and making statements like 'Bob, have you thought about gravity? When you drop something, what proof have you got that the ground does not come up to meet the object, instead of the object going down to meet the ground?' Bill Pearson recalls visiting the Baxters at Brighton in 1941 when James was in the fourth form: 'Mrs Baxter talked proudly of "Jum" who came in from school before we left. I recall the sharp sensitive profile, the soft pale complexion and an odd impression of a boy snug in his parents' affection, but at a distance from it and from all of us.'[5]

Mr Ted Hayes, Baxter's fifth form English master in 1942, remembered him as a quiet, attentive boy, who participated well in discussions. Hayes was impressed with the range of Baxter's knowledge and, when the class studied phonetics, with his fine ear in detecting differences of pronunciation. He was well-spoken with a pleasant voice and a good vocabulary, and he had a special gift in paraphrase and précis, getting easily to the heart of the matter. In class exercises like parody – something he very much enjoyed and was good at – he showed a keen sense of humour. Baxter had no reputation at high school as a poet. A few knew that he scribbled verses and on one occasion a poem written for a class exercise had 'Excellent' written heavily beside it. But the English syllabus placed great emphasis on grammar, something which did not interest Baxter. Though he could not be bothered working at revision, he came second in English. His essays were especially good. Another teacher, Dr Basil Howard, to whom Baxter was able to relate well, said that other boys put in an essay of four pages, but Baxter wrecked his weekends with fifteen page documents. When new boys joined the form, Baxter was reserved towards them, preferring the company of those he knew.

Because of his fine speaking voice, he was put in the school choir and remained there a whole term before it was discovered he could not sing in tune. As his mother said, 'He hadn't a note of music in him.' Nor could he draw. One day he said to Bob Craigie: 'I'm terrible at doing anything with my hands', yet he thought that the ideal was to work with both your head and your hands. Often Baxter brought no lunch to school. He would buy a pie if he had the money, but if not he would go without. Bob remembered that he often bought fish and chips after school, perhaps as an insurance against the irregular hours of meals at home. During lunch-time he would either read in the library or play chess, for he was a member of the chess club. Sometimes he would sit by himself in the quadrangle with a book or chess board. To the sports-minded majority, it seemed an odd alternative to outdoor games.

From his four years at King's, Baxter is remembered as a well-built, but not muscular boy, with a pale, almost feminine complexion, and strong, very blue eyes. As he loped along with his long arms and slightly hunched shoulders, he was rather ungainly. Throughout high school he was in the top class of his year and usually well up in it – in the third form he was fifth in a class of twenty-four, though he declined to twelfth out of twenty-five in the fifth form. Throughout, English was his best subject, though he was fairly good at History, Latin, and French. Two class-mates recalled Baxter as a boy of short and passionate enthusiasms. He would concentrate on what interested him and skimp the rest. When the class was introduced to advanced algebra, he was consumed with interest for a couple of months, putting in time even outside school hours. He was also a great experimenter, fascinated by chemical formulae, though frequently he did not bother to write up his laboratory book. With chemicals from the laboratory he concocted all sorts of mixtures. Once he made nitro-glycerine and ignited it in the school playhouse, almost setting the building alight.

Generally, however, Baxter was a rather timid, well-behaved boy, who almost never made trouble. During the war there was an influx of women teachers, a new development in a male preserve like King's. Some boys defied them and ragged them endlessly, but Baxter never joined in. On one occasion, just as a young woman teacher was about to come in for her class, he was bundled into a cupboard at the back of the room. Her mystification at the strange sounds, suggestive of an animal much larger than a mouse, was greatly relished by the boys. And Baxter discovered that the way to deal with his tormentors was to go one better and play the clown. Though he often spoke against authority he accepted it in practice. Caning was then part of the system, but Baxter was never severely caned nor in any of the masters' bad books for very long. A companion looking back, and perhaps affected by hindsight, thought that the views he expressed anticipated his later non-conformity. But at school he was not regarded as a rebel. A former master observed that what rebellious energies he had were fully occupied with coping with his companions.

As soon as classes were over, Baxter and Bob Craigie would rush off. It was generally assumed they had to catch the bus to Brighton, so they had a ready excuse for not taking part in organized games. Though these were not compulsory, the school liked boys to join in. When most others were playing or simply passing the time talking, Baxter was gone; so he lost the opportunity of meeting his schoolfellows informally outside class and becoming more acceptable. What he gained was the freedom to go his own way; in the long run this was more valuable in the making of a poet.

Baxter and Bob Craigie walked into town or caught the tram at Cargill's Corner. Sometimes they visited the Athenaeum in the lower Octagon and pored over its fine collection of books, which included many old volumes. Or they would go to the fruit market, or a bookshop, or walk down to the railway station or the nearby Early Settlers' Museum. Occasionally they visited the First Church and strolled around. Baxter was most interested in the Bible and would hold forth on what he had read and what he thought of it. To Bob he did not seem at all religious, and he never went to Church. The Bible was just another interesting book. In those years Baxter even styled himself an atheist. He would say things like: 'What's in this religion? I'm an atheist. What's wrong with being an atheist?' In the poems he was writing at this time he was fiercely critical of the institutional church, which was seen by pacifists as supporting the war. He preferred 'the faith that fired the pagans'. One attraction was:

> The pagan's mystical attitude
> Whence all things have similitude.[6]

Both boys became enthusiastic swimmers and used to go to the tepid baths near the First Church. Normally they caught the quarter to five bus home, but after swimming it was often a rush. There was a little street that led down to the bus terminus in the Queen's Gardens. Baxter took a long time to get dressed and Bob would run ahead. He recalled Baxter emerging from the baths, hair dripping, trousers loose, fly wide open, dropping things as he ran. Sometimes they missed their bus, and had to catch the next one an hour and three quarters later at half past six. On the ride to and from Brighton, Baxter talked a good deal about sex, often coming out with outrageously coarse expressions.

When Baxter started at King's in 1940, New Zealand was at war for the second time in less than thirty years. At the end of the previous year great excitement had swept the country when the New Zealand cruiser HMS *Achilles* took part in the Battle of the River Plate off Montevideo. The adversary, the German pocket battleship *Graf Spee*, was scuttled shortly after the engagement. King's took special pride in having one of their old boys on board the *Achilles*.

The situation of the country at large was reflected in the school. As younger masters enlisted they were farewelled during assembly. The headmaster himself was often away, since he was in charge of the main Otago camp for the National Reserve. The arrival of women teachers and the return of older masters, to release men of military age for active service, reminded everyone of what was expected from patriotic New Zealanders. The school magazine for 1940 observed: 'Although this is only the fifth year of our life as a school, our Old Boys are already doing their part, with most of the older ones in training camp and a few even on active service.'

Photographs of those in the armed forces were displayed in the new Assembly Hall where there was a large chipboard map of the world. During assembly a master would go to the map and explain any significant developments in the war. The 1941 magazine published a full page photograph of the first Old Boy casualty. It also made clear the expectations of the school: 'It would be quite safe to say that the majority of our present senior boys are eagerly looking forward to the day when they can play their part in defending home and country and in ridding the world of the present forces of evil.'

At the breakup in 1940, Baxter's first year at King's, Mr W. Downie

Stewart, a former Cabinet Minister who had once been acting Prime Minister, recalled what it meant to be a citizen of the British Empire, 'the greatest political miracle in the world', as he described it. 'The Dominions,' he said, 'knew Britain was fighting for freedom of thought and freedom of conscience and against the oppression of smaller and weaker nations, militarism and aggression.' His viewpoint received a local habitation in the school cadet corps, which allowed boys to express publicly their solidarity with the war effort. Every year Baxter was at King's, four full days were devoted to cadets, and army instructors put in an hour a week during the first and third term. 'Every boy we train,' an officer harangued the school, 'is another nail in Hitler's coffin.' On Anzac Day 1940, one hundred and twenty senior boys turned out at the Cenotaph and for the function in the Town Hall. On the evening of the fifth of March, the whole cadet battalion attended a recruiting campaign. The school paraded in uniform again during the Queen carnival in support of the Army Queen.

Before Baxter was enrolled at King's, his father had gone to see the headmaster. To his credit, Chisholm readily exempted James from cadet training. But in such an environment there could be no escape from the pressure of his peers. Barracks, as cadet training was called, took place early in his first term, from the nineteenth to the twenty-second of February. The thirteen-year-old boy quickly felt the isolation that was part of the price of nonconformity. Mercifully, war conditions that year meant the school was without military uniforms. Over the next three years it was different, with khaki replacing the school uniform during barracks, and on the days for cadet training throughout the rest of the year Baxter stood out by appearing in civvies on the bus, at assembly, and during classes.

His refusal to take part in cadet training confirmed for his contemporaries what they already believed – that he was a born member of the awkward squad. He did not conform to what is blandly described as the normal way of doing things. Nor did he take part in sport, nor in any community activity. Even in ordinary things he was something of an oddity. His brief-case was so much larger than anyone else's that his school fellows wondered how he could possibly fill it. In addition he was generally regarded as a day-dreamer. Everyone who recalled Baxter testified that he was a loner. One or two said they felt sorry for him.

Schoolboys are notoriously intolerant of eccentricity. During his years at King's, Baxter was given a fairly hard time. Sometimes he was bullied. Boys would grab his brief-case and throw it up on to the roof of the bicycle shed. When he climbed up to retrieve it, they would pull off his shoes. Once they refused to give them back until he got up on a table and danced a jig. At times they would tip out the contents of the brief-case, and end up scragging him. His reaction was not at all ill-tempered, and he was not regarded as being aggressive. Sometimes he would enter into the sport by affecting to scowl and mutter: 'I'll get you for this.' The role of the baddie at bay helped him to cope.

To Archie's dismay, the Labour Party, led by his old pacifist ally Peter Fraser, had introduced conscription. When Terence was called up he appealed against military service, and his case, which came before the court around Christmas 1941, was fully reported in the local papers. Archie appeared as witness, as he was to do for five of his nephews. Terence was asked: 'If the authorities gave you a guarantee that you would not be called upon to bear arms, would you do non-combatant service?' It was the same offer that had been made to his father during the First World War. He replied: 'I would not trust it.'[7] Pressed further he said he would refuse such service. He was sentenced to Defaulter's Detention for the duration of the war. James was then fifteen. His brother had been taken away almost as soon as he came of age, and this was interpreted by the family as a sign of hostility towards Archie.

From the unfriendly outside world Baxter retreated to his own house, where his mother saw there were plenty of books. He became 'the book-bred one', as he later described himself. Reading and writing gave him a world which he could inhabit and control. In that protected enclosure he could marshal his resources against the harsh reality 'beyond the palisade'. A poem of that name, written at the age of fifteen, contains the exhortation:

> 'Seek out thine own abode
> By solitary sun.'

And it ends with the resolution:

> Yet shall I hold in all
>   The faith that none may see –
> The inmost citadel
>   Of strong integrity.
>
>   (CP 4)

His resolution was strengthened by the example of a father whom he revered. Another poem written at about the same time opens:

> O mild preceptor of my early youth,
>   True father still in action, word and deed,
> In whom I find the archetype of truth –
>   For this, my love and gratitude thy meed!

In the poems he was writing on the war, he was one with his father in seeing its futility: 'the battle done/One further mud-patch won', and in lamenting the needless slaughter of men who 'have hopes and aspirations like their own'.[8] And he said that but for his father he would not be a poet. A poem 'To my Mother' from the same period calls her 'friend and mother'. It thanks her for introducing him to many 'tales and legends of the past', and for sharing with him 'the full knowledge that thou long had'st known'.[9] The second of the long series of notebooks, in which he entered all his poems, contains verse written in these years. It had a verse from Matthew Arnold as epigraph:

> 'If poets have not, when they make,
> A pleasure in creating,
> The world, in its turn, will not take
> Pleasure in contemplating.'

James was entering more fully into the interests of his parents and their friends than his brother. Terence had been cast into the role of the practical, outdoor, non-intellectual member of the family by the time of his detention. But he proved to be more reliable than his younger brother and much more helpful in giving his father a hand around the house.

In the vacations the family still went away together. The daughter of neighbours who often accompanied the Baxters on holiday recalled that when James was about fifteen they were at Blackstone Hill, some nine miles from Naseby. He rashly swam through a flooded culvert that ran under the road, although it might have been obstructed in the middle by logs or branches. Her father was terrified he would never emerge. She said it was one of the few occasions she ever saw Archie angry. For James it was a way of testing himself against an adversary. He would swim far out into Brighton Bay for the same reason. His parents were coming to distrust his judgement.

By now, James kept wanting to kiss his young companion, but she said she would have preferred to be kissed by Terence. At this age, with no sisters and little association with girls, James was unable to develop a relaxed and natural attitude towards them. He remained shy and withdrawn and was easily disconcerted. In 'Winter River' he wrote of his youth:

> I never liked it much.
> I did not venture
>
> to touch the thick blonde matted curls
> of those man-swallowing dolls, our big sisters.
> I had no sister.
> Their giggles made me tremble
>
> and coast away to the bathing shed latrine
> in itchy summer torpor,

furiously inventing a unicorn
who hated the metal of Venus.

(CP 378)

At high school his peers did not understand Baxter, nor realize the deep loyalty he felt towards his father and brother. Though he was considered unusual it could not be said that he was ostracized. The boys respected his intelligence and recognized him as a good speaker, who thought out what he said. There was no great hostility towards him because of his pacifism; everyone knew his whole family thought like that, though he was often taunted, 'Conchie, Conchie!' The attitude of the boys reflected their parents' support for the war; those who had relatives killed in action felt resentful towards him and his family. When Japan entered the war, the danger had come closer to New Zealand and on occasions feelings ran high. Baxter recalled: 'I remember the time when a crowd of boys of my own age surrounded me in a shelter shed at school, shouting abuse and inflicting a certain amount of physical violence.'[10] But by and large he experienced a fair degree of acceptance, especially as he advanced into the higher classes. At sixteen he wrote to a friend: 'At school I get a certain amount of opposition as I am the only fit one not in their military cadet corps, but in arguments I usually come out on top.'[11] With the confidence of later life he gave his views on cadet training:

> The school had a militant and active cadet corps. On days when the school as a body had dressed themselves in khaki fancy dress and were practising with unloaded rifles on the lawns, I weeded flower plots, under the charge of the gardener, in the company of another lad who had weak lungs. The arrangement was a compromise between my parents and the school authorities. It might have been pleasanter to put on the tribal finery, fire empty rifles, remove and replace the magazines, and get oil on one's hands, inhaling the smell of grass clippings, metal and scrubbed khaki. On the other hand, it would have been one more mental jail which I'd have had to climb out of later in life. I could see that the boys I knew became less themselves the more they became members of the corps. Their faces became wooden and their language monotonous. They were entering the borders of the collective fantasy generated by Ares, dealer in souls. My own fantasies were Venusian, perhaps less harmful.[12]

Because of his constant reading Baxter's eyes were often bloodshot during his time in the upper school. He was teased for it, but by then he could look after himself. The earlier badgering and humiliations had been harder to take, but he came to believe they helped his development as a writer: 'These experiences were in the long run very valuable, for they taught me to distrust mass opinion and sort out my own ideas; but at the same time they were distinctly painful. I could compare them perhaps with the experiences of a Jewish boy growing up in an anti-Semitic neighbourhood. They created a gap in which the poems were able to grow.'[13]

A letter to a friend in his last year at the school suggests he had been reasonably content: 'Sixth form life has lost some of its attractions for me since I discovered that "free" periods are never free. Nevertheless, I like it.'[14] At the end of that year, the lower sixth, without any public examinations to prepare for, decided to get up a concert for the rest of the school. Baxter volunteered to do the Highland fling. The clown fully met the school's expectations and his performance brought the house down. In *Canta*, July 1948, he wrote of King's: 'By the time I'd been there a year or two I was counted all right and a bit of a dag. And I made friends with one or two that were a bit like myself . . . My last year at school I began to like it a good deal. There were always the masters saying, "I don't expect the 4th form behaviour from 6th form boys", but even they were human at times. There was no one to bully you any longer and a lot of the time you could do what you liked. In a way I was sorry to leave.'[15]

In 1942, in his third year at King's, Baxter passed University Entrance, gaining his highest marks in English and French, and coming first in the class in English. Though he admitted his marks were 'nothing spectacular', he was very excited at his success, and went around telling everyone. The local milkman at Brighton gave the family a free bottle of cream to celebrate. He returned to school the following year and told a friend that he intended to become a lawyer.[16] At the end of the first term of 1943 his form master wrote that he: 'Seems to work quite energetically in all his subjects and has a good deal more than average ability in English.' He gained his Higher Leaving Certificate, awarded in those days to anyone who had 'substantially completed a course of four years secondary instruction with one year of advanced study higher than University Entrance'. That year he was placed first equal in English. The teachers recognized that in certain areas he was exceptional, and his English teachers commented on his outstanding linguistic ability. From the remarkable number of Old Boys of King's with positions of responsibility in the community, it is obvious there was a great deal of talent in the school. A comment attributed to the headmaster, Chisholm, is therefore significant: 'Of all the boys in the school, Baxter without doubt is the most brilliant.'

The image of a Jewish boy growing up in an anti-Semitic neighbourhood which Baxter used of his time at King's may have over-dramatized his situation. Yet despite what he said in moods of generosity, he was not truly happy there. A Brighton friend to whom Baxter used to speak freely said that he hated the place: the school uniform, the discipline, the emphasis on sport, the cadet training and the constant pressure to conform. Years later, when a master at the school asked Baxter if he could remember anything

good about the place, he replied: 'The library.' On the occasion of the
school's twenty-fifth anniversary, a teacher, with the unquenchable
optimism of schoolmasters, requested a poem. Baxter declined, saying he
had not been very happy at King's and that if he did write a poem they might
not wish to publish it.

Earlier – at the age of thirteen, according to 'A Family Photograph 1939'
– Baxter had a death-wish. The desire for death is also referred to in 'At
Brighton Bay':

> Today I hoisted myself
> Up the rock stair that's called Jacob's Ladder
>
> This end of the bay, shoving through gorse, and stood
> On the smooth edge of the flax-covered cliff
>
> That tempted me to suicide . . .
>
> (CP 371)

In a letter written to a woman friend on 21 June 1960, Baxter presents the
temptation in a different guise:

> At sixteen or thereabouts I used to get down the sawn-off 22 I used for rabbits,
> and put the muzzle in my mouth, and wanted to pull the trigger. Why? Because
> I was a wicked wretch who would soon go insane because of masturbation. I
> was right inside the mad Calvinist judgment crystal; a perfect frame for
> schizophrenia. Why didn't I? Because I feared the void. Because I knew how
> extremely unhappy it would make my parents. Because I thought secretly . . .
> Boy you have never been in love. Wait till then and then decide. Venus was to
> be the Saviour. Sob stuff.[17]

In 'At Day's Bay' he felt grateful to have survived:

> I think of
> adolescence: that sad boy
> I was, thoughts crusted with ice
> on the treadmill of self-love,
>
> Narcissus damned, who yet brought
> like a coal in a hollow
> stalk, the seed of fire that runs
> through my veins now. I praise that
> sad boy now, who having no
> hope, did not blow out his brains.
>
> (CP 309)

In 'Notes on the Education of a New Zealand Poet' he wrote of what this period did for his writing:

> It seems to me, looking back, that the negative aspects of my growth were in the long run of most help to me as a writer. They tempered the axe of intellect, as it were. A writer cannot avoid the task of exploring and understanding the private hell which lies just below the threshold of his own mind. I doubt if he can begin to understand the threefold aspect of the modern world – monotony, atrocity, anarchy – if he has not first done this. But while this growth was going on, I was of course a very quiet New Zealand lad doing this and that in a quiet New Zealand town.[18]

All his life he was to be fiercely critical of the New Zealand system of education. He based his views on his own experience and what he had learnt from the young. The schools fostered many of the attitudes with which he was most out of sympathy. They exerted powerful pressure to conform, and to be different was to provoke ridicule and bullying. Conformity, to Baxter, meant compromise and the loss of personal freedom. His parents wondered if they had done the right thing in sending him to King's, and later he himself speculated on the type of education he would have preferred. Certainly he would have liked it to be coeducational. With the romantic unreality to which he was prone, he added: 'Perhaps – till ten years old, on a farm in the South Island mountains or the Urewera country, learning to handle a horse and a dog and a gun; then, for a year to two, during puberty, in a Maori pa; then perhaps on the coastal boats. By now I might have owned a good fishing launch. One could still have learned to read and write. There is no lack of libraries in this country. But our firms and departments require literate peons for their dreary empires of economic liberalism. So we have universal and compulsory education'.[19] He was aligning himself here with his Baxter ancestors, not with the Macmillan Browns.

During the war years his family experienced considerable animosity from the local community. Neighbours felt that the country was fighting for what the Baxters enjoyed like everyone else, yet they would not lift a finger to defend it. The family became isolated. Older people seemed especially bitter, and on the bus to and from school James felt their antagonism. A young friend of his at the Brighton primary school, who was also from a pacifist family, was taunted at school: 'Your father's got a yellow belly.' She felt that the school authorities made little attempt to protect the children of those opposed to the war. On one occasion faeces were emptied all over the lawn of pacifist neighbours of the Baxters. A friend who had been a radio operator had his house ransacked because he was suspected of sending signals to the Japanese. And suspicion also fell on the Baxters: 'I remember how in my teens, we could not put on the light in the upper room at night, because such neighbours would imagine we were signalling to Japanese submarines.'[20] The wartime bitterness was his first personal experience of the hostility that was part of the family inheritance. The reaction of the Brighton community gave him 'a sense of difference, of a gap – not of superiority, nor of inferiority, though at times it must have felt like that, but simply of difference – between myself and other people.'[21]

During his schoolboy years, Baxter's real life was going on within. He was writing verse nearly every day, and considered that some of it had shape and meaning. But 'I had no tools to deal with the central anguish of a child hurled into the adolescent abyss, at the mercy of his imagination and the impulses of his body; for our civilisation has no such tools to give. It was some time before I could forge them for myself.'[22] We are fortunate to know a good deal more about how these tools were forged than Baxter disclosed in 'Notes on the Education of a New Zealand Poet'.

One of the significant friendships he formed at this time was with Noel Ginn, Terence's hut-mate in the Detention camp, located just off the Shannon-Foxton highway. Ginn had worked for the government in order to save enough money to go to university. His studies were under way when he was called up for military service. Already he had a good general knowledge in literature, religion, and philosophy.[23] From August 1942 until late in 1945 (that is between the ages of sixteen and nineteen), Baxter corresponded with him regularly. He sent Ginn nearly all the poems he was writing, told him what he was reading and what writers were influencing him. Ginn became a kind of mentor for his ideas on literature, lending him books of poetry, and providing a sympathetic and critical audience. And Baxter offered detailed criticism of Ginn's own poems. The letters show how precocious Baxter was in his wide and discriminating reading of modern poetry, and how dedicated he was to the writing of verse. He was getting for himself an education none of his schoolmasters could give.

Baxter's letters to Ginn are fascinating because of the light they throw on his development as a poet. The earliest letter, written on 9 August 1942, contains the first of many references to his own writing. It gives one reason he was writing so much, and speaks of the romantic theme of the passing of time, which was already preoccupying him: 'Throughout my poems there is the idea of the ephemerability of time – as we know it – and, along with this the eternal endurance of what is time, space, matter and spirit combined . . . "The Flame of Grass" is a very negative poem – for negative emotions are most easily expressed and understood. Therefore the preponderance of my poems have a touch of nostalgia or some similar feeling.' On 9 August 1942 he was reading Pound, and a fortnight later he commented on Auden, Spender, MacNeice, Day Lewis, Dylan Thomas, and T. S. Eliot, expressing admiration tempered with dislike of their modernist and Marxist elements.

He had also read a good deal of Wordsworth, whose lyricism attracted him, though he objected to what he considered a certain didactic smugness.

A letter of 21 November 1942 apologized for not having written, since he was working for Matriculation then about three weeks off. He thanked Ginn for a poem by Terence, which he liked, and he enclosed two poems: 'Post-Proelium', an indictment of slaughter, and one in the style of Gerard Manley Hopkins. Dylan Thomas he still found obscure. On 16 January 1943 he made the interesting statement that his poems spoke better than he did. Two months later he was speculating about his future profession. Doubtless his classmates in the Lower Sixth were doing the same. One was to become a doctor, another a Professor of Classics. Baxter was not yet completely decided on law, and he was considering the role of prophet, though his inclinations were plainly literary.[24] He wrote:

> . . . if I see any chance of a job as lecturer or literary critic I'll go for it. The ideal, of course, is Professor of Poetry – but after all, that might lead to narrow-mindedness even more than law. The role of a prophet is a delectable one but would not provide me with a living. However, first and foremost, I will NOT sell my soul. Be easy on that point. If I should find it possible to live by writing I would gladly do so. Yet many men have thought they could, and found it an illusion.
>
> Concerning the Law. It is true that 'the manifestations of evil cannot be passively endured'. Yet the seditious man is no criminal, is usually more 'good' than his judges; the thief (not kleptomaniac) is the natural product of our economic system; the murderer has the precedent of war; the sexual criminal is put off balance by environment, by our mad warping 'civilisation'; the smuggler, racketeer etc. is only a go-getting business-man. Governments do their utmost to plant in us the inabilities to put ourselves in the place of others: we must fight this, fight this till we die, die fighting it. Perhaps the barrister has a place. He is in the system, tries to prevent a few from the unrighteous punishments of the system, which destroy warped humanity and strengthen, not destroy, warping influences. Anyway, Law is a dirty business. I'll do my best to keep out of it. The only reason I consider it is that I might be a good lawyer. I am human, so will often fall from it, but to me the only true Law is the Xtian one – Humanity, humanity, and again humanity. This casts out pain and evil, but not those influenced by pain and evil. Doubts as to the existence of God do not destroy this Law. In the legal system I see, as you see the utter lack of psychiatry, the inhumanity of humans.
>
> In the words of a man influenced by the powerful, poetic (yet blinding) emotion of indignation: 'But this I know, that every Law that men have made for Man, since first Man took his brother's life, and the sad world began, but straws the wheat and saves the chaff with a most evil fan.'

Baxter's philosophical and social views are clearly affected by government policies during the war and particularly by its treatment of conscientious objectors. They also reflect the conversations he would have heard at home between his parents and their friends. His last paragraph shows he could use his own reading to give point to what he heard. The letter demonstrates how early he began to formulate the social philosophy which later he would argue as skilfully as any lawyer. He already considered that the state was failing to embody in social terms any real humanity. In Christianity he had found a standard against which to judge it. His scrutiny of politically organized society would one day lead to a radical analysis in the light of one of the great controlling ideas in his thought, the concept of the Just City. But at sixteen the process had begun. The reference to the thief and sexual criminal illustrates his rejection of the Calvinist view that as a result of the Fall human nature is intrinsically vitiated. Baxter is presenting the socialist view that men and women are naturally good, but seduced by a corrupt society.

He enclosed a poem imitating R. A. K. Mason, and after sending greetings to Terence added that if the war did not end soon he would be joining him. On 16 April 1943 he agreed that his theme was the survival of life. He could never accept the view that life was futile. For him human relationships provided the basis of 'the soul' and he planned to build on his own personality and what he made of the personalities of others.

In the same letter he said he agreed entirely with Goethe on the subject of Great Works and was pleased to have what he had worked out for himself confirmed. It is of interest that he was already reading Goethe who articulated in *Faust* 'the great romantic conflict of the divided self.'[25] He enclosed 'Hill-Top', with the comment that unlike most of his other poems it was written out of experience. He told Ginn: 'At fifteen I lived more in what I read and wrote than in what I saw or did.'[26] From now on, more and more poems were to follow this new direction. But he thought poems based on reading and poems based on actual experience had much in common. He said of his early poem 'The Mountains', written when he was sixteen: 'The poem from reading is very like the poem from memory, and all good poems have much of memory in them; also much of present emotion.'[27] Memory was to be a powerful element in some of his best poems. The principles of his poetic were being established.

Already he was a Blake enthusiast, admiring his 'pure poetry' and the sanity of his theories. Lawrence, too, he had read with enjoyment though he found him irrational on sex.[28] Two of the greatest poems he had read were Blake's 'Tiger' and Auden's 'Lay your sleeping head, my love'. Both were doom poems, 'perhaps I like doom'.[29] He was well aware that the theme of Auden's poem was homosexual love.

By 4 July 1943, a few days after his seventeenth birthday, he had read *New Bearings* by F. R. Leavis, which Ginn had sent him. He liked the criticism of Victorian poets, and was delighted to find Leavis praising the same parts of

'Empedocles on Etna' which had impressed him. He talked enthusiastically about Hopkins, Auden, and Yeats, was bored by Bridges, and expressed distaste for Browning. Yeats was singled out for special praise. He criticized the Georgians, and censured both Eliot and Pound for their obscurity. At this time, what Baxter most admired in poetry was vitality of thought, because he believed it intensified the emotion of a poem. Though he had pronounced authoritatively on many matters in this letter, he must have felt he was chancing his arm because he told Ginn to have no qualms about contradicting him. An undated letter which was probably written early in 1943 advocated combining the strengths of traditional and modernist verse, something Ginn was not achieving. In Baxter's eyes to be unable to appreciate Burns because he was traditional and sentimental was to be a literary lost soul. Early in his seventeenth year he was lamenting his decline as a poet and felt he was not as original as he once was.

Since Ginn was in a Detention Camp, the correspondence was censored. By 11 September 1943 the censor had become restive and complained to Ginn. Perhaps the letters overtaxed his concentration or made him feel inadequate. Baxter responded that he did not have to read his poems, which in any case were rarely subversive.

Despite evidence to the contrary, Baxter wrote that while he was at school he did not write many poems, nor very good ones for that matter. All the same he felt in need of someone capable of appreciating what he wrote. His father could do that up to a point, so could his mother to a lesser extent. But he was glad to have a more intellectual reader such as Ginn.[30] On 2 October 1943 he spoke of one poem, 'In Flames Politic', as an imitation of Yeats and he explained that the merit of syllabic verse was in its cumulative effect. He realized the difficulties of writing, and that he had never been able to say all he wanted to say. The nearest he had come was in 'The Mountains'.

As yet he was not consciously religious and felt he never would be. At the same time he did not believe that human life ended with death:

> Religion can never be my way, for in so doing I retire to my mind and find no true life there; only in meeting others do I find it – and how many can we meet? My advice, for what it's worth is: don't face up to things; lie low; don't think more than you can help, then when the weight is lifted there may not be much to face up to.
>
> Religion to me is not an ardent need for a belief in (god) though in trouble I always seem to find one to murmur to. It is a belief in the sameness & continuity of life; thus, at any rate mentally I would fear pain but not death, for I cannot believe in death.[31]

Of the relationship between the meaning and form of a poem, he wrote: 'If I thought the meaning of a poem was all that mattered, that the verse-form was merely for adornment and easy remembering, I would rewrite all my poems in simple prose. But emotion is the essence of poetry: vowel–music promotes it, rhythm facilitates its flow. Naturally one wants original thought; but it is the emotional force, not the reasoning force, that makes the poetry.'[32] He told Ginn his poems were written to be read aloud.

On 16 October 1943 he was greatly enjoying *The Faber Book of Modern Verse* and considered Yeats to be the best poet included, calling him 'the greatest modern poet the master of the phrase',[33] though Auden, he believed, 'has made better poetry of modern conditions than anyone else I know.'[34]

On 15 November 1943 he again expressed concern for his brother and found his imprisonment 'a sore spot' in his mind. It seemed to him that his brother might have to re-enact his father's experiences, and he was horrified at the thought that Terence would have to suffer physical pain. He himself did not have that kind of courage.

Baxter was deeply affected by the war and its effect on him can hardly be overemphasized. At home it was discussed every day. British papers arrived by airmail, radio broadcasts were listened to and commented on. The mental anguish of relations and friends, either in camp or in conflict with the community because of their unpatriotic views, affected every aspect of life. And it was a long war. Baxter was driven further into his private world where he could fight the dragons with words.

With his school examinations over he was looking forward to going to university the following year. Already while he was at King's he had called in occasionally, and he had visited the editorial office of the student newspaper *Critic*. He reported that he had met some intelligent students, but 'no good poets, no Noels, but such are rare.'[35]

IV
The Making of a Poet

In the New Year of 1944 the family was holidaying in a rented house at Naseby, an old gold-mining town in Central Otago. Baxter had been unusually sociable, joining with the locals in rounders and tennis and swimming. But he liked walking on his own 'among broom and gold–claims composing moral codes', and he always carried a pencil and notebook with him. He was still writing regularly to Noel Ginn discussing his own reading and writing. Many of the poems he mentions, and the age at which they were written, were meticulously entered into notebooks.

At Naseby his holiday reading included Auden, whom he considered 'the best modern' since he first read 'Lay your sleeping head . . .'.[1] It may have been the example of Auden's practice of mythologizing his experience which so profoundly affected the same inclination in Baxter, and helped to make him the most mythopoeic of our poets. He was reading widely and already had a good library of poetry books to which he was always adding. By 20 January 1944 he had bought the poems of Harold Monro, Siegfried Sassoon, and Gerard Manley Hopkins. He admired Monro's 'Bitter Sanctuary' but was ecstatic over Hopkins: 'He is great – that is all one can really say, except for reading him again and again. I may be unusually susceptible to him; anyway he is like the bread, the water of life to me as far as poetry goes (it goes a long way.) . . . "Spring and Fall" I know by heart and repeat mentally and aloud whenever not in company. The sad-made-strength is Hopkins' forte.' Baxter's early experience, his fondness for doom, and his admiration for Hopkins's 'sad-made-strength', help to account for the gloomy tone of much of the early poetry. They also formed a cast of mind that led him to lament and to memorialize.

In February he was delighted to receive from Ginn MacNeice's *Autumn Journal*, and T. S. Eliot's *Essays:* 'Eliot's essays are the best I know on poetry. My tentative efforts in that direction quail when I read him – I have found that it is far easier to write good poetry than good prose; or rather the mental apparatus is different and I haven't developed it yet.'[2] Within a few weeks of receiving *Autumn Journal* Baxter sent Ginn a long poem of over four hundred lines using the metre he had learnt from MacNeice.

Baxter's class-mates at King's were surprised that he did not return to try for a University Scholarship. He had topped the class in English in Matriculation, and was top again in the Lower Sixth. On 19 February 1944 he told Ginn he was leaving school and going to university. His mother encouraged him, but he was determined to take it on his own terms. He still did not know what courses to take, but at university he expected to find people he could talk to about the ideas he was wrestling with, ideas such as the nature of good and evil. But he had many reservations: '. . . why am I going to "Varsity"? For knowledge? – I can acquire for myself as much as my digestion will stand, not undigested slabs. For a good job? – It is what I am, not what I do that matters. For prestige? – a barrier to sympathy.'

Behind his uneasiness was admiration for his father, who was a ploughman, road-contractor, and farmer. In the eyes of his son no one had greater integrity nor peace of mind, and he attributed his father's sanity to the fact that he worked with his hands. The true line of development for such people, he believed, lay in subjectivity. His immediate plan for himself was to 'work at manual labour, keep off drink (which is to the mind and emotions like pouring sand on a sea-anemone), sexually find my own way.'[3]

On 6 March 1944 he enclosed a long Ode, 'rather like George Barker', and proposed that he and Noel publish a book jointly, 'like Wordsworth and Coleridge in *Lyrical Ballads*'. By 12 March he had read *Wuthering Heights* for the first time, and admired Emily Brontë's dramatic skill in putting aside her own beliefs and principles to allow Heathcliff to be his passionate self.

When requesting *35 Poems* by Herbert Read on 18 March 1944 he added: 'Just lately I have been re-reading Dylan Thomas. I find his involved symbolism as difficult as ever, in spite of a sort of emotional reception.' But Dylan Thomas's hour would come. Already Baxter liked his prose, and since his own poetry had reached an impasse, he had resolved to go in for prose:

> I am not satisfied with my poetry: your last letter has, as it were, touched the spark to a waiting fuse. I am casting round for new footholds. Always when I have come to an impasse before I have found a new cycle to swing onto. But this time not. Well, if I stop writing for practice – and I have learned about all I need to as far as technique goes, it is only driving-force I need – I will still write such poems as TO THE SUN, but will move otherwise to occasional prose. Prose is greater than poetry: infinite horizons. My prose technique needs improvement, as I see in studying other writers. I could not be 'a sedulous ape' like Stevenson, but will have to go as well as I can – along modern lines, I think.

At seventeen he did indeed know a good deal about poetic technique, as his poetry notebooks show. The range and closeness of the reading evident in his correspondence with Ginn explain how he acquired it. He was also aware of his own precocity in reaching a point many of the poets he had read arrived at only later. Yet already he felt his scope was too narrow. When he toyed with abandoning poetry in favour of prose, he remained quite sure his vocation was to be a writer. For him, writing, like breathing, was part of being alive.

On 24 March 1944, at the age of seventeen, Baxter enrolled in English, Latin, French, and Philosophy at the University of Otago. He was supported financially by his parents. As Brighton was twelve miles from Dunedin, he still had to find the most economical way of getting in and out of town. He settled for cycling, though the wartime shortages made new tyres hard to get. A letter to Noel Ginn on Easter Sunday, 9 April, gave his first impressions of the university:

> I find 'Varsity very new but have become fairly used to things. The best feature is the 'canteen' where I can get coffee before lectures. English is not very hard, the professor being a Shakespeare enthusiast; Latin (I have been persuaded to take Latin) is rather difficult; French I can stand up to. The two last I mean to pass in; but as I am not taking them for the second year, I don't intend to expand much beyond the lecture-notes and specified books. Still, I read a bit of modern French: Giono (Jean) who has a most powerful style; and numerous prison-reformers on Cayenne . . .
>
> Psychology (1st Year Philosophy) is rather striking. I have done some Exp. Psych. and am waiting to get my lab. book next week – in mild trepidation. I wrote up an experiment on 'interviewing' at length, about 8 pages.
>
> I smoke a bit, not very much; intend later on to 'roll my own' as tailor-made are rather biting. Went to the Freshers' Hop and got one or two long-suffering females to haul me round the floor. It was very enjoyable on the whole.

Dancing was not one of his accomplishments. Its social aspect appealed to him, but his lack of co-ordination made him clumsy. His form-master at King's the previous year, Dr Basil Howard, was now the liaison officer between the secondary schools and the university. It was he who persuaded Baxter to take Latin.

Baxter threw himself eagerly into the literary life of the university, publishing four poems in the opening issue of *Critic*, the student newspaper, which said that 'Hill-Country' was 'powerfully suggestive of the New Zealand landscape and atmosphere . . . not so much a series of vivid scenes, as one swift comprehensive view of the whole drama of the land.' It was virtually a joint effort with Hopkins:

> Yellow broom blooming
> Pollen-heavy. Bees hum
> Come from air there –
> Bare, bleak, blue-peak
> Towers over mountain flower –
> (CP 7-8)

Otago University offered a Macmillan Brown prize for poetry, awarded 'for excellence in verse on a subject which allows scope for imaginative treatment'. That year the topic was 'Convoys'. The competition was open to all undergraduates of Otago University, and to all graduates of not more than two years' standing. Baxter found the topic distasteful: 'a disgusting subject betraying the lack of imagination of whoever chose it.' Once he decided to compete, however, he applied himself. On 24 February 1944 – a full month before he had enrolled at the university – the poem was already written, and he thought it 'a pretty good one'. The general tone, however, might be 'too near to pacifist to ring the bell'. But he was adjudged the winner. Since he was the grandson of the founder of the prize, the editor of the *Otago Daily Times*, John Moffett, published his entry with a youthful-looking photograph of the poet. The poem contained one hundred and fifty-nine lines. After an evocation of the sea, it recalled the hazardous journeys of Phoenician galleys, Columbus's caravels, and 'the iron monsters' of modern battle fleets. It touched on the bitterness, hatred, and futility of war, then moved into a prayer to 'iron fate/That hope predominate'. The poem was well constructed, with sections of long, irregular lines alternating with shorter ones that rhymed. In 'Captains edgy for alarms', the gift for phrasing flashes out. Stylistically the poem is a pastiche of Shelley, Day Lewis, MacNeice and Auden:

> What power drives these convoys?
> For what will the seas loosen their liquid vice?
> For what will men brave bergs of ice,
> Hail and sickness? Is it but the red
> Furnace coal – or oil fed –
> The precise steel shaken by blind steam?
> It is more. It is the ammonite's dream . . .
> Sand-buried forests here grow leaves again,
> The leaves of flame flicker . . . And in man's brain
> Shell-coiled, the form of ships unbuilt
> Born in crude galley and caravel. And blood spilt
> To save the Roman grain-ships pirated.
> There are ships and sailors, the unburied dead,
> Save by the black seas buried; hulks that lie
> In wars sunk, by storms sunk; the high
> Sea-roof above them, bedded upon ooze.
> These are the fates that wrangle in her flues,
> Battle-ship, liner.
>   . . .

'Convoys' is competent and has some of the merits of a prize poem. For a seventeen-year-old with strong pacifist views it was an imaginative feat. Winning the prize within a month of enrolling at the university made him 'pleased, even thrilled (perhaps that is puerile), partly because it is pleasant for my parents. Anyway, an increase to my banking account.'[4] Fellow students writing in *Critic* praised the poem's vigour, and considered it both profound and intelligible. One justly observed that the subject was beyond Baxter's range of experience, though it was on the whole successful. Alistair Campbell, the lyric poet, who was also a student at Otago in 1944, said that before 'Convoys' Baxter had been an ordinary enough student. Now everyone was talking about him. On 4 May a writer in *Critic* commenting on a recent *N.Z. Listener* review of New Zealand poetry remarked that the verse of J. K. B. is Otago's example of 'what possibilities there are waiting to be cultivated'.[5]

Baxter's next triumph was with 'Prelude N.Z.', which won the Literary Society's annual verse competition. With two prizes for poetry under his belt, and the publication of poems of the quality of 'O lands seen in the light of an inhuman dawn', he was setting too hot a pace for some students. Signs of the jealousy Baxter's outstanding talent would inevitably provoke in some other writers appeared in an unsigned letter in *Critic* on 7 September: 'In common with many other students I feel it is a pity that J. K. B., one of our most promising literary contributors, is being used to excess on our Literary Page . . . likely to be on the one hand detrimental to J.K.B. and on the other discouraging to whatever other latent talent we have in O. U.'[6] Baxter's final contribution to *Critic* that year, 'Spring', was a fair rendering of an ode of Horace.

Already in 1944 Otago University had a New Zealand literature group. *Critic* ran articles on R. A. K. Mason and Frank Sargeson. The literary society was capable of mounting a lecture on D. H. Lawrence and another on surrealistic poetry. Baxter took part in a panel discussion 'What is Art?', arguing unexceptionably that the poet must be motivated by deep and sensitive feeling and be a master of words. More interesting was the way he supported his thesis by wide-ranging quotations from poets he admired.

Baxter was remembered by his fellow students as youthful-looking, with a large head and aquiline features. He had full, pink, shapely lips, and eyes that gave his face a great intensity. What was most striking was his resonant voice, described by W. H. Oliver in a poem as a 'golden whine'. Baxter's unusual voice gave him a natural authority. He spoke well and with great originality. He had read more than most of his contemporaries, and his conversation was sprinkled with quotations from the books he had just been reading. All his life he could call up verse at will. Wherever he went he was becoming the focus, and he dominated most groups he was in. He had a good sense of humour, enlivening his talk with witticisms or mimicry of lecturers he found dull. His habitual manner was that of somebody totally absorbed in whatever interested him at the time. He also liked playing different roles. In the photograph published by the *Otago Daily Times* when he won the poetry competition, he looked quite respectable in sports coat and tie. Normally he trailed around in a long grey overcoat.

Some of those who worked in the office of *Critic* recalled that he had the knack of talking easily with people even if it happened that they were not literary. He was able to command attention because he spoke so well and with such originality. At university, Baxter was really coming into his own, and the legend that kept growing until his death took root.

In Baxter's time, Otago University was not a homogeneous place. Students in the faculties of medicine, dentistry, mining, science, and the arts might know very little about what went on outside their disciplines. *Critic* to some extent supplied a bridging of interests, but each faculty had its own concerns. Baxter's reputation flourished in the Faculty of Arts. Boundaries of any sort confined him less than most, but to many outside the Arts Faculty, he was not known.

In a residential university like Otago the pub assumed special importance. In the Bowling Green Hotel students could relax, and there Baxter met people and found an audience. At the Silver Grille, a sort of hash-house in the Octagon where he took his meals, he enlarged his acquaintance by mixing with workers from the city. With his newly found freedom from the discipline of home and school he had begun to drink heavily, and he was undoubtedly affected by the example of George Barker and Dylan Thomas. He was entering the confines of Bohemia.

Before he enrolled at Otago his mother had warned him that some girls might want to sleep with him and that he should keep away from them. Her estimate of her son's character, he conceded, was accurate, but he was to be disappointed: 'No Otago girl ever tried to rape me. For many long months I searched hard for such a siren, without success. Those iceberg virgins never melted.'[7]

This was confirmed by Alistair Campbell, who recalled that though Baxter had a reputation as a womanizer he saw no sign of it. He could not even remember seeing him with a girl. A woman student of 1944 considered that he related well to women. They enjoyed his company because 'he treated you as a person he really wanted to talk to'. Some senior women students lived in Huntly, an overflow annex from St Margaret's, one of the university hostels. Baxter was a frequent visitor there, enjoying a yarn and reading poetry as though it were a Celtic chant. Sometimes he would drop his voice very low so the women would have to listen attentively. In those days there were no poetry readings as we know them today, so the audience was more appreciative. But not everyone, especially those doing medicine or science, could take him as seriously as he took himself.

Campbell was in the same English I and Latin I class as Baxter at Otago. Since Latin had only a handful of students he got to know him well. In his view Baxter was a fair scholar but not particularly gifted in foreign languages. As the year wore on Baxter's early diligence flagged. He would drop into lectures only when it suited him, and his entry could be dramatic. At the last minute he would rush down the aisle with his coat flapping behind him. Then as now, lecturers were variable. One of the best was the Professor of Classics, Tommy Adams, who was also a Presbyterian elder. He was a dapper little man with a rather jaunty manner, who was able to communicate his own passionate enthusiasms. Campbell was fascinated by the books they were studying: the sixth book of the *Aeneid* and the ninth book of Livy. Nor were they lost on Baxter. Virgil's hero, Aeneas, entered his imagination.

One night early that year, on the way home to Brighton, Baxter was pedalling up hill too slowly for the dynamo to light his lamp. A girl cycling down hill without a light collided with him head-on. He was badly concussed and her nose was broken. When the pair went to a farmhouse for assistance they were mistaken for two escapees from Borstal who were said to be in the area. Eventually the family took them in and called an ambulance. Baxter spent a couple of days in hospital. The people at the farm remembered that his main concern was for the girl's injuries.

Psychology fascinated Baxter. He was reading McDougall's exposition of the instincts, and texts of Freud, Jung, and Adler, not in potted versions, but in full. He knew them well enough to be able to argue with the lecturers over their interpretations. When the class was given an IQ test Baxter's was the highest. In his spare time he continued to read widely and study the art of poetry. He told Ginn on 9 April 1944: 'G. M. H. teaches above all compression, which is the great trick, to be learned by all poets; although poetry itself depends on a queer letting-go, trance almost, using reality merely as a peg.' He had also read Herbert Read and learnt Wilfred Owen's 'Strange Meeting' by heart, reciting it whenever 'I get bored biking to Varsity'. On 25 May 1944, despite a certain feeling of depression, and the sense that his writing had fallen off, he was enjoying university and had his 'moments of expansion mostly in the company of the crude'.

During the holidays he travelled with a WEA lecturer and visited the Kaitangata mine. Years later his memories, enriched by discussions with his father, entered a poem called 'On Reading Yevtuschenko':

> When the mine exploded at Kaitangata
> Trucks flew out as if from the barrel of a gun,
> Trucks and truckers, bodies of men,
> Or so my father told me;
> > and far down
> In those dark passages they heard faintly
> The waves of the sea hammer
> Above their heads.
>
> (CP 261)

Of late he had read one of Joyce's short stories and Tolstoy's 'Death of Ivan Ilyich', which he thought 'the best short story in the world'. It taught him the nature of death, the helplessness, the inevitability, and the 'blindness of those whose turn hasn't come yet'. It showed him that people 'might live without God, but they couldn't die without Him'. He had become a man much possessed by the idea of death.[8] He had also read Sargeson: 'who strikes me as able but of a style and plotting too cut-down for this N.Z. society: Europeans have to prune their material: we have to build it up.'[9] Because of the importance he attached to eloquence, Baxter at seventeen was still unable to appreciate Sargeson's achievement. Sargeson admired the style of the nineteenth century novel and its range of effects, but he was among the first to use a sparer, more colloquial style to render the New Zealand experience.[10]

Ginn had criticized Dylan Thomas as a person and Baxter agreed: '. . . an objectionable specimen of introversion – yet would I give worlds to have written his "We lying by seasands" '.[11] Religion is once again on his mind: 'I do not think I will ever become an atheist, coherent personality growing like a tree cannot narrow to anything so dogmatic. I remain agnostic; have often felt that unvague prescience "the whole reconciled with the parts, the parts with the whole", but never the presence or necessity of a God.'[12]

University was going well and in an English examination, 'phonetics and some fairly hard stuff about Tennyson, Browning etc', he scored 85 per cent with only one or two above him.

Disturbing rumours about his behaviour must have reached Ginn and Terence at Shannon, for he wrote in his own defence: 'I really appreciate your and Terry's concern, but I am more solid than you think. I am growing up, changing gear as it were; or setting sail, inevitably shipping a few seas, but will not sink or run aground. What I am trying to say is: don't regard what is partial as entire, any more than you would regard any poem of mine as all I had to say. Tell Terry not to worry. I will find a basis, am finding.' And he was concerned for his brother: 'a lone wolf – dark and sensitive . . . when I do think of him that indescribable grip of consanguinity makes my mind sore.'[13] With luck he hoped to see them both at the end of August.

Baxter criticized Ginn for not shaping his verse enough; and he spoke of his own need to shape and re-shape:

> . . . not to a standard, but till an intuitional dissatisfaction is satisfied: the 'poetic censor' let us call it. I avoid him sometimes, sometimes can press on without him, but always in danger, often in ruin . . . [An] automatic verse-perfection which comes when following a mood. But the same sense for the perfect (a different perfection for each poet) . . . or perhaps not perfection, but 'rhetorical

ring' as Full fathom five . . . will work to order if one keeps one's mind in suspension, waiting for the right word.[14]

His re-casting of 'Rain-Ploughs' was won by this 'second, harder method'. Writing of his poem 'In July' he acknowledged his debt to Auden: 'Auden my master. Auden I consider the best modern poet.'[15] He complained that writing was becoming more difficult, and that sometimes he had to spend an hour on a sonnet. He found the form difficult though rewarding. 'I have sneered at poets who beat out each line on the anvil of thought. Now I do it myself.'[16] An hour for a sonnet is a fast clip, so he must have habitually composed very quickly.

In the second half of August that year Mrs Baxter and James visited Terry in Whitanui, Shannon. As Ginn watched them arrive at the outer gates and walk through security, his first impression was 'of Jim's enormous head, and his loose, almost shambling gait. That head, I thought, is like a lamp held before the body. I thought also of another friend, the Rev. O. E. Burton, who had similar physical characteristics, the slightly arched shoulders and the heavy head projected forward.' Though Ginn already knew Baxter from his letters and from what he had learnt from Terence, there was more to him than he realized: 'What was new was the rich cadence of his voice and the engaging bashful manner contrasting with the quality and authority of his speech. It was the same with his mother.'[17]

O. E. Burton was detained with Terry and Ginn at Whitanui. A Gallipoli veteran, a decorated hero and chronicler of New Zealand military exploits in the First World War, he had become a Methodist Minister and pacifist by the Second. The day after war was declared in 1939, he denounced its futility outside Parliament Buildings and was arrested. Subsequently he was imprisoned for subversion, and unfrocked. He wrote a number of books and an essay *Spring Fires: A Study in New Zealand Writing*[18] in which he said:

> While I was in prison in 1944 I received on the same day and quite independently two letters both asking for my opinion of verse that was enclosed. To one I had to reply as kindly as possible and say very definitely that I thought the writer had not the makings of a poet. To the other, from a boy of sixteen, I could only say that I was not competent to criticize work of such merit, but that in my opinion the only thing that could stand in the way of his becoming a poet of world stature would be some tragic interior movement in his own soul. The boy was James K. Baxter . . .[19]

Baxter presented Ginn with a copy of Joyce's *Portrait of the Artist as a Young Man*, which he considered 'one of the best novels ever written. The part about the Catholic Hell is overpowering.' On his return to Brighton he wrote: 'It was very good for me to see you and Terry. It sort of straightened out things in my mind. And my mother was immensely relieved and rather captivated by the new Terry. But going away was tough – I wrote a poem to try to set down my ideas and feelings; not very good, not very true to life perhaps.' It ended:

> Who killed cock robin? he was a frail soul
> perhaps: could not endure: a cage killed him
> Or turned him, who'd never the head for heights
> to the cynical one
> the heaven-searcher out-staring the sun
> the ravenous eagle.[20]

The poem, as he said, was not very true to life. It treats Terence's situation, not his character, and expressed the apprehensions voiced earlier in a letter to Margaret Hargreave, his Sibford friend: 'Terence is still in detention camp – for the duration it seems, however long that may be. I have a pain in my mind whenever I think of it, he has so much vitality and he's shut up. I don't like to write about it.'[21]

On the way back from Shannon the Baxters spent three days in Christchurch.[22] While they were there, Mrs Baxter brought James to see Lawrence Baigent at the Caxton Press. Baigent had refused military service during the Second World War on the grounds of conscientious objection, and had lost his teaching job at Christchurch Boys' High as a result. Though his health would have excused him even from home service he preferred to stand by his principles rather than claim exemption. Later he worked alongside Professor Frederick Sinclaire and Winston Rhodes in the English Department of Canterbury University College.[23] Baigent recalled his first meeting with Baxter:

I was sitting in what was called the office, which was just a cramped little space inside the front door, just about time to close up. The door opened, this dumpy little woman came in followed by this youth. She marched up to the desk while he stood just inside the door. She said, 'My son has written some poems. I wonder if you would be interested in reading them.' I was a little embarrassed because I had no idea who they were, and we had so many people coming in with bundles of atrocious poems. I said, 'Yes. I'd very much like to look at them. Could you leave them with me overnight?' She said that would be perfectly suitable and left. I don't think she even introduced herself; she certainly did not introduce Jim. Jim just stood there, gazing rather vacantly around him, didn't utter a word and followed his mother out the door. I went home thinking, 'Good Heavens, what am I in for?' That night I sat down and started reading the poems, and got the biggest surprise of my life, I think. I was completely bowled over by them. Next morning Jim himself came along. I said, 'Yes, certainly we'd be delighted to publish a volume.'[24]

When Baxter went to see Baigent that night, they talked until two or three in the morning. Baigent recalled: 'We went through virtually all English poetry from Shakespeare until the present day, backwards and forwards and sideways.' He found Baxter, who was then eighteen, intellectually mature and amazingly well-informed. He seemed to have read everything. It was quite remarkable, and what was especially impressive was his ability to quote so much poetry accurately. Burns was his favourite at the time and they discussed him at length. He had brought his little notebooks with him, and he read poem after poem. 'I think he was up to number one thousand and something and he was writing at that time anything from three to six poems a day. He was in extraordinary spate.'

Baxter's impression of Baigent was confided to Ginn: 'I find him friendly, sensitive, intelligent, poetical views sound but slightly narrow for me.'[25] Baigent helped him to make the selection for the book, for though Baxter knew which poems had to go in, he was doubtful about others. Many of the poems which impressed Baigent were fairly recent. Baxter was very modest, and though he did not consider himself a true poet yet, felt he was gaining control and beginning to express what he wanted to say.

On 17 October Baigent wrote to Baxter: 'I want this first volume of yours to make as sharp an impression as possible upon the few people in the country who care about poetry.' He felt the selection at that stage still did Baxter less than justice, and that as a whole the book lacked weight and that 'Not enough of the poems speak with the authentic personal voice of 'Cry Mourn', 'The Mountains', and 'The Letter'. He apologized for raising the matter when Baxter was caught up in examinations and apprehensive about them. He told Baigent of his disappointments and uncertainties in the language papers. But he had no worries about English or Philosophy. He agreed to include the poems Baigent had suggested and he believed he had 'definitely improved of late, but my style still vacillates a bit and probably always will. Though a good one, I am an amateur from start to finish. Perhaps all poets are. Shelley is the only exception I can think of at the moment.' The following year he hoped to bring out a more solid collection; this first one was 'a poet's progress'.

Another letter to Baigent on 15 November 1944 described the writing of all poetry as:

. . . a process of learning, an exploration of subjective and objective environment. 'Concerning Judy' is faulty where you say. But I am still young and only in the process of discovering what Goethe said: that when one speaks in general terms one may easily be imitated: but when one speaks from personal experience one speaks with an inimitable voice, since at no point is the experience of two individuals the same. I welcome your criticisms; all the same I know my artistic imperfections and try to erase them.

What you say about the possibility of genius is very pleasing to me, though I know not flattery. And in exuberance I would rather err with Burns and Byron than remain firm with Arnold . . .

A couple of months earlier he had been reading Rilke's Duino Elegies, especially 3, 4, 7, and 10, with 'ever increasing understanding'.[26] He felt the poems he had just been writing showed the influence of Lorca, Laura Riding, George Barker, and Roy Campbell.

On 20 November 1944 he was expecting his name to be in the ballot for compulsory military service: he planned to send in an appeal on conscientious grounds. Whatever the outcome he felt it would strengthen his principles.[27] It never came to that, but he did send a letter to the Appeal Board outlining his views on war and his family's history of pacifism.

On the twenty-first of the month he was expecting to see Lawrence Baigent, who is 'rather enthusiastic as midwife – a fine and intelligent man'. *Beyond the Palisade* was printed but not yet bound, and the first hundred copies would probably be ready that month (though in the event the book was not published until the following year).

He had planned to go fruit picking in Central Otago, but the crops had been damaged by frost. Towards the end of November his parents arranged a job for him on a dairy farm at Purakanui on the coast north of Dunedin. They were worried by his heavy drinking. Several times he had been found dead drunk at the back of the Brighton bus after it had reached the terminus. And sometimes he spent the whole night at the bus shelter though it was only a shortish walk from his own home. It was hoped that a couple of months in an inaccessible place like Purakanui cut off from a liquor supply would help to dry him out. He started work at six in the morning and went to bed about half past nine at night. He was in excellent health. He had given up smoking and felt the benefit of it. He said nothing about alcohol, but when he returned to Brighton from visiting Terence, he said he had not seen alcohol since coming down on the boat, 'when I got drunk to avoid being sea-sick – successfully'.[28] Though he was physically fit he told Ginn he retained the 'blight man was born for': 'I used to think it was caused by modern living conditions: I begin to think it may be our intellectual heritage. Still, one can with luck sink into a sort of physical placidity, stop thinking, with sex as guiding star. But mind re-enters the arena, never content with the purely physical.'[29] The family he was living with were Salvationists: 'their calmly hummed hymns of voodoo blood-sacrifice appal me rather'. The daughter, aged sixteen, was not very attractive 'except by dint of proximity'. The family remembered the notebook and pencil he carried everywhere, and how dreamy he was. In general they disapproved of him, and the daughter was warned to be wary. His poem 'The Farm' draws on this experience.

> I remember the rise
> Where Walter and I split old, dry logs with the maul
>
> Below the railway line. The whole farm
> Is hidden somewhere in my guts, as if
>
> I'd swallowed it: the creek, the byres, the haybarn,
> The crumbs of wood and resin in the sawpit.
>
> All tracks led outward then. I did not see
> How bones and apples rot under the tree
>
> In cocksfoot grass, or guess the size
> Of the world, a manuka nut in the sun's gaze.[30]
>
> (CP 271)

In response to Ginn's request, Baxter had sent him a photo which he thought 'a little unfair (vanity requires the explanation). I am not habitually hunched; nor do photos ever capture what depends on animation, colouring, expression.'[31]

V

First Book, First Love

Baxter's erratic application during his one year of full-time study at Otago University brought as its reward modest passes in English and Philosophy. He flunked Latin and French by failing to qualify for terms, a prerequisite for sitting the final examinations. Looking back seventeen years later he offered a witty but inaccurate summation of the year: 'Aphrodite, Bacchus, and the Holy Spirit were my tutors, but the goddess of good manners and examination passes withheld her smile from me.'[1] Aphrodite was indeed to smile on her acolyte, but during 1944 she had hardly noticed him.

Feeling the need early in 1945 for 'more elbow room to get on with living and writing', he decided to leave university: 'the truth is that I have no wish to be an intellectual; prefer not to enter the gate to the Waste Land Garden. I am frightened at the closing up of minds I see, and recognize the same symptoms in myself . . .' But he planned to go on writing as the spirit moved him.[2] He had faced considerable opposition in his decision to leave the university: 'I remember how in my own late teens my parents presented me with a tentative programme for the future – with their generous support I was to obtain a New Zealand degree in English, go to Oxford or Cambridge, obtain an English degree, and then become a scholar and lecturer in English literature.'[3] The offer was not taken up. In a difficult session with his parents his mother said justly that he could always find persuasive arguments for doing whatever he wanted. But the fact was that he was becoming a hobo. She and Archie wanted him to snap out of it and return to university. Though he was shaken, he stuck to his guns. When the meeting was over, he went out 'and wept under a gum-tree on the river-flat below the house'.[4] He recognized his motives 'were mixed and doubtful; but some obscure voice at the back of my mind said: "You are not meant to be a scholar and a lecturer, Jimmy. You would shrivel up like an old, cold potato. You are meant to be someone else, whom you have not yet become, and one of the ways you will find your true self is by writing." '[5] He knew this might sound egocentric, but felt that even if a saint advised him differently, he had to follow his own sense of vocation.[6]

By the fourth of March he had started work in an iron foundry. It was not too demanding, but inhaling iron and enamel dust was unpleasant. During the half-hour interval for lunch he went down to the wharves to visit the crew's quarters on the ships. He climbed about a hundred and fifty feet up a mooring rope to expend his animal energy and to show off in front of a crowd of mill-girls. He went into the crew's quarters but was thrown out. Next visit he brought magazines and a pack of cards, which sweetened them no end. He found the crew simple and rather aloof.[7]

On a visit to the university he had gone into a pub and discussed Hopkins and Chatterton. He met a medical student whom he had once assisted in an affair of the heart by writing a poem for his girl-friend. Now a second poem was commissioned for another girl: '[He] gave me dinner: placed me upstairs in an armchair with a continual supply of rum and gin: and waited for the poem. After about 35 minutes and 14 glasses it arrived, good and pithy, epigrammatic I think. He was entirely satisfied . . .' By drinking in university pubs Baxter kept in touch with the social life of the university. And he had been asked, presumably by the Registrar, to write a university song.

Lawrence Baigent was also unhappy that Baxter had left university and needed reassuring:

> It is necessary to find one's balance, whatever constituents may be necessary for that balance, Though one cannot call one man stupid and another intelligent – yet, broadly, there are the stupid-and-unbalanced whom one sees on all sides; there are the intelligent-and-unbalanced, most writers included; there are the stupid-and-balanced whom I have admired but in whose ranks I cannot be; there are the intelligent-and-balanced, among whom, 'tall and lonely' or otherwise, I would wish to be. Psychological factors, though unanalysable, can be charted; for each person adjustment is unique; and I know what I am doing.
>
> When I read my letters to people, I am always discouraged by the fact that I have in no way expressed the solidity and solidarity of my mind and feelings. The poems do it better. And you naturally enough underestimate my understanding looking on my poetry as subjectively insular, which it is only in part, and less so as time passes. For me leaving 'Varsity is just a necessary shift of ground. Having acquired insight into the falseness of many obligations, I have acted on this where most would not.[8]

The collection of poems they had worked on together was to be called *Beyond the Palisade* and would go on sale about the last week in March. Denis Glover had returned 'from the foreign wars' in time to design the cover, but it was a rushed job and did not meet his exacting standards.[9] Moffett, who had published 'Convoys' in the *Otago Daily Times*, persuaded Whitcombe and Tomb's to mount a window display with a photograph of the author.

The book had a remarkable history. While it was still in the press late in 1944, Lawrence Baigent showed the manuscript to Allen Curnow, who was preparing an anthology of New Zealand poetry for the Caxton Press, *A Book of New Zealand Verse 1923-45*. Curnow was impressed and chose six poems. He would have liked more, but did not wish to gut a young man's first book of verse.[10] Word spread that he had discovered a brilliant young poet and expectations were high. The now famous introduction was already written, but Curnow added a couple of paragraphs about Baxter, the youngest poet in the anthology:

> His poems seem a new occurrence in New Zealand: strong in impulse and confident in invention, with qualities of youth in verse which we have lacked; yet with a feeling after tradition and a frankly confessed debt (besides the unsought affinities) to some older New Zealand poets.
>
> It seems to me that since Mason in 1923, no New Zealand poet has proved so early his power to say and his right to speak. He is directly aware of the great audience that is addressed by a poem in English. That is the hardest knowledge for a New Zealander; if it comes in youth it can only be by some rare accident of talent and circumstances . . . This in Baxter, and some assurance of self and history, has made it possible for him to use and not mimic his English influences – inevitable ones, George Barker, Yeats, Auden – and to write some poems which could only be his and only a New Zealander's.[11]

Curnow's anthology, with his introduction, established him as the leading critic of New Zealand poetry. The excitement, penetration, and cogency of his ideas made him a kingmaker of poetic reputations. It was Baxter's good fortune that *Beyond the Palisade* appeared about the same time as the anthology. Among the 'older New Zealand poets' to whom he was indebted was Curnow himself. The initial impulse for 'The First-Forgotten', for example, had come from him.[12] And the influence of the older poet did not stop there. To the English models mentioned by Curnow could be added Hopkins – a powerful presence in the volume – in poems like 'Rain Ploughs' and 'Hill Country'; Blake, for example, in 'To the Sun'; Wilfred Owen in 'That the World may Know'; and elsewhere, Spender and MacNeice.

A capacity for imitation is part of a poet's equipment. The modernist movement, and critics like Eliot and Bloom, have demonstrated how fruitful it can be. What matters is that a poet fully assimilate the originals. Baxter knew this. He wrote to Ginn: 'Occasionally the sub-conscious remembrance is not of my own image, but of one which I have read and have appreciated as much as if I had written it.'[13]

In his introduction Curnow continued: '. . . he seeks the eloquent rather than the inquisitively precise word. This is weakness as well as strength in a poem like "Prelude N.Z." with its elaborate verse structure, but strength wholly in "Death of a Swan" . . . and "O lands seen in the light of an inhuman dawn".'[14] At times Curnow's reservation (a variation on the Imagist principle enunciated by Richard Aldington, 'to employ always the exact word, not the nearly exact, nor the merely decorative word') has been fastened on, and his praise of Baxter's eloquence forgotten. And he was talking of vocabulary and nothing else. Baxter was young, romantic, and a Celt. The luxuriance of his early language, like that of the early Keats,

81

showed the youthful exuberance with which he was responding to his experience. A large part of that experience had been verbal, acquired from his books and from what he had heard at home. And his familiarity with romantic poets like Shelley affected his conception of the poetic. His eloquence could be cut back in good time. And the question of the appropriate language for a New Zealand writer had occurred to him. It will be remembered that he considered Sargeson's style too attenuated, and that a fuller style was needed.

Five hundred copies of *Beyond the Palisade* were printed. Baigent's arrangement of the poems pleased Baxter: 'In a way "The First Forgotten" begins the book and "Letter to Noel Ginn" ends it. "For Burial in Ground" is just a kind of epitaph. The whole book is as I would like it to be.'[15] From his very first collection he was aware of the special importance of the opening and closing poems. The book was written during the Second World War and profoundly affected by it. The image of a palisade suggests the common peril faced by the beleaguered Baxter clan. And the notions of victim and aggressor recur. A sense of menace, death, and pity for the violation of innocence, broods over the book, becoming explicit in poems like 'Death of a Swan', 'Song of the Sea Nymphs at the Death of Icarus', 'Death of a Man', and 'The Killing of a Rabbit'. Icarus and the unicorn are tragic symbols of himself, and in many poems violence is associated with death. Yet paradoxically in 'What shall we seek for', death is something to be prized. A further paradox is that in 'Letter to Noel Ginn', poetry, his chosen vocation, is seen as life-enhancing:

> Both clouds and houses are a frozen tide
> Till poetry inhabit them with fire.
>
> (CP 28)

The general character of the book is lyrical and elegiac.

The nature of Baxter's life up to *Beyond the Palisade* meant that his sensibility was profoundly affected by the New Zealand landscape. In poems like 'O Lands seen in the light of an inhuman dawn' and 'The Mountains', nature is perceived as harsh and the land as empty and alien. Baxter told Ginn 'The Mountains' referred to the landscape around Naseby, Central Otago, where he had spent part of the summer holidays.[16] The 'whelming bowl of hills' could be taken to be the hills surrounding the Maniototo. The poem develops a childhood perception of mountains as threatening, and as a symbol of an inexorable destiny. The second to last verse, which chooses

mankind in preference to the natural world, is interesting in the light of
Baxter's future development:

> I will go to the coastline and mingle with men.
> These mountain buttresses build beyond the horizon.
> They call. But he whom they lay their spell upon
> Leaves home, leaves kindred. The range of the telescope's eye
> Is well, if the brain follows not to the outermost fields of vision.
> I shall drown myself in humanity. Better to lie
> Dumb in the city than under the mountainous wavering sky.
>
> (CP 9)

The poem is one of those written when he was sixteen. Baxter glossed his
own copy of *Beyond the Palisade*: 'Mountains are mothers', an indication that
at the time he thought his mother's influence was looming too large in his
life and threatening his independence. In 'Prelude N.Z.' and 'Love Lyric IV'
his perception of landscape is modified by history:

> The skyline silhouette was
> no different for the aborigines:
> its inhuman natural curves will
> never alter while
> we watch them.
>
> (CP 24)

Baxter had no doubt about the poetic power of the natural images he
employed so freely: '. . . natural images are poetical, because more emotions
become associated with night or wind than with a gas-works. This is only
a generalisation . . . but great effects are within the scope of natural images
as is shown in Job and Ecclesiastes, and to a most minor extent in my Psalm
of the Defeated. It is a sign of lack of vitality when effects are best achieved
by the obscure or bizarre.'[17] 'Song of the Sea Nymphs at the Death of Icarus',
written at the age of sixteen, in its maturity of thought and technical
dexterity demonstrated Baxter's precocity. It is an individual application to
war of the classical myth:

> Only the old may live
> In their regret and pain:
> Them shall the gods forgive –
> But the young than gods are yet more beauteous
> And are forever slain.
>
> Lament ye for young Icarus,
>   Lament again!
>   For he is youth
> Forever living and forever slain.[18]
>
> (CP 6)

From this first volume, with its skilful use of the myths of Icarus and Lir,

Baxter signalled the direction his poetry would take. He would travel in the company of poets like Blake, Yeats, and Auden, along the path of myth and symbol. Several of the poems, together with his comments, confirm that he was already on the way: 'You are right about The UNICORN. Only a maiden could capture him, by making him lay his head in her lap. The "iron dream" is definitely material sensuousness and existence.'[19] He said that in 'Rain-Ploughs' the 'Angel-Archer' is 'the power of rational life'.[20] Further evidence of the symbolic nature of these poems is the classification he sent to Baigent. 'Hill-Country' is placed under Death, 'The Mountains' under Love, 'Prelude N.Z.' is 'the cradle of life'. 'Death of a Swan' is 'Death-love-totemism', 'The First-Forgotten' is 'Death-Birth', 'Rain-Ploughs' is 'Birth from Death'.[21]

Beyond the Palisade illustrates Baxter's considerable technical skill and control of a variety of verse forms. Representative of the best work is the finely rhetorical sonnet 'Death of a Swan':

> Fell the wild swan: from havenless crags of sky
> Fell to no cool lagoon of summer flocks
> But bruising river-ice: she fell to die
> Beside a winter shore and wolfish rocks.
> Fell the wild swan to ice and lay thus weakly:
> The tower-shadows hung compassionate;
> Night like the river flowed till day came bleakly . . .
> Hooded and frozen, her webs spread full: of late
> The piteous bill moved, clogged as snow sank.
> Vaulting pinions, the immense heaven cloven
> To blades of sunlight, where now? She dead and dank,
> And one with ice, snow-down to feel, wind-woven.
> No baptismal save sleet; no Erin, priest-word repeating;
> Lost Child of Lir, heart frozen in faint beating.
>
> (CP 30)

Baxter explained the mysterious reference to the 'Lost Child of Lir' in a letter to Ginn: 'from the Irish legend of the children turned into swans who wandered for 300 years till released, and dying after baptism.'[22]

This first collection, sporting Curnow's bouquet, established Baxter's reputation. He became a celebrity. The *N.Z. Listener* reviewer was astonished at his maturity and the poet Basil Dowling sent him a most complimentary letter.[23] Charles Brasch, poet and patron, took him up and was to remain a good friend critically and financially for many years. But one reaction displeased Baxter: 'I object to "authentic voice of 40s" for only lately have I been world-aware. Indeed from 15 to 17 (from which period comes most of *Beyond the Palisade*) I only knew at times there was a war on.' On one level his claim to be oblivious was nonsense. His mother was preoccupied with the war and Terence was in detention from the time James was fifteen. She spent a great deal of time collecting information on those who were sentenced to detention, arranged for them to receive visitors, and raised money to send them books and food parcels. She was a very active member of the Peace Council and of the Howard Reform League which worked to improve prison conditions. She assembled material which was used for various representations to the Government on behalf of those in detention. Archie spent hours counselling young men who had been called up, and often appeared as witness for them when their appeals against military service were being heard. That took a great deal of preparation. The home activities, and the frequent discussions that went with them, created the atmosphere in which James lived from day to day.

Yet at one level he did try to insulate himself from the war, as from something painful, and that drove him further into poetry. On the charge of pessimism he had a point: 'And, truthfully, who can in honest and sincere introspection be soulfully optimistic? . . .' and he thought it better to err with Burns and Byron than fall in line with Brasch. He knew he was over-reacting and that his vanity was easily pricked. He admitted that the theme of pride was pretty basic with him: 'atavistic ancestor-worship, but very satisfying poetically . . .'[24] His style was changing and he thought that a poem like 'In City Night' gave a trace of things to come.[25]

Baxter proposed to spend Easter 1945 at Baigent's Christchurch flat in Cambridge Terrace near the Bridge of Remembrance. It was difficult to get a seat on the express from Dunedin, and Baxter queued from 4.30 a.m. to 8 a.m., passing the time talking to people. Many were turned away. When he was told by the girl in the ticket office that there were no more reservations, he put on his 'best smile, asked her if she couldn't do something about it, and she produced one from nowhere.'[26] Baxter brought to Christchurch a new collection, 'Cold Spring', which he thought better than *Beyond the Palisade*.[27] In fact none of its contents appeared in his next published collection. Baigent introduced him to some of his artistic friends, Allen Curnow and Basil Dowling, Rita Angus the painter, and the musician Douglas Lilburn. Lilburn agreed to set Baxter's 'University Song' to music. All these artists were to become important friends, and Baigent got to know Baxter better. He also suffered from his loquacity. Baxter talked all the time. Even when he went to the toilet he continued to talk through the closed door. Both men slept in the same room, and the only way Baigent could stem the flow was by pretending to be asleep. As soon as he woke up a voice started again from the other bed.

After his return to Dunedin, Baxter told Baigent he had done him a lot of good; 'more than anyone else has ever done'. He was feeling happy, 'generally stable and forceful'.[28] A good singer was to sing his 'University

Song' at the Capping concert. But he had been riled by a correspondent who repeated the charge that there was too much despair in *Beyond the Palisade*: 'I think moralistic criticism of psychological realism is foot-and-mouth disease in the poetic herds . . . And why call a fairly subtle but impermanent death-mood self-pity. Birth, copulation, and death, says Eliot's Sweeney. I'd be bored, answers Doris. And speaking seriously, death-poems and love-poems are the world's best.'[29]

By late June Baxter was still rolling iron at the Green Island foundry where he worked until September. His wages were £2.6.3d a week. Now he had shifted from store work to range-fitting he made a few extra shillings. When he turned nineteen he would get a further rise of ten shillings.[30] Most of his workmates were much older, and they were surprised at how well this fresh-faced youth was able to cope. They were hardened drinkers yet he could keep up with them in the pub as well. Already he was restless and planned to go up country on a sheep-run in the spring 'in search of fresh air and perfect fitness.'[31] And he hoped that when he got back into the stride of poetry again he could develop a new style.[32] He sent Baigent another collection of poems, his third, which he considered was not as spectacular as 'Cold Spring'.[33] Prompted by admiration for Fairburn's poetry, not by the magazine he edited, *Art in New Zealand*, he sent him four sonnets, all of which were printed. About July or August of 1945 he had an affair with a young married woman, 'intelligent and good-looking'. When her husband found out he took a tolerant view of the affair, but insisted that it stop. Psychologically Baxter felt it did him a lot of good, though he did not say how.[34]

He left the foundry for a job at Wanaka Station, in Central Otago, arriving on the evening of Monday 17 September. Before the large station had been divided up for housing it ran from the foot of Mt Iron on one side to the foot of Mt Roy on the other. It skirted a sizeable portion of the lake and offered magnificent views of mountain and water. By the time Baxter arrived the high country section of the block had been sold and they were running both sheep and cattle on the flat, and installing irrigation. Three married couples worked on the property as well as the single men, who were housed in a building containing the bunkhouse and cookhouse. Work was from eight to five, with Saturday afternoon and Sunday off. During lambing they worked longer hours.

Baxter's duties, as recorded in the station journal kept by the manager Mr Charlie Harris, were with the sheep, drafting, and picking over crutchings and dead wool in the paddocks. Another job was top-dressing. Stripped to the waist Baxter would stand on the back of a lorry and feed the superphosphate into a hopper. He also acted as a rouseabout, gardening, cutting lawns, cleaning the woolshed, clearing out ditches and swamp. After a month on the station he wrote to Baigent that though it was a hard life, he was very fit and clear-headed. And he had not been drinking. The scenery was splendid: 'lake, snow-mountains, green willows under a huge sky – lucent is the word. Infinitely preferable to iron dust.'[35] But he was missing his family. His dreams brought that home to him more than his conscious thinking. The hardest things to get used to were the smells, sheep's wool, the damp ground etc.'[36] It was still cold and in October they had snow, which was very hard on the new-born lambs. On the first of the month he wrote to his mother that though he was not reading much, he was doing a good deal of thinking and finding that as his mind clarified he was losing his problems.[37] He was enjoying the country, though he was not doing any writing:

> In spite of the inevitable monotony and isolation of outside work, I'll have to incorporate it in my scheme of living somehow. It is much more satisfactory, satisfying than the town. Just to walk along the mountain, look down at the lake, round up sheep, smell, hear, see, is more than work as love is more than sex. Later on, separating stinking sheep dags from wool, I have to recite to myself to gloss over the unpleasantness of it. Am not writing just now, no poems, since no need of self-justification. Also it's when they're finished growing for the year that trees make flowers.[38]

It was a simple life with good meals, plenty of eggs, meat, and vegetables. Once he was present at the castration of a calf and had 'rarely felt so ashamed of myself and the whole human race.'[39] As he settled into his new routine he began to read again. He requested from his mother a copy of Ezra Pound, 'a pinkish covered book', and was borrowing three books a week from the public library. One was Richard Llewellyn's *How Green was my Valley*, another A. S. Neill's *A Dominie Abroad*. Neill confirmed his own views on education by telling him 'that the running fight I'd put up against education from the age of five onwards might well have come from a kind of sub-conscious wisdom, and not from any source of malign perversity'. Neill's name was inscribed 'with reverence on the wall of my spiritual bomb shelter'.[40]

Washing clothes was one of his chores. He told his mother he was careful not to boil the woollens but needed some tips on how to get the dirt out. To distract his mind while he was plucking the wool off stinking sheep, he psychoanalysed himself: 'Remembered things that happened before I was 3; even recovered some beautiful bits of fantasy. It is marvellous what comes to the surface when you set off the depth-charges. What a writer one would make if one could write at 3! All the pure poetry that gradually gets tamped down to a bare surface and stage for clichés.'[41] He drank water when he was thirsty since the country pubs were very strict about under-age drinking. He was nineteen and in 1945 the legal age was twenty-one. He had also grown accustomed to the absence of women, persuading himself that he had become 'friends with hills and trees'. He philosophized to his mother:

> Though I'm quite capable of infatuation, I think I could do without women. Excepting you and one or two others, they do not attract me as persons; though I am over my earlier shyness. And it is intolerably humiliating to be attracted by someone you don't like as a person. So I stand back with a nice smile and my heart in the highlands. Protracted childhood, some would call it; I don't think so. Rather my own version of being grown up. Good for poetry. Not so good for marriage; but one can take that when and if it comes. The split between wife and art comes to all artists. The only unbearable thing being an arty wife. I am trying to be self-honest. What one is at 19 will not be fundamentally different from what one is at 40. The gentle and intricate music of the normal social pattern is not the music at the heart of poetry, which is the wind, pollen-bearing, infinitely desolate and all-embracing. One can remain outwardly a usual citizen; so these matters are not of interest and importance only to oneself – until the capacity to love another person completely is called upon. Even then it matters little, for few loves are complete.[42]

Conscious of what his down-to-earth mother would make of that, he conceded that he had been 'Soliloquizing on what is usually left unspoken. Poets have a certain licence to be queer birds anyway'. At nineteen none of his assumptions had yet been tested. But they are interesting because they never really changed: there is an inevitable tension between marriage and art; poetry flourishes outside the normal social pattern; most human love is disappointing.

On Labour Day he was on the beach of Lake Wanaka collecting driftwood. The weather was perfect: 'You could hardly imagine how beautiful the lake was. Scarcely a ripple right to the feet of the snow-mountains. And the dry shingle overgrown with poplars and willows, the dead wood and broken branches coming to life again everywhere.'[43] He also told his mother that though his writing was sometimes gloomy he was fairly contented. 'The inner man is always melancholy otherwise I wouldn't write poetry', and he was 'always expecting an apocalypse despite diatribes to the contrary'. He sent a sestina modelled on Sir Philip Sidney, but felt his own was stronger and moved more easily. He requested a copy of A. L. Rowse's *Poems of a Decade*.

In a letter from the same period he confided to Baigent: 'I grow up, not painfully, am losing something of that hectic adolescent attitude. But will continue to be a poet, since whatever I do know or don't know, and no matter how thick a skin I may acquire, I understand symbolism. Can look back quite objectively on all the poems I have written; some of them are surprisingly good.'[44] He told his cousin Antonietta, Viola's daughter, that he was glad she got so much pleasure from words, but he advised her to keep poetry in perspective. No books, however wonderful, could compare with even a stupid man who could 'see, hear, teach, taste, smell, and love and understand'.[45] As the extracts from the correspondence show, his new-found independence had allowed him to come to terms with his parents, and develop a certain aloofness:

> Having found my own feet, I am friendly with my parents again, no latent antagonism since I no longer accept their standards. Complete self-honesty is perhaps the only morality. The Christian basis *Love your neighbour* does not seem essential to me, if active feeling is intended . . . Aloneness of the individual is I think symptomatic of a highly developed civilisation. Oversharpness of sensibility. Not a characteristic of men. Hence *We must love one another or die* only when we step a long way from the animal pattern. Mutual pugnacity and simple anger can be invigorating; not these, but paranoia permits war.[46]

Because he much preferred outside work to his university studies, Wanaka Station suited Baxter. In its magnificent surroundings he had plenty of time to reflect. And he felt a new stability. But he missed the stimulus of intellectual company and knew that he needed it. 'My father, I know, lived until he was over 40 showing only a fractional part of his thoughts and feelings to those among whom he lived. I have not got his drive or outward self-sufficiency; and am for good or ill bloody intellectual.'[47] A friend of Baigent's suggested that Baxter apply for a job at the Caxton Press and the idea appealed to him. With his knowledge of poetry and 'large vocabulary' he felt he was qualified. He mentioned the proposal to Baigent, but the suggestion came to nothing.

Baxter sent Baigent a foreword to a new collection. It expressed his attitude to poetry in the latter part of 1945:

> The introduction of classical allusions occurs for symbolic purposes, the allusions containing for me in each case a powerful private significance. It may seem strange that verse assumedly modern, should be rhetorical or bear any resemblance to that of the Romantic era. I believe (as do both Spender and the later Auden) that the root of poetry must always lie in personal emotion, and that rhetorical gestures may be a truthful and natural mode of expression for this emotion. Dynamos and skyscrapers are no more essential to 'modern' poetry than were ruffs and wars with Catholic Spain essential to Elizabethan poetry. They may nevertheless quite naturally acquire an objective or subjective significance in the mind of any poet, and thus occur as an integral part of his poem. Birds, flowers, air, earth etc. must remain the staple and permanent poetic images because of their never-diminishing evocative intensity. If Spender uses the word 'ocean', this does not mean that he is necessarily imitating the

nautical Masefield or the romantic Byron; it means simply that he is writing –
and, being Spender, is probably writing powerful and original poetry.

In a word, the modern poet is not a species distinct, and may be taught by
Burns as readily as by Eliot . . . The distinguishing mark of the best modern
poets is an unprecedented degree of self-honesty.

He was sufficiently self-critical to hope the foreword was 'not too priggish'
and independent enough to add: 'not that I care a damn anyway – will say
what I think fit, and let the poems stand up for themselves.' The emphasis
on self-honesty was to become central to his literary criticism.

When I visited Wanaka Station in 1983, Mr Bill MacPherson, who
succeeded Charlie Harris as station manager, was still there. He
remembered Baxter vividly from the days they worked together. To him
there was something special about this fresh-faced, pleasant young man,
who was a good worker and got on very well with the others. Nor did he
remember him as a heavy drinker or womanizer but as temperate and clean-
living. Off the station, of course, it was not difficult to have some private
life. In a late poem 'At Wanaka' Baxter looked back:

> I remember how I walked to Luggate once
> To get drunk, and waded lost
>
> All night beside Mount Iron, through
> The wrong fords under a mottled moon.
> (CP 346-7)

He would go with the others on outings, and may have visited the
neighbouring Matukituki valley. Once an insurance agent turned up during
haymaking, an inappropriate enough time to do business. Seeing Baxter take
out a good insurance policy, the others, who knew he was no fool, followed
suit. With the women he had a great reputation as a reader of teacups.
Rarely would they have heard the leaves interpreted with such imagination
and authority.

Accidents occur on all farms. One day, a machine too big to pass through
a gate proceeded nevertheless, carrying the gate with it and part of the
fence. Baxter took the blame, admitting: 'My mind was elsewhere.' The
driver also accepted responsibility. One worker, an ex-sergeant major,
made himself very unpopular by a manic insistence on keeping the bunkhouse meticulously clean. Baxter's indignation, fuelled perhaps by memories
of cadets at King's, blazed out: 'He has an authority complex, and expiates
his obscure sins by washing out the huts whenever possible. He has quite
wide knowledge, but like all authorities, a mind strong like a taut wire, and
crystalline accumulations amounting to paranoia . . . You know how people
can get on one's nerves in a confined space. It takes all kinds to make the

world, but one can usually choose one's companions.'[48] Baxter left Wanaka Station on Thursday, 15 November. One of his last jobs was to muster the sheep for shearing. He rode around on 'a stumble-footed pony without a saddle'. The preceding month he had written 'High Country Weather', one of his best known poems, nurtured by his central Otago experience:

> Alone we are born
> And die alone;
> Yet see the red-gold cirrus
> Over snow-mountain shine.
>
> Upon the upland road
> Ride easy, stranger:
> Surrender to the sky
> Your heart of anger.
>
> (CP 34)

The war ended on 15 August 1945, but it still kept Millicent busy. She had always taken a great interest in refugees from the war zone. Among them were the Osterreichers, who had fled from Hitler's Germany in 1939. After the war, Mrs Osterreicher set up a relief organization to send food parcels to her homeland. Millicent and her friends proved her strongest allies. Over the space of a few years some eight thousand parcels were sent. The Osterreichers' son Paul, who later became a prominent campaigner for nuclear disarmament, was often in the Baxter household as a boy. He found it a place of immense intellectual stimulation, with people always coming and going. He liked Archie and admired what he stood for, and was fascinated by 'his sustained silence' in the house. At the age of fifteen Paul read *We Will Not Cease* and was profoundly influenced by it. At King's High he had been a regimental sergeant-major, but by the time he had left school he had become a pacifist under its influence.[49]

At the end of 1945 Terry, who was still in detention, was given a fortnight's leave before being commandeered into the Gear Meat Works at Petone. Noel Ginn came down to Brighton with him. From Ginn's account it was a time of great excitement and much confusion. 'The air was thick with the names of dispersed friends and acquaintances, much news, always change. Jim was part of this ferment, but his disorientation was from a different base. There was exhilaration as we talked of poetry, of life and world affairs, there was much humour also, and I was learning of Jim's first forays into the realm of sex.'[50] Given his limited opportunities at Wanaka, Baxter was presumably making capital of his earlier success with the young married woman. But he knew he could not compete for attention with the new arrivals who were greeted as heroes. Some of them, remembering what they had heard about him, took a severe view of his behaviour. They thought him an unworthy son of a father like Archie.

The effect of imprisonment on Terence was profound. From having been outgoing and sociable, a person who related easily to others – much better than his brother, in fact – he had become moody and withdrawn. He seemed to have lost faith in society. In the family, of course, he was regarded as a man in the same mould as his father. Archie was very proud of his son's good looks and strength of character. And he knew better than anyone the cost of refusing to conform. Terence's relationships with his peers were affected, and when it came to finding a job, he was at a disadvantage. Everything was weighted heavily in favour of ex-servicemen. There had also been a displacement in the home. His brother was now older and Terence noticed the amount of time he spent discussing poetry with his father. The subject was clearly of passionate interest to both of them. He felt excluded and later confessed to a certain amount of jealousy. He decided to yield his brother's chosen territory, though it had interested him once. More and more it became alien to him as he was driven to develop his own skills in making and doing.[51]

But his life was about to change. That summer of 1945/1946, a young woman, Lenore Bond, had gone out to Brighton to work at the guest-house 'Trevose', owned by close friends of the Baxters. She became friendly with Millicent and began going out with Terence. His previous relationships with women were short-lived and it had been a problem to find someone who could relate easily to his mother. He enjoyed being with Lenore, and she was already a friend of Millicent. Both James and his mother were very keen on the match. When the marriage eventually took place on 22 August 1947 in the South Dunedin Baptist church, Lenore felt she had married the whole Baxter family. She became the sister James never had, and for Archie and Millicent she was like a daughter.

By the end of March 1946, Baxter was working in the Burnside Freezing Works. Over Christmas he had been drinking heavily but had gone on the wagon for most of January in deference to a medical student he had been keeping company with. A reading of Jung's *Modern Man in Search of a Soul* and *Psychology of the Unconscious* was leading him 'in the paths of righteousness', and giving direction to some of his poems: 'The death-theme no longer dominates – despite an unsuccessful falling in love with the "P. D." of the poems. I think I toughen in fibre and am achieving a separation from my parents'.[52] His heavy drinking broke out again and his habit of not coming home at night led to clashes with his mother. He felt his father was more understanding. An uncollected poem of the period recorded a breach between him and his mother:

> I that was nearer thee
> than the leaf is to the tree, the stone to the bedded stream
> walk upright and alone.[53]

Baxter often visited the university, drinking in the Captain Cook, and attending parties. One medical student in particular (not the P. D. of the poems), became more important to him, and they saw each other often. He would ring her up: 'It's J. K. B. here', and then come around and read poetry in her room. She liked that, though she did not feel any emotional attraction towards him. What amazed her was the range of his reading and the speed with which he grasped the key ideas in very diverse material. She was flattered at the attention of a man regarded as a prodigy.

During 1946 and 1947 Baxter's drinking problem was at its worst. Sometimes he got drunk 'for many days together' (CP 235). He seemed to have lost direction. The restlessness inherited from his Baxter ancestors showed in the way he drifted from job to job, and he had a history of being sacked and taken back. Typically he would work for about six weeks, collect his pay, and then go on a spree for a couple of weeks. A student friend remembered that Baxter, after spending the morning in the pub, would meet him in the afternoon. He would throw his arms around him and say, drawing out the 'o' sound in 'booze', 'Let's go on the booze'. Usually they went to the Captain Cook, but sometimes they drank in the Bowling Green, a pub often referred to in Baxter's reminiscences. After a drinking bout Baxter was not a pretty sight. His face would go a deep purple and there was a white line like a collar where the discoloration stopped. After he dried out he would return to work. For nourishment he would take a quart bottle of milk, drink a little and break a couple of eggs into the rest. The occupant of a flat where he often turned up to stay the night recalled that in 1946, when he was working at the iron-works again, he would leave about 7 a.m. and on the way to the bus he would drink milk from the bottles outside the houses.

At parties Baxter held the floor and declaimed. He paced about the room with his head thrown back, occasionally ruffling his hair until it stood on end, and talked and talked. In fact he was liable to be still going strong when everyone else had either gone home or lapsed into torpor. Terence spoke of his brother's habit of addressing not the person but the idea. He felt that often he was just an audience, not someone who had a personal relationship with his brother. Most of Baxter's friends suffered from his fluency. Monte Holcroft met Baxter in 1947 and was impressed by his ability to reel off 'long passages from Wordsworth, Coleridge and Shelley, then changing abruptly to the poems of Allen Curnow and Denis Glover, which he seemed to know completely.'[55] As his reputation grew, people with similar literary aspirations used to flock around him. Then his relatives and close family friends melted away. He attended student parties and events like the annual Riggerstring ball. 'The Riggerstring was the annual Boat Club Ball, a real hooley, the best and the worst hop of the year. It was held in a boathouse on the waterfront. Mining students bellowed in the cloakroom while the couples lunged above their heads. The dead marines rolled down the stairs or spun from the top windows to plop in the salt sober harbour. The year before the police had had to be called in'.[56]

During 1946 and 1947 Baxter became acutely aware of the problems of his sexuality, and he came to this largely through Terence. His elder brother was good-looking and girls had always found him attractive. The family knew this, and it was a source of pride for Archie. As Terence grew up his sex appeal was one of the liveliest sources of his self-esteem. Sex appeal continues to elude definition, but in Terence's case it could be described as something romantic and elusive. Women invariably responded to it. James had none of this special attractiveness for women, though it was a quality he greatly envied, and the deficiency was the more painful since he was naturally demonstrative and affectionate. Terence was also an accomplished dancer, which James was not. At dances he tended to sit around and talk. Yet he had some success. One girl, who was five years older than him, thought that he was as 'beautiful as an angel, with his wonderful sea blue eyes, his golden fair skin (he blushed like a girl) and his flashing smile, and I was fascinated by his lively voice and his ability to reel off his own and others' poetry'. There was little that was sexual in her attraction, and it was always like that. Whenever he tried to chat girls up they would appear most interested, then, just when he felt he had made an impression, out came their problems with some other man. His advice was earnestly sought as to what they should do. He felt he was only a convenient and sympathetic listener. Whenever he took a girl home to Brighton, even intellectual or artistic girls, they usually fell for Terence. His self-confidence was shaken and he wondered about his sexuality. This is clearly significant for his poetry since he believed that 'There is a close connection between the state of a man's sexual impulse and the poetry which he is likely to write'.[57]

His sexual anxiety may also help to account for a brief homosexual affair with a university lecturer. In the forties such matters were rarely discussed in public, but they interested him, as a former student of psychology. He knew that homosexual relationships had developed in the detention camps, for instance. After the war, one of his friends had a serious and long-lasting relationship with one of his cousins. He may well have wondered if he was homosexual himself, and if this was the reason for his lack of success with women. From his own account there were other homosexual episodes in his life, and though he couldn't be called a homosexual, he had some difficulty in coming to terms with his sexuality throughout his life.

Baxter often discussed the nature of marriage with a woman friend. Both were admirers of Adler and agreed that romantic love was mostly an illusion. They saw marriage as something domestic that had to be worked at, and the way to build up a relationship was through mutual respect and affection.

Baxter took no interest in politics during 1946 and 1947. Terry's fiancée Lenore belonged to a radical group of politically active students and tried without success to get him to attend. The nearest he came to it was when he became interested in one of the girls in the group and hung about to see her.

The many jobs of these years were not especially significant in themselves for Baxter's development, but their cumulative effect was. The texture of lives spent in an urban environment, the privations of the poor and underprivileged, were learnt at first hand. He had acquired the knack of mixing easily with all classes of people. Because of his father's influence, he already had a deep sympathy towards the 'ordinary working man'. Now he began to see him more clearly as decent and loyal, refusing to 'kiss the boss's arse' as he fought for independence and self-esteem. And from him he learnt that mastery of the vernacular which enabled him to use across many registers the real language New Zealanders speak.

Venus, so long delayed and looked for, showed up at last in the person of Jane Aylmer, a medical student at Otago University. Her appearance was striking rather than beautiful, but she was undoubtedly very attractive. She moved in a fast set and was said to have broken a few hearts. Her father, Stanley, was one of the Labour Government's first special area doctors and was prominent in left-wing politics. An articulate atheist, he was a virulent critic of religion. Bill Pearson, in his novel *Coal Flat*, took him as the model for Dr Alexander, the Marxist theoretician for the striking West Coast coal-miners. Like her father, Jane adopted atheism, and her views on morality were very liberal.

At that time Latin was part of the Medical Preliminary Examination. Knowing Archie Baxter's pacifist and socialist views, Stanley wrote and asked him to recommend a Latin tutor. Archie suggested James, who despite the fact that he had not even passed first year Latin, relished the assignment. Baxter fell passionately in love and haunted Jane's flat in Castle Street: 'I couldn't stay away from her and counted the hours by her coming and going. She rode continually in my mind like a night-haired Venus making a home of the sky'.[58] The image was appropriate for she was a skilful horsewoman. They became lovers and in 1946 he wrote for her one of his most acclaimed early love poems, 'Let Time be Still':

Let Time be still
Who takes all things,
Face, feature, memory
Under his blinding wings.

That I hold again the green
Larch of your body
Whose leaves will gather
The springs of the sky.

And fallen from his cloud
The falcon find
The thigh-encompassed wound
Breasts silken under hand.

Though in a dark room
We knew the day breaking
And the rain-bearing wind
Cold matins making.

Sure it seemed
That hidden away
From the sorrowful wind
In deep bracken I lay.

Your mouth was the sun
And green earth under
The rose of your body flowering
Asking and tender
In the timelost season
Of perpetual summer.

(CP 52-3)

When Jane visited the family at Brighton, Millicent found her good-looking, but not the right girl for her son. Jane admired his genius but did not feel he was right for her either. Baxter made most of the running. One of her comments struck home for he recorded it in a later letter: 'If you were more often sober you would be a nice, sensitive bloke'.[59] But by then it was not a compliment he felt he deserved. He saw himself rather as 'an old pig looking over the wall of the sty at the freckled bums of the girl pigs passing, and

snorting gruffly through his nose.'[60] It seems that Jane felt sorry for him. The
following year they had their first quarrel:

> Above the weirs, on the Leith Stream's bank.
> A streetlight flashing on
> The muscled Leith water; your acrid tears
> Of rage at something I had done or said —
>
> (CP 262)

Later that year, at a party in George Street, Jane fell in love with the man
she would marry. Baxter's most passionate and satisfactory relationship
with a woman in these early years was over. And it had been broken off
against his will. The anguish of having loved and lost remained with him for
a very long time. One poem in the sequence 'Songs of the Desert' of 1946-
1947 has the intensity of Marvell:

> Though usage and oblivion do us part
> And your womb be barren, from no fault
> Of nature but our own devising art
> Like labourers that sow the field with salt,
> Yet I go heavy from our naked bed
> With that quick child fathered by grief and you
> Which shall endure, as amber, being dead
> Outlasts the living forest where it grew.
> Having no heart, these words cannot decay
> As your young body shall and tender eyes,
> Nor like true children go their careless way
> Forgetting us for an obscure sunrise –
> But men shall murmur, 'These are his and hers,'
> When we both lie in our foul sepulchres.
>
> (CP 58)

But already he had met the young woman who was to become the most
significant person in his life. Jacquie Sturm, a young Maori of the Taranaki
tribe, came to Dunedin from the East Coast of the North Island. She had
been brought up by adoptive parents, a Maori father and a Pakeha mother.
Both were strong non-conformists and Jacquie was one of the very few
Maori then studying for a degree. At a time when returned servicemen and
those with degrees had preferential entry into the medical school, only the
exceptionally gifted student had any chance of one of the remaining places.
Jacquie passed her Intermediate year, but not with high enough marks to
gain a place against the fierce competition. Her strength was not so much in
the scientific subjects as in the arts. She switched to a B.A. course and
developed a special interest in psychology.

By 1947 Baxter had fallen under the spell of Dylan Thomas and carried the recently published *Deaths and Entrances* 'in the inside pocket of my working coat – drunk and sober – until those poems were part of the structure of my own mind'.[61] He would spout them when the mood took him, even to complete strangers. Two that were often in his mouth were 'Ballad of the Long Legged Bait' and 'A Winter's Tale.' Another friend remembered his playing her the records of *Under Milk Wood*. Baxter's delivery of the poems resembled a chant, a style derived, perhaps through Archie, from the lilting speech of his Highland ancestors, and from what he made of Dylan Thomas: he even wore the same kind of navy polo-neck sweater Dylan Thomas wore in a well-known photograph. In a gesture worthy of the Welsh bard, he celebrated his twenty-first birthday by crawling into the *Prince of Wales* hotel: 'on my hands and knees, dead sober, and barking at the ulcerous Scots barman. He heaved me out on the street. I had returned with a young policeman, whom I told that I had been refused a drink though I was over age, and left them wrangling at the bar.'[62] On another occasion when Baxter was in his cups, and not even a student, he sat in the front row of a university lecture on Shakespeare and forcefully challenged the Professor of English. Perhaps he was challenging the dead grandfather who had once stood on the same rostrum.

To many of his contemporaries this youthful-looking poet, who wore in all weathers a long overcoat buttoned up to his neck, was a true genius. But alcoholism had deeply affected his character. Baxter's critics regarded him as self-centred, self-indulgent, and always posturing. One thought him 'a fake Dylan Thomas'. His drunkenness was obvious enough, but his reputation as a womanizer is harder to document, though it received a fillip in 1947 when the first year class in Geology made a field trip to Dunedin's Flagstaff Hill. Half-way up they saw Baxter in the bushes with a girl. The class of some sixty students filed silently past with unaverted eyes.

He was still reading widely, and since he was often unemployed, he had the time. He would go into Whitcombe and Tomb's and spend the day with his nose in a book. Sometimes he just skimmed. A friend was once reading *Eyeless in Gaza* when Baxter called. He looked at her place, asked what had happened so far, then sat down and finished the book. A student remembered his earnestly recommending Samuel Butler's *The Way of All Flesh*, saying: 'It will change your life'. The drift of Butler's argument is that everyone must live as they choose, and not as others would like them to live. Butler's hero, Ernest Pontifex, is the eldest son of an obsequious mother and of an authoritarian, tight-fisted, professional Christian, who revels in 'his power of plaguing his first-born'. Ernest grows up taking on trust everything he is told by those in authority. Gradually he learns to rebel, but not fast enough to prevent the collapse of his life when he is imprisoned for indecent assault. He then realizes that his one chance is to separate completely from his parents and their puritanical standards, which had been reinforced by his public school education. He becomes a writer determined to say 'a lot of things, that want saying which no one dares to say'.

In 1947 Baxter too was rebelling against his parents, though they were some distance from those of young Pontifex. He felt the need to make a clean break. Despite his irregular habits of sleeping out in various flats, and on at least one occasion in the bomb shelter below the Octagon, he used always to return to his Brighton home. There his behaviour was roundly criticized by his mother, never one who hesitated to speak her mind. Already Baxter had the knack of picking up with unusual people and bringing them home. Worse still, they sometimes just turned up. Terence was resentful that complete strangers were being foisted on the family without any warning. Baxter's regard for his father was unchanged but it had to be reconciled with legitimate aspirations for adult independence and personal freedom. Before 1947 was out the relationship was memorably expressed in 'To my Father', an eloquent, rhetorical poem. The relationship with his father is admiring, but as the son of a man like Archie, Baxter rebels until he can win through to his own integrity:

> There is a feud between us. I have loved
> You more than my own good, because you stand
> For country pride and gentleness, engraved
> In forehead lines, veins swollen on the hand;
> Also, behind slow speech and quiet eye
> The rock of passionate integrity.
>
> (CP 65)

The illness referred to in the second verse 'too long/In love with my disease' was not one of the body; Millicent Baxter believed it referred to her son's view that he was too much attached to his family to have the independence he needed as a writer. She thought he had picked up the idea from some of the books they had both read. The fourth stanza of 'To my Father' is especially interesting:

> You were a poet whom the time betrayed
> To action. So, as Jewish Solomon
> Prayed for wisdom, you had prayed
> That you might have a poet for a son.
> The prayer was answered; but an answer may
> Confound by its exactness those who pray.

The poem was Millicent's favourite among her son's many poems. It stands like a monument to the memory of the man they both loved.

VI
A Seeding Time

This was unquestionably a seeding-time, when I became a man of sorts and ploughed under everything I had ever known, as a farmer ploughs in autumn before the hard frosts arrive.[1]

Baxter set off for Christchurch at the end of 1947. His ostensible reason was to start a new university career at Canterbury University College. In fact he wanted to visit a Jungian psychologist.[2] And he needed more freedom than living with his parents, or even in the same town, would allow. But it was difficult. He was living away from home for virtually the first time. Wanaka had been different because that was only a temporary absence, and there he had had a secure job and full board. Now he was on new ground and had to rely on his own resources. He felt less sure of himself.

Jacquie Sturm had also moved to Christchurch. When Professor Sutherland came down to Dunedin from Canterbury University College to deliver a set of lectures on psychology, she had been so impressed she decided to shift to Christchurch to study with him. Baxter had not liked the idea and tried to dissuade her. Now he was glad she had come. Christchurch was new for her too, and it was the first time she had lived outside a hostel. They did not live together but they saw a lot of each other and did many things together.

Baxter already had a base in Christchurch and liked what he had seen of his Caxton Press acquaintances, especially Lawrence Baigent. He told Baigent that his reason for coming to Christchurch was that he and Rita Cook would be there and that they were the people he most enjoyed talking to. He also knew Leo Bensemann, printer, painter, and calligrapher; John Drew; Dinnie Donovan; and the printer and poet Denis Glover. Caxton had published *Beyond the Palisade*, and he had contributed to their sporadic journal *Book*, a forerunner of *Landfall*. The Caxton Press had been a new phenomenon for New Zealand. Its passion for excellence in typography was inspired by the example of Bob Lowry in Auckland in the thirties, and the production of books of quality became a matter of special pride. From 1937 on, the Caxton Press had entered a period of steady production following the policy set out in one of its catalogues, that the most useful work to be done was to make known any promising literature written by New Zealanders, and to provide a rallying point.

By 1947 Caxton had among its titles: *When the Wind Blows* by Frank

Sargeson; M. H. Holcroft's three essays, *The Deepening Stream, Timeless World,* and *Encircling Seas*; Allen Curnow's *Island and Time, Sailing and Drowning,* and *A Book of N.Z. Verse*; Denis Glover's *Wind and the Sand*; A. R. D. Fairburn's *The Rake-Helly Man*; Basil Dowling's *Signs and Wonders*; and Baxter's *Beyond the Palisade*. Poetry was well served though there was little profit in it for the Press. A welter of manuscripts was submitted and selection was difficult. Glover was astonished to find that 'far more people wrote verse than ever dreamed of reading it'. At the Press in Victoria Street the atmosphere was relaxed, with people drifting in and out. Sometimes the staff would just sign off, and repair to the nearby Gladstone or Albion Hotel. But the long hours they put in at work meant their standards did not suffer. In March 1947, the year before Baxter moved to Christchurch, the Caxton Press had published the first number of *Landfall, A New Zealand Quarterly*. Its editor was Charles Brasch, a man of meticulous standards and, within certain clearly defined boundaries, of excellent taste. Almost every day he gave some time to editing.[3] Brasch made the promotion and development of the arts in New Zealand his vocation, and *Landfall* was his instrument. It achieved a reputation far beyond New Zealand shores. Brasch profited from the new and informed interest in New Zealand literature generated by Curnow's anthology, the writings of Monte Holcroft, and the series of studies published by the Government to commemorate the centennial of New Zealand in 1940 (one study was E. H. McCormick's *Letters and Art in New Zealand*). Then there was the excitement of the new books from the Caxton Press.

Brasch was fortunate in both his personal circumstances, which made him financially independent, and in his friends. In James Bertram and Harry Scott he had exceptionally well-endowed advisers. Bertram had taken a First in English at Oxford, and his travels in Europe and Asia had given him international perspectives useful to a New Zealand journal at this time. Harry Scott had been in the same detention camp as Terence Baxter and was now a lecturer at the university. In his introduction to *Landfall Country*, Brasch named him with Bertram, Glover, and Leo Bensemann as one of the 'four people without whom *Landfall* would never have existed'.[4] He was later to die tragically in a mountaineering accident. Brasch dedicated *The Estate* to him. For printers, *Landfall* had men of the calibre of Bensemann and Glover.

Brasch had already met Baxter in 1947 and knew that Caxton had published his book of poems two years earlier, when he was only eighteen:

> He looked less than that now with his fresh round face and very clear eyes, and the frankness and warmth of his smile were quite unselfconscious. He stooped, or slouched rather, holding his head forward between his shoulders, but kept his

heavy overcoat on even over lunch at the Savoy so that I could only make out that he was fairly thickly built. He left the university, he told me, because he was not interested; he seemed content to take casual labouring jobs which he said left his mind free, and to lead his own inner life. He wrote a lot, showing me a fat notebook from which he gave me a couple of poems to read. He seemed to have an untroubled, quite unassertive assurance that he was a poet and was accepted as one . . . outwardly he appeared to be untouched by the world, by the impossible choices, incompatibilities and guilt that are forced on us; he seemed to live and write out of the original freshness of his perceptions and emotions. How incongruous a pair we made, I thought as we walked along the quays, he with his clear-eyed directness, I in the complicated mesh of my guilts.[5]

Brasch was later dismayed to hear Baxter say during a talk at the university that Dylan Thomas was a poet and a genius because of his drunkenness.

In New Zealand cities, with their relatively small populations, the vitality of artistic life depends very much on a few people. From the mid-forties Christchurch was an exhilarating place for the arts. Glover, Curnow and Dowling were there. Brasch was a regular visitor from Dunedin and he used to stay at Harry Scott's flat, a focal point for many writers and academics, in Dorset Street, near Park Terrace. Fairburn came from Auckland occasionally; and R. A. K. Mason paid a visit. Painting flourished, especially through what was called 'the Group'. Formed by a few Christchurch artists who wanted more freedom than was allowed by the Canterbury Society of Arts, 'the Group' gave younger and experimental artists a chance to exhibit. It also invited painters from all over the country to take part in its annual exhibition, which was for years the best and most comprehensive in the country. The catalogue was designed and printed by the Caxton Press. A foundation member of 'the Group' was Baxter's aunt, Viola Macmillan Brown, who had trained at the Slade.

Prominent artists in the city were Rita Angus, Colin McCahon, Olivia Spencer Bower, Leo Bensemann, Evelyn Page, Doris Lusk and W. A. Sutton, all of whom exhibited work with 'the Group' in either 1947 or 1948. McCahon, Lusk, and M. T. Woollaston exhibited in both years. The musician Frederick Page and the sculptor Francis Shurrock were also in the city. Risingholme, an old Victorian Gothic house which had once been owned by Pember Reeves, became a community centre with classes in crafts like pottery and wood-carving. Caxton's premises were a centre for artists and writers, and the parties held there were events. The paintings of Leo Bensemann, the space given to artists in *Landfall*, and the publication of books, like Mervyn Taylor's woodcuts of indigenous subjects, all helped to place the Caxton Press near the centre of Christchurch's artistic activity. Rita Angus's fine portraits of Bensemann, Lawrence Baigent, Douglas Lilburn, and Betty Curnow, Doris Lusk's portrait of Bensemann, and

Bensemann's own portrait of Rita Angus, indicate the network of relationships.

Baxter, the 'marvellous boy' of New Zealand poetry, was warmly welcomed. His arrival aroused high hopes and much speculation about whether he would fulfil his promise. It also stirred the usual literary undercurrents of suspicion and jealousy. His arrival in a well-established artistic scene with its own hierarchy caused a displacement which required some adjustment. For some, like Glover and Bensemann, and to some extent Curnow, the great literary personality of the time was Rex Fairburn, poet, critic, humorist, raconteur par excellence. A tall, athletically built man with a commanding presence, his voice had wonderful projection. With little effort he could make himself heard in any part of a room. He was excellent company. Once when he was in full spate in a Christchurch pub the whole bar stopped to listen. On another occasion a postman came in for a drink and, realizing that Fairburn was not of common clay, threw down his mail-bag, and settled in for the afternoon.[6] Whenever Rex visited Christchurch his friends treated him royally. On a celebrated occasion they met him at the airport wearing firemen's helmets and driving the Electricity Department's electric car. They hired the Heathcote Arms for the night and squared the police. They even arranged for a pipe band. Glover with his outrageous sense of humour and verbal dexterity, which made him one of the most celebrated wits of his generation, was also excellent company. He and Fairburn were splendid foils for each other. Both were great talkers and liked to hold the floor. Glover remembered Baxter:

> . . . making a continual habit of turning up from Dunedin. And at eight in the morning when I repaired to the printery I would sometimes find Jim sitting on the doorstep in a very good severe Anglican frost. He was wearing some sort of hugger-mugger coat, no doubt stolen from the St Vincent de Paul's Society, and eating a crayfish – There he was, this cherubic, innocent-faced, baby boy from Otago. He'd say, 'Let's go and have a drink.' I said, 'I was just going to say the same thing myself.' So we'd wander off. He was totally addicted to alcohol. He found strong drink liberated him from all the toilsome world around him and enabled him to carry on with his real vocation of writing.
>
> Because of his cherubic face, young, beautiful and smooth like a new born apple, he was often asked by the barman if he was over age. He would reach into his pocket and pull out his birth certificate. I thought, 'Oh God, here I am bringing a callow youth into the pub.'[7]

Sometimes Glover would while the afternoon away with Baxter whose talk he found brilliant. Once, when he brought him home to dinner, Baxter recited 'accurately practically everything I'd ever written'. He would talk over his poems with Glover and learnt the need to be sparing with words, especially adjectives. Glover also warned him not to be too much under the shadow of Yeats. A few years later Baxter said that he had outgrown Glover, who felt this was as it should be. A longer apprenticeship might have saved him from the diffuseness of a good deal of his earlier verse and taught him to work his material more carefully. Glover admired Baxter's mind, which could look at all sides of a question, and he was a magnificent expositor. He never tried to win Glover over to his way of thinking, but he would contradict him mildly. He enjoyed Baxter's talk but 'his sheer bad behaviour' was too much even for the old sailor, who found him the most troublesome friend he had had in his life. When Baxter was drunk and introduced to well brought up young women anxious to meet the rising poet, he sometimes behaved outrageously: 'What I would say insidiously out of the corner of my mouth, he roared at the top of his voice and grabbed them.'

And he was 'a marvellous borrower of monies. One would simply feed money to Jim as a loan, saying good-bye to that. And he almost drove us poor printers mad. He would ask: "When are you going to get my book out? Because I've got another three for you." There are people who can write faster than the printing machine can whistle, and who can't understand why the book isn't out like the *Evening Post* Sports Section.'

Glover regarded Baxter in Christchurch with a 'mixture of real love and great misgiving, tinged with utter dislike'. He considered him devious, and clever enough to put something over him. Though he admitted to some twinges of professional jealousy, he granted that he never doubted Baxter was a great poet. Both Millicent and Terence felt that Glover, because of his heavy drinking and life-style, was an unfortunate influence on James. Glover, with Burns, Dylan Thomas, and George Barker, certainly confirmed the observation that drinking and creativity often went together. And for the present Baxter found the relaxed, self-indulgent approach to life too seductive to be able to make the necessary discriminations.

A member of the Caxton Press admitted, 'We all drank too much – an occupational hazard of printers and blacksmiths.' True to the character of the alcoholic he had now become, Baxter went to extremes. Some regarded him as just 'a drunken little slob', a real nuisance in a pub because he had to be looked after and kept out of trouble. And he had some reputation as a bludger of drinks. They thought him, in Dr Johnson's phrase, 'not a clubbable man', but self-centred and lacking a sense of humour. Compared to Fairburn he was dull company, nor did he help matters by continually reaching into the pocket of his long overcoat and pulling out a poem. In addition, he had no appreciation of painting or music.

He followed not 'the god Apollo's golden mean' of rational living, but the way of Dionysus which exalted the instincts and the emotions. One grudge he held against society was its habit of reducing everything to intellectual terms. And he had a low opinion of the university, considering it unduly cerebral and a threat to the artistic and creative life. As he put it in 'Envoi' [to 'University Song']:

> *Per ardua ad astra:* blind
> Inscription from a catacomb.
> *Lost, one original heart and mind*
> Between the pub and lecture-room.
>   (CP 52)

Though Baxter recognized that he was more intellectual than instinctive, his intellect was intuitive rather than analytical, and his inclination was strongly towards the instinctive. His anti-intellectualism, so often expressed, was a rejection of all that intellect represented: prudence, moderation, control, calculation, and all that could be subsumed under academe. This came from his conscious identification with his Baxter ancestors rather than with his mother's family, and it was nourished by his reading of McDougall and Jung. His anti-intellectualism was an externalizing of the rebellion that was taking place within himself.

Yet he was drawn to Canterbury University College, which became his centre in 1948. He attended lectures intermittently, though he was not entered on the College's books. He took a prominent part in the literary life on campus and, when the first number of *Canta* came out for the year, he appeared as Literary Editor with the address 'any pub'. Bill Pearson, a quiet, modest, thoughtful ex-serviceman, who was doing an M.A. in English, was editor. Poems by Baxter that appeared in *Canta* were 'Virginia Lake', 'To my Father', and 'Song for an Old Soak'. Baxter also contributed articles. One morning he turned up at Baigent's around 6 a.m., asked for coffee, then sat down and wrote a piece on Sargeson for *Canta*. Lawson was admired for seeing 'the grinding monotony of rural and industrial labour without the rosy spectacles of conventional optimism', and Baxter lamented the loss of 'that strong and original voice whom circumstances combined to stifle'.

On 13 July, Baxter spoke to a large audience at the Literary Club on the poetry of Dylan Thomas, praising him for saying not 'what he thought he ought to say but always what he wanted to'. 'He has had the rare courage to tackle honestly his deepest personal problems' and was 'making himself by self-expression in poetry'. He identified some characteristic themes of Thomas's poetry including sex, both as a creative and destructive principle, death, and sin. His work was 'rather an exploration than a record – a reaching out rather than a classification' and 'his symbolism has an emotional content only achieved by the greatest poets'. His devotion to Thomas was well known. It was clear that the themes he admired and identified in

Thomas's poetry were the very themes he was trying to incorporate in his own work. That year he contributed three poems to *Review*, Canterbury College's annual magazine, and edited the third number of *Canterbury Lambs*, an occasional publication.

At the end of 1948, Pearson's successor as editor of *Canta* thanked those who had worked with her, but omitted to mention Baxter. A special page headed 'Free Lesson in Self-Advertisement' allowed the staff a free-for-all on their colleagues. The pie in Baxter's face was:

> Mrs Baxter's little Jim
> Got immersed in sex and sin.
> When the pangs of doubt grow violent
> Beer's the universal solvent;
> But in between the rum and vomit
> A poem flashes like a comet.

'Mrs Baxter's little Jim', an expression suggested perhaps by that first visit to Caxton, was often used to cut Baxter down to size. Like the squib, it was said to have come from Glover.

The Little Theatre was the focus of the strong student drama society, which had been built up at Canterbury College in the forties by Ngaio Marsh, the well-known writer of detective fiction. A tall, slim woman, with striking features, reddish chestnut hair, and hazel eyes, hers was an imposing presence. She had trained at the School of Fine Arts as a painter, but her real interest was in amateur and professional theatre and she had a passion for Shakespeare. Her personality, her sense of the ridiculous, and her enthusiasm greatly endeared her to the young, who crowded around her. At Canterbury she directed a series of celebrated productions which included *Hamlet*, *Othello*, *Henry V*, and *A Midsummer Night's Dream*. When Baxter met her she was friendly towards him, though he found her 'rather a managerial woman' with exacting standards.[8] Strong women still threw him off balance. They reminded him too much of his mother. In July he took a small part in Jean-Paul Sartre's *The Flies*, produced by John Pocock and Pamela Mann. To accommodate the play to the small stage 'the crowd' was reduced to Baxter and a companion. He doubled as the Idiot Child and at rehearsals took the part of a soldier as well, leaping to attention when he was there. Baxter liked 'the smell and feeling of the stage. It is a world in itself. One has a sense of power playing a part, even a minor one.'[9]

He had been impressed by Allen Curnow's play *The Axe*, specially written for the Little Theatre. He told his parents that he came along slightly tipsy with Glover and was in the 'right frame of mind to appreciate the play'. After the audience had gone, he danced his version of the Highland fling before a group of applauding observers. Then he 'danced just for fun (now a waterfall, now a tree, now a ploughman, now a hunter). Energy like electricity or heavy water in my limbs flowing out of my shoes and fingertips and the sheer delight of expressing something. And no one objecting.'[10] Though not much of a dancer, he wasn't going to waste an audience. And the dance was a key into an idealized childhood. He referred to this incident in the first verse of 'Poem by the Clock Tower, Sumner', published in the 1948 number of *Canterbury Lambs*:

> Beside the dark sand and the winged foam
> Under the shadow of the naked tower
> Play the wild children, stranger than Atlanteans.
> For them the blazed rock hieroglyph burns clear:
> Bear dance and bull dance in the drenched arena
> To the sun's trumpet and the waves' crying.
>
> (CP 73)

New Zealand universities have always reflected the attitudes of the communities they serve, and Christchurch was conservative and class-conscious. A student at the School of Fine Arts, attended by many upper class Anglican girls, remembered Baxter in his grey herring-bone overcoat down to his boots, coming to sit at her table in the Students' Association cafeteria. His conversation was stimulating and witty, though what he said was worlds away from her concerns. Her companion took umbrage that a scruffy-looking oddity like Baxter should have the cheek to join them. In her circle Baxter was regarded as a rather desperate sort of person. She had even heard that the reason he always wore a long overcoat was that he had nothing on underneath and that he used to go around flashing. This was just gossip, but he certainly had a flair for generating rumours. The overcoat, in fact, solved the problem of what to wear, and he had grown up in the cold South. At the Literary Club his clothing was not much different from that of other students, though he never wore a collar and tie.

Through *Canta* Baxter had become a close friend and drinking companion of Bill Pearson, who observed that he could strike up an acquaintance with the most unlikely people. He communicated easily with ordinary workers. From the way he greeted all sorts of people in the pub it was apparent he had an astonishingly detailed knowledge of their lives. He was not at all self-conscious, and would read a poetry book at the bar as though that was the most natural thing in the world. To casual enquirers he described himself without embarrassment as a poet, and that was accepted. He was not regarded as any sort of freak.

Pearson and Baxter were both friends of the painter Colin McCahon, who had come to Christchurch in 1948. He was living with another painter, Doris Lusk, and her husband at 52 Hewitts Road, Merivale, while his wife,

the artist Anne Hamblett, lived with her parents. McCahon had an outside
shed which he used as a studio. It was a difficult period for him financially,
with a wife and three children to support. He made jewellery and frames for
miniatures, and did as much painting as he could. From 1948 came such
paintings as: *Takaka Night and Day; Green Plain; The Virgin and Child compared
to a jug of pure water, and the Infant Jesus to a lamp*. McCahon attracted many
visitors. When Baxter and the poet John Caselberg visited McCahon in the
spring of 1948, McCahon asked him: 'What are you, a poet or a prophet or
what?' Baxter and Pearson became frequent visitors.

On Friday nights, and often on Sunday afternoons, Pearson, Baxter, and
McCahon used to meet in the United Services Hotel, next to the Post Office
in Cathedral Square, and have long drinking sessions. Often they were
joined by Lawrence Baigent and sometimes by the bookseller and writer
John Summers. According to Pearson, the trio shared:

> . . . a dismay that the times which in our memory had seen Stalin's purges,
> world war, Guernica, Belsen and Hiroshima offered neither peace nor
> likelihood of accommodating the idealist hopes we thought we had lost. We
> remembered *Darkness at Noon*, and read Graham Greene, talking in terms no
> longer in vogue of natural man and original sin and of eros and agape and caritas
> and the sin of sloth or despair to which he felt especially prone and called by its
> medieval name *accidie*. The truths that we were finding out were old ones, and
> humbling: that the seeds of oppression and violence lay in the nature that we had
> in common with other men, and a recognition of the supreme value of
> compassionate love – truths that explain the compassion Baxter could feel not
> only for the victims of authority but for its agents. We were drawn to the
> security and conviction that religious orthodoxy offered, envying the Middle
> Ages their simplicity of belief.[11]

Pearson admired Baxter's 'sympathy and insight, his tolerance and common
sense, his heavy oblique humour and his endless image-spinning talk'.

McCahon considered Baxter a warm person, original, and with
stimulating ideas. He did not laugh much, but when he was amused there
was a twinkle in his eye and a quick smile. He thought Baxter was very
complex, a person at once self-centred and capable of great generosity. His
scurrilous talk did not bother him, it was part and parcel of the man and did
no harm. He agreed that Baxter was very much a Romantic in his
aspirations and ideals. Baxter greatly admired McCahon's integrity, his total
dedication as an artist, and his refusal to compromise. And he made a spirited
defence of McCahon's art, in an article he wrote for *Canta*, 'Salvation Army
Aesthete'. The title came from a remark Baxter had made to him as they
passed a hoarding outside a Salvation Army citadel: 'Your painting's like
that'.[12] The article is the more interesting since Glover did not get on well
with McCahon and disliked his work. Baxter had to disagree with one

friend to support another. Fairburn, too, had dismissed McCahon's experimental cartoons as 'graffiti on the walls of some celestial lavatory'.[13] Baxter commended McCahon's fire and originality, and the way he captured 'the raw harsh quality of so many New Zealand ranges. He is expressing the sour and struggling piety that lies behind the blank mask of Presbyterianism'. Fairburn knew a great deal more about painting than Baxter would ever know, but when it came to defending his friends, Baxter was often more perceptive than their critics. He and McCahon had something special in common. Of Brighton, Baxter was to write:

> Here first the single vision
> Entered my heart . . .
>
> (CP 135)

And it was when McCahon was driving over hills from 'Brighton or Taieri Mouth' to Taieri Plain that he had his own vision:

> I saw something logical, orderly and beautiful belonging to the land and not yet to its people. Not yet understood or communicated, not even really yet invented. My work has largely been to communicate this vision and to invent the way to see it.[14]

McCahon was experimental and innovative in a way Baxter was not, but both artists pursued their vocation as visionaries, romantics, and masters of symbol.

That year Baxter often visited Doris Lusk to see McCahon, and to have a meal or a much-needed bath. When he turned up he was usually alone. He was clearly drinking too much and she disliked his behaviour when alcohol induced a maudlin mood in him. At such times he would clumsily try to seduce any woman who was present. She admired his poetry but not his behaviour.

Both Denis and Mary Glover and Allen and Betty Curnow had young families, and they were always welcoming to Baxter and Jacquie, often inviting them to their homes for meals. Albion Wright and his wife were also friends. This group of couples supported each other and went to the same weekend parties. However, Jacquie felt that she and Baxter moved like babes in the wood within this sophisticated group. At times they found people slightly over-protective or patronizing. Baxter was influenced by many people, and one or two, though not at all well-known, were important to him. One was described as a complete cynic — disillusioned, dissipated, without idealism or scruple. Whatever Baxter said or did was scornfully dismissed. Baxter seemed to need people like that, and there were always one or two in his life. Their cynicism sharpened his thought and gave it a certain robustness.

To support himself that year Baxter had a series of jobs. He worked at the Sanatorium from 24 March until 30 June 1948, living in the porters' accommodation supplied by the North Canterbury Hospital Board. When he tendered his resignation, the authorities tried to persuade him to stay on, but he had had a very bad cough for some time and was concerned with the risk of infection from tuberculosis, a much more dangerous disease in those days than it is now.[15] And the 'women bosses' he found niggling and authoritarian. He got on well with the patients and admired the qualities they developed in coping with their malady. For his twenty-second birthday on 29 June he asked his parents for a copy of Nietzsche's *Zarathustra*, 'an intuitive kind of philosophy, rather like that of Blake in his "Marriage of Heaven and Hell", and as it doesn't try to be all-inclusive it is more valid than most philosophies'.[16]

In November he was proof-reading for the Christchurch *Press*, a job he got through the good offices of Allen Curnow, who was on the staff. The work was pleasant enough and he liked the boss. But it did not 'help the fight for clarity' which he found a 'constant and prodigious struggle'.[17] He worked from 8 p.m. to 2 a.m. and often slept through until midday. That year he also became a freezing worker. These steadier periods of employment were interrupted by casual jobs like grinding brass taps. After three days of that he was fired by the foreman as 'bloody useless'. Free-lance journalism seemed to him his best prospect to make a living. He would not have to 'prostitute' himself the way he felt a writer on a salary had to. And he knew his 'capacity for turning out a quite impressive screed at a moment's notice'. In general, he was reasonably happy. But he had some bad patches and needed help.

The psychologist he had come to Christchurch to see was Mrs Christeller, a Jungian. In the sessions he had to do most of the thinking and scrutiny of his 'self' because the analyst would not impose anything on him. Though she did not solve his many problems, he thought the experience valuable because it gave him self-confidence and a better sense of responsibility.[18] And they both agreed that he had found a balance he had lacked.

That year Baxter made do with some pretty rough accommodation. He rented 'a little dog-kennel of a place' in Webb Street, Merivale, for 'eight bob a week'. In bouts of depression, he was occasionally more strongly tempted to suicide than he had been at any other time in his life. Neither he nor Jacquie had much money. They often went to milk bars and bought milkshakes, or to the pie-cart for pies, hot tomato soup with toast, or for tea and wafer-thin slices of white bread smeared with butter. When they had no money they simply went without. The romantic notion of starving in a garret was all too real. Jacquie was slightly better off because both her professor and lecturers kept an eye on her and sometimes had her home for meals. Baxter would pick up quarter-smoked women's cigarette butts, tinged with lipstick, undo them and roll them again.[19] Yet:

> Hunger for light sustained me there
> Under the sign of Dionysus-Hades,
> In a kennel with a torn gas mantle,
> Alive on milk and benzedrine . . .
> (CP 216)

A friend who called one day found him asleep between two filthy mattresses, with no sheets and no blankets; he was obviously cold. On the floor were empty cans and a half-eaten tin of baked beans. At one end of the room was a kind of tallboy. The top was spotless, and writing-paper and pens were neatly laid out. It was the only clean place in the hut. The friend and his companions went into Ballantyne's Department store and bought Baxter a jersey for seven and sixpence. Not all his visitors were so beneficent. A dead-beat, whom Baxter had put up in the shed for a day and a night, stole his best suit and all the books he could carry. But Baxter would not go to the police.

Wherever he lived, whatever he worked at, his preoccupation was poetry. He talked about it endlessly and was absorbed in it to the point of obsession. In a roomful of people you could hear his steady drone behind the conversation. At other times he would just sit in a chair and take no part in what was going on. It seemed that he was asleep or had passed out. But he was likely to be meditating or composing a poem which he would later copy into one of those thick black notebooks he carried in his overcoat pocket.

That year the contrast between external behaviour and the inner world of thinking and feeling, characteristic of alcoholics, was strikingly illustrated by his second volume of poetry, *Blow, Wind of Fruitfulness*, published by the Caxton Press in 1948. The rich, complex inner life it revealed demonstrated how much more complicated the split was in Baxter than in many others. The selection was made by Denis Glover, though the last seven poems were added after he had finished his work. Of the thirty-six poems in the book, only four were written in 1948. Of them the two most notable are 'Letter to Noel Ginn II' and 'The Cave'. Most of the others, twenty-three in all, came from 1946, and seven from 1945.

The volume continued the exploration of themes begun in *Beyond the Palisade*: death, war, loss, time as destroyer, and the need for some defence. Like the first poem in Baxter's earlier volume, the opening poem in *Blow, Wind of Fruitfulness*, 'Thistle', pays homage to his Scottish ancestors. It is done indirectly by choosing a verse form made popular by Robert Burns. The elder poet's 'To a Mountain Daisy' is acclimatized in a New Zealand setting. 'Thistle' declares Baxter's personal stance outside normal New Zealand society, resolutely individual, independent, even anarchic. The link with Scotland continues with the celebration of John Baxter in 'Elegy for my Father's Father'. But there was a new element in the poems as well. Unable to believe any longer in the perfectibility of man or in the myth of inevitable progress optimistically presented by writers like H. G. Wells, he had come to accept the Genesis myth as the ultimate explanation of humanity's predicament. The sense of disinheritance consequent on the loss of Eden, so central to 'The Bay', was emerging as one of the great controlling ideas in his poetry.

> On the road to the bay was a lake of rushes
> Where we bathed at times and changed in the bamboos.
> Now it is rather to stand and say:
> How many roads we take that lead to Nowhere,
> The alley overgrown, no meaning now but loss:
> Not that veritable garden where everything comes easy.
>
> And by the bay itself were cliffs with carved names
> And a hut on the shore beside the Maori ovens.
> We raced boats from the banks of the pumice creek
> Or swam in those autumnal shallows
> Growing cold in amber water, riding the logs
> Upstream, and waiting for the taniwha.
>
> So now I remember the bay and the little spiders
> On driftwood, so poisonous and quick.
> The carved cliffs and the great outcrying surf
> With currents round the rocks and the birds rising.
> A thousand times an hour is torn across
> And burned for the sake of going on living.
> But I remember the bay that never was
> And stand like stone and cannot turn away.
>
> (CP 44-5)

'The Bay' is an idyllic memory. Its physical features are sharply observed – the katipo spiders 'so poisonous and quick'; 'the great outcrying surf / With currents round the rocks and the birds rising'. But the past, so vividly recollected, has to be put out of mind 'for the sake of going on living'. The reason was given in Baxter's comment on a line from his poem 'Prometheus': 'Soon shall the mad mnemonic crow take rest'. The 'crows', he said, are the memories of past moments rendering man unable to face the present.[20] Behind the childhood paradise of 'The Bay' is 'the veritable garden where everything comes easy'. The lost Eden now dominated his imagination.[21] The final impression communicated by the poem is a sense of longing for this lost inheritance. The feeling is widely enough shared but Baxter has given it particular force by the intensity and sharpness of personal memories.

'Sea Noon' skilfully evokes the mood of undefined melancholy sometimes induced by the New Zealand landscape: 'the grey smoke of rain drifts over headlands', 'So stand the dull green trees bearing the weather'. The poem is a celebration of friendship and a lament that it cannot cure humankind's essential isolation. The same sense of loneliness runs through 'High Country Weather' ('Alone we are born and die alone'), and 'Prometheus', for whom the only hope is the oblivion of death. In 'The Antelopes', gentleness and grace are menaced by aggressors who seek to kill the antelopes, which symbolize youth under threat – as in the third part of Auden's *New Year Letter*. Baxter had read Auden's poem by 1944, and these lines may have given him the impulse for his own poem.[22] 'Catullus at the Grave of his Brother' is an early example of influence by a poet who was powerfully to affect the much later sequence 'Words to Lay a Strong Ghost'.

In 'Christmas Poem' Baxter pleaded:

> You who have heart to pray
> Pray for the children lost
> Within a haunted forest
> No path for turning back:
> (CP 37)

Baxter, too, felt he had lost his sense of direction. In 'Morning and Evening Calm', with its use of incidents from both the Old and New Testaments, he was moving towards a religious faith accepted with difficulty. In his earlier poem 'The Mountains', Baxter had chosen to 'go to the coastline and mingle with men'. In this volume, 'Haast Pass' confirms that choice. New Zealand landscape is caught with wonderful precision. Here it evokes the evanescence of a mood that shifts from rejection to commitment:

> In the dense bush all leaves and bark exude
> The odour of mortality; for plants
> Accept their death like stones
> Rooted for ever in time's torrent bed.
>
> Return from here. We have nothing to learn
> From the dank falling of fern spores
> Or the pure glacier blaze that melts
> Down mountains, flowing to the Tasman.
>
> This earth was never ours. Remember
> Rather the tired faces in the pub

The children who have never grown. Return
To the near death, the loves like garden flowers.
(CP 62-3)

Baxter's title poem 'Blow, Wind of Fruitfulness' is a yearning for a creative life which has become by the end of the poem a desire for immortality. The maturity of thought and the use of language as personal utterance in the new collection is evident if the two letters to Noel Ginn are compared. The first followed 'a more romantic vein', in the second the pressures of his life have entered deeply into the poetry. And he is now capable of self-irony:

> I was a lamp,
> A kind of beacon to you then, you said –
> Since then the wick has grown a trifle damp.

There is a new humility:

> but I
> Live by extremes. The madman and the saint
> Have both (I fear) the same extremist taint,
> And both are mad to Madame Butterfly.
> Being no Francis, I can scarcely paint
> A halo – 'poet's licence' is my cry.

The earlier attitudes to the working man, influenced by Auden and Spender, and romantically heightened by the *bonhomie* of the bar, have become illusory. There is a new realism as they yield to experience:

> It was my dearly held delusion once
> That labouring men were better than their betters
> And needed only to throw off their fetters
> For Eden to return to Adam's sons.
> Since then I've worked with them; and they're go-getters ...

Reluctantly he accepts that he does not belong with them:

> So I have found alas that my true station
> Is still among the academic crew
> Whom I despised for undue cerebration
> That leads to withering of the heart and thew.

The last verse formulates the antinomies in that struggle for wholeness he would engage in all his life:

> There is a kind of reconciliation
> With buried selves and seasons ...
> (CP 70-2)

Blow, Wind of Fruitfulness was published to general acclaim. Alistair Campbell believed that it immediately established Baxter as the leading poet of his generation.[23] Allen Curnow reviewed it for *Landfall*. It is a measure of

Curnow as a critic that in his review he saw so clearly and expressed so unequivocally Baxter's merits. He praised his 'natural eloquence' and called Baxter the most original of living New Zealand poets. He placed him in a central position in that tradition of New Zealand verse so lucidly enunciated in the preface to the Caxton anthology: 'The way in which certain conceptions of his country haunt the background of Mr. Baxter's poetry, having receded from the positive foreground of older poets, encourages the belief that something of continuing effect was achieved by them: it is, of course, a shared achievement, which needed good poets for its beginning, as it has waited for a good poet to point towards a consummation.'[24] He also realized that Baxter's fluency and exuberance needed more restraint, and justly observed that some 'poems are too good not to have been better'.

Despite the acclaim his book brought him in 1948, Baxter shared with Pearson and McCahon a deep disillusion. In the aftermath of the war and the revelation of Nazi atrocities they suffered 'a fundamental shock, a derangement in that area of the brain in which stable ideas about humankind and its possibilities are kept'.[25] They felt the need for a religious faith and the form that appeared most attractive was Catholicism. For Pearson the moment passed and he looked elsewhere for a response to the human predicament. Nor did McCahon make any religious commitment, though his great respect for Catholicism probably dated from these Christchurch years.[26] But Baxter had been travelling towards a religious faith for a long time. His brief phase of adolescent atheism had yielded, according to his personal notes in *Rostrum* in 1946, to 'Pantheist or thereabouts', and his politics were 'anarcho-syndicalist'. In the course of that year Baxter would sometimes telephone Lawrence Baigent and sound so low-spirited that, though he was desperately busy with his university teaching, Baigent would drop whatever he was doing to make time for him. Guilt, sin, and death obsessed Baxter, and he was forever quoting poetry about them. On one occasion Baigent pointed out that not all religious poetry was of that kind. He instanced Traherne, of whom Baxter had never heard. That night Baxter kept insisting that guilt was an inescapable part of life and was what chiefly impelled people to God. Baigent took down Traherne's *Centuries* and read a few passages. Baxter looked at him in disbelief: 'That's not true,' he said. 'No Christian could feel like that.' And he was utterly disturbed for the rest of the night – as though one of his fundamental beliefs had been shaken.

For a Christian, reality is conditioned by two cardinal facts: everyone inherits that separation from God resulting from what is called by analogy with personal sin, Original Sin; and everyone is likewise included in Christ's redemption.

Baxter's guilt complex probably stemmed from his alcoholism and his sexual experiences and was exacerbated by a sense of loneliness. Awareness of his moral failings carried him further towards an acceptance of the Christian doctrine of Original Sin as an explanation of human depravity. He talked about it constantly as something crucial, and had no sense of the joy or celebration found in religious poets like Herbert, Traherne, and Hopkins. By concentrating on the Fall, rather than on a readily available salvation, Baxter developed a tragic conception of human nature as flawed. This emphasis, congenial to his temperament, reinforced the melancholy present in his poetry from the beginning. The notion of Original Sin became crucial to his thinking. Throughout his life he refined and deepened his understanding. It was a decisive factor in a conversion accelerated by a wide reading of religious books. C. S. Lewis particularly impressed him, clarifying his thoughts and strengthening his resolution. Baigent considered despair a prime impetus in Baxter's religious conversion. It was perhaps the impulse behind 'Song for an Old Soak', a poem he worked on from 20 June 1946, and which first appeared in the August *Canta* of 1948. It contained a prayer:

> Jesus and Mary, make
> The springtime come again
> Somewhere sometime, or take
> The burden of my pain.
> I seek the green inn
> Where life and death begin.
>   (CP 76)

Almost forgotten is the uncollected 'City of God', published in *Canta*'s last issue of 29 September, which includes the lines:

> City of God within my soul abiding
> From where all waters flow to nourish me
>
> Pity us Lord, that we are unbelievers
>
> City of Love, deliver us from fear.

Baxter was baptized an Anglican on 4 November 1948 at St Michael and All Angels in Oxford Terrace. Jacquie was a witness. Early that morning he turned up at Baigent's place and said: 'Lawrence, you haven't any nugget, have you? I'm getting baptized today and look at my shoes.'

Religious conversions of prominent people, in New Zealand as elsewhere, are not greeted by their co-religionists as the spectacular triumphs for Christianity those with no stomach for conversion sometimes believe. The minister who received Baxter had only vague memories of the event. Another, fresh from a course in classics at Auckland University, and who was ordained in Christchurch in 1948, did not know for some time that Baxter had been received. He could not remember anyone at St Michael's mentioning him.[27] The chief importance of the event was for Baxter.

How carefully Baxter weighed up the various modern views of mankind before making his own commitment can be deduced from a talk, 'Choice of Belief in Modern Society', that he gave to a students' congress at Curious Cove four years later.[28] He began by saying that since we face death at every moment we have no real security in this world. We should therefore take stock of our lives by deciding what is of permanent value. Artists can help the discrimination by contributing their fragmentary intuitions of what is true. Baxter scrutinized prevailing world views – what he called the comfortable view which dismisses suffering and atrocities as inevitable; the idyllic view that mankind has been corrupted by civilization and finds the remedy in a retreat to the wilderness; the Promethean view, following Prometheus the fire-bearer as technologist, which believes that science will in the long run deliver us from moral and material bankruptcy, and 'One will be happy without being good'. His final category, the revolutionary view, overvalued people's good will and altruism.

All these views were rejected. Optimism, for example, did not touch 'the deep sense of isolation and malaise, of meaninglessness which explodes inwards and produces those symptoms which go by the name of neurosis and psychosis'. And the work of artists, the testimony of saints, and our own experiences at moments of moral crisis, point to the 'fact that our feeling that great wrong is done and great good can be done, is truth, and the comfortable view an illusion'. Pertinently he asked: 'Can we believe that human nature has really changed since the time of the Roman Empire or Ghengis Khan?' He argued to the acceptance of a disastrous flaw in our human nature, the view 'held by Dante, Shakespeare; by Tolstoy, Dostoevsky; in part by the Greek dramatists – I mean the view that man is a moral being whose suffering proceeds from his denial of the light of conscience within him; and that this denial is universal.' For Baxter the truth and force of characterization in the classics sprang from their recognition that we are moral beings capable of free choice and inescapably responsible for what we choose. The desolation of the tragic hero moves us because it is something we all share to some extent. We share too his dignity as a person, which all other views of human nature whittle away.

The final emphasis of the address was on that relationship between people with which all morality worthy of the name is concerned. Against what he took to be the greatest public danger in New Zealand – State worship, he set the example of Francis of Assisi standing naked before his bishop and recognizing no claims before the love of God in his heart. The thrust of the whole talk was towards action: to share the physical and spiritual suffering of others as the way to the regeneration of humanity.

What Baxter regarded as central was the effect of Original Sin on human nature; the Reformation emphasis on individualism, with the private conscience privately formed as the supreme arbiter of right and wrong; and the importance for true religion of social action – especially in the form of active compassion for those who suffer. It is noticeable that Baxter did not employ in his talk any of the traditional formulations of Christian doctrine, but characteristically expressed religious ideas in his own words. He knew that traditional terms often meant nothing to an increasing number of people. The challenge was to present what he believed in language that could be understood by those with different assumptions.

'Choice of Belief in Modern Society' made plain Baxter's conviction that the artist is concerned with the truths by which people live, and that he believed actions both public and private are accountable. With this view the role of poet and social reformer easily merge. In the history of English poetry he could easily find illustrious precedents.

Towards the end of 1948 Baxter once again felt he had come to terms with his parents and had broken 'some invincible umbilical cord' and could see them both clearly for the first time 'without any mistrust and feeling of insecurity'.[29] And whatever the myth he created in his poetry or prose: 'I'm inclined to think, too, that I had a singularly pleasant upbringing; probably if anything, you and Daddy were too easy on me – I must have been rather irritating at times.'[30]

The ghost of Jane Aylmer, whom he had lost at the end of 1947, still haunted him and for a good part of 1948 he was still licking his wounds. He told a Christchurch friend that whenever he saw a young woman like her he felt faint. For years her memory would keep surfacing in his poetry.

But Baxter had grown very fond of Jacquie Sturm, and late in 1948 he asked her to marry him. That October, he wrote to his parents:

> She is a very fine girl, and I feel entirely at home in her company . . . I have grown fond of her. Not 'infatuation', just seeing more and more how much character and meaning she has. I might marry her in a year or two — but that is by no means certain, it will depend on how we both feel then. It is strange, the fact that she is a Maori draws me to her rather than repelling me. Still, you can be quite easy about it. There will be no marriage of necessity in my case . . . Also her 'pakeha' foster-parents have no love for me, since they have set their hearts on her being an intellectual prodigy, and regard me as a feckless intruder.[31]

Neither of their families was keen on the marriage. Jacquie's parents had hopes of a better match for someone with her ability and education. They knew that she was highly regarded in the Psychology Department at Canterbury College, especially after she had demonstrated that European-devised intelligence tests were unsuitable for Maori children because of significant differences in their cultural background. Her parents appealed to her Professor to intervene. He knew of an expedition about to leave for Antarctica for which a writer was needed. He suggested to Jacquie that Baxter might be persuaded to take the job.

At Brighton too, there was little ecstasy. At that time, even a Pakeha family as liberal as the Baxters had difficulty in accepting their son's marriage to a Maori. The opposition merely strengthened the young couple's resolution. Jacquie resented the interference and Baxter stepped up the pace of their courtship. He pursued her everywhere, even into her lectures, pushing past other students on the benches to reach her side. The lecturers were annoyed because he had no right to be there, and he and Jacquie had several rows. Denis Glover advised Jacquie that Baxter was not an ideal husband. He did not have a steady job or a home, and he drank too much. She was undeterred.

Amid the general turmoil Jacquie passed her exams, Baxter held down his job, and he continued to write. They went to see Jacquie's parents and Baxter wrote of the visit: 'I think her mother found me not as bad as she expected, she has grown to accept me in the last two days.'[32] Her father did not want to see him at first, but he relented later.

They were married on 9 December in St John's Cathedral, Napier. Baxter was twenty-two and Jacquie was twenty-one. She looked charming in white, her father came out of hospital to give her away, and James borrowed a suit for the occasion. Years later in *Autumn Testament* he expressed what he felt about their prospects:

> I was a gloomy drunk.
> You were a troubled woman.
> Nobody would have given tuppence for our chances ...
> (CP 539)

VII
The Young Married Man

After the wedding the couple lived with Jacquie's married sister in Wellington. The necessary adjustments of married life, and the many small tensions generated by sharing the same living space, made this a trying time. Baxter was often on the defensive. But within a couple of months they had moved to 'a nice house with a foul rent' at Park Road, Belmont, in the western Hutt Valley. It was a quaint little cottage, and fully furnished. For heating they had an open fire and Baxter would collect and saw up wood from the banks of the nearby river. They had an outside toilet with no light and for washing there was a copper and tub. They did not have a fridge, but both of them had been brought up simply and their requirements were modest. Baxter was working at the Ngauranga abbatoir and brought in £8 clear a week. They were expecting a baby and already Baxter was calling it John McColl.[1]

At Belmont life was suddenly very grim. It all came as rather a shock to Baxter. He was working hard at the abattoir and doing overtime. He worried about paying the rent and the grocery bills. Since they had no car, he cycled to work. That was good for his health at least, as for some time he had been suffering from an embarrassing bowel infection. Neither he nor Jacquie had parents in Wellington, so there was no question of running home when they got into difficulties.

Baxter consoled himself that he was no longer alone and that troubles over money, lodging, and the attitudes of relatives were something that concerned his wife as well. In some ways life was wonderful. He was delighted with Jacquie, with her enthusiasm and her skill as a housekeeper. She was able to feed them both for about two pounds ten shillings a week. She was able to buy a rabbit for 1/6d, and Baxter could bring home sheeps' hearts, liver, kidney, and sweetbreads from the abbatoir.

The Baxters were fortunate in their neighbours. James and Jean Bertram became close friends. James Bertram was lecturing in the Department of English at Victoria University College and was a friend of many leading New Zealand writers, such as R. A. K. Mason, Dan Davin, and Charles Brasch. But the neighbours who helped the Baxters most in this first difficult year were Arthur and Shirley Barker. They had a big house and were financially better off than the Baxters. Their passion was music and Arthur was a fair poet. Later, when the Baxter baby was born, Shirley would mind the baby while Jacquie was away at lectures. And Arthur was an invaluable foil to his younger friend's idealism. He could be devastatingly cynical and was unwilling to commit himself to any particular cause or belief, as Baxter was able to do.

Jacquie's baby was due mid-year, and when she went into hospital, Baxter visited her every day. When labour was imminent he 'disgraced' himself by 'weeping profusely', and when it began he was convinced that either Jacquie would die, or the baby would be born deformed as an 'Old Testament reward' for his sins. All went well, and Jacquie gave birth to a healthy girl on 18 June 1949. She was baptized into the Anglican communion and christened Hilary Anne. Her god-father, Colin McCahon, presented the family with his painting of Mary and the Child Jesus called 'there is only one direction'. For years it hung in the Baxters' living-room.

While his wife was in hospital, Baxter had been getting his hand in by washing, changing, and feeding a friend's baby. He thought he might eventually become 'a man about the house'. Now he enjoyed being a father and found himself becoming more attached to Hilary every day. He told his parents: 'I don't know very much about her yet. She seems so fragile and small that I am afraid to touch her. It is a great privilege to have a child to look after.'[2] Hilary was a beautiful baby, yet with 'a distinct Baxter half-ugliness, reminding me of Uncle Jack'.[3] To another friend he confided that baby-minding 'was a great thing for knocking hot air out of the mind and hysteria from the feelings'.[4] The poem 'Charm for Hilary', which expressed 'the continual undercurrent of anxiety' over a new baby, was written to pin over her cot.[5]

In 1949 Baxter was adjusting to his new life with Jacquie. Over the previous four months he had stopped drinking, realizing that 'it was time I stopped playing the fool'.[6] But his illusions about marriage had been shattered: 'I used to think marriage had a lot to do with sex, find it has practically nothing. Affection, harmony, even washing nappies or worrying about money are far more central. A shared endurance test, not a garden of Greek statues.'[7] He told Charles Brasch that for the first time in his experience, verse was no longer the most important thing in his life, and that the displacement was 'probably salutary'.[8] Though his domestic duties left him no time for fantasy, he had kept on writing. Wellington , a bureaucratic city, was a very different place from Christchurch. Baxter was not as well known there as he was in Christchurch, where he lived in a somewhat unreal world on the fringes of the university. But there were people who would give him great encouragement and it was not long before he met them.

He was invited, almost as the number one exhibit, to the soirées of Maria Dronke, held in a small room of her house in Hay Street, Oriental Bay, or at her studio in Lambton Quay. Hitler's anti-semitism had driven Maria and her husband John, a former German District Court Judge, to seek asylum in New Zealand. She had the aura of a cultivated exile whose real country was not Germany but the German language, and during the Weimar Republic she had explored its complexity with some of the best people in theatre. When Maria arrived in Wellington in August 1939, she was still at the height of her powers. Her personality and *grande dame* manner were as formidable as her reputation; and she was not a woman to be crossed. Through public recitals of astonishing projection, and through her work as a teacher of speech and drama, she became a moving force in the cultural life of the capital. And she trained some of New Zealand's best actresses. At the gatherings in Hay Street or Lambton Quay, Baxter met senior school pupils, young undergraduates, drama students, musicians (including his old friend Douglas Lilburn and the singer Dorothy McKegg), as well as theatre people like Richard and Edith Campion. For this circle and many outside it, Maria was a vibrant presence. In the years immediately after the war, she represented for many in Wellington, and even further afield, the aesthetic values they had missed during the war.

With her flair for languages, Maria quickly became familiar with New Zealand poetry. In her public readings she included poems by Mason, Curnow, and Baxter alongside those of Keats, Shakespeare, and T.S. Eliot. Between 1945 and 1948, many owed their first introduction to the poems and plays of Eliot to her. At the soirées, guests would read, and Maria also took part. Richard Campion remembered seeing Baxter there: 'hair sticking up, a bathed pink and white, looking absolutely like a cherub – a clever cherub, soft-mouthed, bright blue eyes, ears sticking out, like someone looking through the garden hedge at what was going on.'[9] Maria introduced Baxter as a poet, and among the younger members the word generated some excitement. For them poets were magical people, and for many magic surrounded Baxter.

Hella Hofmann (Helen Shaw) had invited Baxter to contribute to her collection of essays on Frank Sargeson, which was to be called *The Puritan and the Waif*, and since he was now finding more time to write he accepted.[10] The piece was finished within three months. When it eventually appeared, Sargeson wrote to Baxter saying that Maurice Duggan had several times remarked on its brilliance, and that he agreed. He added: 'You paraphrase much better than I write.'[11]

Baxter continued to speculate on the nature of a writer's vocation. On 27 May 1949, while addressing the Literary Society of Victoria University College, he gave as his answer to the question 'Why Writers Stop Writing': fatigue, lack of time, but above all an inability to find meaning in the world. The solution he proposed was to embrace orthodox Christianity, though he knew that was an unpopular choice.[12] He himself was writing all the time.

On a rainy night in November 1949, Baxter was confirmed as an Anglican by Bishop Owen. The Bishop, an ex-naval chaplain, offended his pacifist views by comparing the reception of confirmation to entering the navy. Yet Baxter realized that the Church is more than the views of its clergy, and that faith rested on creed, liturgy, and sacrament, 'which began before and will outlast nationalist feeling. Some day the Church will break her uneasy marriage to the State.'[13] He was troubled by the rudimentary nature of his own Christian commitment and conceded that the metaphor of the Christian soldier made good sense if it was properly understood. Pacifism itself, he believed, could find in Christianity the purity of motive without which it risked becoming sterile. Baxter's mind continued to be preoccupied with the problem of evil in human lives, and in one letter he speculated on where the 'thread of rottenness in one's character starts from. Once I thought . . . it was because people didn't get a chance to develop their potentialities for good, were born good and mis-educated into rottenness. Now I think rottenness is basic. As Paul says "For the good that I would I do not; but the evil which I would not, that I do." It is a terrible statement, but the beginning of clear thinking.'[14] Later that year he told his parents he was becoming something of a conservative and no longer believed in progress through social upheaval: 'Of course there's the fine element in socialism (compassion for the oppressed), but this is apt to shift into fantasy, leaving only Envy of the oppressor. The old problem – can impure motives produce a social good? I'd say No. We're none of us good enough to be like Christ with the money-changers. Our indignation is rarely righteous.'[15]

But there were more pressing problems than these large questions. The family had to leave their rented house in Park Road at the end of the year, and Baxter confided his anxiety to his parents. They had been a great support in the early days of his marriage, and though they were not affluent had sent gifts like blankets. He assured them of his gratitude and said that they were the first people he wrote to when he had time. Now they offered to share their house at Brighton. Though he was very appreciative, he declined since he was planning, on the advice of Arthur Barker, to enter Wellington Teachers' College the following year. His parents then offered to put up the money for a house. He would not hear of it, settling instead for a loan to pay a year's rent.

Teachers' College, he felt, would break him into academic work again, and he was resigned to the fact that any job has some 'harshness of routine'. He had also come to realize what his place in society should be:

I don't belong and never have belonged to the 'working class', much as I admire their virtues of patience, tolerance, and charity. By nature I prefer a scoundrel who knows and appreciates Shakespeare to a good man whose faculties have withered from neglect. Of course, more than either I prefer a good and wise cultured man. Daddy knows that the gulf between cultured and uncultured is greater than that between good and bad. He has always been lonely among his relatives. It is all a matter of manners and interests in common. I'd find it harder to condone bad manners in Jacquie, than lying. We all tell lies but we don't all put our fork in the jam. – This lengthy explanation is just to show why I must get a white-collar job.[16]

In 1950 the family moved to what had been the original farm house at 105 Messines Road in Karori. They shared the house with an elderly widow whom Jacquie found very accommodating, though she disapproved of some of their friends. They shared the kitchen, the bathroom, and the outside toilet, but had separate sitting-rooms and bedrooms. They had no telephone. There was a copper, a tub, and a wringer, but no washing-machine. Baxter collected wood from the adjacent Karori reserve and made sure that they always had a good supply. The family recalled that he was very skilful with an axe, a mallet, and wedges, and he could set a fire beautifully. They shared responsibilities for the upkeep of the grounds, though they had their own garden where they grew a few vegetables. Baxter was not a bad gardener.

After Hilary was born, Jacquie had had a miscarriage and she did not enjoy good health. Yet she persevered with her degree. Baxter had a drinking problem, and was becoming well known as something of a drinking artist. Privately, Baxter felt vulnerable because of his low income, their lack of financial resources and the fact that they were at the mercy of landlords. Some of them disliked tenants with children, and he suspected some, at times, of racism. Baxter did what interviewing was necessary himself. At Messines Road they were offered a two-year lease, but, in fact, they stayed in the house for four and a half years.

I. A. Gordon, a Professor of English at Victoria University, was a near neighbour. He was to give Baxter unwavering support. But the people who had most effect on the Baxters' lives at this time were the Millers. Harold, the university librarian, and Edith were both very committed High Anglicans, and it was through them that the Baxters had found their new home. Mrs Miller took them under her wing and was especially kind to Jacquie. She held open house every Sunday between two and five, serving a substantial afternoon tea of home cooking and elaborate sandwiches. Jacquie and Hilary, who was still in her push-chair, attended most Sundays. The Millers' son, John, was a research student in history and he became a close friend of Baxter's. Chess had become popular in Wellington in the 1950s, and many coffee bars had set aside special tables for players. Baxter and John used to play chess by the hour and talk. They would also go for long walks, something Baxter greatly enjoyed. Through Edith, Baxter came to know George Hughes, an Anglican priest who had taken up the Chair of

Philosophy at Victoria early in 1951. Hughes heard his confession on and off for a number of years. He also celebrated the Eucharist fairly regularly at Baxter's parish church, the Church of St Mary the Virgin. They became friends, though Baxter could be something of a trial, especially when he turned up at midnight in an intoxicated state.

Baxter did not go to Training College that year but continued at the abattoir. He soon threw that in, and on 6 March he became a temporary postman. Before long he was complaining that his sou'wester and waterproof gave him little or no protection against the drenching Wellington rain.[17] However, the new job allowed him more opportunity for poetry. He told his mother he knew in which part of the streets every phrase in a poem was composed. He was still drinking heavily. Denis Glover was in a bar one day when Baxter came in and:

> upset the whole mail-bag on the deck. I don't know whether he threw it or just knocked it over. There's the mail sacredly to be delivered in Her Majesty's name throughout all of those outlandish suburbs in Wellington, up a hill in Khandallah or somewhere. There it is, all swimming in beer . . . he takes no notice at all. He's making some point and he goes on having another few beers. His cobbers, however, were pretty decent blokes. Do you know they picked it out of the wet puddles on the deck and they jolly well went and delivered it themselves. Jim didn't care, didn't know, didn't thank them.[18]

The mail was often late and people used to ring up and complain. He ceased employment as a postman on 17 January 1951. From his own account, he was sacked 'when the bosses found me asleep dead-drunk with my head on a full satchel of letters in the Karori post-office.'[19]

In 1950 Baxter resumed the academic studies he had abandoned in Dunedin five years earlier. He enrolled at Victoria in Greek History Art and Literature.[20] His marks in the terms examination on Literature pleased him, since he had not been able to give the books much time. He told his parents the results allayed his fears that his brains were 'too rusty to do the work'.[21] I was in the same class as Baxter for part of that year and recall Professor H. A. Murray, a man chary with his praise, saying that one of the answers on Homer was as good as any he could remember. I assumed the answer was Baxter's, already so inward with the world of the poet whom the Muses loved above all others, 'though they had mingled good and evil in their gifts robbing him of his sight while lending sweetness to his song'. Jacquie, too, had resumed her studies and had taken on the much more formidable assignment of an M.A. in philosophy. She was to pass with First Class Honours, and wrote a thesis commended by the examiners as of exceptional merit. Baxter's own courses did not interfere with his vocation as a poet and he studied what suited him. At that time he was reading the poems of

Thomas Hardy and, despite their melancholy, he admired their vigour. From Hardy he learnt 'how to use the more desolate and uncreative moods which make most writers silent'.[22]

Victoria University College had a lively literary society in those years. Its random publication, *Armadillan Absolute*, was edited by Eric Schwimmer, and succeeded by the journal *Hilltop*, the brain-child of J.M. Thomson, W.H. Oliver, and their friends. One reason for the journal's existence was the desire to publish the verse of Alistair Campbell, which had greatly impressed them. At a time when there were few opportunities in New Zealand for publishing verse, they aimed at printing 'as much poetry, fiction, polemic and scholarship, as we, in fallibility, judge good'.[23] And they accepted contributions from outside the College. The *Hilltop* group also included Pat Wilson, Alistair Campbell, Louis Johnson, Lorna Clendon, and Judith Wilde. They met at J.M. Thomson's flat at 301 Willis Street, to discuss the contributions that had been sent in. Baxter sometimes attended meetings, but he was never at the centre of things nor interested in editorial matters, though he contributed five poems to the first number of *Hilltop*, published in June 1949.

Hilltop's modest format gave way to the much more ambitious style of *Arachne*, which folded in 1951 after its third number. History has vindicated the good taste of the editors. Besides the work of the Wellington group, their two magazines published poems by Charles Spear, Kendrick Smithyman, Charles Brasch, and a short story by David Ballantyne. An anthology of writers associated with *Arachne* had also been planned, 'to focus on the important new tendencies, and will contain a detailed introductory essay seeking the principles behind them'.[24] But the promise was never fulfilled. In *Recent Trends in New Zealand Poetry* Baxter spoke of *Arachne* (née *Hilltop*) as a 'ground for testing crops' and as providing a forum for younger writers to exchange ideas.[25] The same lecture showed he was well aware of the broad meaning given to the word 'group' as applied to these writers. Like many other artists, Baxter was not capable of being much more than an associate.

In 1950, at Monte Holcroft's invitation, he began reviewing for the *N.Z. Listener*. In *Landfall* he published some of the best of his early poems: 'Wild Bees', 'The Morgue', and 'Poem in the Matukituki Valley'. By now he was attending social functions at the Wellington Teachers' College and had met members of the staff, such as W.J. Scott, Anton Vogt, and Pat Macaskill. They found him a great talker and a heavy drinker, and knew of his socially eccentric reputation.

On 1 February 1951, Baxter enrolled at the Wellington Teachers' College to train as a primary school teacher. The College was then situated in Kowhai Road, Kelburn, not far from the university, with which it had close links. About one hundred and fifty yards down the glen were the Art and Craft and Science buildings, and below them in Ngaio Road were other buildings to accommodate the growing number of students. In Baxter's time, under W.J. Waghorn as principal, a liberal tradition flourished in the College. When a lecturer asked if he might take his students to the National Library during teaching hours, Waghorn replied: 'Wherever you are with your students, I will know you are where you should be. Tell the Office.'[26] W.J. Scott, the Vice-Principal, was also well known for his enlightened views. A man of strong intelligence and reserved manner, he was a quiet, detached figure, universally respected. He was a powerful ally for students of ability who found it hard to fit into the system, shielding them and nursing them through difficulties. Scott became a leading educationalist and a co-founder of the Council for Civil Liberties. He had learnt the secular morality he propounded from his reading of Bertrand Russell. In the writings of F. R. Leavis, he discovered the critical method he employed in the teaching of English. Through two small pamphlets he made Leavis's methods known to a wide range of students in and out of College.

As the person charged with maintaining discipline, Scott emphasized the need to combine a sense of personal responsibility with the development of an independent, enquiring mind. Since attendance was compulsory and the timetable covered the whole day, the College was more like a secondary school than a university. Students were liable to be fined for unauthorized absence, and the staff were expected to uphold the regulations. Yet most students enjoyed a fair amount of freedom, as long as they could show that what they were doing was worthwhile.

This was a period of vigorous cultural activity in the history of the College. Waghorn himself was a painter, and the art mistress, Doreen Blumhardt, was a skilful potter. But the liveliest of the arts in the College was literature. Scott set high standards for the writing of prose, and the science lecturer, Baxter's old neighbour, Arthur Barker, published some competent versions of Ronsard. Yet the moving spirit in the literary life of the College was a brilliant, independent, Peter Pan figure – Anton Vogt – whose family had emigrated from Norway when he was twelve. Though he had little formal education, he was able to cut straight to the heart of any matter under discussion, and he excited students by persuading them that they could write. His enormous vitality and enthusiasm, his all-night parties, and a house that was always buzzing with people, made him a dominant figure. He was the kind of person that could flourish, perhaps, only in a small institution like the Teacher's College of the fifties.

Vogt was a powerful stimulus for the practising writers in the College. One was Louis Johnson, whose first volume of verse, *The Sun Among the Ruins*, had appeared in 1951.[27] He had worked as a journalist for *The Southern*

Cross (a newspaper sponsored by the New Zealand Labour Party), and when it collapsed had decided to enter the teaching profession, thus enrolling in the one year 'pressure cooker' course designed for mature students. He met Baxter on his first morning at College, and was to become his best friend for some years. Both men were married and older than most of the other students. Johnson was fertile with publishing schemes and enlisted Baxter's help. In the literary battles ahead, they would be on the same side. It was usually Johnson who blew the trumpets and marched around the walls, but Baxter was the one who could breach them. Baxter was a reliable friend and always supportive of Johnson. For him, Johnson's best poems cut through experience 'like a buzz-saw'. In 1952 Alistair Campbell, who had made his reputation as a poet with his first collection, *Mine Eyes Dazzle*, returned to Training College and came to know both Johnson and Baxter well.

Some emerging writers at the College felt overshadowed by this group of established poets and were resentful. But the student anthologies of the time show that they were left adequate space. On Thursday afternoons, the time devoted to club activities, the Literary Club met in a prefabricated hut down in the Glen. It became a centre for what was dubbed 'the Glen group'. Outside speakers, like Denis Glover, were occasionally invited. Some members of staff disapproved of these students and complained that they were receiving preferential treatment. Scott and Patrick Macaskill, an English lecturer, defended them, believing what they were doing was valuable. Scott's attitude was that as long as they did not become obstreperous, they should be left to their own devices.

With his literary contacts already established outside the College, Baxter saw little of the Glen group. Sometimes he would address them on poetry or anatomize a poem. They thought he knew more about poetry than anybody they had met, and the range of his reading astonished them. Club afternoons held little interest for experienced writers like Baxter and Johnson, who headed off for the National Hotel in Lambton Quay. This hotel has now disappeared, but lives on as the Hesperus in Baxter's poem 'Lament for Barney Flanagan'. Alistair Campbell, who often drank in the National, thought that drink made Baxter more relaxed and amiable, and that when he had 'a few under his belt there was no one to match him'. Some of the younger students, however, found his flow of sexually explicit language shocking. As Baxter's alcoholism took wings, Campbell found him less pleasant and inclined to be aggressive.

Another favourite watering hole was the Grand Hotel in Willis Street, where a group from Training College used to drink on Friday nights. Sometimes Baxter turned up at College on Monday morning with a pale complexion, red-rimmed eyes, and wearing the same clothes as on the previous Friday. His friends encouraged him to shower and drink coffee before attending lectures. Baxter managed to control his drinking during the week, and was not seen under the influence of alcohol during working hours. He succeeded in carrying off many different parts.

Like others taking a degree at the university, Baxter was exempted from some Training College courses. Patrick Macaskill had made his study available to students at any time he was teaching. Baxter used it frequently, even when he should have been elsewhere. Once when Macaskill asked what he was working on, he replied: 'Well, I write an exercise every day and I write a poem when I feel like it. I send my exercises to *The Listener* and they usually publish them.'[28] In conversation he was often cavalier towards editors, even those who, like Holcroft, were generous to him. He was practising a wide range of poetic forms so that when he needed them the skill was there. Macaskill saw him working on the lyric sequence, 'Cressida', which was published in *Landfall* and admired by Brasch and Glover. Macaskill's dominant impression of Baxter at Teachers' College was of a man who kept to himself, 'following his star very carefully'. What he remembered best was Baxter's conversation, which often turned on his reading. One particular memory was of how the tragic elements of Hardy's *Jude the Obscure*, with its delineation of the lonely, original figure, fascinated him. So too did the ideas of the ancient Greeks on virtue and responsibility.

Once, as Baxter came out of a lecture, Macaskill asked him if he had taken any notes. 'No,' he replied, 'I did not hear anything worth noting.' This was not arrogance, Macaskill believed, but his characteristic honesty. He also recalled that on the few occasions Baxter attended his English lectures, he had the good manners to remain and never walked out. In class he took a full part in discussions, speaking quietly and establishing a good rapport with other students. When loose statements were made, he would expose their weakness firmly but gently. He was able to take issue with ideas and not with people. When a fellow student showed him some poetry, he told him that he had not suffered enough to write well. He said that his own best writing was produced as a response to stress; when he felt he had to record his dissatisfaction in some way. He was an amusing colleague with a good sense of humour and was always ready for a bit of fun.

W. J. Scott found him a gentle man with a deep kindness towards others. He considered Baxter's behaviour during his time at the College quite impeccable, apart from the drinking outside working hours. When Baxter visited him at home, Scott was astounded at the eloquence with which he discussed the philosophical and moral questions that were troubling him. One of his first impressions was of Baxter's intense feeling for religious experience, and for the contrast between good and evil in the world. As they talked, Scott found that Baxter was more concerned with expressing his own ideas than with listening, though he was capable of discussing a question and of presenting a good case for what he believed. One of his preoccupations at that time was the question of the existence of the devil and his influence on human affairs. Another lecturer, who knew Baxter well, was surprised to learn later that he had been an Anglican. He had noticed his interest in theology, but would not have described him as a religious person.

The limits of the liberalism professed by the Teachers' College were severely strained to accommodate Baxter within the teaching profession. At a staff meeting the question was asked: 'Do you think Mr. Baxter will somehow become a teacher?' Ray Chapman Taylor responded: 'Become a teacher? He's already taught more New Zealanders than any of us.'[29] It was even suggested that he be psychoanalysed. Anton Vogt enquired: 'Who do you think is going to deal with the psychiatrist when Jim Baxter has dealt with him?'[30] Vogt knew Baxter well. He found him a many-sided man, sometimes lugubrious, deeply religious, as well as being the author of bawdy verse. 'There was even something angelic about him. Sometimes I think he developed from a sort of Shelley boy to a sort of Tolstoy man very very fast. And it may be true of him and Curnow and perhaps no other writer I've ever known – these two – that for them indeed "In the beginning was the word".'[31]

W. J. Scott was familiar with the staff's opinion of Baxter, and with the reports on his performance in the schools when he had been out on section. He considered that while Baxter was never a vigorous teacher, he was certainly a thoughtful one, and able to stimulate his classes to think and talk in quite a useful way. The amiable Patrick Macaskill admired Baxter's compassion and the tolerance he showed to children. The special report sent by the Teachers' College to the Department of Education at the end of Baxter's course read:

> Academic: He has a first-rate mind, capable of probing experience quite profoundly and interpreting its meaning with fine insight and originality. Considering the nature of his gifts, which make him the intellectual superior of both his fellows and his teachers, he has adapted himself to the simpler climate of thought and experience of the College very well.
> Personal: With his extraordinary sensitivity and depth of feeling, he is subject to pressures and tensions unknown to the ordinary person, and sometimes finds the steady, hum-drum routine irksome . . .
> Professional: Rated by associate teachers good. Has fine understanding and feeling for children, but a little too gentle in manner, too deliberate in speech to be effective with an ordinary class. With a few children could be a first-rate educator.[32]

The unsigned report was written by Scott. Baxter never saw it, but a few years later he paid his own tribute to Scott, who:

> seemed to see clearly that Teachers' College and Education were not the world, but necessarily limited schemata simplifying the difficult and ambiguous lives of people . . . More personally, I rarely felt at ease at Training College being near the centre of the manic-depressive booze mill from which by the grace of God I have walked out sane; but you more than any other person there helped me to adjust, as far as I did adjust, and that because you have not accepted the role of father-figure which we teachers so fatally tend to accept.[33]

The demands of his training helped Baxter to develop a personal stability which the shifting nature of his previous employment had been unable to give. And his family responsibilities were growing. On 29 October 1952 his second child, John McColl Baxter, was born. Jacquie Baxter stressed that her husband took his family obligations very seriously. When he fell down he felt guilty. She recalled that once, when she suffered for some time from severe arthritis in her hands and could scarcely lift the baby, she had to leave the soiled linen piled up in the tub for Baxter to wash when he got home from work. He did it without complaint.

Baxter was living in two worlds, the domestic world with his wife and two small children, and the literary world where he received so much adulation. The two worlds merged to some extent in friendships, like that with Louis and Pat Johnson, who then lived in Newtown, and with Alistair and Fleur Campbell who lived in Tinakori Road. And there were other important friends, like Erik Schwimmer and his wife. But the dichotomy remained.

On 10 December Baxter completed his course at the Teachers' College. That same year he collaborated with Anton Vogt and Louis Johnson to bring out a joint selection, *Poems Unpleasant*.[34] He always supported the publishing ventures of his friends. The volume enhanced his reputation within the Training College, but hardly outside it. The poems he contributed, exploring themes close to the experience of his fellow-students, are well made and thick with images. At times they suffer from diffuseness and a strong moralizing tendency. The best is 'The Homecoming'. It was Vogt's idea to bring out the joint volume, but his own offering reveals no more than a minor poet. His contribution to the writers who passed through the Training College in the fifties was as catalyst and animator.

Nothing contributed more to Baxter's standing in the literary world than his brilliant performance at the New Zealand Writers' Conference held at Canterbury University College from 8 to 11 May 1951. The Conference, part of the celebrations to mark the centenary of the foundation of the Canterbury settlement, was organized by John Garrett, professor of English at the College, and two of his staff, H. Winston Rhodes and Lawrence Baigent. 'Writer' was interpreted broadly, though a good number of New Zealand's leading creative writers were also there. Most of the limited funds went to pay the expenses of a distinguished Australian writer, Vance Palmer, so there was little left to pay the way of New Zealanders. Fairburn, for instance did not attend but sent instead a wry telegram: 'No fare, no Fairburn.'

Baxter's lecture, *Recent Trends in New Zealand Poetry*,[35] given in Room 15 on the west side of the front quadrangle of the old university building, galvanized the conference. Garrett, an Oxford graduate who had come to New Zealand from Canada only two years earlier, thought it as eloquent an address as he had ever heard. What impressed him was Baxter's youthful idealism and his grasp of the problems confronting New Zealand writers.[36] W. H. Oliver expressed what many felt when he wrote in *Landfall* of the 'almost magical nature of his performance, the power over people made up variously of honesty, pure and precise wording, and the originality of the thing said.'[37] Baxter appeared to him to possess an eminence far beyond his years. D. M. Anderson wrote in Otago University's *Critic*: 'Baxter was 19 when he emerged as an important poet, now at 25 he takes his place as the profoundest critic we have. It is an extraordinary achievement.'[38]

The lecture was confined to the years since Curnow's 1945 Caxton anthology, and concentrated on five events that marked a significant evolution in New Zealand poetry: the establishment of *Landfall*; Alistair Campbell's first book of poetry, *Mine Eyes Dazzle*; Basil Dowling's third book, *Canterbury and Other Poems*; Ursula Bethell's *Collected Poems*; and Allen Curnow's verse play *The Axe*. Baxter related all five to the history of New Zealand poetry. His argument was that poets in the nineteenth century, and many of those in the twentieth, failed because they were unable to meet the country on its own terms. He indicated briefly the nature of the achievement of the poets of the thirties, and paid tribute to Fairburn, Curnow, Brasch, and above all to Glover. He argued that 'a new and valuable stereotype is in the process of being formed: the view of national history held by the poet who has grown up in entire acceptance of his environment, truly inhabiting the country.'[39]

The scope of the address was greatly enlarged by his attention to the function of the artist in society. Given that the pioneering dream of a just city had not been realized in New Zealand, and that our 'island is in fact an unjust, unhappy one, where human activity is becoming progressively more meaningless',[40] it was 'reasonable and necessary that poetry should contain moral truth, and that every poet should be a prophet according to his lights'.[41] After evoking the great images of the city and the wilderness, he made the famous statement that the modern poet:

> should remain as a cell of good living in a corrupt society, and in this situation by writing and example attempt to change it.[42]

The phrase 'a cell of good living' Baxter had probably come across in Eric Gill's *Autobiography*, where he wrote:

> And if I might attempt to state in one paragraph the work which I have chiefly tried to do in my life it is this: to make a cell of good living in the chaos of our world.[43]

The general conclusion of Baxter's lecture was optimistic: 'I believe that recent events in New Zealand literature indicate that men and women of goodwill greater than mine may yet speak prophetically and sanely to a wide audience.'[44] Baxter feared he might overvalue the formal aspects of poetry, but throughout the address his concern was not with poetic techniques but with ideas, for verse form seemed to him 'a tool for sharpening ideas'.[45] Poetry for Baxter was not a free-floating artefact cut adrift from its human context. Poetry was embodiment, and what was embodied was the vision that came out of his whole cultural matrix. With such broad parameters, his vision could affirm the goodness and significance of all that is human. Aware as he was of 'The importunate horror of knowing the world as it is/ Unpardonable', he could love it just the same. As a poet of embodiment, Baxter's poetry is in the same tradition as Blake and Yeats. Like them, he saw poetry as revealing what lay behind the appearances:

> Both clouds and houses are a frozen tide
> Till poetry inhabit them with fire.
>
> (CP 28)

Seeing the poet's role as prophetic, he believed 'More than aesthetic order is required in any problem involving truth, even the "truth of poetry".'[46]

Baxter was never in any danger of reducing the art of poetry to the indulgent describing of arabesques. It was too central a human activity. Whatever he may have said in controversy with critics who, he believed, overvalued form, he knew very well its importance. Stanzaically his work shows considerable variety. But he was not a technically inventive poet. His lifelong practice was to pick up from other poets what suited his immediate purposes. That is why we do not find the metrical subtlety and variety in his verse that can be found in the work of some other New Zealand poets, such as Curnow.

133

Recent Trends in New Zealand Poetry was published in 1951 by the Caxton Press, and was a landmark in New Zealand criticism. Baxter summed up in a balanced and perceptive fashion the achievement of his predecessors, and acknowledged that the writers of the thirties had established the foundations of a national literature. For the text of his address he had chosen some lines from their high priest, W. H. Auden. He also aligned himself with the aspirations for a just society that had preoccupied older writers like John Mulgan and Frank Sargeson.

The Conference was the first large gathering of writers since the war, and the sense of the need for a new start was widely felt. Sargeson recalled that 'Glover in his blatant way used to say, "Remember you'll be pre-war – you'll be completely out of it now – forget that you ever put pen to paper." '[47] Glover was to be refuted comprehensively, but the remark indicates the prevailing mood. Baxter, with his strikingly youthful appearance, seemed to be the one who would show what the new form of New Zealand writing might be. For many, he was the 'marvellous boy' who had been predicted by Curnow in his poem written in 1940, 'The Skeleton of the Great Moa in the Canterbury Museum, Christchurch':

> Not I, some child, born in a marvellous year
> Will learn the trick of standing upright here.

His sense of continuity with the tradition, the high seriousness with which he spoke of the writer's vocation, his own poetic achievement, all combined with his personal charisma to inspire and exhilarate.

At Training College and elsewhere in these years, Baxter had become well known for his bawdy verse as well as for his serious work. He composed and delivered his erotica with some appetite. He was a clown out to entertain his audience, a rebel against the primness of his Victorian upbringing, and he was driven, as he admitted to Brasch, by his own unresolved sexual tensions.[48] Before him was the example of his hero Robert Burns, whose book of bawdy poems, *The Merrie Muses of Caledonia*, was still hard to come by. Baxter had managed to get hold of a copy and pored over it. By the end of 1951 he had written enough bawdy verse to be able to offer a selection to Harry Orsman, the lexicographer and student of the vernacular. Orsman sent them off to the editor of a projected 'Sexual Ballads of the English-speaking Peoples', which was never published. A fair number of Baxter's bawdy poems are still in private hands throughout New Zealand. One substantial collection is 'The Frog Beneath the Skin', which contains among its twenty poems 'The Rumbustious Bad Young Man'. The collection has two epigraphs, one from Blake: 'The road of excess leads to the palace of wisdom'; and one from Karl Shapiro: 'For the lips of the newly

born are warm and pure, but the lips of the dead are lewd and cold.' Baxter
liked having things both ways. He did not take his 'bar-room verses'
seriously, and they later caused him some misgivings. In one of his notebooks
there is a poem from 1961, 'A Repentance for Pornographic Verse':

> My bar-room verses I would justify
> Because they used the salt of the common tongue;
> But any weather-freshened farmer's eye
> Could see they were dry chaff and dung . . .[49]

When his teacher training was finished, the Teachers' College allowed
him to go full time in 1953 to Victoria University College, on full salary. He
passed Latin I and Philosophy II with very modest marks, but failed English
III because of his inability to handle the compulsory paper in Old English. He
simply had not done the work.

In 1953 the Caxton Press published Baxter's third major collection of
verse, *The Fallen House*. It included poems written in the late forties beside
more recent work, including five pieces completed in 1951. Many poems,
including 'To My Father', 'Virginia Lake', and 'Poem in the Matukituki
Valley', were already familiar from earlier publication in periodicals or
student newspapers. It was the rain of Wellington that stimulated the
memory of the Otago beach scene in 'Rocket Show'. 'Wild Bees', of which
the first version was written in 1941, was completed in the capital.

The Fallen House was Baxter's most accomplished book to date. He
showed the capacity to adopt a variety of roles and to carry them off with
an enviable virtuosity. The dominant theme of the book is loss, and the
feeling that holds it together is grieving. This springs largely from that acute
awareness of the loss of childhood innocence and vision possessed once in the
'Garden of Eden'. This theme is apparent in 'Virginia Lake', a poem based
on a memory of the magical world of a child, where:

> the red-billed native birds
> Step high like dancers.
>
> (CP 74)

and

> This was the garden and the talking water
> Where once a child walked and wondered
> At the leaves' treasure house, the brown ducks riding
> Over the water face, the four winds calling
> His name aloud, and a green world under
> Where fish like stars in a fallen heaven glided.

135

'Poem by the Clock Tower, Sumner' is instinct with the exaltation of childhood's perceptions over those of adults. In such poems, innocence has succumbed to the grief of experience and sharpened the poet's yearning for a lost paradise. The insight of the French writer, polemicist, and pamphleteer, Léon Bloy, has fermented in his blood already: 'There is only one sadness, to have lost the Garden of Eden, and only one happiness to find it'.

'Poem in the Matukituki Valley' came out of a two-week stay, early in January 1950, in the Mount Aspiring hut near Wanaka. Baxter had been commissioned by the New Zealand Film Unit to write a verse and prose script for a film to be made by the internationally known photographer, Brian Brake, 'The Ascent of Mt. Aspiring'.[50] Adverse weather throughout the expedition meant the climbers did not reach the summit, and the film was never made. In the long wait for the weather to clear, Brake and Baxter had many philosophical discussions. The grandeur and variety of the Western branch of the Matukiuuki Valley and the neighbouring mountains are sharply observed and set down. The land is:

> matrix and destroyer
> Resentful, darkly known
> (CP 86)

and the natural world confronts the poet with the question:

> what are these
> But His flawed mirror who gave the mountain strength
> And dwells in holy calm, undying freshness?
> (CP 87)

The response is evasion, escape into the city where the land's intimations of the eternal world can be forgotten. Baxter told Brasch that 'the true source of my Matukituki Valley poem lay in my marriage quite as much as in the Matukituki Valley'. He added that married people get from their marriage strength to write good poetry, not about their respective partners but about quite other matters: 'Marriage is one of the great human reservoirs which conserves the water of life. It is built one always hopes to last a life-time. But the "conserving" factor is necessarily conservative, and as such, tends to be anti-aesthetic.'[51]

'Wild Bees' employs a common Baxter strategy, learnt perhaps from Wordsworth. An experience is recalled, vividly realized, then pondered until it yields its meaning. In personal terms the method helped Baxter to arrive at a philosophy of life based on his own experience. A key idea in that

136

philosophy is expressed with magnificent resonance at the end of 'Wild Bees':

> But loss is a precious stone to me, a nectar
> Distilled in time, preaching the truth of winter
> To the fallen heart that does not cease to fall.
>   (CP 83)

Loss was precious because it led to detachment from all that would impede his ascent towards truth. And he had the humility to realize how much he had to learn. The phrases 'the fallen heart', 'the mansion ruinous of the human heart' in 'The Morgue', and an expression in the following quotation from 'Rocket Show', extend the meaning of the title poem 'The Fallen House'. The heart and its mysteries would always preoccupy Baxter. They are unforgettably expressed in lines that interpret the experience of 'Rocket Show':

> As I walked home through the cold streets by moonlight,
> My steps ringing in the October night,
> I thought of our strange lives, the grinding cycle
> Of death and renewal come to full circle,
> And of man's heart, that blind Rosetta stone,
> Mad as the polar moon, decipherable by none.
>   (CP 81)

The Fallen House displays remarkable technical virtuosity. There is rarely any sense that Baxter is constrained by the difficult metres or by rhyme. The words move musically in verse which is a fit medium for a poetry of celebration and yearning. In such poems the lessons in versification learnt from Yeats have become so integrated into Baxter's technique that the verse carries his individual accent. There are echoes from 'Under Ben Bulben' and 'Easter 1916' in a poem like 'Temple Basin':

> Invisible multitude of the wind horses ranging
> From peak to mitred peak, from cloud to tumbling cloud.
>   (CP 75)

Other poems show the influence of Hardy. One reason he responded so sympathetically to Hardy, 'trained in the college/of the heart's despair' (as he expressed it in 'Defence of Romantic Love') was that he shared the acute sense of loss which informed the older writer's verse. Both poets had in their temperaments a strong vein of melancholy. 'Revenants' employs one of Hardy's intricate verse forms, and other poems are influenced by his attitudes and language. 'The Fallen House' is typical of Hardy's method of organizing a poem. It holds the past and the present in conjunction to mourn better what time has taken. The regularity of stanza form and the beat of the verse throughout the volume, Baxter's use of place names, alliteration, the interplay of double and single rhymes, and diction such as 'no forefarer's foot-mark treading' and a 'once-fair steading', clearly show his debt to Hardy.

After two years at Teachers' College and a year at Victoria, Baxter, accoutred as he was, became Assistant Master (Scale 1) at Epuni School in Waterloo Road, Lower Hutt on 1 February 1954. He considered the pay of £45 a month quite good. It was better than the £32 a month at the abattoirs. That year Epuni had three hundred and eighty-five pupils, most of whom came from a state housing area. It offered classes from the Primers through to Standard Four. Only four teachers from the previous staff had returned, and Baxter was one of eight new recruits. The headmaster, John Clifton Ward, knew Baxter, who had already been at the school as a trainee teacher. Ward was aware of Baxter's reputation as a hard drinker, but he admired his powers of application, and the way he related to the children. He was happy to have him back on a permanent basis.

Baxter, Ward observed, was inclined to be reserved until people knew him, whereupon he became very sociable towards them. He said little at staff meetings unless his view was expressly requested. Epuni school is well situated with the classrooms facing north. The minutes of a staff meeting record Baxter's request for curtains to reduce the strong light, and on another occasion, he requested two lengths of curtain for an open cupboard to improve the appearance of his classroom.[52] During lunch-hours he sometimes swam with Ward at Point Howard, though he was never known to take part in any other sporting activity.

Baxter was apologetic about his poor class control. One afternoon he came to tell Ward that half of his class had taken to the gorse-covered hills near the school, and he felt sorry that they had disobeyed him. In the Physical Education period, Baxter proceeded slowly from his Standard I classroom to a spot in the playground. His progress was impeded by some thirty children leaping and cavorting around him. Ward could observe little organization in the sessions. There was nothing of the sergeant-major about Baxter. The spectacle was one of intense animation and of children enjoying themselves immensely.

We know Baxter's own feelings during his first couple of months at the school from a letter to his parents:

> Have now been school-teaching for nine weeks and the first desperation of it has worn off. The class is now thirty-two equally divided into sex, standard one and average age about seven to eight. They are still to a large extent babies; but it

is a Standard One teacher's job to make them less so and to teach them the basic skills of writing and arithmetic. On the whole though, I like the children. I would rather not see them in the classroom but somewhere elsewhere. One's attention is so much directed to keeping a routine going, and the whole class working, that one can never do much for the individual child; indeed, the children who are the most trouble, and whom one keeps in after school or sends to the headmaster to get the strap, are often the ones from whom one would get the best results if only one knew how. Am not really scared of the children any longer; but I seem to spend all my time teaching, preparing for teaching, doing Latin, travelling or sleeping.[53]

The exaltation of the difficult child, the outsider, would always be typical of Baxter's attitudes. The care he took over the preparation of his classes was borne out by his workbook, not now extant, which Ward thought was beautifully kept. In the freshness of its approach it was quite unlike those which usually pass for workbooks.

Baxter came into his own when he was teaching English. He had the ability to fire children with enthusiasm for poems, and he wrote some especially for them. He showed them the fun they could have by building up verses together. Ward made full use of him to help the children develop a liking for poetry, and he asked him to visit other classes. When Ward left Epuni to become headmaster of Taita Intermediate, he sometimes invited Baxter to take a class in poetry.

Without Baxter's knowledge, the verses he had written for his own pupils were eagerly collected and widely used in Hutt Valley schools. Ward had a full set and was keen to see them published. Baxter offered them to Pegasus Press who turned them down.[54] They were not to appear until the posthumous volume *The Tree House* was published in 1974, without doubt the finest volume of children's poetry produced in this country. Poems like 'The Growly Bear' could only have been written by someone who understood and liked children.

> The growly bear,
> The growly bear,
> He lives in the cupboard
> Under the stair.
>
> His hat and his boots
> And his breeches are brown,
> And he sleeps all day
> On a brown eiderdown.
>
> At night he goes walking
> About by himself
> To gobble up the honey
> On the kitchen shelf.

You can hear him growling
Wherever he goes,
But just what he looks like
Nobody knows.

(CP 604)

When he was supervising the playground, Baxter would walk about slowly, engrossed in a book and quite oblivious of the children frisking around him. At lunch-time he would send a pupil off to buy his fish and chips. He would place the parcel carefully under his left arm (which also held his book), tear a hole in the newspaper, and with his right hand pick out chips and pieces of fish. As he moved around, a group of curious children trailed after him.

His inbred dislike for teaching was gradually dispelled, and he found his permanent job preferable to that of a relieving teacher. He could not be 'sent out at a moment's notice from here to Timbuktu'. Ward told me that inspectors from the Department of Education were concerned about Baxter's performance as a teacher. His own view was that the problem of class control, stemming from Baxter's very personal approach, would disappear in time because of his great affection for the children. But it was an approach that made heavy demands on his energy.

While Baxter was still a student at Victoria, Professor I.A. Gordon invited him to give the Macmillan Brown lectures. They had been set up and endowed by Baxter's grandfather and administered by the University of New Zealand, and could be given in any of the University Colleges. Macmillan Brown had specified that they were to be given on 'my books or on topics arising from them'. Mercifully those conditions had not confined lecturers like Dan Davin who spoke on the novels of Joyce Cary. Baxter gave his lectures in June 1954. They were published the following year under the title *The Fire and the Anvil* and dedicated to Frank Sargeson. The first of the three lectures discussed the formal aspects of poetry, and figures of speech, and offered personal criteria for judging a poem. The second touched on the nature of poetic inspiration and discussed what gave a poem significance. It also contained a good deal of Baxter's personal philosophy. The final lecture, which Baxter regarded as the best and most balanced, dealt with symbolism in New Zealand verse and drew its examples from a wide range of New Zealand poets.

The judgements were challenging, and enough was said to make discussion worthwhile. Baxter did not sustain an argument in the manner of analytical criticism, but adopted an impressionistic approach. This allowed him to follow his own interests, literary, social, and psychological. The weakest sections were those where he assumed the mantle of an academic, the strongest, those where he gave his personal response. The rhetoric was more persuasive because of his unobtrusive manner on the platform and the earnestness with which he spoke.

The published lectures were mostly well received. James Bertram, who had been present when they were given, wrote with his usual generosity that they were lively and good-humoured as well as embodying 'a great deal of shrewd observation, some genuine if not very precisely formulated literary insights'.[55] For Robert Chapman, historian and anthologist, the book was 'the most important critical work on New Zealand poetry since Eric McCormick's *Art and Letters in New Zealand.*' For him, Baxter had shown the place our poetry had reached. The lectures offered 'a convincing picture of what a poet at home in New Zealand would sound like when thinking about his work and surroundings.'[56] But E.A. Horsman of Otago University, a precise and rather reserved scholar, wrote a severe review in *Landfall*, censuring what he took to be simplistic exaggeration and pseudo-history. Baxter's own judgement, expressed with the self-deprecation of many of his private utterances, was inscribed on John Weir's presentation copy of *The Fire and the Anvil*: 'This confused and sincere book still expresses a good deal of what I feel about the artist's vocation . . . and most of it was written between or during savage drinking bouts.'[57]

The lectures formulated Baxter's concerns as a writer in 1954. It had become centrally important for him that New Zealand should be a community of people with a spiritual identity, shared at least to some extent by both writers and audience. Ten years earlier, Fairburn, too, had called for 'a common consciousness, a common set of values.'[58] Baxter indicated the pressures society exerted on writers to make them conform, pressures he would continue to resist. The seriousness towards the vocation of a writer which he had expressed in *Recent Trends in New Zealand Poetry* persisted: 'The work of a writer is one of liberation – not the persuasion to good or evil, but the liberation of the creative will of both himself and the reader to do either . . .'[59] Of special interest to a biographer is his warning against 'the personalist heresy of equating a writer and his work',[60] along with his statement that 'To save (in a purely aesthetic sense) his soul, a poet must be more honest than his everyday cowardly or jocular self.'[61] The point of the parenthesis, *pace* W. H. Auden in his first version of 'In Memory of W.B. Yeats', is that for salvation in the full sense, presumably more will be required from a writer than writing well. From his statement that the self in poetry is 'a projection of complex associations in the poet's mind', it can be inferred that the poet's mind as well as what it produces, can be usefully examined.[62]

Baxter's style was enlivened by his never-failing talent for an original and pertinent image: 'The proto-type of the active poet is not, to my mind, the

magician or dreamer – rather the emu, who digests stones and old boots
. . .'[63] A couple of months after giving the lectures, he regarded them in the
same way that he regarded his address at the Writers' Conference, as 'charts
of progressive knowledge of aesthetics rather than statements of dogma'.[64]

The letter to his parents in which he wrote that is remarkable for its
analysis of his personal development up to 1954. He felt that his thinking and
his life were both embarrassingly unsystematic. He was not even writing
poetry:

> . . . because I never seem to have a settled and full grip of the various problems
> of work, life with Jacquie and the children, and actual or potential writing.
> There is much one can be thankful for in personal relationships. But I do not
> easily find peace of mind and some such peace is necessary to build work and
> marriage securely. It comes, I think, from having 2 minds – the one careful,
> considerate and awake to necessary obligations; the other egotistical, erratic
> and much at the mercy of feelings. Love in marriage I know is pretty central;
> but it seems to be a product of many things including one's own perseverance.
> Religion often serves to sharpen one's existing problems. I have many ghosts of
> past folly or ill-doing which are not laid readily – a not unusual condition for a
> man to be in – but I have always perhaps expected happiness on too easy terms.
> The readymade schemes – to drink only tea; to work to a set routine – are about
> as useful as firm resolves to control one's temper. I think I will always have on
> my hands more than I can conveniently deal with. A clearer vision and a lack
> of egotism are what I need most, more than money, artistic reputation, or a
> first-class job. It is difficult to whittle down egotism when one's line of country
> in art requires a close, even solitary preoccupation with one's own feelings. It
> is difficult to keep the rules, even the basic ones, when one is concerned often
> so much more with the 'feel of things' than with the rules. To want to be a good
> man is one thing; to want to be a good poet is another. I hope they are not
> imcompatible, for if so I may well not make the grade.

A note at the end of the letter cautioned his parents not to take too much
notice of these 'vaporings' as there was 'a good deal of toughness in the
Baxter hide and character'.

Late in 1954 the family shifted to 166 Wilton Road, an old school house,
large, empty, and very cold. But it was all theirs. The children were very
excited when they arrived at their new home. They ranged through the
house stamping and shouting, and John, at two and a half, dived out of a
window and fell head first on to the concrete path. He soon recovered.

Wilton Road was a landmark for Baxter and Jacquie. The more spacious
environment seemed to free them up. After four and a half years of sharing
a house, they no longer had to worry about anyone but themselves. Their
degrees were very nearly behind them, and Jacquie had started writing.
Financially they were better off, and both had come to terms with the new
people they were becoming.

The same year, 1954, a new periodical called *Numbers* appeared, with Baxter, Louis Johnson, and Charles Doyle as editors. It represented an attempt to cock a snook at the rigorous standards of *Landfall*, and at 'old Uncle Charlie, the sheepdog of the flock'.[65] The philosophy behind *Numbers* was to see a much greater range of New Zealand writers in print, and it also set great store by 'internationality'. Ten issues appeared between 1954 and 1959. Though it had its triumphs, it was never a serious alternative to Brasch's quarterly. Johnson did most of the editorial work, and he managed to keep the periodical afloat with skilful handling of meagre finances. He often gathered his writing friends together at his home in Epuni and Charles Doyle's memories included parties where Baxter recited 'whole stretches of Dylan Thomas's *Deaths and Entrances*'.[66] Doyle knew Baxter well in the early fifties. For him, the pages of *Numbers* were as good an indication as any of Baxter's life at this time. Certainly Baxter's contributions reflected his alcoholism, his growing commitment to Christianity, the relationship between his life and art, the problems he was having with his poetry, and his domestic difficulties.

By December 1954 Baxter was 'fiendishly tired'. Besides his literary activities and his teaching, he had been studying part-time at the University, passing Latin II but failing English III for the second year running. The language of Alfred the Great was again his undoing.

Baxter's drinking, and the sexual irresponsibility that went with it, had given him a reputation as an antipodean Dylan Thomas. In the early fifties his more extreme bouts of drinking took place on his visits to Auckland, where his drinking companion was frequently Bob Lowry, printer and sometime editor of the irregular left-wing journal *Here and Now*. In 1955, by his own admission, Baxter had once got drunk with Bob Lowry for nearly a fortnight: 'We were stuck at the bar like two octopuses in an aquarium.'[67]

Lowry lived in a fine old house on the slopes of One Tree Hill which had belonged to Colonel Wynyard, sometime Superintendent of the Auckland Province and Acting Governor of New Zealand. Part of its colonial charm was a large ballroom with french windows opening on to a large patio. Outside were large old oaks, a plum tree, and wisteria. The romantic and spacious setting was ideal for the rollicking good parties that were famous in Auckland in the early fifties. They usually began in the ballroom on Saturday night, and as people flaked out they simply stayed since there was no shortage of accommodation. Lowry virtually kept open house for printers, writers, painters, and musicians, and for the Auckland intelligentsia. There was much good talk, well oiled by half-gallon jars of red wine from the Henderson vineyards. In the background the strains of Brahms or Beethoven, the Lowrys' favourite music, issued from their old wind-up gramophone.

Lowry, a close friend and drinking companion of Fairburn and Glover, was himself a great raconteur, with all the attributes of a good host. The atmosphere of his parties was as relaxed as could be found anywhere in Auckland. Baxter, his mouth stained with red wine, played with dash the role of the 'rumbustious bad young man'. And he seems to have had no difficulty in finding sexual partners. There also appear to have been homosexual episodes. His sexual irresponsibility affected a dislocation in his imagination between sexuality and love.

A society that frequently dismisses sexual deviation as of little account can also be severe on those who adopt its attitudes. The number of women with whom Baxter had sexual relations fell well short of the one thousand and three of Don Giovanni in Mozart's opera. A letter written late in Baxter's life mentions some thirty-five. His case would hardly have interested the compilers of the Kinsey Report. Baxter's aspirations outran his performance, and both in verse and conversation he was capable of telling 'tall stories of girls that he had never known'.[68] His reputation for debauchery, which still lingers, rests largely on these Auckland visits.

Baxter's drunkenness was not always as dramatic as it was in Auckland, where so many others competed with him to be the centre of attention. One well-known meeting-place in Wellington for journalists and literary people was the Britannia Hotel in Willis Street. Drinking sessions often went on all afternoon. An observer noted that though Baxter was drinking gin heavily, he was for the most part quiet and well-behaved. Louis Johnson was one who never saw Baxter roaring drunk, though he would finally reach a stage when he would pass out. Another acquaintance recalled 'that he seemed to be watching you and watching himself'. In his drinking as in much else there was a good deal of play-acting. Johnson thought it unfortunate that a young man should receive so much adulation: there were simply no models to guide his behaviour.

He was a married man on a modest wage with two small children and a wife to provide for. Yet sometimes his fortnightly pay was spent in a few hours and he had nothing to take home. The strains on his marriage were immense. Yet Baxter was too intelligent, too sensitive, to be ignorant of the misery his drinking was causing, or of the damage it was doing to himself personally and as a writer. As he told Brasch: 'Drunk I am either a bore or a savage or both.'[69] He was also much afflicted with guilt. And his excesses were damaging his health. In the early fifties he had gone to a doctor about pains in his chest. He was told the trouble was with his heart.

What was the reason for Baxter's alcoholism? It cannot be accounted for merely in terms of exhibitionism, though that was part of it. Alcoholism is today regarded as yet another of the illnesses that flesh is heir to. Some authorities believe it to be inherited. If that is true, the dice was loaded against Baxter. His paternal grandfather, John Baxter, had been an alcoholic, and he regarded him as 'his looking-glass twin'. Alcohol was also a way of screening out suffering, anxiety, and his own sense of inadequacy. Many people use drugs in the same way. Baxter came to see the force of the comparison with them, and would draw on what he was learning himself to free others from their dependence. Another element in his alcoholism was a romantic idealizing of Celtic bards like Burns and Dylan Thomas. Drinking was also the readiest way of asserting his independence from his parents, especially his mother.

He had tried to give up alcohol without success. He realized that evasion, posturing, and living for oneself was to live in an illusory world. He longed for the realism to confront life. But his good resolutions were short-lived. The hard-drinking milieu which he found congenial made it impossible to make the break. The first step was to analyse the nature of his malady, and that took time. He wrote to a friend:

> I certainly thought that grog was only the second of my problems – the first seemed to be a total inability to keep my fly buttoned, even when I would consciously have much preferred to – or even more specifically, a free flow of violent language at the worst times possible, a tendency to rape my hostesses at most parties I went to, and a recurrence of homosexual episodes, which things combined made life at home impossible and sat on my back like a mountain . . .

> The core of the whole matter seems to me to be that when boozed or recovering from booze, I was Jamie(2) a very pathological deadbeat whereas without booze I am Jamie(1) no beauty but functionally sound. As long as I took Jamie(2) seriously as a possible life-form I remained a long way up the beanstalk; only when I realized that Jamie(1) was me, not half-me but all me, did life begin to fall into place. Booze turns us into schizophrenics (I speak of alcoholics . . .) split men.[70]

What made the decisive break possible was joining Alcoholics Anonymous. Late one night towards the end of 1954 he stumbled into a house and rang the bell. When the owner opened the door, he saw a man sitting on the top step with his arm around the family dog. When this stranger was brought inside, he immediately launched into Francis Thompson's poem 'The Hound of Heaven', which dramatizes the ex-drug addict's guilty evasions and final conversion to Christ. Baxter declaimed the poem in its entirety, some one hundred and eighty-two lines. The owner of the house was a leading light in A.A. Although he was well used to drunks this one was clearly at the high water mark of literacy. He sat out the performance quietly, then they talked. Baxter was persuaded to attend an A.A. meeting.

His first night in St Andrew's Presbyterian Church on the Terrace was not auspicious. A person who was present recalled her impressions of this softly spoken, boyish-looking man, who came in wearing a felt hat and a blue shirt. He was reading the big handbook of A.A., the movement's gospel, with great concentration. When his turn came to address the meeting he kept asking questions and appeared dissatisified with the answers. His new friend, whose dog had been transmogrified in Baxter's imagination that fateful night, guided him through his early days in A.A. and gradually he was won over.

The A.A. organization became an extremely important part of Baxter's life. The people he had most to do with at this time were from A.A., and he kept open house for them at Wilton Road. Jacquie could not pretend to have liked it.

In 1955 the Baxters were able to buy a house at 41 Collingwood Street in Ngaio. James's Great Aunt Hetty[71] had died, leaving James a substantial legacy. Baxter was her favourite nephew because he was carrying on the family tradition of scholarship as a famous poet. Since the money was a windfall, it seemed only fair to share it, so Baxter decided to divide it into three parts; one for his parents, one for his brother, and one for himself. He knew that his parents would refuse the offer, since both their sons had young families, but he told them that another trip to Europe was just as important to them as a new house was for him.[72] Joining Alcoholics Anonymous seemed to have been another decisive step in his long journey from the early egoism to a genuine concern for others.

The movement's basic assumption, that alcoholism is a disease over which the alcoholic has no control, matched Baxter's own experience. He was attracted by the assurance that anyone who really wishes to attain sobriety can do so. The basic strategy of alcoholics coming together to support each other harmonized with his still vague aspirations towards community. He could accept that one alcoholic can influence another as no one else can, because the alcoholic speaks out of personal experience. More challenging was the claim that for an alcoholic the only course is total abstinence. As the A.A. handbook puts it: 'Whether you are dry one year, ten years or fifty years, you're still one drink away from a drunk.'[73] The handbook also rejected the romantic notion, which Baxter half-believed, that artists of genius conceive their best projects when drunk.

This least programmatic of men was confronted by a programme of twelve simple but demanding spiritual steps, some of which were to prove crucial to his development. The first stated: 'We admitted we were powerless over alcohol – that our lives had become unmanageable.'[74] Baxter found it hard to admit that this was his situation. It demanded too much humility. He wrote to a friend: 'The main difficulty I had in getting hold of the A.A. programme was not so much innate stupidity, as a deep reluctance to admit to myself or anyone else that I was an alcoholic – a kind of shrinking violet attitude which hardly fitted in with my habits of abusing my friends (verbally); dragging my hostesses out the door, absorbing whatever grog I could lay hands on; and generally shouting down all opposition.'[75] The two great cohesive forces for A.A. are the instinct for companionship, and religion, interpreted in a broad sense. The second step, which appealed to Baxter's strong religious sense, is that members come 'to believe that a Power greater than ourselves could restore us to sanity'.[76] At the fourth the alcoholic makes an honest moral inventory of himself. By the fifth he 'Admitted to God, to ourselves, and to another human being the exact nature of our wrongs (i.e. wrong-doing).'[77] These steps parallel the Catholic practice of confession. The similarity was even clearer in an earlier form of the A.A. programme when there were only six steps. Three were 'moral inventory, confession and restitution'. Baxter responded readily. The handbook encouraged that natural candour which made him confessional in writing and speech. Many of his letters contain an astonishingly frank account of his failures.

At step eleven the alcoholic sought to improve his conscious contact with God as he understood him through prayer and meditation. He prayed for knowledge of His will and the strength to carry it out. From now on meditation became a regular part of Baxter's life. But what contributed most to his later work for drug addicts, and to the creation of the Jerusalem commune, was the twelfth and final step. This insisted that helping others was the very foundation of any rehabilitation.[78] Baxter took the programme very seriously. The hours he put in with fellow alcoholics developed his caring for those living on the margins of New Zealand society, the down-and-outs, prisoners, and the disenchanted young. Ideally an A.A. group should have as little organization as possible, for the leaders are only trusted servants and do not govern.[79] Members were also warned that problems of money, property, and authority could divert them from their 'primary spiritual aim'.[80]

As far as Baxter was concerned the movement was: 'A good show . . . For the first time in my life I feel free of acute depressions, anxieties, dreams of judgement etc . . . I have A.A. to thank that I am not in gaol, under the sod, or in a permanent residence in a natty little villa up at Porirua.'[81] It was a great relief 'to enter A.A. and find that most of the members have been similarly cantankerous, dour or suicidal when drunk. Things fell into place, as the saying goes. There was a spell when everything seemed rather black and white and grey to me; but nowadays the world looks pretty good most of the time, and I have no ambition at all to become a lay preacher.'[82] He said he had heard that alcoholics must undergo a personality change to lose the compulsion towards grog, but he was unaware of any such alteration in himself. He did not find the twelve steps easy: 'In my own case I took them slowly, haphazardly and reluctantly, making excuses, wasting time and deceiving myself; yet over a period of seven years they removed entirely from my life the alcoholic compulsion and brought in its place a workable pattern of behaviour.'[83]

The central group of A.A. in Wellington met at St. John's Presbyterian Church in Willis Street and Baxter attended regularly every Thursday night. When the chairman called on people to speak he often noticed Baxter, especially if it was a meeting open to the wives and husbands of members. Many recall what an impressive speaker he was, sincere, original, and quietly spoken. What he said ranged far beyond the usual account of a person's life and drinking history. He enjoyed these occasions, for he could blend his testimony with his philosophy and lace what he said with humour and self-irony. Although he preserved an unobtrusive presence at A.A. meetings, and was never a group representative at gatherings, he became a respected figure in the whole movement. And A.A. changed him. The anonymous style made him less egocentric. When he addressed meetings he was fond of pointing out that in the A.A. programme there is no 'I', only a 'We'. And he stressed that an alcoholic cannot recover without help. For those who hung around outside the doors after meetings, looking not for sobriety but money, he was a soft touch. His deep belief in people made him vulnerable. But often his trust and compassion effected surprising changes.

Counselling is considered to be important by A.A. Baxter was skilful at detecting what lay behind the surface problem. Even outside the framework of the meetings he did not spare himself. He would go off to a coffee bar and talk over the problems of anyone who consulted him as if he had all the time in the world. His approach was gentle and unthreatening. He would never say 'You'll have to pull yourself together,' but rather, 'Let's look at why you have this problem.' He took a special interest in the most desperate cases. His readiness to spend time with them shamed even members who had been in the movement for years. He was one of the first to see the need for a place where the most advanced cases could walk in from the street.

Counselling women was more difficult because he was always likely to become emotionally involved. In 1957 he wrote with characteristic earthiness: 'Woman trouble is perennial; it comes with the spring, every spring since Eve first tucked the apple down her bloomers.' Yet he was learning to manage. He wrote to his mother:[84] '. . . one has to cope with the reflexes of the nervous system and the imagination . . . the best thing to do is to pray a bit for a pure intention, ignore the reflexes, and above all laugh at oneself. People – I at least – get bogged down by taking themselves – myself – seriously. It's no good getting in a flap.'[85]

A group from A.A. visited prisons regularly and Baxter visited both Mt. Crawford and Wi Tako. He knew from observation that many crimes were related to excessive drinking. Some prisoners would not attend these officially arranged A.A. meetings, feeling they were being badgered by the prison staff. But Baxter was well received. He had the knack of getting on well with those who were offside with the bosses. The prisoners liked his sincerity and frankness. And he spoke their language. From that time until the weekend of his death, visiting the imprisoned was to be a regular part of his life.

The extent of Baxter's personal commitment can be seen in his involvement in the case of one Eddie Te Whiu. Baxter used to take the train each day from Wellington to Epuni, and although he sometimes missed it, he was generally punctual and seldom away sick. One working day, towards the end of July in 1955, he visited Patrick Macaskill at the Wellington Teachers' College. When Macaskill asked 'Why aren't you teaching,' Baxter replied: 'I took the day off. There are more important things to do. A boy is going to be hanged so I've got up a petition.'

Macaskill asked: 'Have you seen the Headmaster?'

'No, but I know he's free and can take my class.'

The boy, Eddie Te Whiu, was a twenty-year-old Maori who had broken into the house of an elderly widow at Ngararatunua, near Whangarei. He was desperately in need of money and had not eaten for a couple of days. When the old lady disturbed him, he struck her several times on the head with his closed fist, and forced a pillow over her face to quieten her. She died from strangulation. At his trial it was stated that Te Whiu came from Sweetwater, 'a poor village', and that he was one of twelve children. Like ten others of his family he had been under the care of Child Welfare. The defence argued that Te Whiu had not intended to kill, but panicked when he was surprised. After a trial of three days, he was sentenced to death on 27 July 1955. The assistant counsel for the defence, D. S. Beattie (a future Governor-General) prepared an application for commuting the sentence to life imprisonment.

The case attracted great public interest, and a number of petitions for leniency were presented to the Executive Council. They were signed by many people Baxter had known at the Teachers' College and University, such as W. J. Scott, Pat Macaskill, G. E. Hughes (the professor of Philosophy), and Kenneth Quinn of the Classics Department. The appeal was based on Te Whiu's youth, his unstable family background, and the opinion of the trial judge that Te Whiu had not intended to kill. The petitioners conceded the crime was a grave one and that the jury's verdict was just. The appeals failed. Te Whiu was hanged at Auckland prison on the evening of 18 August 1955, little more than three weeks after he had been sentenced.

'A Rope for Harry Fat' was Baxter's response to Te Whiu's hanging. It is one of a number of successful ballads on public themes, as a single verse illustrates:

> Te Whiu was too young to vote,
>   The prison records show.
> Some thought he was too young to hang;
>   Legality said, *No.*
> Who knows what fear the raupo hides
>   Or where the wild duck flies?
> 'A trapdoor and a rope is best.'
>   Says Harry Fat the wise.
>
>   (CP 163)

Baxter had already expressed his empathy with alcoholics in his 1953 ballad, 'Lament for Barney Flanagan'. Roy Fuller, an English poet who was to become a Professor of Poetry at Oxford, said that it sounded a note unheard in England for a long time.[86] Baxter's original was Dooley Frost, the licensee of the National Hotel in Lambton Quay who collapsed and died in his own bar. The details of the ballad were mostly invention, and five hundred copies sold in the Wellington pubs in a couple of days.[87]

As Baxter struggled towards his new ideal of total abstinence, he experienced the 'massive disturbances and irrational fears of an alcoholic who is drying out . . . a process that may take, on the mental level, not a week or a month but many years.'[88] Jacquie found the process very difficult. She tried to keep her expectations as low as possible, otherwise she inevitably felt disappointment, even outrage. Nor did it help Baxter to feel that he had let her down. She had to live with A.A. and apart from it. Alcohol was Baxter's problem and he had to solve it.

Against all the odds, he eventually succeeded in achieving sobriety. But he was to feel the effects of alcohol until the end of his life.

VIII
The Path to Rome

To the embarrassment of the English Department at Victoria, Baxter had failed English III two years running. In 1955 the Old English component, which had been his downfall, was still compulsory. But this time, with the aid of a private tutor arranged by the Department, he was successful, and graduated B.A. The degree was conferred in May 1956. He enrolled for an M.A. in English as a part-time student in 1956 but did not proceed. Baxter appears to have regarded his degree merely as a meal ticket. He felt that the higher learning had had little effect 'except a negative one, upon the processes that make me tick as a writer. Writing, in my case, has proceeded entirely from Lower Learning, learning who one is.'[1] That is not learnt in a lecture room or library.

On Anzac Day 1956 Epuni School observed a simple ceremony with the laying of wreaths. Instead of inviting an outside speaker, Baxter was asked to read and explain 'In Flanders Fields'. According to Ward, he read it 'coolly and well, but without too much emotion'.[2]

At the end of the first term, Baxter resigned to become a sub-editor at the School Publications' branch of the Department of Education. When Baxter left, Ward wrote him a reference praising his integrity and honesty of purpose, his friendly nature, and his ability to fit in easily with his colleagues. He said he counted those children who had the privilege of being taught by him very fortunate.[3]

Looking back on his days at Epuni, Baxter recalled how much he hated reprimanding a child for the kind of language he himself would use at home. Yet he did it and disliked what he did as hypocrisy. The regular routine of school teaching did not suit him. He was too individualistic, and his temperament was too restless to be satisifed with any job for long. The lure of freedom was too enticing to allow him to settle.

Baxter's appointment at School Publications began on 16 May 1956. His salary was £935 a year. School Publications, one of the new developments in New Zealand education following the Great Depression, aimed to provide schools with material written from a New Zealand, rather than a European, perspective. The avowed aim was: 'To make New Zealand seem to its future citizens more important and more worthwhile than anything else.'[4] The Branch's responsibilities included publishing bulletins for the primary and post-primary schools and also the *School Journal*. The *Primary School Bulletins* assumed special importance because the school-leaving examination, the Proficiency, and the syllabus that went with it, had been abolished. The New Zealand historian, J.C. Beaglehole, had said in a public lecture: '. . . you can see the right seed sprouting if you will look in the right place . . . I am not sure that the School Publications Branch does not hold the New Zealand future in its hands.'[5] It was recognized from the beginning that if the Branch was to succeed, 'native authors of something like genius' would have to be found.

In 1956 the Branch was housed behind the old wooden Government buildings in Lambton Quay in Wellington. Later it moved to a building on the corner of Willis Steet and Ghuznee Street, at the other end of town. There Baxter had a ground-floor office with a door opening on to the street. Through a window he could observe everyone who came and went, though he gave no sign of doing so. A large bag of peppermints on his desk indicated that, like many reformed alcoholics, he was replacing one source of sugar with another.

His job was to produce primary school bulletins for children between the ages of nine and thirteen. The original expectation was that the Branch would bring out twenty a year. One of Baxter's editors thought that they could produce ten, although in fact the annual output had never been higher than five. In Baxter's seven years at the Branch, six was the maximum produced in a single year, and the average output was four. He himself wrote a bulletin, *Oil*, in 1957, a supplement to *A Dairy Farm* by Ray Chapman-Taylor in 1960, and a vividly written bulletin *The Trawler* in 1961. For another bulletin he compiled a glossary of Maori words. But his main work was editing. In 1960 he also acted as editor of the junior section of the *School Journal*.

He was especially interested in publishing stories for Maori children. One of his first duties when he joined the Branch in 1956 was to prepare Roderick Finlayson's *The Return of the Fugitives* for the press. He told an enthusiastic correspondent that for personal as well as more general reasons he wanted to help Maori children to adjust to the 'double role they are eventually required to play – I mean that the Maori child (often without a *pa* background) is in its growing up subject to a double pressure: a pressure to "become pakeha", and a pressure to "be Maori" .' He praised Finlayson's understanding of Maori culture – 'its hierarchical strength, its ritual order, and its promotion of a closer unity of body and mind than is possible to pakehas.'[6]

The Maori people had played little part in the thinking and writing of the earlier Baxter for the simple reason that until his late teens he had never met a Maori. Even by 1952, for example, he considered it foolish to rhapsodize over Maori culture: '. . . at the end of a process which began when the first whaler met the first Maori; to praise the results of a tribal unity which our own deadpan civilisation has torn to shreds . . . We are not likely to take more from the Maori than we have already taken – a number of museum artifacts, their land and their dignity.' As a writer, he thought the myth of Odysseus just as applicable to New Zealand as the myth of Maui, and much better known to an English-speaking audience. He said he spoke with some feeling because his wife and two children had 'their adequate share of Maori blood'.[7] But it was necessary to be realistic. Yet by 1956 his attitudes had been changed by observation of Pakeha society, and by contact with people like Finlayson.

His admiration for the Maori people increased as he travelled into remote areas collecting copy. He had to travel because the Branch expected him to initiate new projects. To write *The Trawler*, for example, he made a fishing trip round the Northland peninsula. When he was making the arrangements through Roderick Finlayson, he told him he did not mind sleeping on sacks if necessary.[8] He never minded roughing it.

In the last week of January 1957, he attended a Teachers' Refresher Course at Ardmore Teachers' College. Afterwards he went on to Motukiore in the Hokianga. It was quite unlike any part of New Zealand he had seen before: 'mangroves like hair along the estuaries, and the whole great sluggish sea invading the land.'[9] From that trip came the poem 'At Hokianga', just as poems like 'At Akitio' came from other trips. He stayed with the Rosses at Motukiore. Ruth Ross was in the process of writing her pioneering bulletin, *Tiriti O Waitangi*, which challenged the received European version of the Treaty. It was a well-researched bulletin and Baxter was instrumental in seeing it through the press. The Ross boys, who were both under ten years old, were enchanted with Baxter. Their mother was reading them R. L. Stevenson's *Catriona* at the time, and he told them a secret — that one of his McColl ancestors had murdered 'The Red Fox'. When he left there were floods of tears. He had, however, misjudged the parents by launching, almost as soon as he arrived, into a long and involved bawdy story. For the rest of the weekend the atmosphere was strained.[10]

When he was writing another bulletin, *Oil*, the staff of the company where he did the research regarded him initially as a joke, since they knew he was a poet, and what would a poet know about oil? But he won them over by his obvious interest, and by the searching questions he asked. He disliked working in an office more than he had to, and would go off to a coffee bar with the company's representative. His conversation ranged well beyond oil and he spoke freely of his problems with sex and alcohol. His resonant voice and detailed exposition made their table the focus of rapt attention.

Baxter's correspondence with his authors clearly shows that he kept his readers firmly in mind. He instructed contributors not to pitch the level too high, because he wanted standard five children of modest ability to be able to follow the bulletins without guidance. And he knew that what they enjoyed was concrete detail, not intellectual exposition.[11] He wanted a proper balance between information and interest because unless the children's attention was held, the information would not be communicated. But he also expected the bulletins to be accurate. In Social Studies he preferred a regional approach, which would uncover 'patterns of behaviour in a given district'. If he was doing a bulletin on Seddon, for example, he said that the West Coast's life-style would loom larger than Seddon's imperialism. He thought this procedure corrected the tendency of the educational system to sacrifice a 'wholeness of outlook to a segmenting, classifying view of life.'[12]

Baxter proved to be a very responsible editor. To one contributor he wrote: '. . . as it stands it is much too strong meat for the schools. To say this, goes against my inward man, who judges aesthetically; but my outward man, teacher and editor, knows that teachers want first and foremost a bulletin on mining, and not something which in parts has the uninhibited force of D. H. Lawrence's "Sons and Lovers". So much against the grain, I must ask you to chip, chisel and amend.'[13] But, he conceded, he would never demand this of a contribution to a literary magazine.

Baxter reminded another contributor that he had to tread warily in an official publication.[14] He was conscious of the sensitivity of the children, even though that really meant the 'sensitivity of Mum and Dad and the teachers'.[15] At times he declined work from leading writers, some of whom were his friends, and he could be quite firm in insisting that scripts be changed. In one story about an accident, he would not allow the father of a child to be killed, because of the distress it could cause a child whose own father had been killed in the same way.[16]

Once, a Senior Inspector complained of 'a regrettable error of grammar, in the use of the verb "fall" instead of "fell" for cutting down trees.' Baxter's boss responded that when the bulletin was in preparation, Baxter had queried the term. The author, Ruth Dallas, had replied that bushmen in Southland, old and young, always said 'falling' and never 'felling'. Since they also said 'maiden bush', not 'virgin bush', that expression was also retained.[17] The incident indicates Baxter's independence of mind and the kind of surveillance he was under.

Baxter's powers of imitation, always remarkable, displayed a brilliant technical virtuosity in a collection of verse parodies he wrote at this time. The seventeen poems that make up *The Iron Breadboard* (1957) parodied New Zealand poets of two generations, and revealed what a shrewd literary critic he was. Parodies as good as these require the parodist's sharp perception of the distinctive way the originals achieve their effect. Some pieces, like those on R.A.K. Mason and Charles Spear, are masterly. The parody of his own work gave a fair inventory of his preoccupations up to 1957: ancestors, Original Sin, death, sex, grief, and the need for love.

These years also offer a good indication of Baxter as a family man. His son, John, found him very huggable, and would often sit on his knee. As early as John could remember, Baxter read to both children every night, and this continued right into John's teenage years. The Doctor Dolittle books were popular when the children were small, and they sometimes served as the inspiration for plays in which the whole family took part. Later, John remembered Baxter reading them Kipling's *Jungle Book*. Both Hilary and John acknowledged the love of literature their parents had given them, and they were always surrounded by books. They also found many of their parents' visitors entertaining; people like Barry Crump and Jean Watson were natural story-tellers.

Baxter was a creative parent who was able to produce any number of toys from odds and ends. The children's memories include cardboard boats, aeroplanes, and animals, and golden syrup tin telephones. Baxter played with them outside, flying kites, building forts, and climbing trees, and he would clamber to the top of the highest trees just to please them.

They remembered questioning Baxter on all manner of things while doing the dishes in the evening. Because of the extraordinary general knowledge their father possessed, they were always sure of an answer. John remembered falling asleep to the sound of Baxter's typewriter almost every night. And he had memories of his father pacing through the house, reciting lines from the poems he was composing.

Fourteen of Baxter's poems, collectively called 'Songs of the Desert', appeared in *The Nightshift, poems on aspects of love* (1957), along with work by his friends Charles Doyle, Louis Johnson, and Kendrick Smithyman. Thirteen of Baxter's poems had been written in 1947 or 1948, and were lightly censured by Erik Schwimmer as 'a series of loudly intoned approximations'.[18] The final poem, 'As kites rise up against the wind', written in 1957 and strongly influenced by Lawrence Durrell, is easily the best.

> As kites rise up against the wind
> Out of the past I summon Pyrrha,
> Girl of plaited wheat, first
> Mentor of love revealed in dying.
> (CP 62)

By now things were beginning to fall into place for Baxter. He had got the better of his alcoholism and come to terms with his domestic responsibilities.

He was writing steadily with varying degrees of success. But he was not satisfied with the state of his religious belief. Now most of his energies went into that. One day in the second half of 1957, Baxter stopped me in Lambton Quay and asked: 'What are your reservations about Anglicanism?' I replied, as any Catholic of the period who was aware of Leo XIII's bull *Apostolicae Curae* which declared Anglican orders invalid would have replied: 'I do not believe that Anglicanism has an authentic priesthood.' He immediately responded: 'If I thought that I'd become a Catholic tomorrow.'

It was not long before he acted. In September he wrote to Roderick Finlayson: 'It seems to me that it is time I became a true Catholic. There will be various difficulties along the road; though a secret desire in which I trust is leading me along that road, most private feelings and many intellectual habits pull against it.'[19] One serious obstacle had been described in *The Fire and the Anvil*: '. . . the gulf between the battlements of the Church Militant and the stony ground below where men struggle often with the same basic problems under different names, yet fear to accept orthodoxy lest their present armour should be called intellectual arrogance and stripped from them.'[20] In John Weir's presentation copy Baxter wrote opposite this passage: 'This was my point of tension before conversion.' He asked Finlayson, who had already converted to Catholicism, to pray for him, because without divine help he could not even begin.

For some time he had been paying visits to St Mary of the Angels' Church in Wellington. It was staffed by priests of the Society of Mary, a congregation established in France in the early nineteenth century, which still draws its distinctive spirituality from its French founders. All the congregation's early missionaries in New Zealand were French. On 17 September, Baxter lit a votive candle before the statue of the Virgin Mary in the Lady altar. He then went over to the presbytery to keep the appointment he had made with Father George McHardy SM, a curate in the parish. The priest, who was neither literary nor intellectual, had not met this well-groomed, youngish man, nor read any of his poems. He recognized him simply as someone he had often seen in the church praying before the altar of the Virgin. After listening to him for a while he said: 'What you need is instruction.' Father McHardy's normal method of instruction was to take the prospective convert through the creed, the commandments, and the theology of the sacraments. He used as his basic text Canon Cafferata's *The Catechism Simply Explained*, first published in 1897, a catechism which had gone through many revisions. In those pre-Vatican II days, it was still widely used for the instruction of adults. Like all catechisms, it was far from a nuanced exposition, but undoubtedly people knew where they stood. The weekly instructions began in September and ran until January 1958.

Father McHardy found that Baxter had read widely about Catholicism and had received considerable guidance from Pat Lawlor, a Catholic with a deep piety of a traditional kind. He decided that the best approach was to allow Baxter to expound what he knew, and then comment when it was necessary. Baxter spoke with his usual eloquence, and the priest was amazed at his knowledge. He had no doctrinal difficulties, but asked for more instruction on some areas of Catholic belief such as the Eucharist. Baxter liked especially the teaching on the forgiveness of sins and on the place of the Mother of God in the plan of salvation. He had none of the difficulties experienced by those who imagine that Catholics regard Mary as equal to Christ. It was her humanity and compassion, her bond with fellow creatures like himself, that attracted him. She made more human the conceptual world of Aquinas and Maritain, and he felt she freed him from a 'self-centred intellectuality'. In a discussion of the relationship of Jung's four faculties in the human psyche (intellect, feeling, sensation, and intuition) to the production of poems, he linked Mary with intuition and with the sensation that leads to it.[21] She was at once the ideal mother he felt he had never had, and a woman to whom he could relate without the complications of physical sexuality that had often bedevilled his friendships with other women. With Mary he developed an easy and unambiguous relationship. Father McHardy remarked that the Catholic understanding of Original Sin had given Baxter an imaginative and intellectual framework for what he had learnt about human nature from personal experience. It became the unifying principle in Baxter's thinking.

Over the months of instruction, the priest found Baxter modest and remarkably open and accepting. He was sincere, though inclined to swing from one extreme to another in his life. And his language was a mixture of the cultivated and the crude.

At home Baxter's marriage was under severe strain. In the early years, a period that was virtually a struggle for survival, Baxter and Jacquie had been very dependent on each other. Now, in more prosperous times, they were tending to go their own way. Jacquie had almost come to terms with Baxter's dramatic change from drunkard to full-blown member of A.A. But the heightened sense of responsibility towards her and the children, which she naturally expected, did not appear to be part of the transformation. The new energies seemed to be going into strangers. Baxter was zealously recruiting members for A.A. and now, out of the blue, he announced he was going to become a Catholic. This was a real shock to Jacquie because he had not even mentioned that he was taking instructions. She attended the Anglican church, Hilary had been going to an Anglican Sunday school and John had been baptized into the Anglican communion when they were at Karori. Now, it seemed, all that had to be put aside. It was the last straw in what Baxter freely acknowledged had been a long series of 'injuries, alcoholism, and gross mistakes'.[22] Then there had been grave clashes of temperament between them.[23] Often Jacquie did not know what Baxter was thinking, and instead of bringing up his difficulties and talking them through, he kept them to himself. They did, however, enter his writing.

In one of the much later Dunedin poems, Baxter looked back at

> three buried selves: child, adolescent,
> the young, unhappy married man.
>
> (CP 385)

'The young unhappy married man' of these years appears in a poem like 'Letter to the World' of 1955. It dramatizes his domestic anguish and tries to use poetry to effect a reconciliation: 'Take again this wordy ring'. A short story, 'To Have and to Hold', published in *Numbers* in 1956, is closer to the bone. It is based on a simple domestic incident, a wedding anniversary on which Jack, who feels his marriage is dying, is sent into town by his wife to do a message. He has a few beers in the pub where he can join in 'the small-talk that reduced every wife to a comic antagonist and moral censor'.[24] When he gets home his wife has dressed herself up and laid out a special lunch. She has been waiting for half an hour and, realizing that he has been drinking, she storms out shouting 'Oh I hate you! You spoil everything, everything'. The story is fiction, but the situation and the setting of the Collingwood home ('the calm, bird-thronged bush towered over him on the path to the road'), clearly reflect Baxter's frame of mind at the time. And it was one he confided to several friends: his failed romantic expectations from marriage; his sexual frustrations; the 'leaden irritability' which lay on his mind; the drinking to relieve physical tension. Jack's real pleasure in attending to his baby daughter and his efforts to please his wife by buying her a red rose also parallel Baxter's own life.

Baxter and Jacquie separated in October 1957. His poem 'The Watch', which speaks of 'That bad year when we were both apart', shows how remorseful he felt. However contradictory his behaviour had been in the past, however much he had complained about Jacquie to friends, he remained loyal to her and spoke of her as a fine woman. And he hoped for a reconciliation. During the separation they never took outings together, but Jacquie made arrangements for him to see the children at weekends. He took the train to Ngaio, she took the train to town, and their trains crossed. Baxter would walk up to the house where the children were waiting. He could do what he liked in the house and often they made hokey-pokey together.

Both Jacquie and Baxter received much unsolicited advice from friends. Jacquie was told all sorts of things about Baxter which she would have preferred not to hear, and it was pointed out that now she was seeing him in his true colours. Their in-laws were simply puzzled.

This was a difficult time for the whole family. The children, especially John who was very close to his father, were very upset. Sometimes he was sent home from school in a distressed state. Jacquie was forced to take on a part-time job which finished at 2.30 p.m., allowing her to be home in time for the children when they got back from school. The family had enough to eat, that was about all. And the mortgage had to be paid. Baxter lived at 17a Boulcott Street Flats and then at 212 Sydney Street West, near the Western Park Hotel, not far from the musician Douglas Lilburn. Jacquie was better housed, but not as free as he was, and both parents were very concerned about the children. Many years later, Baxter believed that a temporary separation from the family might be desirable for a recovering alcoholic.[25] To some extent he was rationalizing a situation about which he felt guilty.

In December 1957, Baxter stayed for a week at the Cistercian monastery of Our Lady of the Southern Star, Kopua, Hawke's Bay. He was impressed by the communal way of life devoted to prayer, manual work, and silence. It gave him a fresh appreciation of contemplation and of the importance of penance. In the new year he was back in Wellington for his reception into the Catholic Church. Following what was then normal practice to insure against any deficiency in an earlier baptism, Baxter was conditionally re-baptized at St. Mary of the Angels on 11 January 1958. Usually baptism is followed by first confession and Wellington offered a wide choice of confessors. Baxter could, if he wished, find a Redemptorist father available at St. Gerard's monastery high on the hill above the harbour. But he feared that the Redemptorist 'might massacre me with a big stick – so instead I went to a Marist priest whom I knew by report to be a holy and gentle old man – and after he had lifted the edge of the dish-cover and peered at the dog's breakfast underneath, he said – "Well, you've had your ups and downs, more downs than ups I suppose; but from now on it'll be more upward." – and absolved me. The incredible gentleness of the Church is more powerful than gelignite.'[26]

One thing the poet William Blake admired about the Church of Rome was that it alone taught and practised forgiveness of sins. Baxter was strongly attracted to confession. The Mass, too, with its emphasis on sacrifice, community worship, and Holy Communion, which Catholics believe provides strength to lead the Christian life, became very important to him. From now on he was for long periods a daily communicant. The doctrine of the Communion of Saints both living and dead, where 'saints' meant all those who had chosen Christ as Lord of their lives, also greatly appealed to him. It was the model of what community might be, and it could accommodate his ancestors.

Baxter's conversion to Catholicism was the climax of a religious quest which was already under way when, as a sixteen-year-old, he had discussed his response to religion with Noel Ginn. A.A. was crucial to his religious development. Though not a religious organization, its methods owe much to Christian thinking and practice. And it does a good deal more than help people give up alcohol; it forces them to take stock of their lives. Another crucial phase was his conversion to Anglicanism, though he came to find it an unsatisfying faith. He told Father McHardy that he was grateful to the Anglicans for what they had done, but he was not at home among them.

> The cross, the surplice and the book,
> Conceal a permanent question mark,
> Under a vault of Dartmoor stone
> The soul is itching in the dark,
> Drunk on your doorstep I mistook
> The wine of an English Platonist
> For God's blood in the Eucharist[27]

Those sentiments were developed in *the flowering cross*:

In that time of transition I was much troubled about the possible validity of Anglican Orders; and I think the crucial pivot of my own conversion was this experience of the Presence of Our Lord in the Blessed Sacrament. If – whatever the sincerity and holiness and doctrinal orthodoxy of many Anglicans might be – if the Anglican Church did not actually, and undeniably possess this Treasure and the Catholic Church did possess it – then where my treasure was, my heart would have to be also, and there was no place for me to go except to that Church who is the guardian of the Blessed Sacrament. Certainly logic played a part in my conversion, and the realization that the magisterium (teaching authority) was necessary if the faithful were to be preserved from error; but the heart went before the head, love before intellect, and my heart has been content since that time to rest in the actuality of Our Lord's Presence. I have never regretted for a single instant the day when I was received into the Catholic Church.[28]

Even when he converted to Anglicanism some felt it would be only a matter of time before he took the path to Rome. About his switch to Catholicism he wrote: 'the Protestants asked me to have an opinion; the Catholics asked me to believe. And I could see that the only possible certainty on matters which lay beyond the reach of human reason must come from belief. And in that instant I bowed to the magisterium and I believed.'[29] His religious journey which began with 'that utter lack of credulity, that abyss of scepticism' which he considered made him a modern man, led him inevitably to some such conclusion. Paradoxically, because he doubted all substantial good, it became possible 'to believe in the Unknown God who is also the Son of Man.'[30] About a month after he became a Catholic he spoke with a new humility:

> The gas has come out of my air-balloon and I am back on the dry solid earth. This longing to be a somebody has deep roots in my nature: it is a cancer, not a plant. But now the longing to be a nobody, to be lost among the mountains and rivers of the Mass, stands beside it, planted by God – and the two may well wrestle till I die, when, as Yeats tells us, *at stroke of midnight God will win*. Do you know why He made me a Catholic? Because I am like a diabetic and cannot live without His insulin; without conscious continual contact with Him I'd be a lost man; and He knows this and will not let me go even when I struggle like a child that wants to leave its mother's arms.[31]

Contact with God is more intense in prayer. Each day Baxter recited the Rosary, and often he made the Stations of the Cross. Mary and the passion of Christ were central to his piety.

Baxter's conversion was not a highly charged emotional experience. What emotion he felt was quickly dissipated. By 1 March he was writing to Pat Lawlor of his sadness at the 'frequent absence of religious emotion', and thought that God was weaning him from such consolation so he could take a more balanced view of Him and the creation. But he was not worried and assured Lawlor: 'I am a Catholic for good, Pat – the Church is my home, the only situation from which this bad old world makes sense.'[32] Two years on he confided to Finlayson that he found it impossible to 'be happy at all without God'. He was meditating on the Resurrection of the Body: 'that loveliest of all doctrines; and carry what weight I have as best I can. Sin never leaves me, the dogs are all round me with their mouths open.'[33] But he realized that was as it should be. Otherwise he feared damnation because of his pride.

Sometimes his faith found flamboyant expression. Once, in Harry Seresin's coffee bar in Lambton Quay during the late fifties, he stationed himself at a table overlooking the street and made a huge sign of the cross as he audibly whispered grace before eating. At a big society wedding in St Mary of the Angels he made the Stations of the Cross with manifest devotion during the marriage ceremony. The reaction to his histrionics varied from irritation to amusement. Even taking into account his remarkable capacity to be utterly self-absorbed, he always seemed to be both actor and observer. Catholic, like reformed rake, was seen by some as just another role.

It might be supposed that a natural rebel like Baxter would prove to be a natural heretic. That did not happen. But the Church in New Zealand had never had a Baxter. He had to find in the history of Christianity itself the sort of Catholic he wanted to be. Sometimes he was attracted to the reformed alcoholic Matt Talbot of Dublin, sometimes to St Francis of Assisi, or St Benedict Joseph Labre.[34]

> When Benedict Joseph Labre
> Lay in the streets of Rome,
> Some thought he was a holy man,
> Some thought he was a bum.
>
> (CP 337)

Baxter's religious aspirations included Gospel simplicity and the courage to affirm his faith in the circles in which he moved, though he was well aware of how cynical those circles could be. But there is no doubt that he overdid it. He was often the butt of ironical sallies, and like most people with a mastery of words, he would have preferred to call the shots. His reading of religious biography had taught him that humiliation was the royal road to humility, an indispensable virtue for anyone professing to be religious. Yet many of his friends, though not believers, were people of goodwill. He taxed even their tolerance by flaunting his Catholicism. His fellow writers were variously accepting, disappointed or angry. Friends considered his personality changed after his conversion and that he was less self-centred. Members of A.A. said he had found a new peace. He had become more caring towards other people. But his new faith made reconciliation with his wife less likely.

Baxter's first collection of poetry after his conversion to Catholicism, *In Fires of No Return*, was published in England by Oxford University Press in 1958, and became a Poetry Book Society's choice. Despite that accolade it was a disappointing book. Many readers assumed his conversion had crippled his art. In fact all of the poems had been written before he had become a Catholic. But some were written after he had given up alcohol, and that may well have been part of the trouble. Experts say that one thing all alcoholics have in common is a sense of conflict. Much later, Baxter told John Weir that though he had never written verse while drunk, 'some qualities of violence and tension in my work no doubt derive from my having the explosive emotions common to alcoholics'.[35] By entering A.A. he had resolved many of the tensions that had given power to his writing.

Baxter often anticipated the reactions of his critics. He knew that some assumed that his Catholicism would restrict his creativity. He took a different perspective: 'I am just beginning to realize – there is no such thing as a Catholic poet – meaning, our Catholicism does not free us from an ounce of the burden of darkness, blindness, weight, pain, of the world we live in. The Faith gives us of course an entirely accurate aerial view of the countryside over which we have to travel; but in the poem, as in all relationships, we have to cover that ground yard by yard on foot.'[36] Though his difficulties as a poet remained, it is still true that Catholic religious experience matched perfectly his own modes of thinking and feeling, because it is a sacramental encounter with God in the events, objects, and persons of every day.

The first of the three sections in the new book reprinted some strong earlier poems, and the second contained some previously uncollected poems. Recent work was confined to the third section. 'To God the Son' (1955) shows Baxter could not yet write religious poetry. The sentiments are unexceptionable, but the tone is strained and his poetic muscles seem to have seized up. In the new work there are strong sections such as the opening lines of 'At Akitio', but the poems rarely form a satisfying whole. The difficulty he had in making his poems cohere is illustrated by 'Auckland', whose glittering pieces are roughly assembled. Baxter relied on ideas to structure his poems. Too often in this volume the controlling ideas are not there, and many of the ideas he has have not yet been sufficiently assimilated to be compelling. He needed to live longer with his material to find a perspective that would enable him to speak with the old assurance. Lacking that, the poems too often give the impression of tired and windy utterance.

In Fires of No Return was not well received by critics. To some extent Baxter shared their dissatisfaction. He confided to one of his friends in A.A. that he wondered whether a return to the bottle would loosen his thought. Baxter could always accept criticism of his work, but he was irritated when Charles Brasch remarked that the third section of *In Fires of No Return* was not well chosen. He replied that he did not think Brasch's literary judgements were more than about 60 per cent right, though he conceded he might well be in the same boat. The trouble was that both Brasch and Curnow mistakenly thought they were more than 90 per cent right, and that *he* might well be right on some of the poems about which they were wrong.[37]

As a poet, Baxter seemed to have lost direction. But he was too resourceful to be confined long in any cul-de-sac. Even as he took his bearings, a new development crucial for his future art was well under way. Already he had written dramatic poems like 'The Hermit', 'Prospector' and 'The Rented Room'. And in his lyrical sequence *Cressida*, published in *Landfall* in 1951, Baxter had shown a dramatic gift for seeing and feeling through the persona of a young woman. Now he entered the field of radio drama, which was still in its infancy in New Zealand. His play *Jack Winter's Dream*, was written 'for the speaking and the singing voice, and for radio',[38] the medium for plays in those pre-television days. There was no national forum for drama apart from productions by The New Zealand Players. The Broadcasting Service had both resources and the larger audience.

The play was produced on 26 September 1958 by the New Zealand

Broadcasting Service, under the direction of Bernard Beeby.[39] The music was composed by Ashley Heenan and played by the National Symphony Orchestra of seventy players, conducted by John Hopkins. The play contained songs and a rich interplay of voices of different accent and pitch: the full resonance of Bernard Kearns as narrator, the gravelly voice of Ballarat Jake, the soft Cornish accent of Will Trevelyan, and the Scottish accent of the half-crazed Preaching Lowry.

Jack Winter, drunkard, rabbiter, swagman, station rouseabout, 'winter-walking Adam', beds down for the night in a shanty pub in Abelstown, a deserted Central Otago gold-mining town. The play unfolds within the convention of a dream that turns to nightmare. In an interview published in the *N.Z. Listener*, Baxter said he had tried to write a play with an authentic setting that would come across on radio. Since it developed from a yarn, the narrator was of special importance. Dylan Thomas's *Under Milk Wood* had been his springboard. He had the record and played it many times for friends. He especially admired the resonance of the words. His own play had three separate themes: 'Age in the person of Jack Winter; death, in the murder of the young miner; and love – in the scene between the young miner and the pubkeeper's daughter. One of the three miners staying at The Drovers' Rest (Preaching Lowry) could be called the conscience of the piece.'[40]

The stage version, first produced by Richard Campion in the Memorial Theatre, Victoria University College in 1960, and the film version, made by the National Film Unit in 1979, brought out other elements in the play. On stage, and especially on film, it turned out to be beautifully visual and haunting. Campion's effects included New Zealand bird calls, something novel to audiences familiar only with European and American sounds. He thought the play was full of interesting characters and was held together by 'the web of Baxter's delight in heavy-booted men', tramps and down-and-outs, people very different from himself. There was also an uncanny sense of a spiritual world behind the appearances, a world shot through with the macabre.

Bernard Kearns, who played in both the radio and the film versions, thought the play took archetypal human experiences and metamorphosed them into characters of mythic proportions. The haunting quality of myth was built up by word and image:

(A wind) shuffles in flat slippers among graves and pines on the island of earth left by the glassy shovels and the swivel gunning hoses. And the Chinamen in exile there, lying down light and lank under a clay quilt, hear it ruffle above them like the swaggering bandit waves between them and China.[41]

Kearns spoke of how it felt to be in the play: 'Suddenly you are nowhere else, you're in Central [Otago] and in the nineteenth century. When you think of the Chinamen working along those river diggings, you can't escape it.'[42]

In a passionately involved way Baxter used to read Lawrence Durrell's lines on the *Deus Loci,* the god of place. *Jack Winter's Dream* illustrates how acutely he experienced that sense of the landscape and weather of Central Otago which he had known from childhood. The knobbly schist rock focused a sense of timelessness, of elemental forces. And it carried the associations of the gold-rushes.[43] To the cast of the radio programme the play seemed very much New Zealand's own.

Baxter further expanded the associations of place by an idea familiar in myth: 'that the shedding of blood christens a place, makes it part of the soul and imagination of man; that the natural world shares in our guilt, agony and perhaps redemption.'[44] The place where innocent blood was shed had to be purified. The events that troubled Jack's dream are carefully re-enacted to create a ritual of exorcism. The ceremony over, Jack can die in peace. Mythic figures speaking New Zealand vernacular counterpointed with poetic language, the violent action, the strong infusion of melodrama – all foreshadowed key elements of Baxter's later drama. As a play for radio, the chief emphasis was on what was said, not on the effects that come from the interaction of characters on a stage. This too would be typical of all his drama.

Jack Winter's Dream was an event. Before it was broadcast the *N.Z. Listener* gave it a feature article and the production itself was enthusiastically received. Richard Campion said that after the stage production Douglas Lilburn remarked it was the first time he had felt at home in the theatre. Frank Sargeson, though he felt there should have been more drama at the level 'accessible to the more hick-minded', was generous:

> Have since carefully re-read your script, which is superb as poetry – I mean it's all poetry. Only poets can write prose like that, and perhaps it's just as well. The language I try to write is intended to be the thinnest of veils – without which, paradoxically, reality can't be discerned. At least not on paper. But in your prose you thicken language so that it becomes part of the reality one is searching for . . . Jack Winter is I think a superb name, and both name and man are to me rich symbols. The time-trick which puts him inside the wall is a very clever invention, and beautifully worked out.[45]

Such responses more than made up for the lukewarm reception of *In Fires of No Return.*

IX

Baxter in Asia

After the separation from Jacquie, Baxter went through a period of grieving, but he was always hopeful of reconciliation. He knew that this could not be hurried, that he had to wait 'without resentment for things to take a turn for the better'.[1]

The chance came when he was offered a Unesco Fellowship to visit Japan and India. His brief was to take part in a conference in Tokyo to discuss school textbooks, and then to study any Indian equivalent to School Publications. It was hoped that the visit would lead to an infusion of more Asian material into the School Bulletins. Baxter was granted leave with full pay, and his fare and travelling expenses were covered by the Fellowship. He asked Jacquie to go with him and put the past behind them. Jacquie accepted. He felt she was brave to be prepared 'to have another go at things'. And he knew she would need the unqualified love and support he had previously been unable to give.[2] Since the Fellowship provided for his expenses only, it was agreed that Jacquie and the children would come to India at a later date. With a view of 'mud flats and mountains', Baxter flew out of Auckland on 16 September 1958.

Typhoon Ida hit Tokyo almost as soon as he arrived, flooding the streets and smashing the houses like kites.[3] He was staying out at Roppongi, a fashionable quarter, and was not in any personal danger, but the courage and resourcefulness of the people in the stricken areas impressed him. He found the conference strenuous. Unesco's delegate from Paris asked him to write a paper on Teaching Aids other than audio-visuals, and when he was absent Baxter kept the notes of the meeting. He also led a working group. A Japanese professor asked him to go through his paper polishing up the English and drafting the conclusions. A poem Baxter had written on the typhoon was translated into Japanese and circulated among the delegates. He won over an aggressive, anti-colonial Iranian by inviting him to have a drink. As a Moslem he presumably drank the same non-alcoholic champagne as Baxter. With a Professor Karasawa he often discussed the different branches of Buddhism, thus initiating a lifelong interest in the subject. The professor helped him to understand the Buddhists' point of view and join hands in friendship with them.[4]

A few days after the conference ended, Baxter dispatched a large quantity of written material to his Wellington office. About the same time he sent the final report to Dr. C. E. Beeby, the Director of Education, to whose personal intervention he owed the Fellowship. He also enclosed a long letter giving his impressions of Japan.[5] He remarked on the enormous technological developments and the complete absorption of 'democratic methods of education'. Both were occurring against a background of widespread suffering caused by the economic crisis and by the dislocation of traditional patterns of behaviour in the aftermath of war. Japan was changing so rapidly that many were bewildered. This was especially evident among the young. Baxter visited a group of training college students and found them left-wing without being Marxist. Japan had not yet been able to arrive at the 'stable middle-left' position which existed in New Zealand. He said that if he were Japanese and not a Catholic he would probably share the students' opinions. Behind a 'rigid shell of manners' he found the Japanese very much alive. The feeling for beauty, which led them to provide perfectly carved chopstick rests even in ordinary eating-houses, made him feel like a clumsy child. He was especially moved by the vitality and warmth of the country people, and the cleanliness and tidiness he found even in the poorest homes. He told Beeby: 'It offends me that these were the people on whom the bombs were dropped at Hiroshima and Nagasaki.'

The Japanese were at a difficult stage in their history:

> . . . like people in a bamboo boat on a rough sea – there are such boats in one of their paintings, with incredibly towering waves above them. The rough sea, or the dragon, symbolizes chaos: chaos is always close to them, held off by a bamboo fence, and not the least when they wake to hear pneumatic drills at work in the ashy Tokyo dawn. To them at heart our Western processes of thought seem to belong to that chaos. The most spectacular results of Western technology they have so far seen have been the giant bulldozer and the atom bomb. We will only win their confidence by learning to understand *their* ways of thought – not to change it or exploit it, but in order to meet them more than half-way with respect and even love.

The East didn't need bulldozers, he wrote, nearly as much as the West needed what its Asian neighbour had to offer. The Indians also impressed him. They cut almost as much ice at the conference as the Japanese, but for a different reason. India owed her influence to a stance of 'studied neutrality' and the special poise she had achieved between East and West.

Beeby was planning a Unesco Conference for 1959 and Baxter recommended that the New Zealand organizers should not think of themselves as teachers of those in the 'underdeveloped countries'. It would have to be their seminar. A paradigm for action might be learnt from Pakeha attitudes to the Maori, whose point of view had not been sufficiently allowed for nor understood. For the meeting in Wellington some Maori should take part in the workshops. That would be in line with the policy already being acted on at School Publications, where a beginning had been made in presenting Maori culture to both Maori and Pakeha children.

During the conference, Baxter was asked informally if he would go to the United States for several summers to work on a children's encyclopaedia for Asian countries. The Ford Foundation had offered to put up the money. But Baxter was never ambitious for personal advancement. He effectively ruled himself out by telling Beeby that although he was much attracted by the offer, there were other colleagues in School Publications much better qualified. He felt he should be getting on with his own job in Wellington. Though the invitation to take part in the American project was never taken up, it confirmed the excellent impression Baxter made in Tokyo.

To get a little peace and quiet after the conference, and to reflect on his experience, Baxter shifted to a house of the Columban fathers at Choshi City, a fishing port about ninety miles from Tokyo. The Columban priest who welcomed him at the railway station met a 'sleepy, disoriented individual'. During the week Baxter stayed, he would snuggle down in an armchair, head back, eyes looking into space, as if he saw what he was describing. Even with no eye contact the priest felt Baxter was speaking to him in a very personal way. The account of his spiritual journey, of how God was working in this 'vessel of clay', absorbed him. When Baxter related his marriage difficulties, he spoke of his wife with great love and gentleness. And he saw the forthcoming visit to India as crucial to their marriage. Especially striking was his trust in Providence. The priest later said that he was deeply affected by Baxter's visit, and felt he was a better person because of it.

In those days, Choshi was a poverty-stricken place with an extensive red-light district which catered for the crews of the large ocean-going trawlers. Just before Baxter arrived prostitution had been declared illegal, and as a result had fallen into the hands of criminals. The problem was very much in the air during his visit. Flirtation with vice had not lost its fascination after he became a Catholic. Baxter explored the place, and afterwards quietened his conscience by moralizing. Some incidents entered his poems. The poem 'Eioko' explores the anguish of a nightclub hostess he met at the Capa Cabana, 'a well-furnished annexe of Purgatory'.[6] Eioko's life parallels 'The lies/The coffee-house adulteries of the West'. But the comparison worked in her favour. She was assimilated to the Japanese virgin martyr who 'hung head downwards for sixteen days over a pit of smoking charcoal, her temple pierced so that blood could flow, holding her back from the peace of death':[7]

> For Eioko, a deadlier martyrdom,
> At drunken midnight tables

Displayed like butcher's meat, unable
To yawn at will, or smoke or frown or sit . . .
(CP 196)

Eioko's suffering is vicarious for her people, and like that of the virgin martyr brings them grace. And despite the misery of her life, she remains compassionate: 'Sharing her rice bowl with a child more poor.'

In the Japan of 1958 any Westerner was likely to incur some of the blame for the bombing of Hiroshima and Nagasaki. Baxter found it a relief to be able to say that he had helped word a petition to the New Zealand Government against nuclear testing.[8] Nevertheless, 'For a Child at Nagasaki' carries a sense of guilt he cannot altogether escape:

Having seen an ocean of fire and then
An ocean of ashes, her mother's head
On the ground in the pumpkin field, Eioko lies
Under a stone in Akagi. Not yet ten
She liked bean jam. You guardians of the dead,
Comfort this child, so young in your mysteries.
(CP 254)

The phrase 'She liked bean jam' communicates the simplicity of the child's life and wonderfully intensifies the sense of outrage.

After three weeks in Japan, Baxter flew to Hong Kong before stopping over in Bangkok. He found the Thai capital: 'A green place full of canals and short dark lovely people.' On a hot night he was lying awake in his hotel room bathed in sweat, despite the fan. He got up and went out for some air. A girl with a ribbon in her hair approached him, but he told her 'No thanks, honey, it would make me sad, it would remind me of old times. Come and have a feed with me, though.' While they ate the girl poured out her troubles, her unpaid rent, the American lover who had deserted her. Baxter put all the money he had on the table and divided it between them. After more talk they walked back to his hotel where he thought 'I can leave her now. She has what she needs, and I think I'll be able to sleep.' But she touched him on the fly and they walked to the sprawl of shacks where she lived. They made love in a room where there was only a bed, a mattress, and a pack of cards. At the airport next day, a great blue and red lizard fell from the roof on to his shoulder. Thailand, he believed, had restored his sexuality, and on the lizard 'was the sky-and-water demon who had entered my heart. But confession in Delhi healed up the wound and left only a scar.'[9] 'Air Flight to Delhi' returned to the incident:

The old ideograph of peace
Tempted me, with card-playing

169

On a hard mattress, light between
Bamboo slats. Such love is contraband.
(CP 193)

Much later he wrote of the experience: 'This is not ugly, but sad . . . Love
with sex, as I know it, is always sad.'[10]

The day Baxter arrived in India, Jacquie and the children flew to Sydney
to catch the *S.S. Strathmore* for the twenty-day voyage to India. Baxter met
the ship when it berthed at Bombay, and he and Jacquie were reunited on
board. There were many things to work out, and compromises to be made.
Baxter was Catholic, Jacquie was not, and she had no desire to become one.
They had to find ways around their religious differences, and they felt it
would be easier to build a new relationship in a different country, without
an audience of curious friends and confused relatives.

The family travelled together by train to New Delhi and took a small
house near the Muslim quarter. They also employed an Indian servant,
Adam, to do the cooking. Although they had read books about India, they
were quite unprepared for the heat, the smell, and the dust. What most
affected them was the extreme poverty of cities like Calcutta, where people
died in the streets and were ignored by passers-by.

For the first time in his life, Baxter was conscious of belonging to an
ethnic minority. All around them were some of the most disadvantaged
people they would ever see. However, even the street-sweepers of the
untouchable class had an air of incredible joy about them. So did the brightly
dressed women, so graceful in their movements, who carried baskets on
their heads and picked up with their feet dried cow pats for fuel. And they
seemed prepared to love even those who did not share their sufferings.[11]
Baxter felt he had much to learn. Images of the Indian and Japanese poor
were to linger in his mind for many years before being memorably recalled
in the Jerusalem books.

India was also a very demanding physical environment. Baxter's job took
him to Bombay, Madras, and Calcutta. He could have travelled first class in
air-conditioned carriages, or at least in those with fans. Yet he preferred to
go second or third class, along with the people who slept on the floors or on
the luggage racks. He was beseiged constantly by beggars, to whom he gave
the savings he had made by not travelling first class. Often he gave more than
he could afford, and he would find himself without enough money for food.
He would then have to make do with a handful of dates from an open stall
on the railway station. He never felt satisfied that what he gave was more
than a drop in the ocean, and he despaired at the beggars' suffering.

By exposing himself to a diet and lack of hygiene with which few
Westerners could have coped, he damaged his health. He had already

developed amoebic dysentery while in Thailand, and it grew steadily worse. By the time he left India, he was a very sick man. Yet a kind of intellectual toughness enabled him to continue sharing the experience of an ordinary citizen's life in India. The country fascinated him, and at the same time disoriented him in the way alien cultures often do:

> the town, the tombs, the heavy eaves
> As cold as Rome and twice as foreign.
> (CP 198)

He felt an unfamiliar horror:

> Lepers in the gateway
> Hold out their cups and bandaged palms.
> (CP 198)

And he was constantly comparing what he saw with things in his own country. The effects of the Fall were less mitigated in the East.[12] The flagrant nature of misery in India and its sheer scale shook him. His extreme sensitivity meant that he registered impressions with an excruciating intensity, the way most people feel only when they are keyed up to their highest pitch. Everywhere people were being exploited. Under the iron Howrah Bridge over the Ganges at Calcutta the boats carried: 'the loot of many lives':

> The rupee god has trampled here;
> The poor implore a Marxist cage.
> Dragon seed, the huddled bundles lying
> In doorways have perhaps one chilli,
> A handful of ground maize.
> King Famine rules.
> (CP 194)

The ominous expression 'dragon seed', evoking swords of violent rebellion, reflects the situation in India as Baxter found it. Over a country angry with industrial unrest fell the threatening shadow of China. The Indian Communists were seen as agitators preparing for a revolution. If they won the next general election it was generally believed they would invite China in. Baxter was caught up in the political turmoil. He had met some Communist writers and artists and been deeply challenged by them. Because he wore a reefer jacket he had bought in Hong Kong, he was often mistaken for an American. When he spoke, people thought he was an Englishman. India had received her independence from Britain only eleven years earlier, and reaction to the British Raj was still strong. Looking back on his visit he explained his difficulties to an Indian friend:

> I do not think I had ever considered myself a 'Westerner' until I first went to Japan and then to India . . . in India I frequently found myself saddled with the responsibility for the wounding and repellent racial and social snobbery of 'the English'. . . . I remember hearing [an Indian writer] open out on this subject. It would have been useless to cry out . . . 'Look, I am no Englishman, I am at one with you in this' . . . for only friends of long standing really know one's credentials . . . one stood in English clothes, with an English face and manner of speech, a background fairly close to that of England, and an English level of income. Do not imagine I am criticizing [him] – (or any other of a great many Indian people I met) – it was right for them to speak the truth; and it was in the long run extremely good for me to be shaken up, but often very tough at the time. It was like being taken to task (or, more often, forgiven) for the faults of a boorish cousin by the people whom he had insulted . . .[13]

His discomfort was compounded by an excessive desire to 'belong', when it would have been wiser to accept the simpler role of observer and visitor. He always preferred to affirm rather than deny, and he had a remarkable capacity to see past apparent differences to the truth that others shared. He could accept that the Communists, too, were struggling for a just society.

Since four-fifths of the population of India then lived in villages, he was determined to move outside official circles and spend some time with ordinary Indians. He made a thirty-hour train journey from Calcutta to Delhi, travelling second class and conversing with the passengers. In the villages he found the people warm, hospitable, and surprisingly well-informed politically. Baxter as a guest, and a polite one, saw no doubt what people wanted him to see, and his experience was mainly confined to Bengal. In the villages he was impressed by the powerful cohesion of family life, something he found lacking in the towns. The villagers were poor, but deeply in communion with their environment. They had an aura of well-being that he attributed to lives led in harmony with natural law. To illustrate what he meant he quoted with approval the romantic account of Bengal written by the son of the Bengali Nobel prize-winning writer Rabindranath Tagore: 'Groups of women with their earthen pots poised gracefully on their hips, coming down the ghats: children swimming boisterously, splashing water at each other: fishermen with their innumerable ingenious devices engaged in trapping fish: peasants loading their harvest on to boats till the brims almost touch the level of the water . . .'[14]

Baxter found that the *Sadhu*, or holy man, of the village was revered. He was a 'highly intelligent, broad-minded, and practical man, with a training of some twenty years in yoga and meditation. His manner towards the

172

villagers was unfailingly gentle, warm and courteous . . . No trace in him of the showman or bogus prophet.'[15]

One *Sadhu* he visited lived in a grass hut alongside a temple. A full-faced, sturdy man of about fifty, he was neatly dressed with long brown hair and a beard. He wore wooden sandals that left callouses between his toes. He talked freely with the villagers and moved among them distributing herbs and giving advice. He advised a woman with a black dress and silver ankle-rings about feeding her baby. When Baxter and his friends arrived they were given Indian sweets. He was impressed by the *Sadhu's* replies to questions: 'Morality? The lines separating one peasant's field from another's.' 'God?' 'Each man can become God, as soon as he forgets himself.' He admired too the way the holy man related to a squirrel that was frisking about and to a calf that was chewing its cud. The easy commerce with all comers, the physical greeting of the touching of the guru's feet when visitors arrived and departed, the Franciscan attitude towards animals, even the living beside the temple, all were to find parallels later in Baxter's community at Jerusalem.[16]

A modern ashram, a centre for study and religious devotion set up by Rabindranath Tagore, fascinated Baxter. But he was well aware of the vulnerability of the gurus on whom the ashram depended. They were 'instructors, men regarded as holy by others; and to Western eyes it may seem that holiness can be acquired too cheaply in India. A poet, a teacher, a political leader, any person with unusual talents, some integrity, and a message to convey, can put on the cloak of a *guru* and gain a following. Gandhi knew the danger of this to the *guru* and always advised his disciples to regard him simply as a fellow-searcher for truth and justice.'[17] This was written in 1961. Before the decade was out, Baxter was to face the same problem as the Indian holy man.

Tagore and Baxter had much in common. Both were playwrights and poets in the romantic tradition. Both adopted a similar approach to the social problems that come from the juxtaposition of two cultures. Baxter approved of Tagore's educational principles which emphasized psycho-logical freedom and creative expression through arts and crafts.

He also shared Tagore's 'genuine loathing for academic education' and admired his attempt to revive the style of the forest schools of ancient India, where 'students were instructed by gurus in the open air'.[18] Baxter admired especially Tagore's efforts to harmonize concern for the individual with 'the powerful communal endeavour of modern India'. He was able to cross barriers of caste and money to approach villagers on equal terms.[19] Whether either man perceived the reality of modern India, or romanticized it, is an open question. Those who believe they misread it point to the communal discord that flared in the post-partition riots of 1947, the massacres of

Muslims by Hindus and of Hindus by Muslims. Tagore and Baxter were idealists. It can still be said that given the complexity of relationships in a country as diverse as India, the views, within certain boundaries, were well grounded. In any event, what was significant for Baxter's life was his personal perception of India. That was what shaped the ideals he would try to realize in New Zealand.

Against the attractive features of village life, Baxter set the horrors of a city like Calcutta. This focused his attention on what he had come to see as the general nullity of New Zealand life and on the effect cities had on people. In 1962, about three years after returning from India, he would write: 'Tomorrow I will go through five tunnels into the great ditch called Wellington City, whose own quiet inanity is much more terrible than any vial of plague an angel could empty on it; and I will swim there with other newts through office and coffee-bar, and watch other newts trying desperately and angrily to climb up high straw ladders; and I will light the gasfire in my hutch and work the type-writer like someone playing the banjo with his feet.'[20] And he was to write of New Zealand cities:

> The city is a dirty mother,
> She does not care for anyone . . .
>   (CP 186)

For the New Year 1959, there was a great deal of sunshine in the Baxter household. India had indeed drawn the family together. Now Baxter could accept as true his mother's opinion that his love for Jacquie had not been whole-hearted. He realized that his many complaints against her were a form of adult tale-bearing, childish rather than malicious, but objectionable nevertheless. Jacquie was 'a good woman, through and through, straight as a die, a good wife to me and a good mother to her children.' In India, day after day, for weeks she had dressed the head of the child of their washerwoman which was covered with sores. By the New Year the last one had disappeared. And there were other instances of her kindness. In the past he had discounted or overlooked them. He admired her relationships with other people, which were generally much better than his own. At long last he felt he was beginning to learn from her, and he was looking forward to a happy life in her company. What he felt was not passion, it might not even be love, but it was something that might well enable them to survive the small irritations and crises that would inevitably come their way. Becoming a Catholic, he believed, helped him to straighten out his life and to understand the nature of marriage better. Now he saw husband and wife as 'watercourses, canals, each one irrigating the other's life.'[21] Yet, later that same year, he told Brasch that during the separation from Jacquie he had

174

learnt something 'for the first time in 10 years: the profoundly temporary nature of human affections and the solitude which is the real element of freedom. It was a weaning, a growing up' that had not reversed itself.[22]

When Baxter's overseas leave expired on 29 April 1959, he returned to his job as Assistant Editor with School Publications. His time abroad had been one of self-discovery and he was right in believing that he had changed. He spoke often of the poor in India and became very depressed. To an Indian correspondent he wrote: 'The images of India never fade in my mind; they were too deeply implanted, whether true or false. It is so difficult to tell.'[23] He had also left behind some good friends. And the Baxter's cook in New Delhi, Adam, had become very attached to the family. His wages had been generous enough to enable him to support several relatives as well as himself. When the time came to leave India, Adam insisted that Baxter bring him and his family with him to New Zealand. Though this was impossible, the Baxters helped him for many years by sending him money and gifts.

After his return from India, Baxter thought the children had 'benefited in all ways' from their time abroad and were as 'lively as crickets'. Later, Jacquie often spoke nostalgically of Delhi. Neither she nor Baxter thought they would ever split up again. Jacquie remembered thinking: 'this man is my husband and I want to spend the rest of my life with him.'

Physically the visit to India took a lot out of Baxter. His health had deteriorated and he was continually tired. A month after his return to Wellington he wrote to a friend: 'My own condition has been poor for the past few months.' The illness he contracted in Asia may have been the beginning of a deterioration in Baxter's naturally strong constitution.

In 1958, before he left for India, he had said in 'A Writer's Vocation': ' . . . a vocation is a calling, a way of life which a man must follow in order to become his true self . . . I am a writer by vocation; also a husband and a parent. But writing and married life are undoubtedly two vocations whose demands I am obliged to fulfil in order to become myself, the man God intends me to be . . .' By smothering their gift writers might lose 'the key to their own interior life.'[24]

Now he had a clearer idea that part of a writer's responsibility, however desperate a character he might be, was to keep criticizing his society. The visit to Asia had given him a new perspective. He was able to define his social values and become more aware of what threatened them. His wife told me that after India writing was no longer the main thing in his life. His chief concern became people and how to help them. But his writing would obviously be an instrument. He began 'a search for images and symbols adequate to our predicament.'[25] Once over Howrah Bridge, the road ahead was clearly signposted.

He felt a new relationship with New Zealand: 'It is very good to be back in this country. The air seems clearer and more glittering. I have discovered a love for New Zealand which I never knew I had.' But he soon realized he was looking through rose-coloured spectacles.²⁶ He had to enter the lists in defence of the periodical *Numbers*. A row had blown up with the State Literary Fund over a story by Richard Packer in the issue of February 1959, and the press had been making much of it. *Numbers* had received a grant from the Fund, and it was being argued that public money ought not to be used to subsidize salacious material. In a letter to the *N.Z. Listener* Baxter asked if a writer must narrow his or her 'vision of life to the point where no published work can risk offending the susceptibilities of an unstable thirteen-year-old or an unlettered journalist? . . . The shadow of Calvin rests still upon the hearts and minds of our countrymen, dividing grace from nature, and refusing our artists their legitimate entry to the garden of a mature vision of life.'²⁷ But his eloquence did not carry the day. *Numbers* lost the grant it needed to survive. Baxter always fought against literary censorship. His views on censorship of the arts were transmuted into the memorable poetry of 'Perseus', written years earlier in 1952. Since the subject was again topical, the poem would be included in his next volume of verse, *Howrah Bridge*. At the end of the poem, Perseus, having slain the monster Medusa, renders:

> back to benignant Hermes
> And holy Athene goods not his own, the borrowed
> Sandals of courage and the shield of art.
>
> (CP 130)

In that shield Perseus had viewed without danger the reflected image of the monster, who turned into stone any living person who looked at her. For Baxter, as for John Henry Newman in *The Idea of a University*, a book which he knew well, art inoculated a reader against evil. Confronted nakedly in life it might prove too virulent.

After an earlier airing in *Landfall*, poems recording Baxter's Asian experience appeared in the collection *Howrah Bridge* (1961). All were written by 1959. On the dust-jacket he said: 'the first part was written some time ago by a man who thought he was a New Zealander; the second part, lately, in the past two or three years by a man who had become almost unawares, a member of a bigger, rougher family. The poems in India mark this change.' Baxter's poems were rarely published in the order of their composition. But he usually arranged them with care. In *Howrah Bridge* the central sequence of seven Asian poems is preceded by eighteen poems, and followed by another eighteen. The early poems lead into the sequence and those that follow it lead out. The Asian poems are not documentaries, but icons. They evoke elements of an experience that flows over to the non-Asian poems in the volume. The Tweedledee and Tweedledum inconsequence of National Mum and Labour Dad in the poem called 'Ballad of Calvary Street' comes partly from his sharpened perception of New Zealand politics. Soon after his return he wrote to an Indian friend: '. . . it was exhilarating, as well as disturbing, to be in an atmosphere where politics meant ideals, enthusiasms, and even at times a life-and-death conflict – so different from our situation here where politics are drearily linked to the pay packet and our leaders tend to be above all votecatchers.'[28]

Howrah Bridge presents a man aware of his disorientation and the need to take his bearings. The task was to diagnose and release what he called in a cryptic phrase 'a secret sorrow not confessing to'. The opening and closing poems of a Baxter volume are usually signposts to what is happening throughout. *Howrah Bridge* begins with 'The First-Forgotten', on his Scottish forebears. The poem acknowledges his origins and tries to come to terms with what he has inherited. Other poems record high points in the development of his present consciousness. There are childhood memories of places sacred to him, like 'The Giant's Grave' along the Brighton River, and Hardy's Boscastle. Poems like 'The Mountains' and 'Haast Pass', with their decisive choice of humanity over the natural world, were included because Asia had confirmed that choice.

From the order of poems in his poetry notebooks, it is apparent that a disturbing poem like 'Schooldays' was written around the same time as the Indian poems. It was occasioned by a visit to a private boarding-school for Anglo-Indians, St Thomas's, which placed great emphasis on English educational traditions. Baxter's note on the school in his Asian diary, 'early exile of English children from their mothers', confirms that this was the stimulus for a poem that distils the anguish of his lost boyhood at Sibford.

The poems that follow the Asian sequence accept that the personal problems faced in the first section of the book remain. 'Sisyphus' locked in his own selfishness, materially well-endowed but unhappy, faces the choice between suicide and a life spent for others. There is the bitter rejection of sex in 'A Clapper to Keep Off Crows': the feeling behind the poem, I suggest, was sharpened by remorse for the encounter with the Bangkok prostitute. 'Be Happy in Bed' reflects the same melancholy and guilt:

> Sex taught him sadness: like St Lawrence
> Roasting on the grid of conscience:
>
> (CP 200)

As he tries to discover his true self, he bolsters his courage by adopting a new perspective towards the past:

> Put off the past: you have endured it,
> Enjoyed, or else confessed it.

But he is realistic enough to know that its effects remain.

The dedicatory poem 'For Kevin Ireland' that opens Section II of *Howrah Bridge* adopts the doomed posture that always attracted Baxter:

> *I am by force of blood and star*
> *One of the maimed immortals who*
> *Tread a pathway to the fire*
> *Where affliction makes them whole.*
> (CP 186)

In the fifties Denis Glover had remarked: 'There goes Jim Baxter, carrying his grave with him and ready to leap into it by appointment.' Because of the remorse Baxter characteristically bore the quip was not unwarranted.

A recent convert like Baxter, confronted on all sides by the diversity and pervasiveness of religion in India, was naturally challenged in his own faith. In 'Madras', a poem not included in *Howrah Bridge*, he compared himself to St. Paul on the road to Damascus:

> On the sea road from Madras You found me,
> Led me to the doubting cave,
> The *Sitio* of true belief,
> Wounds not my own imprinted there . . .
> (CP 197)

His religious faith was complex, despite the simplicity with which he sometimes expressed it. 'The doubting cave' is an image of his questionings, and the *Sitio* the quest for a fulfilment not yet experienced. In India, as elsewhere, he was preoccupied with the nature of true living. The 'massive music' of the carvers of 'the lion-pillared/temple pyramid and burnt-out pharos' in 'The Carvers' 'taught us what to be.' For strength in the struggle, he turned to the Holy Spirit, seen as dark because mysterious:

> Dark Spirit, their Instructor,
> For whom our sleepless hungers burn,
> Shine in the casual labyrinth,
> Explode the debris of our lives.
> (CP 195)

These lines link with 'For Kevin Ireland' in their felt need for purification. 'Be compassionate!' is the moral imperative demanded by the poems:

> These wounds that I must understand . . .
> (CP 193)

The position of 'To Our Lady of Perpetual Help', as the last poem in the volume, gives it a special emphasis. Christianity was never an abstract system for Baxter, but a matter of personal relationships. This particular title for the Virgin was especially important to him: 'Mother of Perpetual Succour, under that title you came to me when I lay broken among the thorns, simply because I called on your name . . . You have laughed my sullenness away and shown me the beauties of your everlasting garden. You have never abandoned me for a moment, in spite of my rebellions and treacherous follies.'[29] 'To Our Lady of Perpetual Help' is also significant because of an incident in Calcutta where he saw a leper dying beside a fruit stall near Howrah Bridge. Though he felt a sense of revulsion, he went over and gave the dying man a few coins. An Indian policeman asked: 'Why do you give him money now? It is the last time.' Baxter wrote:

> . . . here Christ was coming down from his Cross on the pavement beside the fruit markets; and now no one was there to receive His Body except myself and the policeman. And the only true alternative to his fatalistic irony would have been for me to sit down beside the leper and to take his head on my knees and wipe his face with my handkerchief; and afterwards to have washed his body and prepared it for burial. Who am I to speak of brotherhood when that is the thing I could by no means bring myself to do.

Baxter's only resort was to pray to Our Lady for strength in his weakness, for she has 'power as well as beauty beyond measure.'[30] Some fourteen years later, the poem numbered 36 in *Autumn Testament* showed how deeply the experience affected him:

> This fine windy morning I think about
> The leper lying beside the fruitstalls in Calcutta
>
> Under the shade of the great bridge. The oil-stained bandages
> Around his limbs, the flies moving slowly
>
> In and out of his nostrils, over his eyelids;
> That lion face of dark mahogany
>
> Turned up its brow to the overlying cloud
> Behind which Rahm might live, from which a few spots

Of rain aspersed the pavement. I threw some coins
Into his tin dish. The policeman, built like a Maori

Guarding the fruitstalls in his khaki shorts,
Said, 'They're no use to him.' But the man was not quite dead.

When he was younger he should have had a gun.
There or in Karori, the sickness is, not to be wanted.

(CP 558)

Stylistically the Asian poems in *Howrah Bridge* are profoundly affected by Lawrence Durrell, whom he now found a better guide than his old master Yeats. He had come to see that 'the images (or sensory units, let us say) of a poem are the stones from which it is constructed, while the rhetoric is the mortar that holds them together. Durrell, unlike Yeats, makes do with the minimum of mortar.'[31] A comparison of two poems, Baxter's 'Pyrrha', which appears in the *Collected Poems* as the last poem in the sequence 'Songs of the Desert', and Durrell's 'A Portrait of Theodora', makes the point.

There is, too, the influence of Durrell's unrhymed couplets in a poem like 'Elephanta'. In his contribution to Charles Doyle's *Recent Poetry in New Zealand*,[32] Baxter acknowledged his debt to Durrell and to Robert Lowell; to Durrell for loosening up 'the chains of association', for helping him 'to avoid heavy aphorisms about Time or God', and helping him to keep his eye on the sensory image. Lowell taught him to express the 'violent experiences of the manic-depressive cycle'. Both had led him nearer to his true subject. Stylistically, Lowell encouraged Baxter's fondness for rhetorical phrasing and operatic rhythm, as in 'A Family Photograph 1939', written in the same year that *Howrah Bridge* was published. 'Guy Fawkes Night' is so much in the rhetorical manner of the middle Lowell that it could pass for his work:

I saw the freckled children burn their guy
In dry November by the reddened waves
That wash the doorsteps of the dead. Our graves
Are tinder. Look, the sacking falls apart,
The straw will catch as the leopard flames jump high
And grip the squib-plugged heart
Of the poor guy. The dead who have no names
Are shouting, *Miserere!* from the flames . . .

(CP 259)

Baxter could always assimilate whatever lesson the poetry he was reading had to teach.

▲ The New Zealand Writers' Conference, Christchurch 1951. Included are: Baxter (fifth from left); Anton Vogt (sixth from left); John Garrett (eighth from left); and Denis Glover (third from right). *John Reece Cole Collection, Alexander Turnbull Library*

The 1951 intake for Wellington Teachers' Training College. Baxter is in the back row at the far left. *Private Collection* ▼

◄ Baxter, *c.* 1953. *Brian Bell*

▲ Charles Brasch, Baxter, and Basil Dowling, 1952. *Private Collection*

▲ Baxter and Louis Johnson in the garden at Wilton Road, Wellington, *c.* 1954. *Private Collection*

▼ Baxter and a friend from A.A. in the *Man Friday* coffee bar, Wellington, *c.* 1955. *Hocken*

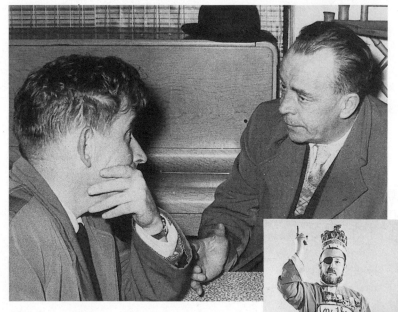

Bob Lowry in his prize-winning costume at the Arts Ball in Auckland, May 1963. *Private Collection* ▶

James and Jacquie celebrating Baxter's graduation, 1956.
Private Collection ▶

▼ James K. Baxter, late 1950s. *Alexander Turnbull Library*

▲ Baxter with Jacquie, Hilary, and John in Wellington,
late 1950s. *Private Collection*

▲ Baxter and his class at Epuni School, 1955. *Hocken*

▼ Baxter with Jacquie and her mother, Mrs Sturm, at Plimmerton, Wellington. *Gordon Brown*

▲ With Hilary in India, 1959. *Private Collection*   ▲ James K. Baxter, 1961. *John Ashton*

▲ Three Baxter families at Brighton, Christmas 1960. Front row: Hilary, John, Cathy, Helen, and Kenneth. Back row: Jacquie, Millicent, Lenore, Archie, Terence. Camera: James. *Private Collection*

X
Pig Island Letters

In August 1959 Baxter was learning to drive a car and had bought an old Hillman Minx.[1] He became a reasonable driver, though he often forgot where he had parked the car. The family went on frequent outings to beaches and other rural areas. One Christmas, the Baxters drove up to Rotorua with Jacquie's mother to stay in a rented house. It was a long drive, and Baxter was very anxious about the safety of his children and his mother-in-law. He seemed to dread the prospect of a mechanical breakdown or puncture in the same way that anyone else might dread a physical injury.

Outwardly his domestic life was happy, but the writing of the period suggests a deep disquiet. 'Mr Baxter's Evening Liturgy', written in 1959, presents a man who speaks from what he feels is his living hell. He is sexually frustrated ('soon we'll both retire . . . And dream of porcupines'), and the poem ends with a phrase which shows his indifference to the horrors of the next hell — 'Timor mortis non conturbat me' (The fear of death does not disturb me). 'Spring Song of a Civil Servant' goes further and depicts the author as a frustrated Othello:

> Underneath my fishbone armour
> Beats a wild Othello's heart
> And between the cup and saucer
>
> Many a savage dream is born
> Of Desdemona's eyeballs popping
> (CP 206)

The month in which these poems were written is unclear as the notebooks do not date them. The turbulence of 'Mr Baxter's Evening Liturgy' and 'Spring Song of a Civil Servant' is present in a few adjacent poems in the same notebook.[2] The violent imagery suggests that Baxter was still having difficulty with his home life. However, it is just as likely that he was also influenced by his romantic view of the artist, as represented in a parable which appeared in *Numbers* (March 1957) by a character who

> will never be content this side of the grave, for the spirit of turbulence in his heart will reject every custom, law and institution, asking from man and nature an impossible harmony. Yet his songs are the fruit of that harmony, which he knows best by the pain of absence. He will always jerk against your yoke; and you will always find him hard to bear.[3]

An insatiable restlessness ran deep in Baxter's nature and would continue to erupt throughout his life, carrying him in directions many found bewildering.

He wrote a letter to his parents in May 1959 which spoke of his bad habit 'of pouring out . . . subjective melancholia' in letters. He thought the cause 'the egocentricity which it is a lifelong labour to overcome.' He realized his poor health acted as a contributing factor (dysentery is a debilitating and depressing illness), and he conceded that Jacquie herself was never completely well. Nevertheless, he was hopeful: 'There is nothing at fault between me and Jacquie: my feeling that there was sprung from the stupid perennial expectation of a return to the garden of Eden.'[4]

His domestic situation had not prevented him from writing a new play. Richard Campion, who had produced *Jack Winter's Dream*, remembered Baxter turning up in an old gabardine coat with the script of a play typed on government paper. Campion was the right man to consult. After training as an actor at the Old Vic, London, he had returned to New Zealand with his wife Edith, a fellow student at the Old Vic, and they had established the New Zealand Players in 1952. The company survived until 1960, when it was finally accepted that the enormous expenses of touring on a professional scale were too heavy to be met by private money. Even in the heyday of the Players it was necessary to take risks carefully, but the Campions were always ready to chance their arm with New Zealand artists. Richard had often commissioned music for amateur theatre.

In 1956 a New Zealand revue, 'Free and Easy', included songs by Denis Glover and a few pieces by Bruce Mason, who also wrote some of the music. 'Free and Easy' attracted good houses, and it began to be realized that local productions could reach out to a large group of people. Campion invited the composer David Farquhar to compose an orchestral suite for a production of Christopher Fry's translation of Anouilh, *Ring Around the Moon*. The music was a great success and gave Farquhar his big breakthrough as a composer. A dance suite from the work became the most frequently performed piece in the repertoire of a Wellington musician, Alex Lindsay.[5] By 1959 Campion, with all his skill and experience, had left the Players and was teaching at Wellington College. Now he could mount plays he had been unable to risk in commercial theatre. He still believed passionately that New Zealand theatre would not exist until there were New Zealand playwrights.

The script Baxter showed Campion was called *The Wide Open Cage*, a New Zealand drama in two acts. Campion's assessment was that the play had a beginning and a finish but 'no drive down the valley', and that the characters were not properly worked out. He asked Baxter to add a middle act. A New Zealand play was a rare thing in those days and the last thing Campion wanted was a flop. The obvious danger was that if the play was too metaphysical it would be very difficult for the audience to get involved. Campion pointed out that as a producer it was his duty to look at the play from the point of view of a hardbitten audience, who nevertheless wanted to be delighted and were ready to be sympathetic. He made a number of suggestions for Baxter to think about. When Baxter came back with the revision, everything Campion had said had passed through the prism of his vision and become his own invention. Campion believed he had allowed his warmth and love for people, for life, and for sex, to flow into the play. He felt excited, and secretly resolved that from now on if Baxter brought him a play he would always do it. It seemed 'a kind of commitment'. He admired Baxter as a poet, but he also liked him as a man because he was modest, quiet, and with some indefinable quality that made him special. He felt privileged to work with him.[6]

When the play finally reached the boards Baxter said in the programme:

> This play has no message. It simply holds up a mirror to certain relationships among people. *The Wide Open Cage* is life itself; or, if you like, the inordinate love of creatures. The people in the play are each in their different ways trying to find happiness in other people; except for the priest, who is out of the running, and Hogan, who loves nobody. The fact that three of the people are Catholics is really incidental. Catholicism brings to a head certain problems of freedom and involvement which are latent in all human relationships. To those inside the cage release seems to be the death of love.

The characters live in sordid surroundings and are rather seedy, but their vitality is never in doubt. Nor is there any doubt about the presence of important elements of Baxter's own character. And his difficulties in relating to women were being worked out. He was attracted by them and they liked him, yet he was unable to establish an easy relationship at a deep level. This tension added greatly to the force of the play.

Jack Skully, ex-sailor, ex-alcoholic, ex-Catholic, forced by a heart attack to drop out from active life, is the kind of character Baxter found congenial. Skully is a warm person to whom people naturally respond; he is also something of a philosopher. Despite a strong streak of anti-clericalism, he remains religious and talks easily of God, the crucifixion, and hell. Alcoholism no longer troubles him, though he is aware that only one drink stands between him and Ben Hogan, a roaring Irish drunkard. Sex continues to preoccupy Skully. His girlfriend, Norah Vane, an Irish-Maori prostitute, is accommodating towards him, but is also drawn to Hogan. Most of the characters carry a burden of guilt. For Norah, it is the memory of murdering her first child. A Redemptorist priest, Father Tom, moves in and out of the action as a symbol of the stable centre from which Skully, Norah, and Hogan have strayed. Then there are the teenagers, Ted and Eila, with their frustration at not finding a satisfactory relationship: and Ma Bailey, Skully's landlady, who is in love with him and is defensively scornful towards his visitors. In the way these characters live in separate, guilt-ridden worlds, they have the same isolation as their counterparts in a morality play. Hogan and Skully represent the two sides of natural man, the one optimistic, god-fearing, life-enhancing, the other life-destroying. The third act of *The Wide Open Cage* becomes more and more a war between these two opposing selves.

In a discussion following the first performance, Baxter said he had rejected a neat plot in favour of a poetically satisfying scheme of 'the eclipse of the forces of light by the forces of darkness'; and his approach was psychological rather than sociological. Like *Jack Winter's Dream*, the play has a strong element of melodrama, something Baxter found attractive. He wrote to his mother on 7 November 1962: 'I can't really sift the lurid quality out of what I write. I would have been happy in the days of melodrama: SWEENEY TODD THE DEMON BARBER and so on . . .'[7]

Campion mounted the play in a small studio in Drummond Street, Wellington, on 19 November 1959. 'This funny old converted house' seemed to Campion ideal 'because it was the heart of Jim's country, – odd, derelict, cops, priests, things happening; booze-ups, and violence round the corner: steep little streets and steps, rain, the sound of tramcars, washing on the line. His kind of country.' Staging the play in a tiny theatre, where the audience was close to the action, was an advantage for a play with such intimate material. And of course it was as much to do with things of the spirit as with murder, sex, and the rest of it.

Campion gave the play as much realism as possible so that the audience would not feel they were in a world made up of 'high-falutin poetic symbolism'. With Don Ramage, the art master at Wellington Boys' College, he built an open-sided New Zealand cottage with rusty corrugated iron. This allowed the illusion that the characters had just come in off the street. Sacks of gravel were brought in so that when people walked towards the house you heard the crunch, crunch; and water drummed on the roof during the shower.

Some very good actors were available. Bob Renner, who played Skully, had served on a sailing-ship *The Pamir*. He was a real character, with a broken nose, black hair, and staring eyes. Skully in the play is just off the ships and has been all round the world in a big wind-jammer. When Renner spoke of his sea experiences, his words had the authenticity audiences recognize immediately. Mary Nimmo, who played Norah, had been in Bruce Mason's *The Pohutukawa Tree* shortly before. Others in the cast were Grant Tilly, Barry Hill, and Thane Bettany, who gave an explosive performance as Ben Hogan. Possibly for the first time in New Zealand theatre, Campion put a naked woman on the stage. He kept the lights well down, considering the needs of the play were sufficiently met, and that this would reduce the risk of an outcry. The nudity was not for shock effect, though Baxter was always looking for ways to unsettle people's assumptions.

When word got around that something special was happening in Drummond Street, the theatre was packed night after night. It became a privilege to get a seat. The season could easily have been extended beyond the scheduled run of three to four weeks. Campion hoped the play would be filmed so the whole country could see it. John O'Shea of Pacific films was enthusiastic, but the plan came to nothing.

The play received a great deal of publicity. There was a full page review in the *N.Z. Listener* and it was discussed in two consecutive issues of *Landfall*. One contributor, James Bertram, who had taken part in the discussion in the theatre following the performance, described the play as explosive in treatment and style with 'the disturbing and perhaps valuable quality of exposing areas of experience most New Zealanders prefer to conceal if they cannot evade them.' The *N.Z. Listener* reviewer thought it would be the year's most talked about play. For Bruce Mason it was 'the most exciting night in the theatre that year.' The play was performed by a small company at the Washington Square Theatre, New York, in December 1962. Baxter had visions of thousands of dollars flowing his way from TV and movie rights. But he did not really think that would happen. 'Ambition,' he said was 'the disease of middle life.'[8] In fact he received almost nothing.

Campion revived the play for Unity in March 1973. He felt he was groping in the original production partly because he was handling new material. The first time he concentrated on character and the dramatic action, the second time he felt he had a better grasp of the other elements.

After the success of his first straight stage play, Baxter brought Campion *Three Women and the Sea* in 1961. Irene Esam, a Wellington actress who had emigrated from Russia as a child, seemed to Campion to realize the role of Sophia so skilfully that it turned the play from an ordinary domestic comedy into 'something that disturbed the waters of the mind and feelings. Baxter wanted to communicate that once in a while somebody very special comes along and opens up new horizons, reshapes people's lives and then disappears'.[9] The last play in which he collaborated with Baxter was *The Spots of The Leopard*, written in 1962, but not produced until 1967. This was a revue with characters drawn from the Wellington streets. Campion thought it rather loose-limbed, a play of impressions.

In the course of producing four of Baxter's plays, Campion became a close friend. Though he had abandoned his early beliefs as a member of the Plymouth Brethren, he was not unfamiliar with Baxter's ideas, and was able to bring the actors to understand what lay behind the plays. At times, Baxter joked about the spiritual dimension. He said to Campion: 'Oh God, I don't know . . . I suppose you think here's me with another priest play and with Irish Catholics.' Campion would reply: 'Yes Jim, it's a bit of a bind. Can't you give us a straight play sometimes?' 'Well,' Baxter would say, 'It's what's on my mind.'

Campion shrewdly perceived there was something of the priest about Baxter. People would talk over with him things they mentioned to no one else. And the thrust of his plays was towards the reconciliation of people's lives with a spiritual ideal. The structure of the plays, too, is more parable than story. Because most New Zealand audiences resist anything that smacks of preaching, the priestly element hindered Baxter from becoming a popular playwright, yet as Campion observed: 'He was also a priest pretending to have hairy feet. He could dance to the devil's tunes, and knew that people would rise and join in the goat dance.' An example is the sophistry of the dictator, Captain Starlight, at the end of *The Starlight in Your Eyes*.

Baxter genuinely liked to please an audience and hold their attention, and he appreciated that one difference between a poem and a play is that in a theatre people hear the words only once. They can't go back and read what was said. Campion found Baxter a director's delight. Baxter believed in the Shakespearean tradition that the text was sacred, but Campion respected that, and relished the discipline of fidelity to the words. He liked especially Baxter's ability to throw in a joke or something very human when things were getting a little heavy. This, too, Baxter had learned from Shakespeare, in whose plays there is no comic relief, only comic intensification. In *The Wide Open Cage*, for example, Hogan, drunk, goes out to relieve himself. When he reappears on stage, the toilet seat is hanging around his neck. At that point the play demanded something outrageous so the landlady could become really angry. 'And it's a very good dramatic picture. A real shithead entering with this thing around his neck. It's hilarious and it's also symbolic, because in social terms Hogan is at the very bottom of the dung-heap. There's very little going for him, and he's dangerous as well.' The scene where the Maori skull talks to Hogan reflected for Campion Baxter's conviction that Maori culture is bound up with the land and rooted in a living tradition.

During rehearsals Baxter would occasionally sit at the back of the theatre, his hands thrust into the pockets of his old gabardine raincoat, a cigarette stuck out the side of his mouth. His eyes were half closed and he wore a slightly amused expression. Seeing his plays come off the page was a 'bit like visiting the circus. Goodness, they're the monkeys, and that's a giraffe, and to think you are the embodiment of what I've dreamed up.'

Campion seemed to him a kind of magician. After Baxter left Wellington for Dunedin, he never again worked with him on a play. But it was Campion who established him as a playwright.

In 1960, John Weir, a Marist seminarian, published a poem in the *N.Z. Listener*, 'Letter from Waimarama', which was addressed to Baxter. This was the beginning of a long friendship between the two men. While Weir was still a child his father had been killed in the Second World War and Baxter saw himself as a surrogate father.[10] Weir later wrote a thesis on Baxter's poetry based on their extensive discussions and correspondence, and ultimately he was the editor of Baxter's *Collected Poems*.

The publication of Allen Curnow's *The Penguin Book of New Zealand Verse* in 1960 was the occasion of a literary controversy. Baxter became passionately involved. Readers compared the Penguin anthology with Chapman and Bennett's *An Anthology of New Zealand Verse*, published by Oxford University Press two years earlier.[11] Baxter's meagre representation is only three poems more than Curnow had allowed him in his 1945 anthology. Yet since then, Baxter's poetry had been published in *Blow, Wind of Fruitfulness* (1948), *Poems Unpleasant* (1952), *The Fallen House* (1953), *Traveller's Litany* (1955), *The Night Shift* (1957), *Chosen Poems* (1958) and *In Fires of No Return* (1958). Baxter, never a person to push his own barrow, said he was reasonably satisfied with Curnow's selection. He would have been justified in feeling aggrieved. Over the intervening years, Curnow had developed a lasting antipathy towards Baxter, the roistering bard. Having backed the emerging poet heavily, his disappointment was the more bitter. He had too much integrity to make his personal feelings the criterion for selection in the anthology, but his attitude to Baxter disposed him to be more critical. Yet even as he tried to cut him down to size he predicted in his introduction that Baxter 'will continue to enjoy the widest repute in his native land'.[12] And he hardly believed that New Zealanders had a depraved taste.

The new poets of the fifties considered that the Penguin anthology misrepresented the state of New Zealand verse. When they first heard of Curnow's proposed selection some threatened to withdraw altogether. Baxter felt later that was what he should have done. What stopped him was a fear of falling into personal acrimony, a wish not to inconvenience Curnow personally, and the knowledge that Curnow's intentions were honest.[13] The main objection was not so much to Curnow's ill-proportioned selection, it was to the theory of New Zealand poetry on which it was based. That view Baxter and his friends regarded as 'self-conscious New Zealandism'.[14] He summed up his attitude in a letter to Brasch: 'The trouble with Allen as a critic and editor is that he is right within his frame of reference, but the frame of reference excludes the actual growing-points of quite a number of other people, who are not really much concerned whether they are New Zealanders or not.'[15]

Until he went to Wellington in 1948, Baxter had regarded Curnow's introductory essay to the Caxton anthology as 'a clear-cut and unbiased view of New Zealand poetry'.[16] Some phrases in an article he wrote in 1946 read like Curnow: 'our real lives are rooted in these islands', 'a poet or an artist must choose here and now whether he is a transplanted Englishman or a New Zealander.'[17] Baxter's early verse illustrates, as well as any, Curnow's view of New Zealand poetry.

Through his contact with the Wellington poets, Baxter changed his opinion. He brought to their cause his considerable personal prestige and a range of reading at least equal to Curnow's. And he too had pondered the question of what a national literature might be. He agreed that its material lay just outside the back door, and that if New Zealand poets were to ignore New Zealand, it would ignore them. He accepted the force of Curnow's mystique but questioned 'its universal validity as a New Zealand experience.'[18] Many poets would write differently from those Curnow admired simply because they wrote out of a different experience; the New Zealand situation was only a variant of the condition of Westerners. And he quoted with approval Johnson's quip that New Zealand and Europe were joined under the sea. He argued that Curnow's myth of insularity, which made New Zealand an island in time and human culture, was valid for the thirties, and fruitful for Curnow personally. It was quite inadequate for the new concerns with suburbia, domesticity, and urban living that characterized the poetry of the late forties and fifties. No less than the poets of the thirties, the new poets were effecting a revolution in New Zealand poetry. Their poems were beginning to make cities clear to those who lived in them, and they had introduced into New Zealand poetry fresh sources of imagery.[19] And they were writing satire as well. Baxter blamed Curnow for failing to take account of the massive shift that had taken place in our poetry. Curnow's theory had exalted what Baxter called the 'poets of transition'. They included Mason, Fairburn, Brasch, Glover, and Curnow himself. The new anthology, in Baxter's view, presented merely a personal view of our poetry, and a distorted one.

Baxter judged the Penguin anthology to be a failure as an act of criticism, and thought the earlier Chapman and Bennett anthology a better book. He liked the inclusiveness which followed from their assumption that by the fifties poets here could feel free 'to deal directly with the concerns of poetry everywhere.'[20] Baxter regarded Curnow's views as constricting. The passion in the controversy was not generated by literary theory alone; some poets were ready to rebel against an acknowledged expert, and exhibited a desire to dislodge Curnow and what he stood for in order to make room for their verse.

Baxter was still having trouble with his own writing. In December 1960 he told Charles Brasch he was doing his best to make his marriage work. He thought that he and Jacquie had an equal amount to offer each other, and an equal amount to suffer. In their own way they loved each other and would be able to stick together. The children remained the strongest bond between them. He mused, 'Well, time passes, and we both keep on growing.' He wondered what Brasch would make of the poems he had just sent him and added that his domestic situation made writing more difficult: 'You must know well the problems of going on writing honestly while one's life moves into narrower and stonier stretches.'[21]

On 5 September 1961, in the course of describing for the Chief Inspector of Primary Schools the progress of six bulletins, Baxter spoke of the thorough editing, amounting to rewriting, that one manuscript had required.[22] Baxter was a conscientious editor, and would go through a manuscript page by page and indicate to the writer what parts needed to be pruned or reshaped. He wrote to one writer, his old friend Noel Ginn, 'I suggest that you work through the script again, making another draft in handwriting, before working on the typewriter; it restores the sense of fluidity.'[23] To encourage Ginn in his personal difficulties he characteristically admitted that he had similar problems in his own life: 'You can be sure that I live like Elijah, always on the point of giving up hope of coping with work, family and life itself, but fed by ravens nevertheless; and so I understand any difficulties you or another person may have'. Baxter's relaxed manner encouraged personal responses from his contributors. The novelist Ruth France wrote: 'As regards being a writer of novels – it's just about as bad to be a New Zealander as it is to be a woman; there's always the extra hurdle to surmount; it's a question of audience, I think, and we can't all reach the heights of universality.'[24] Other discussions of manuscripts indicate the sense of partnership that existed between author and editor. Baxter's tone was friendly and he sweetened his reservations with humour. He told the author of an outsize manuscript: 'See if you can put it in the Turkish bath.'[25]

Editing, he found, was hard work. He asked a predecessor in his job if he too had felt the need of 'three brains and six hands to keep all the bulletins moving forward smoothly at the same time?'[26] Some people thought his job was a sinecure, a benevolent Government's way of giving him time to write. In 1962, a friend asked him how he was coming to terms with his editorial responsibilities. He answered that the Director of Education looked on him as 'an amiable donkey who occasionally excreted lumps of gold.' One of his colleagues, however, was interrupted every morning at about half past eleven by Baxter, with a new poem he had just typed. He found the interruptions something of a nuisance. There was also an alcoholic friend who used to visit Baxter regularly at work for counselling. Baxter's main job, his colleague felt, consisted in being a poet, a member of A.A., and a man struggling with his own problems. The poets in the Branch were seen as having something of the character of wandering minstrels. Baxter and another man were once reprimanded by the Chief Editor for being downtown instead of in the office. While his companion stood there sheepishly and raged inwardly, Baxter accepted the reprimand meekly. Then the other man went upstairs to his office while Baxter went off to the pub.

While the general tempo of work at School Publications in Baxter's day was not frenetic, there is evidence that he was a conscientious and efficient editor. Official reports on his work were always favourable. In one questionnaire his boss, Mrs P. M. Hattaway, was able to reply in the affirmative to questions like 'Is the probationer careful, diligent and efficient in the performance of all duties? Is his conduct completely satisfactory and health good?' Under 'Further remarks' she added: 'Mr Baxter has very strong qualifications for the position he holds and is doing excellent work.' He was clearly reliable, taking only three days sick leave over a five year period.[27] And his extraordinary facility with words meant he could do his job with comparative ease. When he was composing, he worked very quickly. According to one of his colleagues, Baxter could do in a day what would have taken another person a full week, and he would do it better. He typed rapidly, with one finger dancing over the keyboards and with his tongue stuck out. Once he began to work, nothing could distract him; when the job was finished, he lost interest. An art editor, who usually went to see the printer before the sheets were printed, once persuaded Baxter to come with him as the author of that particular bulletin. Hardly had they arrived in the printer's office when Baxter fell asleep. After the business was finished the printer nodded towards him and asked, 'Who's he?' 'Oh,' said his companion, 'He's the author.' On another occasion the layout of a bulletin fell awkwardly, with a couple of words isolated by two pages of photographs. Baxter was asked if he would take them out. 'What!' he retorted ironically, 'You expect me to tamper with the text?' He was quite happy to leave such matters to the person responsible for layout.

Baxter's relaxed attitude made him an easy person to work with. He never complained, and when there was trouble, he took no part in it. At staff meetings he had nothing to say. He kept what he thought for *The Bureaucrat*, his satirical play on the Branch. In it a committee, chaired by the Director himself, agreed 'that the use of the dash in place of the semicolon was a practice that would have to be stamped out.'[28] Baxter did not attend office parties nor enter into the small talk of a publishing house. Colleagues found him pleasant but rather abstracted. One, who used to read to Macmillan Brown when the old professor's eyesight was failing, noticed in Baxter the same kind of remoteness from ordinary life. Like his grandfather, he was wrapped up in his own thoughts.

While the Branch was in Willis Street, Baxter's neighbour was Antony Alpers, the biographer of Katherine Mansfield. After reading Alpers' life of Mansfield, published in 1953, Baxter remarked with a sly grin: 'You thought you could have done better than Murry, didn't you?' Alpers found that in his professional judgements Baxter could put his finger easily and lightly on the essential point.

Baxter continued with his own writing. On 7 November 1962 he told his mother that he had recently written a series of prose sketches, which became the novel *Horse*. A month earlier he had described it as a tragi-comic novel with a certain element of 'self-portrait', and said that he intended salting it away for a bit.[29] The hero was 'my Pig Island version of natural man, that is, in theological terms, the fallen Adam who remembers, as if in a dream, his first state.'[30] There is more of the comprehensively fallen Adam in the book than of Eden. The dominant influence is clearly Dylan Thomas's *Adventures in the Skin Trade*, to which both the language and the outrageous situations are indebted. Baxter had reviewed the book for the *N.Z. Listener* in 1956.[31] The title *Horse* may well have been suggested by Jung. For him, the horse is an archetype of the unconscious side of the human psyche, and of 'the lower part of the body and the animal drives that take their rise from there.'[32] Baxter described his book as 'unpublishable', and indeed it wasn't published until thirteen years after his death. It is a convenient introduction to the world of Baxter 'the roaring boy', and it anticipates the concerns of *Pig Island Letters*.

Baxter resigned from School Publications on 27 March 1963, after thinking about it for some time. As early as 9 February 1962 he had told John Weir: '. . . I am tired of lending my brain to Caesar and having it returned fagged and filthy . . . now it seems he (God) requires a better thing – that I should sell only my labour, not my brain, in the urban brothel, and be free to look on the faces of other men and praise Him when I so desire . . .'[33] From that point on, his shifts in direction were to be interpreted as the will of God, and he tended to consign areas he had once inhabited to the City of Destruction. Whatever else the School Publications Branch of his day was, it was hardly a centre of godlessness, and after all, he had become a Catholic while he was there. But he was writing to a priest, and he was always very conscious of his audience.

A senior official in the Department of Education remarked, on learning of Baxter's resignation from the Branch: 'I shudder to think how much it cost the tax-payer for every line Jim Baxter edited.' The Chief Editor, who knew better, wrote in a testimonial that he was a first-rate editor and that some of the bulletins he wrote were unique.[34] On 11 March 1963, Baxter commenced duties as a postman on the permanent staff of the New Zealand Post Office, Wellington. The duties of his new job were simple and clearly defined, and they could be fulfilled without any sense of personal compromise. He said it was the work he liked best. As a postman he had plenty of time to think, to compose poems, and even to pray. It was outside work, he enjoyed walking, and it kept him fit. With typical romanticism, he imagined that he resembled Robert Burns following the plough.

Baxter reported to the old Post Office in Featherston Street at seven o'clock each morning and sorted the mail in his box according to streets. He worked in the large sorting-room with some fifty other posties. Conversation was lively. Baxter was notable for his resonant voice and the point of his contributions. And he used the full range of the dialect of the tribe. One postie, a man of some education, described him as one of the most brilliantly obscene people he had ever known.

The posties of that period were an extraordinary bunch of people. Several were young university graduates at a similar stage of personal development: Robert Oliver became a musician, Arthur Everard a film-maker and film censor, Ian Macdonald was to be a Mozart Fellow in music, and Alan Lonie a poet and publisher. Becoming a postie was their way of rebelling against society's expectations. With few intellectual pretensions they could accept the valuation which placed them at the bottom of the Post Office's hierarchy. Their chief concern was to find a sense of direction in their own lives and what they had in common with others. They were all reading Jung, whose language became for them a kind of lingua franca.

Baxter was regarded as an inspiring mentor who had lived through experiences they hardly knew about. It was possible to discuss any topic with him without embarrassment; he could articulate with marvellous precision their problems and aspirations, and he knew Jung well. The fact that he had no ready-made answers attracted them because it meant they did not have to make any commitment. One person compared Baxter to a good confessor who understood others because he knew himself so well, even his own fears and pusillanimity.

Baxter was well liked throughout the Post Office. His seniors admired his intelligence and were proud to have on the staff a well-known writer who was also a university graduate. Despite his distinction, workmates found him remarkably free from intellectual snobbery and he would talk to anybody. He would stop acquaintances in the street, invite them into a coffee bar, and plunge into a lengthy monologue. At times his voice dropped so low it could hardly be heard, then suddenly he would get up and walk away. He had clarified his ideas. He needed an audience more than he needed friends. Peter Bland, a poet and actor, knew Baxter well between 1958 and 1965. He believed the monologues were part of Baxter's sense of isolation, and of his need to communicate with a sympathetic listener. 'He loved an audience not because of the actor in him, but because of the prisoner in him, or even the impassioned priest.'[35] He thought Baxter lacked tact and could be very naïve, but he did not consider him 'big-headed'.

Each postal district is divided into walks, and over a period of time a postie works in several. The poem 'Postman' refers to Walk Seven in the hilly Wellington suburb of Khandallah. The roads 'built for the helicopter/ or bullock dray' made the going strenuous. But the hills, the valleys, the occasional glimpse of the harbour, made the walk attractive, especially when it was fine and there was no wind. Dogs, a well-known hazard for posties, nipped at his heels 'from paranoid love'. He wrote in one of his popular ballads:

> There's the heave and the drag, the weight of the swag,
> The kids that yell out as you pass,
> And a bloody great big boxer dog
> With his nose stuck up your arse.[36]

He made friends with one dog by giving it food. It used to trot along beside him and keep other dogs at their distance. With residents Baxter was always ready to pass the time of day. But obviously he lived in a world of his own.

Normally the mail arrived around ten o'clock in the morning, or by one o'clock at the latest. When Baxter was on the walk it rarely arrived earlier than three. Once it was delivered early enough for a householder to comment. He simply replied: 'Today I started from the other end.' One woman remembered seeing him sitting under a tree gazing into space with the mail-bag beside him. There is some truth in Maurice Shadbolt's characterization of Baxter as the most distinguished and dilatory postman Wellington has ever known.[37] But he was conscientious. Once he was observed doubling back to deliver a letter he had overlooked when he could easily have taken it back to the Post Office with other undelivered mail, as happened with registered letters when the householders were out, to be delivered the following day. Circulars were another matter. They had, of course, been paid for like any other mail. But their weight and apparent irrelevance were resented by many posties, and sometimes Baxter did not deliver them.

Before joining the Post Office he had toyed with the idea of taking a job on the wharves because he wanted to understand militant unionism:

'probably the most powerful single force of this time.'[38] He got his chance to understand it during the Soap Powder Lock-Out of July 1963. Lever Brothers had arranged to send through the mail free samples of Surf soap powder. Each sample weighed eight ounces and a postie had to deliver fifty samples. This meant an extra hour's work a day without any further remuneration. Most posties refused to deliver it. As Baxter put it in his unpublished 'Ballad of the Soap Powder Lock-Out':

> Ten thousand quid to the G.P.O.
> And never a bob to us.
> And a leaning tower of Surf soap powder
> To carry from house to house.[39]

The Chief Postmaster, Mr P. H. Lewis, argued the samples fell within the regulations governing mail and must be delivered. Those who refused were deemed to have 'voluntarily terminated their own services'. The posties felt let down by the Post Office Association, which said no progress could be made until the posties resumed work and delivered the samples. Meantime their work was done by volunteers from other parts of the Post Office and by outsiders.

On 23 July the week-old dispute ended with a compromise. A van would take the soap powder to the walks and the posties would deliver it after their normal deliveries. The authorities gave an assurance that the postal regulations would be re-examined. The dispute took place within four months of Baxter's joining the Post Office. The way he comported himself during the lock-out established him as a person who could be trusted. He was not an official spokesman in the lock-out, but he had supported his fellow-workers by word and example. His ballad was well received. His letters spoke of the excitement of fighting for decent working conditions when you knew you could be sacked at any moment.

He was heartened to find how the pressure exerted by employers moulded ordinary men and women into a group with one mind and heart. He had never seen that happen before. When it was over he felt 'proud to wear the clown's coat, this uniform', as he remembered the names of his fellow workers in the struggle, and how they were able '. . . to make the sharing of a meat roll or a cigarette an act of love and to avoid the short circuit of anger at the personal opponent.'

The support the posties received from the general public encouraged him: 'the housewives look on their postman as Santa Claus – subconsciously – they like you for air-mail letters and blame you for bills, as if you had the power to determine which they'd get. So when Santa Claus is getting a raw deal, they sympathize with him.'[40] He felt that politically he thought as a unionist and wanted to see every factory in the country run by a syndicate of workers. Two months earlier he had articulated his views at some length:

> The man who works on the emery wheel, making stoves, feels, among 1,000 dissatisfactions and deprivations, one source of joy – the love of his cobbers on the job, a profoundly actual & humorous love, bound up with a common sense of *dispossession* – all wage-earners are, via their ancestors, dispossessed hunters or peasants. But the Boss chooses *private* possessions, instead of the goal of communal re-possession — however difficult and unlikely this may be . . . An industrial union is a group which expresses the solidarity of the dispossessed. The Boss can't enter this — or those who think like the Boss — his office staff — because they have chosen a different road. Many many times I have been healed by the love of my workmates — who did not basically care greatly about profit or efficiency — when I was sad or sick . . .
>
> Do you understand this? It is not 'Marxist' or 'Red-fed' — it is a certain kind of love . . . this love is a v. good thing, even if unions are at times unjust in their way of getting better pay or better conditions. Men rarely strike for more money, in fact, anyway — they strike because the old sense of dispossession has flared up again. So I understand and sympathize with the Commos v. much indeed, though their philosophy is truncated, since they imagine they can love men well without a God to give them the strength for this magnificent, terrible task.[41]

This letter defines Baxter's attitude to the politics of industrial relations. He was always concerned with ideals, not with strategies for action, and the religious terms in which the workers' struggle is expressed are love, dispossession, the notion of a broken community. The letter also explains that sympathy with Communism which occasionally emerges in his writings, and makes it plain why he could never embrace it. Employers doubtless number among their ancestors as many dispossessed hunters and peasants as their employees. But Baxter's insight into the sense of dispossession is both original and psychologically plausible. It was a fresh statement of the doctrine of Original Sin. His belief in love as the true basis of solidarity was to remain central. Despite his involvement in the Soap Powder Lock-Out Baxter still felt uncomfortable with working people. He had earlier expressed some of these feelings in the poem 'Letter to Noel Ginn II' (CP 70-2).

The most substantial poems from Baxter's three years as a postman formed the sequence 'Pig Island Letters', written during September and October 1963. 'Pig Island' is a vernacular term for New Zealand and carries satirical overtones. The sequence was dedicated to his friend, Maurice Shadbolt, holder of the Burns Fellowship in Dunedin in 1963. The poems were prompted by a letter Shadbolt had written to Baxter expressing an acute sense of mental and spiritual depression at the apparent failure of his creative powers. What he said spoke clearly to Baxter's condition. For both men 'the easy dishonesties we all have in the twenties' had by now been 'drilled out by pain.'⁴² As a close friend he could speak honestly; his 'old cobber and co-worker in the mines of Venus' deserved whatever he had on his plate. Baxter acknowledged that he was troubled by the same failure of creative vitality as his friend and he interpreted it as a foreshadowing of death.

> The gap you speak of – yes, I find it so,
> The menopause of the mind. I think of it
> As a little death, practising for the greater,
> For the undertaker who won't have read
> Your stories or my verse –
> Or that a self had died
> Who handled ideas like bombs,
>
> (CP 276)

The menopause is a crisis of middle age, yet in 1961 Baxter was only thirty-five and Shadbolt six years younger. The stance adopted in the sequence is that of a man wistfully regarding his youth and taking stock.

The notion of the 'gap' is crucial to the later Baxter:

> Talking of the gap – I think I had to be prepared to tear off the bandages, not use the poems as bandages, admit the hollow centre to which writing or psychoanalysis inevitably leads one, and make an act of trust in . . . something, someone, quite unknown whose image is the wound and the darkness itself — the Higher Power of A.A., or the Crucified One — but still in a sense unknowable. I mean, very roughly — *The ikons had to go.* Does this make sense? It is useless perhaps to anyone else. But it is a shift away from the aesthetic patterning, so dangerous to artists because it leads to idolatry of the work. The blind, the deaf, the dumb, are one's closest companions from then on. But you will play it your own way, no doubt. The gap is the place where a new self is able to be born. All one can do is to avoid hindering the growth of this strange embryo.⁴³

Poetry had been the centre of his life, almost the god he worshipped. But it had concealed from him his personal destitution. Like his alcoholism, it had wrapped him in a world of illusion. That kind of poetry with its elaborate art would have to go. Having arrived at so piercing an awareness, Baxter felt obliged to follow the new realism initiated with *Pig Island Letters*, which was to reach its flowering in the late poetry. But the wisdom learnt from his previous experience must not be lost. *Pig Island Letters* shows Baxter distilling it. The concern for the 'something, someone, quite unknown whose image is the wound and the darkness itself', which would make the necessary changes in his life possible, accounts for the strong religious dimension in the volume. Baxter said that the first Letter was 'about Dunedin, saying more

▲ James and Archibald Baxter at Brighton, 1968. *New Zealand Tablet*
▼ Baxter on his postman's round, Khandallah, 1965. *Evening Post*

▼ Brighton. *Lloyd Godman* ▶

◀ Baxter reading in the Anglican Cathedral, Christchurch 1968. *New Zealand Tablet*

▲ Portrait by Els Noordhof. *Patric Carey*

▲ Scene from the play *The Temptations of Oedipus*, a Globe Theatre production, April 1970. The set and costumes were designed by Ralph Hotere. *Michael Hitchings, Hocken*

▼ A room in the commune at Boyle Crescent. *Private Collection*

▲ Baxter in his Jerusalem period, *c.* 1969 *Michael King*

▲ Baxter addressing a group of students, May 1972. *Ans Westra*

▲ Baxter at Impulse '72 in Dunedin, 30 July 1972. *Otago Daily Times*

▲ Baxter with Jean Tuwhare the day he died, Sunday 22 October, 1972. *Private Collection*

▲ The funeral at Jerusalem, 1972. *Evening Post*

or less – it's a hell of a place to be in, but perhaps we are most ourselves in the jaws of death and hell.'[44] Another line from the first Letter: 'Wives in the kitchen cease to smile as we go/Into the gap itself . . .' extends the meaning of the 'gap' to include death, and indicates Baxter's awareness that even in dying he would be creating a spectacle.

For a person of Baxter's sensitivity, a social malaise could be experienced as a personal malady. And it was diagnosed in the second Letter as a sickness of the heart:

> From an old house shaded with macrocarpas
> Rises my malady.
> Love is not valued much in Pig Island
> Though we admire its walking parody.
>
> (CP 277)

The poem concludes:

> The man who talks to the masters of Pig Island
> About the love they dread
> Plaits ropes of sand, yet I was born among them
> And will lie some day with their dead.

However frustrating the role of social prophet, he felt driven to assume that mantle. Since a prophet will not be credible unless his own life is in order, the third Letter rehearses his own history of loving. After dismissing his adolescent fantasies he continues:

> In a room where the wind clattered the blind-cord
> In the bed of a girl with long plaits
> I found the point of entry,
> The place where father Adam died.
>
> (CP 278)

The serpent in Genesis presented the act of eating the fruit of the tree of good and evil as the way to all knowledge.

Baxter saw clearly the consequences of what Calvin made of the Fall. It is not good to be yourself if the self is depraved. Personal freedom is suspect, for a corrupt self cannot be trusted with self-determination. Finding no solid foundation within a person on which to build, Calvinism had to look to what was external, and placed its trust in institutions, 'as if these could eradicate turbulence of the passions and put in their place an abstract social benevolence.'[45] For Baxter, institutions were external signs of the Puritan denial of freedom and individuality. And they fostered Puritanism's besetting sin of acedia, which subsumed torpidity, lack of joy, and purpose in life.

When Baxter analysed New Zealand Puritanism, he nearly always fastened on its view of the total depravity of the flesh and its severity towards sexual deviations. Even its literary judgements were likely to confuse the knowledge of the actions of fallen humanity with the acts themselves. A writer who presents aberrations is resented as much as if he had actually been guilty of them. In the third Letter, sexual experience leads to a wisdom not found in his reading. Sex and death are linked, as they are elsewhere in Baxter's writings. In his essay 'The Virgin and the Temptress', from the first half of 1966, he wrote: '. . . to "die" signifies in folk tradition the sexual act.'[46]

In 'Henley Pub' Baxter explored that connection. He told Archie:

It is the Samson and Delilah story in modern dress. A heavy-drinking Catholic commercial traveller, not young, is considering suicide in the bar room of the Henley Pub. This, if you like, is the blindness of Samson about to pull down the world on his head. He remembers his mistress in Dunedin whom he can neither live with nor without . . .
The poem swings between those two great poles of Catholic manhood — the image of the Blessed Virgin (the created world redeemed) and the image of woman seen as the Temptress (nature unredeemed) — no doubt it shouldn't be so. Catholic men should see women as their sisters and co-heirs in salvation, but in Chaucer and Villon and old Dunbar — and in the mind of a modern Irish drunk — the two poles remain separate and standing.[47]

Baxter said that the core of the poem was that people look for something other than mere pleasure in their sensual failings; they look perhaps for 'God's beauty locked in the creation.' The disparagement of women implicit in the notion of temptress made Baxter wary of using the image without modification, because it continued 'a traditional masculine bias against the sexuality of women with which I have little sympathy.'[48] Even the image of Mary as 'the created world redeemed' had to be handled carefully if her womanhood was not to be reduced to a merely static role.

Nor was any symbolism taboo to him if he judged it suited his poetic purpose. In 'The Waves', for example, written in 1963, he had presented the moon as the

. . . horned and processional
Goddess of sexual pain
Who kills the mandrake I.
(CP 287)

Baxter said he also had in mind the Indian goddess Mara, whose necklace was a chain of skulls. The moon is a malevolent huntress whose poisoned arrows could transmogrify him into a monstrous shape, just as Circe once transformed the sailors of Odysseus. And the only woman capable of protecting the poet is blamed as too 'curbed by gentility' to stir. The moon image may show that he was never really comfortable with strong women. Perhaps he feared his susceptibility to their sexuality would allow them to threaten his independence. The White Goddess of Robert Graves attracted him by her beauty and her promise of romantic love, but whenever she appeared he was conscious that she was leaning on her flawless Cretan axe.

In any discussion of Baxter's treatment of women it has to be remembered that he wrote out of a literary tradition which cast women in many roles, including some which anger our contemporaries. Since he was a confessional poet his own experience entered whatever he wrote. His lifelong aspiration as a true romantic was to find

> the voice of one
> Pure waterfall among the boulders
> In the high bush, pouring light on him,
> Or a woman's moon-bright, saving face,
> (CP 228)

When he seemed to find it, he ached for 'the dream behind the dream', to be 'expert beyond experience'. Romanticism had yielded to the harsher realities of marriage, and when he was licking his wounds he could be severe. But it would be extreme to call Baxter a misogynist. He said in a poem as late as 1972:

> To the grass of the graveyard or a woman's breast
> We turn in our pain for absolution.
> (CP 545)

And he did not necessarily regard death as destructive, but as 'the one door out of the labyrinth'. He had a record of consistent encouragement and support for women writers, as shown by his published lectures and private correspondence. And he saw, too, what is now widely recognized: 'It is the woman inside a man who communicates best with women.'[49]

In an unpublished prose fragment he spoke of the years he had spent in the wars of Venus. He expanded on this to John Weir: 'I carry a mass of scars from such attachments – not wished for, but wished on me – and if I had been more prudent I'd have fewer of them. Some are inevitable from being in the world at all.'[50]

Possibly the 'mass of scars' came from his tendency to idealize women. From all accounts he had no real difficulty in relating to women. Yet his habit of mentally separating them from reality and confining them to the realms of his imagination made relationships difficult to sustain. He imposed a burden of expectations on women which they were often unable or unwilling to meet.

Like the woman in 'Henley Pub', Jane Aylmer had lived in a flat in Royal Terrace. But Baxter indignantly rejected any suggestion that the poem was autobiographical. He admitted to his father that he had not been free 'of the faults of the flesh' and that affected the themes that he chose, but the poem was strictly dramatic. He no more had a mistress in Dunedin or anywhere else 'than Burns *himself saw* the witches dance in Kirk Alloway.'[51] Baxter thought 'Henley Pub' was one of the best poems he had written, though few have shared his opinion.

To those who considered him anti-sexual he responded that the 'romantic vitalists (as I once was) want to be told that sex is in itself a source of spiritual life. My own position is more a middle one: that in some circumstances sex helps us, in some circumstances hinders us . . . Mind you, sex and sexual intercourse are two separate things.'[52] In Baxter's writings sex is presented more often as hindering human development. This attitude stems partly from its connection in his mind with death, partly from the frustration he felt in failing to achieve his own personal sexual integration. What he wrote on the matter was often in reaction to the kind of negative experiences he had had in the 1950s.

Looking back at an earlier self is a recurring strategy in Baxter's poetry. He had a strong sense of the *Doppelgänger*, which incorporated for him his multiple selves. To them he adds the mythic presences in his imagination, Odysseus, or the satyr Marsyas, the manbeast in the ninth Pig Island Letter. Marsyas, a flute-player flayed alive by Apollo, is an image of the artist. None of these selves is rejected, all cohabit Baxter's consciousness on their own terms. They are like a company of actors inside the one skin.[53] Their inherent incompatibility gives the verse its tension and, since reality itself is ambiguous, a sense of actuality. Baxter's growth as a person was towards a full acceptance of his whole self. What made that possible was the goodness he perceived in each of its manifestations, however defaced by moral failures. For example, the Bohemian of the sixth Letter, who learnt 'the tricks of water/From the boathouse keeper's daughter' in the fifth, preserves authentic human values even in his lechery: 'The hope of the body was coherent love', and 'a belief in bodily truth rising/From fountains of Bohemia and the night.' The poem is a defence of one of Baxter's earlier selves. Even 'the love that heals like a crooked limb' points to what true love might be. In such terms alcoholism itself, so destructive in Baxter's life, could be seen as 'the winter of beginning'. Frequently the contemplation of the earlier self is shadowed by regret for what has been lost. In the sixth

Letter he quotes Fairburn: ' "No/Words make up for what we had in youth" ', but adds, with his deeper sense of loss, 'For what we did not have'.

In the ninth Letter, Baxter's *Doppelgänger* was given a profounder and more original significance:

> Look at the simple caption of success,
> The poet as family man,
> Head between thumbs at mass, nailing a trolley,
> Letting the tomcat in:
> Then turn the hourglass over, find the other
> Convict self, incorrigible, scarred
> With what the bottle and the sex games taught,
> The black triangle, the whips of sin.
> The first gets all his meat from the skull-faced twin,
> Sharpening a dagger out of a spoon,
> Struggling to speak through the gags of a poem:
> When both can make a third my work is done.
>
> (CP 282)

In this passage Baxter has dramatized the conflicting elements in human nature as two selves. One is the conventional self which does its duty to God and family. The other is human nature seen as fallen, the Bohemian, the rebel. Jung described it as the shadow side of our nature. Either self alone is only half a person because 'each turns away from some essential aspect of life.'[54] To achieve wholeness the poet must marry the goodness and idealism of the one to the strength and vitality of the other. The self is the matrix of art and must be accepted completely, but the source of creativity is the rebellious energy of fallen humanity. This 'enlarges our order by breaking it and allowing it to re-form in another pattern.'[55] This idea is prominent in *The Fire and the Anvil* and *Aspects of Poetry in New Zealand*. There Baxter often referred to the 'disturbing elements' in an artist's personality as the impulse for creative writing, and as an important part of its material. Acceptance or rejection of these elements is a criterion Baxter used in his literary criticism. He could understand why Katherine Mansfield left New Zealand because in the social climate at the turn of the nineteenth century: 'We could not have provided her with the tools of her trade – intellectual maturity and the courage to commit to paper what she had painfully learned of intimate human relationships.'[56]

When Baxter spoke of the disturbing elements in our personality he nearly always meant sexual elements. What inhibited our writers from exploiting them was the 'austere anti-aesthetic angel of Puritanism'.[57] By Puritanism he meant secularized Calvinism. He had reacted against it from his early days in Otago where he considered it all-pervasive. Dunedin was 'Calvin's town'.[58] In 'Notes on the Education of a New Zealand Poet' he wrote of 'the Calvinist ethos which underlies our determinedly secular culture like the bones of a dinosaur buried in a suburban garden plot . . .'[59] At the heart of the Calvinist ethos was Calvin's teaching 'that the Fall is absolute and the natural man totally depraved.'[60] Baxter could not accept that. In his Catholic theology 'the Fall was not complete, and the natural man, though wounded, is still the earth lamp who holds the oil of grace.'[61] The technical theological term 'natural man' stands for our common humanity after the Fall. Baxter sometimes used it to mean the fallen elements in our humanity, as when he speaks of the 'convict self'. 'Wounded' refers to the flawed condition mankind has inherited as a result of Original Sin. That includes a darkened intellect, which makes it difficult to see what is right, and a will that is often reluctant to choose what it ought, because it is troubled by passions no longer under its control.

The fallen man within him, the convict self, was so passionately accepted that it is one of the most important forms of Baxter's *Doppelgänger*. To apply the term to his work is not arbitrary. He used it himself in a letter the year before *Pig Island Letters* was published: '. . . each man's adolescent *Doppelganger* who hangs round his neck and judges him for having got older and colder.'[62] And he offered further psychological grounds for the concept by saying that when he played the alcoholic doctor in Chekhov's *Three Sisters*, he had tried 'to find that subconscious area in myself which corresponded most nearly to the segment of Tchekov's subconscious mind which is the doctor.'[63] Puritanism exalted the rational and distrusted the instinctive because its imagination was dialectical. Baxter's imagination was analogical. That is why his writing, even his conversation, abounded in images. He often noted the correspondences between things and responded to the revelatory power of the natural world. The hidden, the unconscious, all that escaped the net of intellect, became his special concern. In his buried self he looked for the meaning of his life. From its depths he hoped to bring to the surface 'a kind of sub-conscious wisdom'. To do that he relied on the symbol, and on that extended symbol which is myth. The symbol is 'a door opening upon the dark – upon a world of intuitions and associations of which the poet himself is hardly conscious.' And it offered experiential knowledge, not merely conceptual knowledge.

The importance of myth was that poetry of its very nature is mythical: 'it presents the crises, violations, and reconciliations of the spiritual life in mythical form because this is the only way in which the conscious mind can assimilate them.' An earlier poem like 'The Homecoming' illustrates Baxter's handling of formal myth. But he used the word 'myth' in a very broad sense. When he wrote: 'What happens is either meaningless to me, or else it is mythology',[64] he meant that myth was a way of ordering his experience of a world which he encountered as chaos, the disordered world resulting from the Fall. Within every event, every circumstance, lay a significance that the imagination could discover. The fiction of a poem gave it form, so each poem became part of the mythologizing process. The body of Baxter's poetry illustrates his mythopoeic imagination endeavouring to give shape and meaning to his life. That is why John Weir observed that the poetry 'becomes a substitute for an autobiography'.[65] Since myth for Baxter was a verbal construct giving shape to his perceptions, the challenge was to get as close as possible to the chaos of experience. The poet does not reject it nor hold himself aloof. His poem '. . . gives it a form. It gets as near as possible. It has a great respect for this Chaos, this potential, and doesn't try to mutilate it, and it tries to hold up a mirror to it. And then the poem has strength because it is true.'[66] In his best poems Baxter himself has this fidelity to the truth of his experience. As I have written elsewhere: 'I think of him as a good bull-fighter who works very close to the bull. The reality against which he pits his skill is often disturbing, sometimes dangerous, but he keeps close to it bent on the moment of truth.'[67]

A notable comment on Baxter's view of the nature of poetry at this period concludes the ninth Pig Island Letter: 'The poem is/A plank laid over the lion's den' (CP 282). A biblical passage he used as a master symbol for the opening of a play *Mr Brandywine Chooses a Gravestone* clarifies his meaning: 'So the king ordered Daniel to be brought and cast into the lion's den. To Daniel he said, "May your God, whom you serve so constantly, save you". To forestall any tampering, the King sealed with his own ring and the rings of the lords the stone that had been brought to block the opening of the den . . .'[68] The intention of the play, Baxter said, was to present the situation of a quite ordinary man who finds that he must soon die.[69] A central meaning of the lion's den is obviously death, but it also refers to the destructive forces at work in every life. When Baxter was asked by John Weir in May 1971 to comment on the lines, he replied: 'One has to be pretty close to the fire, I think, pretty close to the position of Chaos . . . The nearer you are to it and can survive the better. One critic of my verse, a sympathetic critic, said that I was like a man who worked very close to the bull, a bull-fighter. You almost get grazed by the horns. Perhaps you do. Perhaps the blood is helpful that goes into the poem. But this is just as *man*: one is not doing this as propagandist or anything like that.'[70] Elsewhere he suggested it is in 'the jaws of death and hell' that the poet expresses himself most truthfully.[71] Certainly for many people, he spoke most truly in his poetry when he was crossing the plank over the lion's den.

When *Pig Island Letters* was published in 1966 it was widely acclaimed. The Australian poet and critic, Vincent Buckley, wrote to Baxter from Cambridge to say that he thought it a triumph, and that he had been especially impressed by the 'fluidity of movement together with such precision of feeling' in the syllabics of the third section of the volume.[72] Baxter himself felt it likely he would not write as well again, partly because of the labour involved, partly because poetry is 'something given us, and that may well not recur'.[73]

The last poem in *Pig Island Letters* was an elegy for Bob Lowry, who had died in December 1963. He was aged fifty-one. Baxter, perhaps the greatest of the artists he befriended, wrote: '. . . he lived without social ambition, without money, not concerned with the big names and big ideas, and so the country spoke through him like the breath blown through a flute.'[74] And he provided his epitaph:

> The grass grows long at Waikumete,
> The ink has dried on the printing stone.
> Take no notice, Bob;
> All things burn.
>
> (CP 296)

Jacquie's mother died on 22 August 1963 after spending her last days in the Baxter house at Collingwood Street. Baxter, who was present when she died, felt 'no fear or grief', only 'an awe which has pierced very deep'. Though his mother-in-law had no time for priests, nor for Catholics, throughout her life she had become close to a number of them. Baxter was one. They developed a deep affection for each other, though neither budged an inch in their beliefs. The relationship was a source of great satisfaction to Jacquie who was devoted to her mother. The death brought the couple closer together and Jacquie found Baxter a great comfort. She experienced the empathy that she knew he had often shown towards others in trouble. For his part, he felt she had helped him to see his own parents more clearly. He wrote to them: 'She teaches me who I am', and added: 'I know I have often wounded you in my struggle to become whatever I am intended to be. I regret this. You are my dear ones.' He assured them that he loved them: 'It has always been so and it will always be so.'[75]

Baxter's parents were planning to follow his example and become Catholics. When Archie was in the Mater Hospital in Dunedin recovering from an eye operation, he met the chaplain, Father Stuart Sellar. Archie expressed a desire to learn more about Catholicism and invited the priest to visit him at Brighton. He expected to be able to see him on his own as he did not think Millicent would be interested. To his surprise, Millicent had reached the same point herself. A formal course of instruction in Catholicism began. Archie's responses to instruction were intuitive. Many things were immediately clear and sat comfortably with what he already believed. For Millicent, everything had to be logical.

They were both baptized at St Peter Chanel Church, Green Island, on 3 July 1965. Archie added the name Francis in honour of Francis of Assisi, Millicent took John after Pope John XXIII whose work for peace she greatly admired. Millicent was seventy-seven, her husband eighty-four. James was one of the official witnesses. His parents' conversion had been 'a wholly unexpected gift'. He had hardly even prayed that it would happen, though he had prayed for their general spiritual welfare. Yet he had felt sad to see them grow old and have to endure the failure of their natural powers without the full hope and joy and clarity that could come from the possession of the faith.[76] When Archie and Millicent were confirmed on 15 August the same year, Millicent took for her confirmation name Clare in honour of St Clare, the close friend of St Francis of Assisi. Archie chose Giles, one of Francis's first companions and a man who appears frequently in *The Little Flowers of St Francis*. James was a sponsor and Terence was also present.

Millicent and Archie told James that while they were receiving instruction from Father Sellar his letters to them had been a great help. Now five days after their baptism he wrote to say that their reception into the Church meant a re-arrangement of his own views and a revaluing of his own faith. He warned them not to be discouraged by the bad example of some of the Catholics they would meet 'who are not just weak, imperfect, imperceptive – we're all of us that – but actually lead horrifying lives – are obviously cruel, lustful, avaricious, opinionated, and so on.' They must remember that the Church is the Church of sinners as well as of saints. His experience was that 'The Protestant Churches tend to be an élite – on the whole those who are fighting God get out of them – but in the Church on the whole they stay – and often at last achieve a stable repentance.' To support his advice he quoted from his Indian experience an incident that greatly appealed to him. An Indian friend who was scandalized by the life of a fellow parishioner said to his priest:

> Look, this man goes to Confession on Saturday and to Mass on Sunday, and then he spends the week in the drinking shops and brothels – how can this be?' And the priest said — 'You can't judge him. Maybe the Lord has set him within this circle as if within a jail yard. Maybe this is the road he has to travel to Heaven.' He meant, I suppose: 'sin also is a mystery — or else, some things that appear sin are actually affliction.
>
> But in the main I am always struck and humbled by the goodness of our fellow–Catholics. And certainly the Church is the mother of the greatest saints.

Looking back on their period of instruction, Millicent remarked to her son: 'Father Sellar thought your father a mystic and your mother a metaphysician.' She considered she was in fact merely practical.[77] In a letter to his mother, Baxter recorded his father's feelings when he entered the

Church: 'I'll say just one thing — it's good to know at last what it's all about.'[78]

Baxter served as one of the two P.E.N. nominees on the New Zealand State Literary Fund Advisory Committee from 1961 to 1964. His fellow members were Professor I. A. Gordon (Chairman), Professor J. C. Garrett, Professor E. M. Blaiklock, Dr Margaret Dalziel, and the other P.E.N. nominee, Monte Holcroft. Late in 1963 there was a celebrated row over certain poems Louis Johnson wished to include in the 1964 issue of the *New Zealand Poetry Yearbook*. Two of them were poems by Baxter, 'Henley Pub', and 'The Girl in Yellow Jeans'. Both were later discussed in *The Man on the Horse*.[79] The Committee could not accept the poem in an anthology to be sponsored by public money. Some members considered them pornographic; some just unsuitable; Margaret Dalziel 'left the Committee for good because she thought the controversy nonsensical.'[80] During the discussion Baxter was very forthright, claiming that the committee had no right to touch the words. They were not watchdogs of public morality, but simply people appointed to make literary judgements. His argument was that if the poems were good they would survive, if not they would sink. The rest of the Committee was embarrassed to be lectured at in that way, and one observed that he always had something of the preacher about him. (His grandfather, Macmillan Brown, had once had aspirations to the pulpit.) The Committee decided against the grant. Baxter's first reaction was to resign. He was a writers' representative and the Committee's decision seemed damaging to their interests. In his experience 'works of art are commonly generated by a tension between an artist's vision of life and the social norms of his generation. Without this tension the salt is lacking.'[81] He also believed there were readers 'prepared to stomach improprieties for the sake of a more truthful and robust literature.'[82] He requested permission to be free to use his gun publicly or privately against what he considered 'muddled principles'. This was allowed. But Johnson's *Poetry Yearbook* series, which had run from 1951, ceased with the publication of the eleventh issue in 1964.

The Vietnam war and the New Zealand Government's decision to send troops gave Baxter an opportunity to take a public stand against war, just as his father and brother had done. Though he was never a member of the Wellington Committee on Vietnam, which was formed on 1 May 1965, he attended some of the early meetings. He was among the group of artists, writers, and musicians who signed a petition published in the *N.Z. Listener* calling for the withdrawal of New Zealand troops. He spoke at a large rally in front of Parliament Buildings, introducing himself as a Catholic, a poet, and a worker. His ballads, 'A Bucket of Blood for a Dollar', and 'The

Gunner's Lament', were printed as broadsheets and distributed at protest meetings. 'A Bucket of Blood for a Dollar' flayed the cynical attitudes of politicians and vigorously presented the view of the protest movement that New Zealand policy was being determined by American economic pressure through capital investments and trade.

Baxter opposed intervention in a civil war and thought the West's involvement was 'a militarist crusade based on naive and irrational premises.'[83] His strenuous opposition was based not on any political analysis, but on pacifist and humanitarian grounds. As he wrote later in 'a death song for mr mouldybroke':

> a white baby fried or a yellow baby fried
> they both look like fried baby to me . . .
> (CP 411)

In October 1965 a poetry reading at the Wellington Library Lecture Hall was used as a form of protest against the war. With Baxter on the platform were Barry Mitcalfe, Louis Johnson, Alistair Campbell, and Peter Bland. Some folk-singers also took part. Poetry readings and ballad singing caught on as a form of protest that was taken up in several other centres. Involvement in the protest movement drew New Zealand writers and artists closer together, making them more aware of their social function in influencing public opinion and government policy. Baxter became a close friend of prominent protesters like Conrad Bollinger, a political writer and activist. And a wider public got to know him as an articulate and courageous spokesman voicing the need for more humanity in public policy. Increasingly during these Wellington years, Baxter conformed himself to the poet's role which he had described some years before: 'to make a cell of good living in a corrupt society'.

XI
City of Our Youth

We ride South on a Wednesday
Into the clearer weather . . .

Down to the city of our youth
(My wife and I) . . .
(CP 366)

'Tired of pounding the Wellington streets on a postman's round', Baxter applied, successfully, for the 1966 Robert Burns Fellowship at the University of Otago. He was given a year's leave of absence from the Post Office. Established in 1958 to commemorate the bicentenary of the birth of Robert Burns and to acknowledge the contribution of the Burns family to the Otago settlement, the Fellowship is 'to encourage and promote imaginative New Zealand literature and to associate writers thereof with the University. It is attached to the Department of English.' A Fellow's obligations are not demanding. They might include some lecturing or seminar work, or a course of not more than six lectures. These are to be confined to one term in the academic year and must not prejudice the Fellow's own writing. A study is provided and the salary is that of a full-time university lecturer. Baxter's predecessors in the Fellowship were Ian Cross, Maurice Duggan, John Caselberg, R.A.K. Mason, Maurice Shadbolt, Maurice Gee, and Janet Frame.

Baxter had returned to Dunedin on a number of occasions since moving to Wellington in 1948. Now he was to reside there again after a lapse of some twenty years. His circumstances had changed greatly. He was a married man with two children, a dried-out alcoholic, and a Roman Catholic. And he was a famous writer. Since his parents, his married brother Terence, the Baxter and McColl relatives, and many friends were in the district, it was a veritable home-coming. It was also a vindication after those earlier failures, personal, moral, and academic. One friend who knew him well recalled that when he came back to Dunedin he was a completely different person. He had a centre to his life and had become 'a quiet, brooding man'. In his fortieth year, he was conscious of those 'changes which one is obliged to face at the beginning of the second half of life.'[1]

The family initially lived at 660 Cumberland Street, in a house owned by the university. Baxter's study – 'a sun-drenched Trappist cell' – was a small room in the south-east corner of the library. One lecturer noticed that two of the few books on his shelves were Robert Lowell's *Life Studies* and *The Merry Muses of Caledonia*, the collection of Burn's obscene poems. Lowell's influence on his poetry was profound, and though the output of obscene poems was not as copious as it had once been, Baxter could still produce one to entertain his friends. The atmosphere of the English Department was friendly and civilized. The demands on a small staff required to teach the whole range of English Language and Literature meant that the lecturers were very busy people. They saw Baxter mainly in the corridors, or at morning or afternoon tea.

His mode of thought was not systematic, and the ideas he loved to float were so wide-ranging that people trained in the rigorous ways of scholarship were often critical. With his fluency, and the leisure of the Fellowship, he was a threat to tight schedules. A senior staff member remarked: 'Any time Jim comes in to tea I'm off because we're in for a long bout of Baxter talk.' Half-way through his first year, Baxter wrote: 'I feel that my relationship to members of the English Department has been wholly amicable and positive.'[2] One man was grateful for the sharply perceptive sympathy he had shown in a time of personal crisis. Some years earlier, the Chairman of the Department, Professor E.A. Horsman, had written a severe review of *The Fire and the Anvil* for *Landfall*. Baxter bore him no resentment and maintained cordial relations. He was never a person to bear grudges. That was part of his humility. Horsman, for his part, accepted Baxter's idiosyncrasies with a reserved tolerance; as Dean of the Faculty of Arts, and as a Chairman who believed in keeping his finger on the pulse of his department, his time was fully occupied. Baxter would often come into his office and begin to talk. After a time Horsman would quietly go on with what he was doing, looking up occasionally as the words flowed on.

Baxter excited Lawrence Jones's Honours students by his engagement with the poetry of Thomas Hardy, which he seemed able to quote at will. When a student attacked the harshness of the prosody, Baxter argued that was intentional and quoted some dozen lines from a little known poem to make his point. His marvellously resonant voice and feeling for rhythm brought out the qualities of whatever he quoted. In the seminar, as in many other contexts, he showed a remarkable capacity for apt and striking images. 'Hardy is like a skilful cabinet-maker, who makes beautiful objects; every detail is perfect, but he refuses to fill the nail-holes – he's not going to hide the kind of work that's gone into it.'[3]

Baxter's reservations about his new position were wryly expressed in 'On Possessing the Burns Fellowship 1966';

> And I who wrote in '62
> *Dear ghosts, let me abandon*
> *What cannot be held against*
> *Hangmen and educators, the city of youth!* –
>
> Drink fresh percolated coffee, lounging
> In the new house, at the flash red kitchen table,
> A Varsity person, with an office
> Just round the corner – what nonsense!
>
> If there is any culture here
> It comes from the black south wind
> Howling above the factories
> A handsbreadth from Antarctica, . . .
>
> (CP 335)

His views were developed according to his own brand of nonsense in *Landfall*: 'The main trouble is of course that the Muse, that primitive and prejudiced old Lady, does not smile on Fellowship holders. Our good morals seem to bore her.'[4] The idea that there is a link between immorality and creativity, picked up perhaps from Dylan Thomas, was something Baxter found easier to assert than to demonstrate. The examples of Milton, Hopkins, and R.S. Thomas among others, would have caused him problems.

Writing Fellows at universities vary greatly in their accessibility. Of all the Burns Fellows up to that time, Baxter was thought to be the most available. Students regularly brought him poems for comment, but he never gave any sign that he felt he was being robbed of his time. He also took part in a poetry discussion group, attended by his daughter, Hilary, Charles Brasch, Ian Fraser, Hal Smith, Bill Manhire, and Trevor Reeves. He would always find something encouraging to say about the offerings, though some felt it would have been better if he had said straight out that a bad poem was bad.

On 27 August Baxter applied successfully for an extension of the Fellowship into a second year. The best comment on his relations with the English Department was that both its representatives on the Selection Committee, one of whom was Horsman, supported him. Baxter's submission indicated how industrious he had been. He had written ninety poems, an output which would normally have taken him about eight months. Their quality persuaded him that he had come to terms with the conditions of the Fellowship, since 'I regard the writing of verse as my central and permanent work.' He had also written six talks, which were 'in the main literary commentaries of a personal and anecdotal kind.'⁵ Two of them had been given to students in the English Department. The talks appeared in *The Man on the Horse*, published by the University of Otago in 1967. The book is of special interest for its biographical detail, the attitudes to literature and belief, and the perceptive and individual reading of Robert Burns's 'Tam O'Shanter'. In the third term of 1966 Baxter proposed concentrating on the editing of Macmillan Brown's memoirs, which were still in manuscript. That project defeated him and it had to be completed by someone else. I doubt if he found his grandfather's writing sufficiently interesting. Travelling had absorbed a good deal of his time, and he had lectured to groups at Invercargill and Alexandra. He also gave an address at the Arts Festival at Massey University which he called 'Shots Around the Target'. Though he felt a strong sense of real communication with the students and with some of the staff, much of what he said was as outrageous as it sounded from his own report in *Landfall*:

> I stood on the platform between the Mayor and the Chancellor, like a frog in a bell-jar, sweating but honest and told the assembled students that Kiwis should smoke a bit of marijuana now and then, that we should hold bullfights instead of flower festivals, that the age of female consent should be lowered to fourteen, and that I was tired of seeing homosexual artists being ridden to death by big ugly stupid homosexual policemen.⁶

More pertinently, he said that the pressures towards conformity faced by women in this country were infinitely greater than they are for men. That for a woman to break the pattern imposed on her takes twenty times as much courage. He proposed Janet Frame, who had escaped a lobotomy at the hands of the bureaucrats, as the prototype of the New Zealand heroine.⁷ Another thing necessary to change New Zealand from an art-killing to an art-fostering place was to repeal 'our present barbarous laws against homosexuals'.⁸

In a university town like Dunedin, the protest movement against the Vietnam war was very active. Baxter quickly became involved. He was the only lay person on a panel which met in the main auditorium of the Otago Museum on 1 May 1966 to discuss the 'Ethics of the Vietnam War'. He was introduced to the packed hall by the Chairman, Professor Smithells, as 'Burns Fellow at the University of Otago, and a well-known New Zealand poet, who is a member of the Roman Catholic Church.'

Baxter began by saying that there was a case for the purely pacifist view, which he himself had held with some difficulty. He recalled the Maori chief who told the Governor-General before the Maori wars: 'The blood of man is sacred. It has been shed too much. We are Christians.' Since that view is not convincing to those who feel their life is threatened, Baxter examined the theory of the just war. He argued that in every war in history each side had considered its cause to be just. Nations must negotiate wherever possible. He quoted Pope Pius XII: 'Annihilation of all human life within the radius of destructive action is not permissible on any account.' And that applied whether the war was aggressive or defensive. Examples were the destruction of human life at Hiroshima and at Dresden, and also some of the German bombing of England. The indiscriminate bombing of North Vietnam was, for Baxter, no different from these atrocities. Obedience to the State was no defence, as the Nuremberg trials had shown. One must follow one's conscience. He concluded by quoting Pope John XXIII, who he believed had done more for peace between the communist and the non-communist world than any other Western man in the past fifty years.[9]

Public demonstrations were considered to be the most effective means of protest. Marches began at the Museum Reserve, and proceeded along George Street to end with an open air rally in the Octagon, on a Friday night. The one held on 20 October 1966 was said to be the first public meeting in the Octagon since the Depression. There were three speakers: Eric Herd, professor of German in the University; Archdeacon Millar, Anglican Vicar General of Dunedin; and Baxter. The speeches were given from the stone platform below the statue of Robert Burns which presides over the Octagon. Baxter assured the crowd of some four hundred that had Burns been alive, he would have been on their side. Whenever he spoke of the Vietnam war, what he said was closely followed, probably due to the characteristic Baxter manner as much as to what he said. He did not speak with passion, but quietly enough for the organizers of the march to ask him to use a microphone. Nor did he use notes, and the general impression was not so much of eloquent speech, as of the testimony of a man who had pondered what he said and was totally committed to it. The pacifist history of his family was well known in Dunedin and added to his authority. But for many, the chief reason for his great appeal was his humanitarianism. He was still regarded with a certain awe because of his standing as a writer.

In 1967 a protest of lesser moment disturbed the quiet tenor of life at the university. The Accommodation Officer had received a letter from a member of the public enquiring if the university approved of students of both sexes sharing flats. Since the question had been raised formally, an answer had to be given. Dr Robin Williams was the Vice-Chancellor of a university which depended a good deal on recruiting students from outside the city, and he believed that the views of parents, as they were represented to him, should be taken into account. With the full support of the University Council, he decided to forbid mixed flatting. The student response was a spectacularly mixed sleep-in at the registry. Baxter's 'A Small Ode on Mixed Flatting', written 'to show that though my gonads were wrapped in steel wire, my mind was still mellow',[10] was tumultuously received when he read it at a packed meeting in the University Union. As a broadsheet it sold well. Some regarded his squib as an abuse of his position as Burns Fellow, and accused him of bringing the university authorities into disrepute. Others thought the whole matter was a farce and that the University Council got what it deserved. In the eyes of the students, Baxter had placed himself firmly on their side.

On 1 August 1967, he took part in the poetry reading in the University Common Room to raise funds for medical aid to Vietnam; two days later he was a speaker in a symposium 'The Church and Human Needs in Vietnam'. This meeting, held in the Red Lecture Theatre of the Medical School, was preceded by a meal of reconciliation at which there were Buddhist and Christian readings. In March 1968, he published an article in *Vietnam Quote & Comment*: 'Is Stupidity a reason for Vietnam policy?' A cluster of Vietnam poems, 'To speak truly', 'The Grand Tour', 'a death song for mr mouldybroke', were written in these years.

Members of the Committee on Vietnam, both in Wellington and Dunedin, believed their activities had restricted New Zealand's involvement in the war. For many, the Prime Minister, Keith Holyoake, was a reluctant ally of the United States. They believed he was able to use the size of the protest movement as an argument against any increase in the number of New Zealand troops. More broadly, the movement contributed to that scrutiny of authority and social values prominent among the young in New Zealand during the sixties and seventies. The general questioning was fomented by television coverage of the Aldermaston marches against nuclear weapons in 1958 and 1959 in England, the student protest in Germany and France, and the hippie communes in the United States. The Vietnam protests also affected Baxter's attitude to the police. Like most New Zealanders he was shocked at their heavy-handed approach during the demonstrations against Marshall Ky's visit to Auckland in January 1967. As C.K. Stead described in his novel *Smith's Dream*, institutional violence lurks just below the surface of New Zealand society.

As a powerful speaker against the Vietnam war, a champion of student rights, and a man who was always available for a yarn or to discuss a poem, Baxter was greatly appreciated by the students. He was a colourful and charismatic leader with the aura of great creative achievement about him. And he was extremely open and in tune with the times. In the tranquil, sheltered environment of the English Department he stood out, as he would have done in any department of a New Zealand university of the sixties. Baxter had now entered a phase of his life when increasingly he was to

213

seek advocates and adversaries. One department felt that his use of coarse language in a lecture they had invited him to give was merely a shock tactic; it was taken as lack of the maturity expected from one of his years. But he knew what he was doing. Even before he took up the Fellowship he had written to a friend: 'One has to watch out for the Varsity boys – the embalming process is over before you can whistle, and there you are with a fixed glassy smile in the mortuary parlour – "Doesn't he look nice? He's almost human . . ."' However perversely, he thought the best insurance was 'to speak bawdy on all occasions, on and off the stage.'[11] The documented knowledge prized in the university was very different from Baxter's sometimes inspired intuitions, and he was occasionally regarded, not without a certain jealousy, as thinking that he knew more than he did.

At the end of the second year of the Burns Fellowship, which by regulation cannot be held for more than two years continuously, Baxter was out of a job. Some members of the university, including at least one Council member, would have liked him to stay in Dunedin, but no suitable employment was available. Bishop Kavanagh, the Catholic Bishop of the Dunedin Diocese, who was also on the University Council, approached Baxter and offered him a position with the Catholic Education Office. He was paid the same living expenses he had received from the Burns and a salary of £1,100. The Bishop told Baxter that the diocese could not afford to pay him for more than one year. His job was to teach English to some upper forms in Catholic schools, to write some articles for *The Tablet*, and to assist Catholic teachers by writing supplementary catechetical material for children in country areas. From his office, a poorly lit and inadequately heated room in the basement of the Moran Building in the Octagon, Baxter produced a substantial quantity of material. He presented religious dilemmas in a way that would stimulate discussion, and his text was enlivened by some striking examples. He also gave some lectures to teachers of the Confraternity of Christian Doctrine.

In the wake of the second Vatican Council, Catholic seminaries were beginning to free up. Outside speakers were sometimes invited. Baxter agreed to give one lecture a week for one term to the students at Holy Cross College, Mosgiel. Already he had given them his lecture, 'Literature and Belief'. One of its supporting poems contains the salutary advice to budding priests:

> That long-haired girl upon the beach
> With her eyes half-shut,
> She'd not be there if I'd not found
> A Venus in the heart,
> And if you frown at her at all

Or make the sign of the cross
You'll turn her from a pretty girl
Into a demoness,
But for all that and all that
She is a good lass.

(CP 338)

From conversation with students of the period, I gather that Baxter did
for them what the novels of Graham Greene did for us in far from spacious
times at the Marist Fathers' Seminary at Greenmeadows. By relating the
abstract principles of theological textbooks to lives spent in a pluralist
society, Baxter fostered a deeper understanding of the complexity of men
and women, and advocated as much humanity as possible in dealing with
them. Predictably, some of the professors were sceptical about Baxter as a
moral guide, and saw his contributions as marginal to the main business of
training priests. He also took a few classes in Catholic secondary schools.
Again the reaction varied. Some thought he could have been used more
extensively, others that he had been wished on them by the Bishop, and both
nuns and parents were protective towards their girls.

At the Catholic Education Office, Baxter was a congenial colleague. He
could also be amusing. Once, a secretary was telling others that although she
had never married, she would have liked to have experienced motherhood.
From the next room came Baxter's resonant voice: 'It can be arranged.'
Occasionally he would read a bawdy poem. One woman considered him
egocentric, since everything seemed to begin and end with him; when they
talked together he seemed to be merely thinking aloud. No response was
required, and there were no gaps in the monologue. It never occurred to him
that a one way conversation might be very boring. Even the Bishop did not
escape. When he was recovering from an illness, Baxter turned up at the
episcopal palace at six in the morning and sat on the edge of the bed talking
for several hours. His Lordship experienced some difficulty in following
Baxter's drift. Millicent was a regular visitor to the Catholic Library,
situated in the same building as the Education Office. She, too, was a
compulsive talker. It was generally agreed that the only person who could
out-talk Baxter was his mother. Baxter talked endlessly at this time about
his alcoholism and how much he missed the camaraderie of the pub. It was
clear to his listeners that entering A.A. had been a real, spiritual experience
and was something of central importance in his life. He also spoke frequently
about his family and his concern for them.

While Baxter was still a Burns Fellow, John Kennedy, editor of the
Catholic weekly, *The Tablet*, had approached him for some articles. He was
pleased with the invitation and replied that he had wanted to write

215

something but had felt diffident about raising the matter. He was about to take a holiday with his family to Stewart Island, but was prepared to do something on his return. Kennedy commissioned a review of the newly published *Jerusalem Bible*, which had appeared on 15 February 1967. Baxter now became a regular contributor with a steady stream of articles on a wide range of topics, devotional, theological, and on issues of the day. He also published a number of poems, one of the best being 'The Infant of Biafra'.

Baxter would often come over from his neighbouring office and have morning tea with *The Tablet* staff. The discussion, which often lasted until lunch-time, was very stimulating as Baxter threw out ideas for an article. It was not unusual for him to reappear that afternoon with the draft, or he might bring the finished article in the next day. Occasionally it took several weeks. His output was so prolific that Kennedy established a file of Baxter articles. Even the old pro was astonished at the speed with which Baxter could produce polished work, and he had the discipline to confine himself to the space allotted. The two men had an excellent working relationship. Kennedy's forthright integrity and courage appealed to Baxter's sense of honesty and justice. When an article needed some changes, the staff were impressed with the humility with which the corrections were usually accepted. If the proposed alteration touched something that Baxter regarded as a matter of principle, he would stand his ground, and then he almost always got his way.

In the troubled period following 1965, the year the second Vatican Council ended, Baxter's articles on aspects of the Catholic faith reassured many readers. He was very much in touch with what his readers were thinking and feeling, and he had a flair for expressing quite complex ideas simply and freshly. Usually he had re-thought the theology for himself, so it was largely free from the repetition of traditional formulas. His devotional articles on Mary tapped the deep veneration Catholics feel towards her.

Baxter was well-informed on recent developments in Catholic thought because of the proximity of the excellent Catholic Library, which had been set up and maintained by Bishop Kavanagh. Since Dunedin is a university town, the Bishop felt a special responsibility to see that members of the university had access to the most up-to-date Catholic material. The Library's special excellence lay in the wide range of international Catholic periodicals. Baxter became familiar with contemporary presentations of the Catholic faith, and with what was being said in disputed matters.

The skills needed to write for a weekly like *The Tablet* were those of good journalism. And as every journalist knows, there simply is not enough time for everything written against deadlines to be equally well-pondered. He said himself: 'I was discovering the Faith as I wrote about it, and that I had managed from time to time to isolate, as it were, certain nodules of

experience where the unconscious influence of the possession of the Faith on
my own life suddenly became more conscious and explicit.'[12] It is unfair to
Baxter to present his thought on religious matters mainly in terms of what
he wrote in *The Tablet*, though some of his contributions were admirable.
Though he might denigrate them in another context (such as 'Letter to Sam
Hunt'), he was sufficiently committed to what he wrote to publish in *the
flowering cross* the selection he himself had made from his *Tablet* articles. But
the book may have been put together in deference to Kennedy. After the
book appeared, Baxter wrote to Weir that its articles 'disgust me, except the
one on Heaven.'[13] Perhaps he thought then they spoke the language of the
Pre-Vatican II church, and he had become aware that a new mentality had
emerged. He also knew the difference between his religious journalism and
his other writings: 'When I write for the *Marist Messenger*, I'm well aware
I'm "lying" in a way I'm not in HENLEY PUB – the latter is my truest
contribution to the Catholic body of experiential knowledge; the former
will of course be much more acceptable, but in particular to the *already
converted*. I feel the Lord desires me to fish in troubled waters – among the
Greeks a Greek . . . among the Bohemians a Bohemian.'[14] Two thousand
copies of *the flowering cross* were printed, and it sold out quickly. It has never
been reprinted.

Baxter's situation in Dunedin was favourable for his religious journalism.
He had time at his disposal, a good Catholic library, and well-informed
people with whom he could discuss his contributions. When he moved away
from the city his offerings became less and less frequent, and his attitudes
changed as he became radicalized by the new group of people among whom
he moved. He became activist and sociological. He wrote an article on
abortion for *The Tablet*, which Kennedy found unsatisfactory and returned.
He also included some comments on a similar piece Baxter had written for
The Sunday Times.[15] Baxter said that although he was against abortion, he
knew that what he had written in the article might conflict with Church
teaching. The looseness of his argument, and the inadequate account of the
Catholic position, naturally alienated some Catholic readers. But his main
concern was that existing abortion laws should be taken off the books, a
perfectly legitimate view for a Catholic. He had no obligation to support
particular laws, even though they were designed to lessen the harmful
effects of abortion. Quite simply he did not believe that they did. He saw
clearly the relationship between abortion laws and women's struggle for
equal rights, and he presented sympathetically the case for women who
chose an abortion. Baxter, with his distrust of the State, did not believe its
laws could solve the problem, and he pointed to its inadequate provision for
unmarried mothers. After receiving Kennedy's letter with the rejected

article, Baxter rang Kennedy and agreed that he had departed from Catholic teaching, and assured him that in the future he would adhere to it.

What was distinctive in Baxter's Catholicism is not easy to condense into a few sentences, but it can be said that whatever he did was done in his own way. *The Tablet* staff who knew his religious attitudes, saw that Catholicism was something precious to him, and that his view of it was really quite simple. He brought to his faith, especially in sexual matters, an earthy realism which some found shocking. One woman thought him a very odd sort of Catholic since he did not appear to regard the ten commandments as of central importance; she recognized his strong religious bent, but thought he could just as easily have belonged to an Eastern religion as to Catholicism. When he worked at the Catholic Education Office, Mass was said in the chapel in the building, but she could not remember seeing him there.

'Catholicism's true commodious faith', where even sinners could find a home, attracted him, and he was genuinely touched by its compassion, especially as he experienced it in the Sacrament of Reconciliation: 'My sins do not hinder the axe of his mercy.'[16] Authority, which offered a guide to true living in the many complex areas of human existence, was also important to him. When Pope Paul VI's controversial *Humanae Vitae* on contraception came out in 1968, Baxter, like Malcolm Muggeridge, stood solidly behind it, and defended it publicly. Tradition, in the sense of the continuity of a faith handed down in an unbroken line from the apostles, was something with which he felt an instinctive sympathy. It was the religious equivalent of his identification with his Scottish ancestors.

What sort of a Catholic was Baxter? I have met people who regarded him as a saint, and heard one well-informed priest speak of him as a mystic. Some Catholics resented him as an impostor and hypocrite. I do not believe he was any of these things. When it is said that he could be considered New Zealand's first indigenous theologian, what is meant is his spirituality, not his doctrinal or moral theology. Theology reflects on religious experience and systematizes it; spirituality is less systematic and speaks directly about religious experience. Baxter's theology was simple and old-fashioned and reflected the pre-Vatican II instruction he had received. Paradoxically, for so liberal a man, it reflected a native conservatism in religious matters. I very much doubt that he would have approved of the ordination of women. And he was not open to such developments as married priests. He wrote a witty article, 'Why shouldn't Our Priests Marry?', in support of compulsory celibacy and was congratulated by the conservative Archbishop McKeefry of Wellington.

In the area of sexual morality, Baxter's views were more advanced. His own sexual difficulties led him to contest the normal Catholic restraints. Yet he helped many young Catholics, whose education had sometimes placed a disproportionate emphasis on sexuality, to redress the balance. He admired Pope John XXIII, who threw open the windows of the Vatican to the modern world, but he would also have admired his conservative successor from Cracow, John Paul II. Baxter's spirituality, however, was very different from his theology. When he reflected on his own spiritual experience he was not confined by traditional formulations but was able to express himself in his own way. Whenever he did that, he might write something memorable. The originality and force of some of his insights carried them beyond the confines of Catholicism to a statement of universal truth. His attitude to those who did not share his faith was live and let live. There was nothing of the proselytizer about him. Of his former workmates of the Green Island rolling-mill, he wrote:

> If some of them were atheist
> As their bad luck might be,
> The plague of *convertitis*,
> Let it be far from me!
> Though the grim cogs of Calvin
> Would grind them underground,
> Our Lady loves a careless man
> With a pound and a word for a friend
> For all that and all that,
> And she will watch our end.
>
> (CP 338)

It was not converting others to Catholicism that concerned him. His passionate interest was in converting society to better human values and to more humane ways of acting.

In Dunedin, Catholics formed a small close-knit community occupied with its own affairs. For them Baxter was not a celebrity; some had not even heard his name. He did not take part in social activities like the Catholic Men's Luncheon Club, nor in parish organizations. Most Catholics knew him only through his writings in the *The Tablet*, though of course he had many friends among them, clerical and lay. For the older clergy he was an enigma, and was viewed with some suspicion. The people who knew him best were the young Catholics at the university. He was very devoted to them, spending time discussing such difficulties as the perverse economic situation, which made the early marriages that some of them wanted virtually impossible.

The inner life of these years found its way into poetry. Both for Jacquie and himself Dunedin was 'the city of our youth' and he delighted in its harbour, its cliffs, the 'green flats of weed', the lighthouse and the jetties. He located his origins in the Otago landscape:

> Land of drenched willows, river-flats and farms,
> All of us acknowledge as the matrix
>
> Of whatever grows in us . . .
>   (CP 424)

As always, the sea provided him with splendid images such as one for the breaking waves in 'At Aramoana':

> on the spit
> sheaves of water bow as if
> to the sickle . . .
>   (CP 336)

The Dunedin winter is characterized by a detail:

> The centre of the Octagon
> (Where, this winter afternoon,
> The streetlights burn . . .
>   (CP 361)

'At Kuri Bush' recalls a visit to the site of his family's old farm. He picked up as a keepsake a chip of the fallen chimney:

> That splinter of slate
>
> Rubbed by keys and cloth like an amulet
> Would hold me back if I tried to leave this island
>
> For the streets of London or New York.
>   (CP 370-1)

Duffy's farm, and the cottage where MacKenzie made his boats, were revisited; but he found the world of childhood had disappeared. The Brighton River, where he had paddled his canoe under the Black Bridge, 'is foul weed and sludge/narrower/than I had supposed,' (CP 353) and the bridge itself was now 'under fifty bull-/dozed yards of gravel and dry clay.' (CP 372) But the past, even the distant past of his ancestors, is still vivid. The last verse of 'The Titan' begins:

> And there are others. I cannot hear their voices.
> I cannot see their faces. Not even the jingle
> Of a stirrup, as they cross the river mouth

In late evening when sandflies rise
From rotted kelp. Only a pressure at
The fences of the mind. From clay mounds they gather
To share the Titan's blood with us.

(CP 373)

It was not mere nostalgia that led Baxter to visit the scenes of his childhood. It was a search for a 'lost key'[17], a retracing of his steps in order to determine the point at which he had taken the wrong turning. What he hoped to find is made explicit in 'The Return'. There the mature man visits the Brighton of his childhood 'to get back a full sight of loss.' In 'The Flood' he visits Scroggs Hill:

> It was (I think) my soul's hidden face
> I looked for . . .

(CP 263)

With that face, that of the true man, he associates:

> Joy, glory, primitive charisma

What he finds is the greater self-knowledge expressed by his 'inward guardian':

> All
> Knowledge, my son, is knowledge of the Fall.

(CP 263)

The poet has to accept his fallen nature, reconcile his buried selves and their history. And that includes the failures and the pain of being judged by the ideal from which he has fallen:

> that
> grim boy step by step at watch,
> my judge below the larches

(CP 389)

The 'grim boy' is present in 'Rhadamanthus'. Against his better judgement, he returned to a beach where twenty years earlier he had made love. Such events mattered to Baxter for:

> To love at all is to be haunted
> As stones are haunted by the ghost of water
> Where a creek ran once.

(CP 407-8)

Above the place of love:

> The cliff was a high stone Rhadamanthus
> Washed by the black froth of the sea.

221

He felt judged, but he was never too proud to ask for forgiveness. The wisdom to be gleaned from all these returns is detachment, to be:

> Delivered from a false season
> To the natural winter of the heart . . .
> (CP 179)

By 1967 he could finally interpret the speech of the Brighton River:

> 'Does it matter? Does it matter?'
> (CP 385)

Returning to places associated with the important events of his early life was crucial for Baxter's poetry. He provides a striking example of that intensification of memory which Katherine Mansfield thought was the way to become an artist.[18] And he believed: 'The generative power of poetry comes largely from the rediscovery and revaluation of childhood experience.'[19] Such lines in 'The Return' as 'I have no skill to set down/The perils of a late journey' express a disclaimer found elsewhere in his poetry that has been found strange by some critics. It is no stranger than Shakespeare's feeling of inadequacy, expressed in his thirty-ninth sonnet: 'Desiring this man's art and that man's scope.' Poets of such stature know so well what creative possibilities there are that they feel the extent of their failure.

Baxter's tendency to speak as an old man, not as a man in his forties, surprised many. He pushed a disproportionate number of people through the portals of Pluto. A man of forty could say eloquently in a poem 'The Old Man Thinks of Women', what he could hardly say of more than a few of the women he had known:

> they are either old or dead,
> Gone into the ground, into air and water,
> Who shared with me that irrecoverable strength of youth.
> (CP 406)

And it was true of his ancestors, but not of many others that:

> The dead have now become a part of us,
> Speaking between our words, possessing all our dreams.
> (CP 406)

Of his mental state in 1966 he wrote: 'I wrestled with the ghost of an ancient mistress who came back to haunt me, and got a number of written

222

lectures and some grim, dry poems out of the encounter.'[20] These poems compose the sequence 'Words to Lay a Strong Ghost', written in imitation of Catullus. Some of the Catullus 'translations' made their first appearance in *The London Magazine* under the title 'Seven Masks of Pyrrha'. Kenneth Quinn, Professor of Classics at Otago University and a specialist on Catullus, was a friend of Baxter's and they discussed techniques of translation together. Quinn considered him a passable Latinist and the imitations 'creative translations'. Baxter's approach was the same as that in his earlier translations of Rimbaud, which were published in *In Fires of No Return*. Then he had tried to build up a parallel text to the French. That meant 'melting the poem back to the original ore and re-forging it.' Rimbaud's poems were taken as 'guides, indications', not as 'sacred texts'.[21] That, he felt, was probably the only way he could translate. 'The Counter-Lunch' is a poem against his rival Allius, who is pilloried in the earthy language of the Latin original. 'The Streetlight' is a bitter poem against Pyrrha. 'The Flower' wistfully records:

> I didn't know
> Then how short life is – how few
> The ones who really touch us
>
> Right at the quick –
> (CP 363)

During the Dunedin years Baxter visited his parents regularly in their Brighton home and found them 'more alive than I am.'[22] The old admiration for his father mingled with compassion:

> not always firm on your legs
> at eighty-four. Well, father,
> in a world of bombs and drugs
>
> you charm me still – no other
> man is quite like you!
> (CP 365)

Honesty forced him to say: 'Mother, I can't ever wholly belong/In your world.' (CP 369) And a wooden-framed photograph offered a partial reason for the long rebellion:

> the baby blondish drowsing child
> So very slow to move away from the womb!

223

Yet despite all vicissitudes he feels a sense of unity: 'we're at one in the Catholic Church.'

The relative leisure of the Burns Fellowship allowed Baxter to take holidays with his family at Stewart Island, Naseby, the West Coast, Queenstown, the Milford Track, and Wanaka. But it was a sense of death, evoked perhaps by his return to Dunedin with its associations of his own past and that of his ancestors, which was uppermost in his mind: 'From each place,' he wrote, 'I came back with icy solitary poems that described the landscape in terms of the third and grimmest face of the Muse, which is a skull. There was a bit too much death inside me.'[23] Death startled him when he read the name James Baxter on a Naseby tombstone. He was not ready to die yet:

I'd like to

Have time, time to use my bones a little
Before testing whether the void is kind or not.
(CP 388)

Despite continuing domestic difficulties the family enjoyed some good times in Dunedin, and the many excursions made the period the happiest the children had known. But Baxter still had reservations about marriage:

To mate with a woman is the choice

Containing all other kinds of death
(CP 399)

And in the ironical 'The Perfect Wife', her sex is 'presented like a box of dice/Each Saturday.' Baxter did not condemn marriage, but he feared it as a threat to his development as an artist. He told Weir in 1967: 'What I have feared most in life is never some inward or outward pain, but the situation of being trapped in domesticity, in normality, in that segment of life which others no doubt quite properly find satisfying; I have feared it because it might choke up in me the double source of fantasy and truth.'[24] Yet the yoke of marriage itself taught 'a kind of truth'.

Some of the Dunedin poems point forward. In 'A Small Ode on Mixed Flatting' there is a reference to St Francis of Assisi, and in several poems he speaks of 'Sister Death', 'Sister Water', 'the clouds my sisters'; and the turtle in the Botanical House which is called 'my brother'.[25] There is a close interest in Maori things also. He took part in a tangi and admired the Maori acceptance of death 'as the centre of life', a viewpoint very different from that of the Pakeha for whom death is 'A thing unacceptable to the world we inhabit, in which/No one is allowed to speak of death.' (CP 400) In a poem called 'Man, You Will be Dust', he adopts the Maori stance:

> Death is a kind of life
> As the Maori understood it,
>
> And you who struggled all your life against it
> Become a Maori
>
> (CP 375)

It has already been shown that it was not a lifelong struggle. He was probably referring to his earlier belief that Maori culture had nothing to contribute to his writing. 'The Maori Jesus' shows how much Baxter had already identified with the Maori by 1966, becoming their champion against social injustice:

> The first day he was arrested
> For having no lawful means of support.
> The second day he was beaten up by the cops
> For telling a dee his house was not in order.
> The third day he was charged with being a Maori
> And given a month in Mount Crawford.
>
> (CP 347-8)

Baxter's acquaintance with Maori in Dunedin was limited. His personal knowledge of their problems came largely from his travels, from his work in Alcoholics Anonymous, and from visits to prisons.

Poems such as 'Summer 1967' expressed the need for a spirit of poverty and detachment: 'To want nothing is/The only possible freedom.' 'Mary at Ephesus' is a fine religious poem on the very Catholic theme of the Assumption of Mary into Heaven. The individuality and honesty of Baxter's religious quest is expressed in 'The Flame':

> Christ, who is all men
> Yet has to be discovered
> By each on his own –
> (CP 400-1)

In 'Letter to Sam Hunt' (1968) Baxter spoke for the young against a society that was failing to meet their aspirations, and leading to suburban neurosis in loveless marriages, a theme that had already engaged his attention in *Pig Island Letters*. This theme was to emerge later in the Jerusalem books.

'The Doctrine', which was not published until after his death, is an apparent disclaimer of what Baxter said in his poems.

> It was hope taught us to tell these lies on paper.
> . . .
> We did not believe ourselves. Others believed us
> Because they could not bear to live without some looking-glass.
>
> 'Are they real?' you ask — 'Did these things happen?'
> . . .
> What we remember is never the truth;
>
> (CP 413)

This poem raises questions that are susceptible of a variety of answers. My own response to the question 'Are they real?' would be: 'Allowing for your selectivity and modifications, including your exaggerations, and remembering too that you are a dramatic poet, yes for a large number of your poems.' The account of the relationship between the life and the work already given substantiates that view. At times people were upset by the literalness with which their real-life situation entered the poems. Baxter said some things so often it is difficult to believe that he did not mean what he said. 'What we remember is never the truth' will stand in the sense that what we remember is incomplete, and absolute objectivity is not possible for a human observer. A writer may be in the position described by Wallace Stevens in 'The Man with the Blue Guitar':

> They said. 'You have a blue guitar,
> You do not play things as they are,'
>
> The man replied, 'Things as they are
> Are changed upon the blue guitar'.[26]

Art is concerned with what lies behind the appearances. Baxter had an astonishing capacity for simultaneous belief and disbelief, acceptance and rejection. This was at the heart of his personal struggle to resolve the tensions that racked his life.

Baxter's deepest instincts were with the primitive, and he prided himself that 'these hooves were never shod' (CP 511). He wrote in 'The Muse', dedicated to Louis Johnson: 'it was the Muse, whom you and I/Unhinge by our civility.' (CP 352) And he had closed his Burns Fellowship piece thus:

Lately it has seemed to me that God was trying to say something to me. It is hard to hear through the static of frost and cigarettes and *Tablet* articles and TV documentaries. But it seems to say something like this: 'You poor old sod! I meant you to be a primitive, not a civilized talker at Women's Social Evenings.

You've balled it up. Remember your clan motto:– *Don't die till you're dead.* I know you believe in Me; but that's not quite enough to believe in. Try growing kumaras for a change. I make very few primitives and I like to see them survive. The Fellowship was a conditional mistake. You knew that all along. Why don't you use your radar. I'm not angry about it; I'm only sorry . . .'

Something like that. The Fellowship hadn't exactly done me in. But my asbestos suit had worn through in a few places.[27]

When Baxter returned to Dunedin he had no intention of writing plays.[28] But there were two people in the city with a single-minded dedication to the theatre, Rosalie and Patric Carey. It was inevitable that the three would meet. The encounter was an event in all their lives, and in the history of New Zealand drama. Rosalie was a New Zealander who had trained at the Guildhall School of Music and Drama in London, and then worked with several small acting companies in England. In 1950 she was with the Ring actors at Penzance, where she met Patric. They were cast as husband and wife in the Christmas light comedy for which Patric had designed the set. He was Irish but had been in England long enough to be taken for an Englishman, and for Rosalie his soul was 'as Irish as you could possibly have.'[29] Already he was a brilliant designer and an experienced producer.

The couple married, and since Patric was eager to find a country where he could make a career as a producer, they had emigrated to New Zealand and ended up in Dunedin. After producing the *Medea* in the garden of Willi Fels's house in Lombard Street, which the Careys were renting, they decided to launch out on their own and 'concentrate on the production of important plays, regardless of financial gain.'[30] The nature of many of the plays meant audiences were small, so it was possible to accommodate them in the studio of the Careys' house. But it was becoming apparent something more was needed, and in March 1960, a meeting of some twenty-five people unanimously supported the building of an intimate theatre.[31] There was no money but the Careys made available their studio and the adjoining land. Patric had built Elizabethan stages in local halls several times, and found the open stage and balconies a great advantage. It was decided to incorporate these features in the design of the new theatre, which naturally became known as the Globe. The Careys' home itself was part of the whole enterprise. It was used for dressing rooms, wardrobes and sewing, as well as for rehearsals, and it became a club for all those associated with the Globe. Of the theatre itself, erected in 1961, Baxter wrote: 'The upper part of London Street is high above the centre of the town. One approaches the theatre through a garden with a view of the harbour. Thus the theatre is both part of the town and separate from the town, a physical circumstance that exactly symbolizes the intentions of its directors.'³²

The Globe, with seating for seventy-five people, was ideal for intimate drama. The deep stage allowed entries from a distance so characters could be part of the action before they actually spoke, and entrances and exits were simple and natural. There was no curtain, so plays ended with a dead blackout. Nor were there curtain calls. As Patric said: 'How can you bring the players back after something like that?' The Globe was in every sense a group activity and with its emphasis on literary plays, irrespective of their box-office appeal, it could never become a commercial theatre. Actresses and actors were not paid and they were drawn from all walks of life. In a magical production of *Waiting for Godot*, for example, the cast included a statistician, a psychiatrist, a surveyor, and a schoolteacher. Patric did the casting and was praised by Baxter for 'a type of direction which allows actors the maximum freedom in developing their own reaction to a play, and finding their own emotional and physical pattern of acting.'³³ As the performances were not intended for the general public and the Press was not invited, the Globe enjoyed considerable freedom in the choice of play and in the style of production. As Carey told me, 'In those days an indecent word was an indecent word, and Mrs Grundy was sitting in the front row. You could always tell her to get out as this was your private house.'³⁴

Besides producing most of the plays, Patric also looked after the designing and building of the sets. Rosalie conducted the Globe theatre school, which offered classes in acting and other aspects of theatre. Sometimes Rosalie acted, giving, for example, a notable performance as Hedda Gabler. She was versatile enough to be able to fill in at short notice. She looked after the wardrobe and did the hundred and one chores associated with a small theatre. She also had two small children to look after. The theatre paid for itself, but the Careys had to find some other employment to support themselves.

During the *Marat-Sade* season Baxter came to a performance, and while Rosalie was doing her usual stint in the kitchen at the interval, he burst in and said 'Bloody marvellous, good on you.' He did not stay to have supper with the players after the performance. Three days later he was back with the full text of *The Band Rotunda*. The play had obviously been working in his mind for some time and now the moment had come for it to be put down on paper. Patric read it and said he would do it as soon as there was a gap in the programme. It was produced on 15 July 1967.

For the role of Jock Ballantyne, Patric cast Hal Smith, a newly arrived American who was lecturer in Drama at the university. Smith found his first encounter with the Globe a thrilling experience. There was Carey, 'a maverick producer', who was both exciting and witty, a poet-playwright, and a group of people leading busy lives, who came together for a purely creative purpose. There was no money in it for any of them and they were free from jealousy and self-aggrandizement. An atmosphere of exhilaration and a sense that something new and important was being accomplished prevailed. Looking back on the Globe experience of those years, Smith still considered *The Band Rotunda* Baxter's most fundamental play because it contains many of his basic concepts, 'stated perhaps in the most pure form he ever stated them.' It has his concern for the down-and-outs, like the two men who sleep on the park bench; for the prostitute; for the homosexual Snowy; and for the boy from Mt. Eden. Then there are the pervasive religious issues climaxing in the shocking and superficially blasphemous address to Christ on the cross. 'The material of the play,' Baxter said, 'was subconscious, personal and highly familiar, since I am myself a member of the great tribe of drunks who hold a mirror to the world of chaos we inhabit . . . [The material] was already imbedded in the marrow of my bones. I only had to write the play.'[35] The strong social and religious concerns of *The Band Rotunda* were to emerge again in the Jerusalem writings.

Baxter arrived at just the right time for the Globe. Rosalie and Patric were beginning to get tired and were looking for stimulation. To play a new text was a great experience, especially for a theatre with such high artistic ideals. The Careys profoundly affected the way Baxter wrote the plays. After *The Band Rotunda* he wanted to go on writing for the theatre but said he needed a theme, plots, and a structure to work with. Patric told him that when Eliot was commissioned to write a play for the Canterbury Festival in 1935, he could not find the model he needed in either the contemporary theatre or among the Elizabethans and Jacobeans. He went back to the Greeks and based *Murder in the Cathedral* on them. Patric advised Baxter to do the same and lent him copies of the plays.

Baxter found the advice congenial: 'I think I brought with me to the theatre a subconscious certainty that the Greek myths and legends are never out-of-date since they form that mythical stratum in the mind of modern man which enables him from time to time to make a pattern out of the chaos of his experience.'[36] In a play like *The Sore-Footed Man*, which was produced at the Globe on 4 September 1967: 'Baxter's mythical characters are not those that the ancient Greeks knew, but the rationalized figures stripped of their heroic qualities to which we have become accustomed in the twentieth century. They argue not so much in the style of a formal debate as of a session over a jug of beer.'[37] Fireman, the modern Prometheus in *The Bureaucrat*, is chained to a desk instead of a rock.

The great classical scholar Professor H.D.F. Kitto, a man of the theatre as well as an authority on Greek drama, was then visiting Otago University. Carey introduced Baxter to him and about an hour later they stopped talking. Baxter remarked to Carey: 'That's all I need to know about the Greeks. I've got it all out of him.' In the course of his lecture, 'Some Possibilities for New Zealand Drama', given in 1967, Baxter expounded the view of Aristotle's unities that he had learnt from Kitto:

> But since I heard Kitto speak, my feelings about Arisotle have changed. I realize that Aristotle has suffered from his interpreters. Unity of action means to me that the words express a coherent myth held down by the tent-pegs of local knowledge and experience. Unity of time means that the time a play takes to be performed represents a day in the life of Everyman, that day which is also his lifespan, his permanent now. Unity of place means the stage itself, that narrow universe which is for the time of a play a womb and a tomb, the place where the audience project the communal drama of their own minds, helped in this creative labour by playwright, producer, actors and stage designer. By this process of creative illusion they may perhaps learn who they are, or at least who they are not.[38]

When Baxter saw the *Marat-Sade* he regarded it as an extension of Brechtian theatre. Already in his writings there was something of Brecht's theory of alienation and of the view of drama as a vehicle for social reform. But these theories had to be translated into theatre. Carey told Baxter he would have to take part in a play if he was to understand the problems of the cast, and not write plays that would be technically impossible. For example, players must be given adequate time to move from one place to another. Despite Baxter's objections that it was inappropriate, Carey cast him as the alcoholic doctor in Chekhov's *The Three Sisters*, produced in 1967. His performance was wooden, and he appeared to have no acting talent whatsoever. He just sat about and philosophized. Nor did he manage to learn his lines, but gummed them inside a newspaper he carried about. Carey observed that it was another matter when Baxter was reading his own poetry, then he gave a private performance of great skill.

The two men became close friends. Carey spoke of Baxter as a person of great warmth, the most precious friend he had ever had; yet there were also occasions when he wished he had never met him. A close relationship with a personality as powerful as Baxter's could be disturbing. He could also be very boring on subjects like Maori problems, and made some ridiculous statements. Sometimes with a twinkle in his eye he would stop, look at Carey, and burst out laughing. Carey admired his superb speaking voice: the way he made no pretence to speak anything but New Zealand English: 'yet every vowel was in place, and he spoke in beautifully cadenced rhythms.'[39] Baxter found Carey 'a witty man and a begetter of life in others.'[40]

For Carey the theatre had always existed as a vehicle for the spoken word, and since he saw little significant action in New Zealand society, he wanted to 'create a theatre with action in dialogue.'[41] Baxter, with his mastery of words, was very much his man. Carey remained receptive to whatever kind of play he wrote, believing a producer or director should never dictate how a play should be written. As he remarked, with that attitude we wouldn't have had Webster, or Beckett, or Ionesco. Since he believed in Baxter as a writer he left it to him to create his own form of play. At that phase of New Zealand theatre, it seemed to him that what mattered most was not so much the quality of the play, though obviously that was important, but that we had plays capable of exciting others to the point where exclamations might be made: 'We can write plays here', or 'I can do better than that.'

It was a true partnership. If, for instance, they were doing *The Sore-Footed Man*, Baxter would take away a copy of Sophocles' *Philoctetes* and read it. Then they went down to Cowell's coffee shop in the Octagon and spent up to eight hours there. The proprietor did not receive them with any enthusiasm since his clientele included many elderly ladies. Baxter's language and general manner were too much at odds with the surroundings, and the strategic use of the vacuum cleaner failed to flush them out. They just moved from table to table as they threshed out what Sophocles had done with his play, what Athenian society had in common with modern New Zealand society and the differences in audience response. At the end of the marathon, Baxter knew exactly what he wanted to do and how it should be done.

Baxter wrote his plays straight off. He would work with intense concentration and he made very few corrections. A play would take anything between two days and a fortnight to write; once it was written, Baxter would never alter anything, nor would Carey. In general, Baxter did not attend rehearsals. At the start of the production he met the cast. They would ask what the play was about. He never answered, feeling that was their business. Then he would go away and not be seen until the opening performance. First night was an occasion he greatly enjoyed, and he was often surprised at Patric's interpretations.

A glance at the list of the Globe's productions will show that 1967 was Baxter's year. *The Band Rotunda* was produced in July, *The Sore-Footed Man* in September, *The Bureaucrat* and *The Devil and Mr Mulcahy* in November. The plays were preceded by three of Baxter's mimes performed by two accomplished dancers, John and Barbara Casserley. Barbara had a background of classical ballet, John in contemporary dance. At the Globe Baxter was regarded as a kind of presiding deity, and he developed an almost religious commitment to drama. He could be seen hunched up in the third row at almost every production of his works.[42]

Early in their relationship, Carey told Baxter he would be interested in a contemporary version of *Oedipus at Colonus*, which Sophocles wrote as his final comment on Athenian society. Carey considered *The Temptations of Oedipus* the best of Baxter's plays. He told Peter Harcourt: 'He wrote himself in it, and somehow everything he'd learned. A sense of form like Sophocles' came through, so by that time he really was formulating a plan of action which might have worked.'[43]

The *Listener* critic, Philip Smithells, considered the first production of the play 'the most striking of any play I have seen in New Zealand in thirty years', and some demanding critics shared his view. The set and costumes were designed by the Frances Hodgkins Fellow for 1969, Ralph Hotere, and the music was specially written by the first holder of the Mozart Fellowship, Anthony Watson. The collaboration of the Burns, Hodgkins, and Mozart Fellows illustrates the shared interests that made the whole enterprise of the Globe possible. It was an exciting time in the cultural life of Dunedin. For *The Temptations of Oedipus* Patric Carey built a pure white set, almost entirely out of scrap polystyrene, which highlighted the costumes. The chorus carried white Hotere masks on wands.[44] Smithells had seen a good deal of experimental theatre in Central Europe the previous year and thought the production would not have been out of place in Vienna, Cologne, Copenhagen, Helsinki, or Dresden.[45]

Baxter's audiences at the Globe included a nucleus of stalwarts, who attended most of the productions. They were all middle class: accountants, dentists, doctors, bank managers, and university staff; nobody in the least represented what's known as 'the working class'.[46] Baxter realized this, and peopled his plays with drunks, frustrated husbands, lapsed Catholics, inadequate and misunderstood Greeks. The heroic world was brought very close to the workaday world. Sometimes Baxter treated his material satirically. *Mr O'Dwyer's Dancing Party* was an attack on what Baxter called 'the Remuera'. *The Band Rotunda* is a parable, working out what he had written in his poem 'Ballad of the Third Boobhead', where a conclave of drunks sits in judgement on the town and finds it wanting.

According to Patric Carey the audiences loathed Baxter's plays. They threatened that if he put one on again they would not come. Yet they kept coming back. They disliked the coarse language and the attack on their whole pattern of living. Many were left-wing, liberal intellectuals who did not see why they should be targets. Carey felt the impact of Baxter could be no worse than that of Beckett or Ionesco. In 'Drama Among the Faceless' Baxter wrote of his audience: 'I don't want to cheer them up, I want to make them less despairing. That, in a sense, would be the moral issue; when you make sense of life you despair less.'[47]

The appropriate language for contemporary theatre was a problem Baxter thought carefully about. It had to be prose not verse because he regarded verse as a dead language in the modern theatre. The language of his time at its most vital level was to be found, he believed, 'in the explosive metaphors and jokes of pub conversation', a language which he could still find lying at the bottom of his mind whenever he looked for it. He argued: 'the theatre should and must offer its stages to playwrights who use street language and put aside its remnants of middle class decorum. The reward will be a spoken language that flows easily into physical movement on the stage. I do not envisage an invasion of the obscene: only that the rhythms of popular speech in our time require a certain sprinkling of swearwords and that the creek in general will have to run muddy before it can run clear.' He believed, too, that the only theatres able to risk upsetting the taste of audiences were those that do not exist for financial profit, and did not cater to people's social illusions.[48] The assumptions behind the Globe matched Baxter's own, and his dramatic language has been deservedly praised. His experience of writing for the theatre – the need for swift communication; the sense of freedom in the use of language; the alert observation of audience response – all these were central in perfecting the wonderful naturalness, the clarity and suppleness of language apparent in his last writings.

Despite hostility from his audiences, Baxter had quite a following among the young. To them, a new Baxter play was an event. In the sixties they were looking for someone to represent the revolutionary spirit of the time. Unable to find such a person in the university, they looked to Baxter. Towards them, he was always indulgent. So much of his own youth had been lost through alcoholism that he saw them through rose-coloured spectacles. When Carey turned a play down, as he did *The Runaway Wife*, Baxter took it over to the university and got it performed there. Baxter's works have a great capacity for finding new audiences in each generation. There have been successful revivals of *The Devil and Mr Mulcahy*, with its indictment of religious fundamentalism, and *The Starlight in Your Eyes*, set in the aftermath of atomic war, has again become topical.

Baxter did not develop a dramatic aesthetic, but he did offer a number of insights which show how he regarded the theatre. It has already been pointed out that he believed the effects of the Fall provided the 'communal foundation of dramatic art'. His theatre offers a pageant of fallen men and women. Like the drunks in *The Band Rotunda*, they 'hold a mirror up to the world of chaos which we inhabit', and they helped an audience make sense of it: 'Without the dramatic role, life tends to be experienced as chaos. The unveiling of this chaos is perhaps the theme of all of my plays.'[49] The relationship between drama and poetry was a difficult problem for him and one that he never really solved. But Carey helped him by pointing out that a play was 'a metaphoric structure in which the multiple statements of the characters correspond to the accumulated images of a poem.'

For Baxter drama was the most communal of the arts, and the stage an arena where a community's myths could be enacted and have a salutary effect: '. . . a viable New Zealand drama, if it were to appear, might profoundly modify our social conceptions, our view of ourselves and the world.'[50] Drama was a powerful means of exposing the limitations of New Zealand society. His chief concerns were social and the plays are closely linked. Each one works aspects of the same material. If Baxter's approach was fundamentally didactic, it must be said that many of the best dramatists, from Aeschylus and Aristophanes to the modern school of Osborne, were also didactic. But these writers had the skill to let audiences draw their own conclusions even as they challenged the assumptions behind their judgements. Baxter knew very well the difference between a sermon and a work of art: 'When I write a play I am concerned not with edification, but with dramatic truth expressed through a series of illusions.'[51]

And he realized the importance of distancing his own views from those of his characters: '. . . when a playwright assigns particular words to a particular character in a play, he cannot, without sabotaging the whole dramatic structure, allow those words to contain his own considered view of life.'[52] Those who saw him act on the stage said he was just himself. But he cannot be simply identified with his characters. He said of *The Band Rotunda*: 'I am not Concrete Grady, though Concrete Grady is one of my secret selves.'[53] The plays drew on his experience in some detail, but they also drew on imaginary situations, which in certain moods he found seductive. As well as alcoholism in *The Band Rotunda*, there is incest in *The Devil and Mr Mulcahy*. Hal Smith observed that such scenes were dramatized, exonerated, and virtually sanctified.

Of the three Baxter plays produced by the New Zealand Broadcasting Corporation for radio between 1961 and 1969, *Mr Brandywine Chooses a Gravestone* is perhaps the most successful. Daniel Brandywine is a quite ordinary man who is soon to die. He returns in fantasy to his early years and to the woman he loved but failed to marry. Baxter told William Austin of the NZBC that the play 'relates to some of the things I know best and feel most deeply about. The problem of course is to get this into a dramatic form that will reach others – but I think I've come nearer to solving this than at any time in the past. Louis MacNeice's *Dark Tower* by the way has influenced my thinking about radio to some extent.'[54] When he sent the Corporation *The First Wife* on 1 December 1966, he wrote that *Mr Brandywine* was on 'the theme of the duality of reality and phantasy which provokes for example the common human temptation of adultery.'[55] *Mr Brandywine* is Baxter's version of the medieval morality play, *Everyman*. Like the central character, we are all waiting for death. All Baxter's dramatic material had been allowed to mature in the cask. Commenting on the last of his radio plays to be produced, he said that the theme had been in his mind for several years.[56]

Baxter took rather a limited view of radio drama: 'Radio is good for an intellectual argument. With the stage the audience want more than that but on radio it doesn't matter so much.'[57] Responding to his remark that in the radio production of *Jack Winter's Dream* the words were too thickly overlaid with sound effects, William Austin told him he should view 'radio as an art form using your script as a composer uses a score designed for the instruments of voice, silence, music and sound,' and he should not regard 'the last two as stuck on.'

So original a writer as Baxter could never be merely derivative, yet the Greek plays lack fire and are rather contrived. In them he distanced himself too far from his real subject to achieve the engagement evident in his best plays. Their relative failure at the James K. Baxter Play Festival at Victoria University, Wellington, in June 1973, suggested that transplanted from the Globe, where the audience had been educated by the Careys in classical drama, they did not travel well. On the other hand, plays like *The Wide Open Cage, The Band Rotunda*, and *The Devil and Mr Mulcahy* can electrify an audience with the shock of experience passionately encountered. Many would agree with what Phillip Smithells said in a review of *The Band Rotunda* for the *N.Z. Listener*: 'The dialogue, which is good theatre, is Baxter at his best; it is often forgotten, so good is his verse, that he is also a master of fine prose, and of the vernacular.'[58] Baxter's dramatic achievement depended solidly on two outstanding producers, Richard Campion in Wellington, and Patric Carey in Dunedin. Carey provided the environment in which Baxter could function and he allowed him great freedom. But he considered each play on its merits. He would not produce, for example, *The Spots on the Leopard*, nor *The Starlight in Your Eyes*, which he thought superficial. Carey was too much a man of the theatre to allow any theory to dominate his practice. None the less his formulation confirmed Baxter in his chief dramatic weakness, the habit of placing the emphasis where he placed it as a poet, on the words. He found it difficult to visualize action on the stage. His plays have a static quality that prevents them becoming great drama.

When Baxter gave Carey *The Temptations of Oedipus*, he told him 'This is the last' and that he no longer wished to communicate on that level. Sometimes Baxter spoke of giving up things, even the writing of poetry; this time he meant what he said. Carey accepted the decision without comment. If Baxter did not want to continue writing plays, that was his business. So ended one of the most remarkable and fruitful literary partnerships in our history. But for Carey and the Globe, Baxter would not have written the series of seven plays. A great moment in New Zealand theatre had passed.[59]

Other matters had begun to absorb Baxter. He appeared tired of being a literary person and wanted to embody values rather than merely write about them. Young people had also begun to absorb his life. On the corner of Great King Street and Howe Street there used to be a wine shop with a flat above it. Some young people who were drifting and struggling to come to terms with their lives lived there. One was Peter Olds, a poet, who was recovering from a nervous breakdown. Baxter used to spend hours there advising and talking to them; helping them when they had the DTs or the shakes. As a man of great gentleness he related well to these young people and they liked the way this older person, who was a man of letters and a successful member of the Dunedin community, shared their social iconoclasm. His hang-ups were their hang-ups, their attitudes his. It could even be said that the submerged teenager in Baxter came to the surface. When one young man was arrested for the murder of a policeman, Baxter went to great lengths to secure a leading Auckland lawyer as his legal counsel. With Jacquie and the family he attended the trial, and when the youth was found guilty he visited him in prison.

By 1968 the Baxters had their own troubles. Hilary was having emotional problems, and she was asserting her independence. Neither Baxter nor Jacquie knew what to do and they felt inadequate. John wanted to leave school, and Baxter had opposed it. In the end they settled for some form of private tuition, which did not work out. Later, when John expressed an interest in attending Art School, Baxter took him to Auckland to see his old friend Colin McCahon. Baxter had become even more anti-academic since his time as Burns Fellow at Otago University, and together he and McCahon talked John out of the idea.

Baxter was exhausted, both physically and mentally. Many people made demands on him, people from the university, the Catholic church, the drama people at the Globe, and others from the general community. He found it hard to say no. The output of the Dunedin years was phenomenal as he churned out plays, poems, essays, catechetical material, and public addresses. He was also worried about his parents' health. Millicent had once taken a slight turn during a family meal. Her face went ashen, but nothing was said. She simply took a tablet.

Baxter was beginning to feel burnt out, and he had lost faith in himself as a parent and a husband. His one-year contract with Bishop Kavanagh was also coming to an end.

A friend who met him in a coffee bar early that year found him in a state of euphoria and rather excitable. He spoke of a vision calling him to Jerusalem on the Wanganui River. It was somewhat oblique; he believed he heard a voice or experienced some other form of communication. When Baxter wrote to a friend on 11 April 1968, he spoke of the communication taking place 'about a fortnight ago'. It occurred at a time of acute difficulty in his marriage. His brother Terence's marriage had broken up recently, 'not through any fault on either side but because even the good life in our present society seems to carry within it the seeds of disruption and death.' In a state very close to despair, Baxter had prayed to God for a solution to his difficulties:

> Then I went to sleep. And when I woke in the morning the first thought in my mind — was 'Jerusalem' — meaning not the city in Palestine, but the mission station on the Wanganui River. And either immediately or very shortly after a linked thought came into consciousness — that I should go to Jerusalem without money or books, there learn the spoken Maori from a man whom God would provide for me — whose name might or might not be Matiu — and then (God willing) proceed quietly and slowly to form the nucleus of a community where the people, both Maori and pakeha, would try to live without money or books, worship God and work on the land.

> (b) Two central ideas were linked — poverty (somewhat of the Franciscan kind) and *aroha*, which then seemed to me to be the Humanity of Our Lord, dismembered among the pakehas, in process of being dismembered among the Maoris. The Lord (I speak as if the communication were a genuine one) indicated to me that He had in this country, as it were, two faces on one Head, a Maori face and a pakeha face, that the Maori face was being mangled and hurt by our civilisation, and that He desired me to begin the labour of washing and cleaning it. I was to learn spoken Maori, and assume as far as possible a Maori identity — this because the Maori is in this country the Elder Brother in poverty and suffering and closeness to Our Lord — and it is suitable the pakehas should learn from him not vice versa.'[60]

Baxter's interpretation of the event was that either his reason was temporarily unhinged or else God had given him 'a minor revelation necessary for my own behaviour'. He realized the possibility of self-deception, but felt that if he had been merely deranged it was unlikely he would be feeling 'not only sane but more vigorous and hopeful than I have been for several years.' Going to Jerusalem might also solve his marital problems in the long run. A temporary break with his wife, he believed, would lead to a final reconciliation: 'To stay with the present pattern would mean we would gradually rot apart and not be joined again.' His hope was that 'she who is likely to be taken from me by the process of life on the pakeha side of the fence will be restored to me on the Maori side.' So complete was the change envisaged for his own life that he believed 'James K. Baxter must die. He has served a purpose; but this no longer seems to be God's purpose.' Locutions such as this are a well known spiritual phenomenon. Whether in his case the experience was genuine, or merely the product of the long years of alcoholism, an extremely active imagination, or a deep unconscious need for more freedom than his domestic situation allowed, it is impossible to say. What is certain is that he believed it to be authentic, and that it was an imperative to act.

His departure for Jerusalem had to be deferred because Hilary was pregnant. He was glad at her 'good sense' in having the child rather than an abortion. A daughter, Stephanie, was born in September. She was a lovely baby and he adored her.

When Baxter did leave Dunedin early in 1969 he just faded out. His friends found that months or even a year or two later he would turn up as if he had just been away for the day. His attitude to time, the hour he arrived, how long he stayed, and his sudden departures and reappearances were disconcerting to those accustomed to normal routines.

Both in his life and in his writings, Baxter was a conscious myth-maker. He regretted not having left in Dunedin: 'a hairy legend of the Abominable Snowman to gladden the hearts of the young and offend the nostrils of the old. But I am myself too old to sleep out on park benches; and on the whole I think I made an exemplary Burns Fellow. My misdemeanours were purely verbal.'[61]

XII
The Junkies and the Fuzz

At the end of 1968, after three years, Baxter left Dunedin. 'Valediction', written in December on the eve of his departure, indicates his frame of mind:

> The death-blue sluggish river in the South
> Like veins on a dead man's arm . . . O you hills
> Where I was born, the people at times were able
> To light fires, to keep lamps burning
> For their children to look at.
>   There is more than one
> Schoolhouse looking at itself in a lagoon
> Where paradise ducks come down; but I must
> Describe also a sadness like flint
> Embedded in the eyes of brown-haired children.
>
> It doesn't matter. The country is dragging
> Chains of words, chains of money,
> Decorated with a necklace of petrol bowsers
> And waiting to be blessed by a good
> Psychiatrist. My dreams do not go South.
> Parents, grandparents, the fire you lighted
> Under my arse will keep me moving
> For another day at least. I will go North
> Tomorrow like a slanting rainstorm.
>
> (CP 431)

The poem shows the familiar preoccupations: with origins; Baxter's quarrel with New Zealand society, especially its materialism and education system; and the personal restlessness which from now on never allowed him to stay long in any one place. He was burdened with many anxieties. He felt he had lost touch with his children, now aged nineteen and seventeen, and with their generation, and he wanted to be able to reach out to it again.

On 7 January 1969, he wrote to John Weir from Wellington that he felt the difficulties in his marriage had made some kind of temporary separation from Jacquie desirable. Finally he decided to leave for Auckland and to visit Jerusalem on the way. The night before he left, he called on Father Charles Cooper, a curate in his parish, whose family had lived next door to Jacquie's parents in Palmerston North and had known them well. Baxter told him that his reason for going to Jerusalem was to help his wife discover her Maori roots. He explained that if he had some personal experience of living among the Maori, it might help her to find them. He was not walking out on her, what he was doing was for her sake. He needed to know more about her Maori origins if the impasse described in 'Winter Poem to My Wife' was to be broken. But he also told Father Cooper he was not at all sure he should go, and when asked what he would do if his plans did not work out, he said that he would return to his home in Ngaio. What Baxter said was a plausible explanation. So too were the explanations he had given to others. He always had a great desire to please in his personal relationships, and he tended to tell people what he thought they would like to hear. It would be wrong to accuse him of duplicity. When his different reasons are examined, they can be seen as all of a piece.

He was very naïve. To speak as he did of his hope that Jacquie would join him in Jerusalem was patently absurd. She had taken the responsibility of caring for Hilary's child at that time, and it was impractical to suggest that she take the baby with her. Also, tribal affiliations are very important to a Maori. They are not able to go and live just anywhere. Jacquie's tribe was Taranaki-based, and a different tribe lived at Wanganui.

Twenty years after Baxter left for Jerusalem, Jacquie still did not know what really went on in his mind. She was not at all sure that he knew himself.

Baxter set off for Jerusalem at the end of January. Just outside Wanganui he headed on foot for the rough shingle road winding high above the Wanganui River on the way to Jerusalem and Pipiriki. He walked barefoot as if on pilgrimage, passing the small Maori settlements named by the nineteenth century missionary Richard Taylor, Atene (Athens), Koriniti (Corinth), Ranana (London), and came at last to Hiruharama (Jerusalem). This first visit was short. He stayed in the presbytery with the Catholic priest, and met some of the half-dozen Maori families that made up the Jerusalem settlement. He was well received. Agnes and Wehi Walker, both respected in the community, were especially hospitable. When he left, Agnes gave him a jar of jellied eels and encouraged him to return.

Baxter arrived with the eels at the home of Michael and Dene Illingworth in Puhoi, some forty miles north of Auckland. By now his hair had grown long and he was sporting a beard. He had assumed a new image for a new life-style. The Illingworths and the Baxters had become friends when Michael was in Dunedin as the first Frances Hodgkins Fellow in 1966. But the visit to Puhoi was not merely to renew an acquaintance. Baxter knew that Michael had lived in a community of the Ngapuhi tribe in the Bay of Islands as a young man. For several years his home was the whare of a rangatira who looked on him as his son. And the local Maori had said to him: 'This is your home, this is your people.' Baxter told Illingworth what he planned to do at Jerusalem and asked if it would be imposing on Maori hospitality. He was assured that he would be received sympathethically because of aroha. Illingworth was impressed by Baxter's sensitivity to Maori feelings.

Back in Auckland, Baxter stayed with Hone and Jean Tuwhare at 21 Tiri Tiri Road, Birkdale. Hone Tuwhare arranged a job for him at the Chelsea Sugar Refinery where he worked for three weeks as a cleaning worker before being sacked. His side of the story is dramatized in 'The Ballad of the Stonegut Sugar Works'. When the ballad was printed, the printer became apprehensive in case an action for defamation was brought, and he would not hand over the run. In the end he relented and gave Baxter six copies.

He had many friends in Auckland, but he was still without a home. He met a man called Trixie in the Auckland Domain who invited him to share his flat in Park Road, Grafton. Conditions were primitive. The two men slept on mattresses on either side of the bedroom. A small night-lamp burned all night as a sign that anyone who needed help was welcome. Trixie was a devout Buddhist and often discussed his religion with Baxter.

In Grafton and Parnell, there were a fair number of run-down houses which were rented cheaply to university students. Groups of young people lived there in loose associations of houses. Baxter's group consisted of three houses in Boyle Crescent, and the house in Park Road where he lived with Trixie. Most of their residents were university students, and they all knew each other. Many of them were brimming with energy and ideas, and they liked the free life-style.

The sixties had seen a rapid increase in drug-taking in New Zealand, and Grafton had become well known to the police as a resort for drug users. Well before Baxter arrived there had been arrests. The first New Zealand arrest for possessing LSD was at No. 9 Boyle Crescent. After Easter 1969, Baxter moved with Trixie to No. 7, which had a history of association with junkies, as addicts to hard drugs were called. Now that he was living in a house familiar to drug addicts, he could offer them counselling and a place to stay. Not all those living in the other houses nor in No. 7 were on drugs, but some who stayed there from time to time were heavily addicted. At least two died from an overdose. One was a seventeen-year-old boy, described in the Health Department's first drug report as living for some time before his death at Boyle Crescent, 'an address occupied by and frequented by known drug misusers'.[1] Another former resident of No. 7 was a girl who died in a telephone booth from an overdose of heroin.

With Baxter in residence, No. 7 became very different from the other houses in the cluster. The people living there were not local nor settled, but came from anywhere and would leave at any time. Among them were young drug-takers from quite well-to-do homes. At Boyle Crescent they mixed with others from virtually hopeless backgrounds. No. 7 became a meeting-place. Baxter brought back to the house many people whom he had met in the streets or in the Domain. Though the resident group normally numbered about ten, sometimes there might be as many as twenty in the house. Such a crowd overwhelmed the facilities, making it so difficult to get into the bathroom to take a bath that many gave up trying.

Dress and appearance proclaimed the group. Headbands and tattered jeans were worn like a badge. Most residents grew their hair long partly to affirm their distance from ordinary society. They were also poor and a haircut was something they could do without. But they received much abuse.

There was little privacy. People slept on the floor, in sleeping-bags or on mattresses, often flea-infested, picked up cheaply from a second-hand dealer. Baxter had a small bedroom where he did his writing. But he was also happy to put another mattress on his floor for a junkie who needed special care. The food was of poor quality because there was never enough money. Those who worked in town brought in a little, and visitors occasionally arrived with small gifts. Everything was shared. Each day the local greengrocer threw out a box of fresh green leaves and Baxter asked for them to make soup. From that time on there was always soup on the stove. Some of the community were resourceful cooks. Trixie was esteemed because he could prepare a whole meal out of a cabbage.

The late sixties was a time of intellectual ferment when accepted patterns of living were challenged. At Boyle Crescent, the young endlessly explored new ideas. As in most sub-cultures, they had their own argot.[2] In the house there was a strong sense of caring. Despite the occasional exploiter and self-seeker, inevitable in such circumstances, some found it a marvellous place to live. For the three people who held the place together, Baxter, Trixie, and Gill Shadbolt (like her former husband, the novelist Maurice, an old friend of Baxter's) it was a very demanding life. Day and night they listened to people's often complex problems, talked them through, and offered comfort and advice. And there seemed to be no end to the steady stream of visitors – among them some of the worst cases of drug addiction in Auckland. When Baxter needed a break he often went to Vulcan Lane or the Domain to meditate. Occasionally he travelled further afield to see the Illingworths in Puhoi. Gill Shadbolt went out each day to work for a printer. She spent most of the rest of the time at Boyle Crescent, though she actually lived in Trixie's old flat in Park Road.

Baxter described Boyle Crescent to his parents:

This place is the homing ground of all the junkies in the country – they come here with or without their needles and their pills, from the bin (mental hospital) or the clink (jail) – and I have a bed on the floor in one of the rooms, and collect rent for the landlord, and try to keep the house free of gear (drugs). The fuzz (police) are almost daily callers — I have now reached the stage where they will sit down and have a cup of coffee and talk, like persons (which they are) instead of like characters out of a horror comic.

Results: One long-standing user of drugs, a Maori woman, has come off them. I have put a statue of Our Lady on the wardrobe above the bed, and burn a blessed candle there each night to keep the actual night fears and possible demons away. The drug-users are very demon-minded.

One man, a user of amphetamine, who has been several times in the bin – a safe-cracker, part Maori, with a drug-induced notion that he may be the Second Coming of Christ – has improved a great deal. I put my arms round these people and talk to them. They are often like children lost in the dark.

Constant and good relations with perhaps 200 people, especially among those whose ports of call are the clink and the bin. Few of them would be much over 30. The youngest – a runaway from a mental hospital, again a Maori girl, whom I had from the police till she could hold a job and get well – is 14.

To be here is to be in the fiery furnace – their fears and their forms of agony become mine and keep me awake at night waiting for the squad cars to arrive. Yet the Lord gives me frequent tranquillity and a clear mind to work for and with them, as some kind of elder brother. I find these people basically very good and loving people – but riddled with many fears. Daddy would know what I mean – I mean he would know something of the thousands of basically good but emotionally disturbed people who fill our jails.

I have become them and them me – this is the torment and it seems what the Lord wants of me – to be devoured and consumed by the love of the many.[3]

As the letter shows, he regarded them as good people, believing they came to Boyle Crescent less for drugs than for aroha. To Bernadette Noble, a journalist, he said, 'They find something of it in the common house, the beard, the almost uniform clothes.'[4] He also told her that he was particularly concerned for women, many of whom found no sense of companionship outside their homes, 'only a big society of strangers. There is no village, no tribe. Women go mad in those places. And like the younger ones, when the pain is too great, they turn to drugs.' And drugs he knew were merely palliatives. They 'increase the paranoia – the delusions of grandeur, the persecution. Fear is the death of the spirit. The junkie lives in fear. Fear of his hallucination. Fear of the police. Afraid of fear.' He considered the regular taking of amphetamines as bad as any other drug habit, though there was no law against it.

Baxter and Gill Shadbolt were both deeply concerned over the failure of their marriages, and accepted they were just as crippled as the junkies for whom they worked. All they could offer was emotional warmth and the support needed to help people to change their lives. Although idealistic, they often failed.

After Boyle Crescent Baxter was never again to be a merely private person. The curiosity, not to mention the prurience, of the media was to become well-nigh insatiable. At first he welcomed publicity as a way of drawing the country's attention to a group of people whose needs were not being met. He hoped for communal centres where those who wanted to get off drugs and stay off them could live. The alternative? 'At present, they come out of hospital – and that's it. There's nowhere to go, they haven't got a job. More problems, so they turn to drugs again. The junkie belongs to a very close social group. When he breaks with drugs he also loses his friends, everything.'5 Finding employment presented immense difficulties to those convicted of drug offences. One girl was filling in the application form for a position with the Post Office, but when she came to the question 'Any Criminal Convictions?' she said, 'What's the use? If I write yes I won't get the job.'

In his poem 'Ballad of the Junkies and the Fuzz' Baxter presented the drug-taker's point of view sympathetically. His attitude to the police had hardened considerably since he wrote to his parents in June. He gave his reasons for the change in an article in *The Waikato Times* : The 'three points on which I am likely to criticize the police – if they tell lies in Court, if they use violence either in interrogation or as a private revenge on people they are holding in their custody, or else if they plant drugs or other articles on people and then arrest them for possession of them. In each of these cases the police are acting illegally. I object to this.'6

The 'Ballad of the Junkies and the Fuzz' is dedicated to Baxter's son John, who had become a Buddhist, hence the references to Buddha in the poem. Baxter adopted the stance of Counsel for the Defence, and spoke for those who had no one else to defend them against a society that holds all the cards. No lawyer in such circumstances would make concessions that could damage his case. Earlier, Baxter made plain what he was defending the junkies against. In an interview with a young reporter, Michael King, in *The Waikato Times* (4 September 1969), he spoke of the belligerence of the police towards the junkies, who had often complained to him that the police had beaten them up. Lacking legal redress, they felt helpless. They had no witnesses because only the police were present, and the police would not testify against each other. Nor did drug patients in mental hospitals get any satisfaction when they alleged maltreatment; they were simply not believed because such people 'can be expected to tell lies'. Baxter quoted the superintendent of a large mental institution who had stated publicly: 'Junkies are the scum of society' and that the taking of marijuana went with promiscuity. Baxter complained, too, that it was not uncommon for doctors to give information to the police.

For him, prevailing attitudes were intolerable:

Police are not helping drug users to recover – they only search for drugs . . . I have also learned from doctors and nurses that mental hospitals have no facilities to offer which are successful in breaking drug habits. In my opinion this is because they are treating people as objects rather than subjects. The whole public attitude to drug using is loaded with fear, fantasy and punitive legalism . . . I want the police to be policed and not allowed to run wild. I want communal centres where people who have habits can help others who wish to free themselves. And I want this country to retain the democratic respect for the free will of the individual.

His expectation was that drug-taking in New Zealand would increase 'one hundredfold as the mental dungeons of our society become more oppressive.' The problem, he believed, was already more widespread than was generally allowed: 'The largest number of drug users may well be among the affluent, respectable people who cannot bear the nullity of their suburban home life. The most dangerous drugs, those which are most readily available and used, are amphetamines, which can kill people in four years. I would prefer these respectable drug users not to be abusive about their fellow junkies, who happen to be poor.'

Public statements like these were meant to change society's attitudes to the drug problem, but Baxter did not confine himself to words. He saw his own contribution at Boyle Crescent as the first stage of a Narcotics Anonymous Association in New Zealand. As the name suggests, it would use the approach and techniques of Alcoholics Anonymous.

'Ballad of the Junkies and the Fuzz' takes up most of the concerns expressed in the interview with Michael King. The poem turns on the contrast between the world of the junkie and that of the outside society, which uses the police to enforce its standards:

> In the rickety streets of Grafton where many gather
> In a single house, sharing the kai, sharing the pain,
>   sharing the drug perhaps, sharing the
>   paranoia;
> Bearded, barefoot or sandalled, coming out crippled
>   from the bin or the clink.
> (The windows painted black; yet the black paint was
>   scraped off again) —
> In order that the junkie rock may crack and flow with
>   water
> And the rainbow of aroha shine on each one's face
> Because love is in the look, stronger than lush, and
>   truth is in the mouth, better than kai –
>   (CP 442)

The junkies' nightmare is generated by hallucinogens or by fear of death from an overdose: 'The wing of the black angel is lying over/Us.' And by the terror of being busted by the fuzz:

> But every light on the ceiling of the room
> Is the light of a squad car
> And every noise of stopping and acceleration
> Grinding on the metal of the road outside
> Means for him the fuzz are at the door —
> To break the locks, brother,
> To tear down the wallpaper,
> To empty the cupboards on to the carpet,
> Looking for a single roach.
>
> (CP 446)

The suddenness of a raid is vividly described and the fuzz savagely characterized:

> How strange, man, to see those spruce and angry ghosts
> Suddenly materialize
> In an old house in the middle of the morning
> When several are eating soup, one is playing the
>   guitar, two are talking about nasturtium leaves,
> And the others are snoring after an all-night party —
> Suddenly you see them in the centre of the room,
> The servants of the Zombie King —
> Skorbul the football player with his brown moustache,
> Krubble, who has a habit of crushing fingers in doors,
> Drooble, who is glad to bang girls' heads on walls,
> And one or two other clean-cut eager beagles
> Young poltergeists squaring their shoulders, imitating
>   the TV hero, hoping for a punch-up —
> The fuzz are in the house.
>
> (CP 443-4)

The police ruthlessly expose the vulnerability of the commune: 'They have taken away Maori Johnny, the horsebreaker from/Taumarunui. A keen pot smoker', 'Blind Bob' and 'Young Vikki'. 'She will have her head shrunk and wear a poor dress/and be touched by the Lesbian guards.'

The world of the commune, with its difficulties and aspirations, is set against that of the society which harries them, whose inhabitants are also on drugs, but ones which happen to be legal. Baxter's examples are 'Boys half-lushed' on alcohol, and suburban housewives. This is the order of things the police were invented to maintain:

> It was necessary of course to invent the fuzz
> To fence off the area of civilized coma
> From the forces of revolt and lamentation
> That rise around it, male and female

Ikons weeping tears of blood.

(CP 444)

'Ballad of the Junkies and the Fuzz' is a powerful defence of an inarticulate minority which was viewed by society as threatening.

About the middle of 1970, Baxter padded barefoot into my study at Victoria University and asked if I could get the poem published. He said that the young people on drugs had found it helpful. Four hundred copies were printed, free of charge, by Professor Don McKenzie at his Wai-te-ata Press, which has often used its small resources to help New Zealand writers publish their work. McKenzie printed the ballad himself and designed its cover.

Baxter's view of the commune and its work was not shared by the police. Drugs were becoming a major problem in New Zealand during the sixties, and in 1965 special small squads were set up by the police in the four main centres. Because the Drug Squad took a strong line with addicts and pushers, Boyle Crescent became a prime target, and many arrests were made. There were other problems. At times young people who had run away from home would be sought by the police; some were found at No. 7 Boyle Crescent.

Police raided the place at any hour every other day and did not hesitate to turn its occupants out of bed. To take off the heat, Baxter told the Inspector in charge of the Drug Squad that he did not allow drugs in the house. He was not believed because drugs had been found there. In fact, it was impossible for Baxter to give such an assurance. Boyle Crescent was an open house and anyone could arrive with drugs. Some of the junkies did not wish to break the habit; if Baxter became heavy-handed they would rebel and his whole venture, which depended on their co-operation, would collapse.

The police considered No. 7 extremely squalid. The kitchen table, which had old newspapers for a covering, always seemed to be piled with unwashed dishes and there was filth everywhere. In 'Elegy for Boyle Crescent' Baxter himself spoke of: 'Burst mattresses. Broken chairs. A sofa with half the springs exposed. A table littered with the remains of fifty meals. Cigarette butts trodden into the carpet.'[7] The police were disgusted to find that in the middle of a beautiful sunny morning the residents were often still in bed. No one seemed concerned to tidy the place. According to a senior policeman, such a life-style hindered the rehabilitation of drug addicts. Since the house was a crash pad, the pressure on facilities also resulted in trouble with the Health Department.

Two members of the Drug Squad observed that a number of young girls were captivated by Baxter's personality, and what they called his notoriety, and they suspected he used them for his personal gratification. They considered that when his daughter Hilary was living at Boyle Crescent, he did not exercise the supervision they expected from a father. They also disliked seeing him walking down Queen Street holding the hands of young girls. Neither policeman thought that the commune did much good. Baxter talked to the young people and seemed to do very little else for them. One man, who was a member of the Drug Squad for many years, said he'd never heard of anyone who had given up drugs because of Baxter, though he conceded that some addicts expressed great admiration for him. Personally he disliked him, and said that some of the Auckland magistrates shared his view. This policeman, who was under the impression Baxter was about sixty (he was forty-two), thought that the very look of him was enough to turn people off. 'He was a dirty-looking old bloke with filthy clothes. If people saw him they'd think "Who's that dirty old devil?" ' In his book, cleanliness was next to godliness.

Baxter continually challenged his contemporaries to look through appearances to the solid human qualities beneath. But he was never sanguine that what he was trying to do at Boyle Crescent would be understood: 'How can I interpret the beauty of that house to a culture that has burnt-out eyes and broken ear-drums? I think it has to be said in Braille, as a man under a blanket touches with his fingers, one by one, each muscle of a woman's body. To learn the language of Thou in place of the language of It. A plantation of love on the mountains of the moon.'[8] A senior police officer, with whom Baxter had a reasonably cordial relationship and who saw him in many moods, angry, philosophical, quietly argumentative, said he had dealt with criminals all his life, and the way Baxter used to look at him with hooded eyes suggested he was a very crafty person. All in all he considered him a likeable rogue.

Baxter was never a junkie, though he admitted that he had smoked marijuana occasionally to identify more with the young people. And he believed it was harmless.[9] In the commune he never saw himself as responsible for maintaining authority, much less for imposing moral standards. But as a father-protector figure he went frequently to police headquarters to lay complaints of maltreatment against the Drug Squad. The most shocking allegation in 'Ballad of the Junkies and the Fuzz', one that Baxter repeated in a letter to his parents, was made by a girl who died from an overdose of heroin. In the poem the incident is attributed to a different girl:

> They have taken away Yancy. For a long time at the
> station Drooble kept banging her head on the
> wall. She lost her not yet born child.
>
> (CP 445)

He also wrote a number of letters making similar charges. His information came mainly from prisoners and from the residents of Boyle Crescent. These were, of course, denied by the police. Much later Baxter shared with Roderick Finlayson, his friend and fellow writer, his own fears that he might not have the courage to stand up to what he believed was the common method of interrogating junkies.[10]

Not only was Baxter grappling with the drug problem in the New Zealand city where it was most acute; his influence was also felt in the radical student movement of the late sixties and early seventies. The most colourful and gifted of the protesters was Tim Shadbolt, much later to become the mayor of Waitemata City. Combining a relaxed personal charm and high intelligence with an independent and forthright view of New Zealand society, he was, and remains, a natural leader. In the late sixties he was cutting his political teeth. His book *Bullshit and Jellybeans* (1971), with its call for a just and healthy society, sold over 8,000 copies in the first six weeks after printing. It became a home-grown *Das Kapital* for radical students up and down the country, and it was favourably reviewed in the *N.Z. Listener* by Alexander MacLeod, the editor, despite some reservations about Shadbolt's simplistic approach to the political process.[11]

In Auckland, Shadbolt attracted around him a group of students who lived in a cluster of houses in Parnell on the opposite side of the Domain from Grafton. There were about twenty in the core group, though at times the number might rise to sixty. They were poor, and the run-down houses in which they lived could be rented for about twelve to fifteen dollars a week. They called their cluster 'The People's Republic of Gibraltar Crescent', and the track that led from it through the Domain to the university they named the Ho Chi Minh trail. Someone even painted the name on the Grafton overbridge.

Occupants of these various clusters in Grafton and Parnell moved freely between each others' places. Shadbolt's followers respected Baxter as an establishment figure who had turned his back on respectability by dropping out. They liked his idealism, his wide-ranging criticism of New Zealand society, and what he was doing for people. Many of them also knew his poetry. When Shadbolt was asked if he believed Baxter had really helped the junkies he replied: 'I don't think you can measure help. He gave them the rest they needed, and he put people up when they had nowhere else to go.'[12] Both men were opposed to the Vietnam war, but for different reasons. Shadbolt's diagnosis was political, Baxter's spiritual. Shadbolt blamed the American industrial-military establishment, and New Zealand for aligning itself with it; Baxter claimed the West had debased people by ignoring their personal worth, and that the war was an effect of the spiritual impoverishment that prevails when society's chief concern is material prosperity. Shadbolt's own thinking, like that of everyone else's of the time, was profoundly affected by Baxter. For him, Baxter was a street-philosopher, a man of the streets, who knew whatever went on. Like James Joyce, Baxter 'knew the limbs and bowels of a city of which Yeats knew well only the head.'[13]

In his youthful mythology Shadbolt saw himself and his friends not as street-philosophers but street-fighters, engaged in a political battle. They were always on the move, moving quickly from one part of Auckland to another, and they thought nothing of heading off to Wellington for a demonstration. Every member of the group was expected to be fully committed and active. They had no room for drones. Initially they found Baxter too slow; he thought they were not contemplative enough. But he felt a real affection for them, smiling and saying: 'Young devils, racing around and getting into trouble with the police.' Baxter told Shadbolt that if he wanted to be detached from money, two or three times a year he should wipe his arse with a ten dollar note and flush it down the toilet. Shadbolt said he did this a couple of times and found it very difficult. Ten dollars was almost a whole week's rent.

Gradually Baxter came to realize that Central Auckland was not the place to achieve what he hoped. He believed that if he could get the junkies out of the city for a while they might recover and return to normal living. To help them survive, he needed to develop a new set of values as a counter to the destructive attitudes of New Zealand society.

About July of 1969 he moved out of No. 7 Boyle Crescent and set off for Jerusalem. But he was back in Auckland in time to grieve when his old house was demolished by bulldozers:

> When I saw the bulldozers crash through the walls of the house, for the first time in years I began to weep. In the dust-laden cloud a great wild bird rose and fluttered and died. And the souls of the confessors of the junkie church who had taken an overdose and died in that neighbourhood blazed out to meet it like white stars in a black sky . . .
>
> The weeds are growing high on the site where the house stood. The landlord has not yet erected the new honeycomb of concrete in which people will be able to watch identical programmes at different tellies, not knowing their neighbours' names. When he does, he will get four times the rent that he got from the house that stood there.
>
> Where are the tribe of the young to go? . . .
>
> The house of prudence is different from the house of love.
>
> A part of my heart is buried in the empty section where the junkies' mother house once stood. Because she gave me life when the city was killing me. She taught me that I can become *Us*.

Broken pill bottles and rusted needles are also buried there. The furnace of the winter stars blazes above the spot.[14]

In the thirteenth Jerusalem Sonnet, part of the Boyle Crescent experience lives on in stillness and vividness:

> It is not possible to sleep
> As I did once in Grafton
>
> Under the bright candles of a poor man's wall,
> Under the delicate Japanese image
>
> Of the Man dying whose arms embrace the night —
> Lying curled in rough blankets, perhaps alone,
>
> Perhaps not alone, with the great freedom
> Of a river that runs in the dark towards its mouth —
>
> Oh treasure of the poor, to be loved!
> Arms and eyes I shall not see again —
>
> It is not possible to sleep
> The sleep of children, sweeter than marihuana,
>
> Or to be loved so dearly as we have been loved,
> With our weapons thrown down, for a breathing space.
> (CP 461)

Baxter's experiment at Boyle Crescent ran from April to July or August 1969. To those who were there it seemed astounding that so much could happen in such a short time. How is to be assessed? Earlier residents of the street, some of whom were junkies, felt they had been displaced by Baxter. A few dismissed him as a man on an 'ego-trip' who attracted unwelcome attention from the police. A prominent psychiatrist believed that he had helped a good number of people and saved a few lives. But in the realm of ideas he was a pioneer. He had discovered what is now accepted as the best way of treating drug addiction – to bring those on drugs into a therapeutic community.[15] His approach obviously suited the junkies because many stayed with him, and those who left kept coming back. But in 1969 New Zealand society was not ready for Baxter's idea of Narcotics Anonymous, drug addicts helping other addicts to come off drugs and stay off them. And because he had no skill in organizing a community, Baxter was not the person to put his ideas into practice.[16]

When the Board of Health set up a committee in August 1968 'to enquire into and report on drug abuse and drug dependency in New Zealand', it offered an opportunity for political action to improve the condition of the junkies. Baxter responded and twice made submissions,[17] once in 1969 and again in 1971. His presentation, based on 'limited yet unusually deep acquaintance with drugs and drug-users', developed fully, and with remarkable moderation, his ideas. He added that religious meditation and detachment from material goods seemed to him especially important in helping people to free themselves from drugs:

> . . . it seems to be that drug-users are often people who are peculiarly sensitive to, and feel menaced by, the pervading and imprisoning materialism of our present culture, whether the people concerned are vagrants or suburban householders. In a sense their use of drugs is their means of adjusting – either the drug removes conflict by sedation, or produces temporary pseudo-mystical states, or does both. The fact that most drugs (including marihuana) block off sexual impulses is an added attraction, because many drug-users desire a degree of celibacy.
>
> It would seem to me both helpful and legitimate therefore to offer the study and practice of Oriental religion – and of Christian contemplative habits – as part of the programme of any group devoting itself to self-cure from drug dependency. A materialist emphasis would obviously be self-defeating.

He advocated total separation between hospital treatment and police action, and that police should not use 'violence in interrogation or indeed in any circumstances except brief and unavoidable self-defence.' He wanted a special permanent bureau set up outside the Justice Department to receive and investigate complaints of violence. This would be a way of 'curbing the over-zealous'. When he presented his idea for a communal organization of drug-users, Narcotics Anonymous, he proposed as a title F.L.A.S.H., Fellowship of Love and Self-Help. He thought the name would appeal to drug-users because of the pun (a 'flash' in the head is produced by the injection of narcotics). Publicly and privately Baxter addressed one of the social problems of his time. The values he had been developing at Boyle Crescent under the pressure of strenuous experience, he was to take with him to Jerusalem and articulate unforgettably.

Even a person with Baxter's prodigious capacities could hardly produce a new volume of poetry in a year like 1969. But the collection called *The Rock Woman* was published that year. In the preface he said that the book's 'main purpose is to provide a reasonable sampling of my verse of the past twenty years.' The selection was made largely by Jon Stallworthy of the London office of Oxford University Press from the original manuscript Baxter had submitted, a selected poems which the Press had judged to be too long. Baxter approved the final selection. Until the *Collected Poems* appeared posthumously in 1980, *The Rock Woman* gave a full, if uneven, overview of Baxter's poetic achievement. Forty of its fifty-three poems are taken from the three previous Oxford collections, *In Fires of No Return* (1958), *Howrah Bridge* (1961), and *Pig Island Letters* (1966). Many of the best poems from earlier collections were included, along with twelve previously uncollected poems.

The title poem refers to 'a rock carved like a woman' wet with drops of sea water, which resemble the rosary beads on a medieval statue. Baxter also said that it is a symbol of New Zealand, a hard, bare, stony country which he knew with the intimacy of a lover. Alone with the Rock Woman – characteristically, for this poet of the beach and coast, she is found by the sea – Baxter experienced peace.

The image of the Rock Woman relates each poem in the volume to the larger poetic enterprise in which he was constantly engaged: the struggle to come to terms with himself.

With its references to his marriage, 'The Waves' had been perhaps too personal to include in *Pig Island Letters*. Now it was given a position of emphasis as the last poem in *The Rock Woman*, and in September 1969, he was concerned about what Jacquie would make of it.

But the poem is also about God, first presented as the God of the Old Testament:

> . . . under weed gates the white octopus
> Haunter and waker of the coast
> In storms of genesis contains his power.
> (CP 286)

As the poem proceeds a second image is developed – the compassionate Christ-figure who does not condemn what is. Baxter's life-task is to conform himself to this model:

> How to distinguish from the flux of fire,
> Salt tides and air, some ruler
> Other than octopus, man-killing moon
> Or our own twist of thought, breeds pain.
> Wings of the albatross whose shadow
> Lies on the seas at noon
>
> I take as the type of a spirit bent
> By abstract solitude,
> Accepting all.
> (CP 288)

Baxter told me that what he had in mind in the last three lines was 'moving in empathy with the waves of events; which doesn't mean the will choosing evil . . . grass moves with the wind, bamboo is broken.' Detachment is difficult, and since art cannot preserve what it loves against time's destructiveness, the poem moves towards an affirmation that religious faith is the appropriate attitude:

> Yet hard for human blood
>
> Is the habit of relinquishment,
> Abandoning of Isaac to the knife
> That tortured Abraham. Come now;
> Poems are trash, the flesh I love will die,
> Desire is bafflement,
> But one may say that father Noah kept
> Watch while the wild beasts slept,
>
> Not knowing even if land would rise
> Out of the barren waves.
> That ark I keep, that watch on the edge of sleep,
> While the dark water heaves.

In 1969 Baxter had acted out his own script. The bearded patriarchal figure, who always slept very little, had been surrounded by the slumbering junkies of Boyle Crescent. He had found it necessary to remonstrate with himself: 'You're beginning to think you're Noah. I keep telling myself I'm not.'

XIII
The Two Jerusalems

If that Jerusalem which is unshakeable friendship
with God has not been established first in the heart,
how can the objective Jerusalem of communal charity
be built so as not to fall?

(CP 629)

Jerusalem, a small Maori settlement beside the Wanganui River, comprises
half a dozen houses and a meeting-house. A church, convent, and presbytery
border the marae.

In Baxter's time the resident pastor was Father Wiremu Te Awhitu, the
first Maori to become a Catholic priest. A heavy stroke had left his speech
blurred, but he was well enough to discharge light duties, and he did not
mind the isolation.

The village has a rich history. It was the first mission station of Mother
Mary Aubert, founder of the Sisters of Compassion, and one of the most
remarkable women in the early European history of New Zealand. She may
have been the first Frenchwoman to take a medical course. Her remedies,
her skill, and her willingness to attend the sick day or night made her famous
up and down the Wanganui River. She also left a legacy of nineteenth
century forms of piety derived from her mentor, the celebrated Curé of Ars,
St Jean Baptiste Vianney who appears to have been greatly troubled by
diabolical visitations. The saint's experience was well understood by those
who lived in a place where 'ghosts are real' (CP 541) and where, for fear of
te taipo, the bush demon, the Maori kept the lights burning all night outside
their houses (CP 471).

At the nearby river island of Moutoa, 'the isle of heroes', the Hau Haus,
sweeping down river towards Wanganui 'to drive the white men into the
sea whence they came', had been stopped by Maori loyal to the Queen.[1]

Jerusalem's many associations, including that of the biblical city, were to
work powerfully in Baxter's imagination. From the beginning, he took
considerable pains to articulate his ideal: 'to receive the peace and love of
God, and help others to receive it, in a communal atmosphere.'[2] This had
been in his mind since his 'vision' in Dunedin in 1968. By the middle of 1969,
with Boyle Crescent behind him, he saw much more clearly how it might
be realized. As well as being a poet, he was now a social philospher.

Most of his adult life had been spent in the city and he had seen at close quarters what city life did to people. His main criticism was that it disregarded the worth and dignity of the human person. Its defining question was 'What do you do?' Personal needs were sacrificed to productivity and administrative efficiency.

Baxter believed that many urban–dwellers felt isolated, inadequate, and frustrated in their attempts to create better relationships – inevitably because they lived not 'in a community of neighbours but in a society of strangers.'[3] The result was despair, which Baxter regarded as the commonest disease in the city: 'And each person thinks that he or she alone is suffering from it. Not a theological despair, since theological hope has rarely been present in these souls at any conscious level. Despair rather in the viability of human relations.' He believed that desacralization, despersonalization, and centralization were the three scourges of urban culture.[4]

The dislocation was apparent at all levels. Parents were often 'unable, on account of their anxieties, to shift gear, as their children grow up, from the role of authority to the role of friend.' Marriages were breaking up while people busied themselves in their possessions. Society could not cope with people who had disabilities.

The education system implanted a logical lens in the skull. Whoever looked through it could see nothing sacred – God or people: 'The Mass is an event in comparative religion. A Maori tangi is an event in comparative anthropology. Sex is a physical union of parts of the body. Death is a statistical occasion.'[5]

Ostensibly concerned with equality, secular education imposed conformity. Variety and spontaneity were lost as the young were impaled on 'the stake of an undesired education'. Even schools which professed to impart religious values could make a girl feel a second-rate person if she lost her virginity.

He felt that his own failures as a husband and father were exacerbated by a corrupt society. An alternative was needed, a new Jerusalem. He would prepare a place where his wife and family could join him in a new and simpler life with a good centre. He expressed that hope many times. Jerusalem was an answer to Baxter's own needs, but from its conception it looked well beyond them. It would be a place where certain values could be lived and communicated once a community had been gathered, the tribe of 'Ngati Hiruharama'. That idea was the culmination of his lifelong search for unity.

The notion of a community at Jerusalem had particular appeal to him since he was of Highland descent and married to a Maori. In an article in the *New Zealand Tablet* in 1967 he asked his Catholic readers to examine their attitudes towards the Maori people.[6] In his view it was harder for a Maori to get employment and housing than for a Pakeha. Gradually he came to believe that it was the duty of 'all New Zealand teachers, as far as their hearts will allow them, to soak themselves in Maoritanga and begin to learn the Maori language.'[7] The Maori wars had broken the Maori tribes the way the battle of Culloden had broken the Highland clans, and the process of dissolution continued in Baxter's lifetime with the breaking down of many forms of community in New Zealand. It bore especially heavily on the Maori people: 'In this country Christ has two faces, Maori and Pakeha and the Maori face is being mangled and broken by our inhuman and money-centred culture.'[8]

Yet he believed that the communal life of Maori people in certain parts of the country preserved the values which Pakeha society had lost. In that respect the Maori was the elder brother of the Pakeha. Baxter chose to go to Jerusalem in order to learn from a Maori community. One of the few possessions he took was a Bible in Maori:

> a sacred language
> Dignified by poverty and the absence of lies . . .[9]

He learnt to use it effectively in his Jerusalem writings.

Baxter was further attracted to Maori culture because of its deep spirituality and its belief in gods – powerful spirits and protectors, such as the taniwha of the Wanganui River. The Maori emphasis on feeling rather than on abstract thought was also congenial to him. Christ was too often presented as a middle-class, educated European. A Maori perspective would correct that.

When Baxter returned from Auckland to settle at Jerusalem he was bearded, barefoot, in poor clothes, and carrying a long sturdy stick cut from a tree The youngsters called him John the Baptist. On 17 September 1969 he moved into a cottage belonging to the Sisters of Compassion: ' – two rooms, a stove, a range, even a bath – somewhat palatial I fear – with a plot of ground alongside which I am beginning to cultivate.'[10] Cultivation never got far – it was part of the unfulfilled dream.

Baxter had to go to Wellington to see the Mother General of the Congregation about his extended use of the cottage. She could never have imagined what would be involved in so routine an approval. There he stayed with his family. Jacquie was working in the Public Library and with John's help, caring for Hilary's baby, Stephanie. The visit confirmed Baxter's view 'that my present course of action is the only one to follow.'[11] He returned to Jerusalem.

He soon felt lonely. His thoughts turned to his wife with whom he hoped one day to be reunited. He told his mother: 'I now have a true hope that my wife and I will be together again on earth – not just alongside each other – one in the spirit also. That is all I need to make me able to go on a thousand miles.'[12]

Colin Durning was an early visitor. He had been a close friend during Baxter's tenure of the Burns Fellowship. Influenced by Baxter, he had resigned the Chair of Prosthetic Dentistry at Otago, though he had done important pioneering work in the field. He had then taken a job at a borstal pre-release centre, but it did not go well. As they walked around the hills, Baxter told him that there was no reason in the world for setting up a place in Jerusalem, yet he knew that was what he would do.

After a visit to Auckland he returned with a young man and a sixteen-year-old girl and they lived with him in the cottage. When they left, there were few people to talk to. But out of that silence, he spoke memorably in verse. The 'Jerusalem Sonnets' were sent in batches to Colin Durning with the instruction:

> Keep these 'sonnets' I send you – I'll have no copies here, or not likely – and just at the minute I mean to go on writing a few more, to get myself mentally settled in – so keep them, stack them away somewhere – I asked the Lord about it and He said He didn't mind – I guess it doesn't come under the 'No books' heading – some day they might be of use to other people, if only as a curiosity. If you want to, get copies typed – but I'd rather you showed them to people very sparingly and didn't give them copies.[13]

The poems were an expression of his friendship: 'Those poems I have sent you – good or bad, who cares? – spring from my sense of the spiritual cable between us – and you will see how nevertheless they are all "I" poems! I think we don't have to be ashamed of "I" – the thing is, what does a man know except his own experience? – which includes experience of such bonds – the ship knows only the ends of the ropes that moor her to the wharf, nevertheless they have other ends.'[14] Although the sonnets were not written for publication, Baxter sent: 'A title and a solemn epigraph(!) in case the poems are ever printed. I will not print them; but in time they could be, of course.'

At Durning's suggestion, the original title, 'Sonnets to Colin Durning', was changed to 'Jerusalem Sonnets'. They are written in loose, unrhymed couplets, perhaps modelled on Lawrence Durrell's sequence of fourteen poems, 'A Soliloquy of Hamlet',[15] which Baxter had reviewed for the *N.Z. Listener* a few months before. When Baxter was eventually persuaded by Durning to publish them under the title *Jerusalem Sonnets*, he remarked wryly: 'Now I'll know who my real friends are.'

The setting for the first two 'Jerusalem Sonnets' is the church, and the poet's occupation is prayer. Prayer, in the sense of meditation, is prominent in these poems as activity, and as a poetic technique. 'All experience,' he said, 'asks to be understood.' The prayer and the poetry are two aspects of a spiritual journey on the road to understanding, an effort 'to hack down the wall of God.' At another level, the Jerusalem writings sustain the effort of Baxter's earlier poetry to penetrate to what Rollo May called 'the level of the archetypes where the eternal myths of history such as those of Orestes and Odysseus have their existence' – myth as a key to the understanding of human behaviour.[16]

Through prayer Baxter introduced his social concerns into the tradition of Christian ascetism. In the process they were intensified and enlarged. Poverty, for example, 'the spirit of non-possession', became not only a prerequisite for an equitable society, but part of an understanding of humanity. There is a restlessness in these Jerusalem poems as Baxter questions experience after experience in the search for meaning. He refers frequently to journeys. The restlessness is that of a man looking for something beyond this world.

Prayer sustained Baxter in his spiritual quest. It also provided a way of expressing what his imagination grasped. The reflective character of religious meditation, its careful weighing of particulars, its arriving at insights, is apparent in the *Jerusalem Sonnets*, which move at their close into the formulation of prayer. Sonnets 37 and 38 adopt the pattern of rhythm and refrain which are characteristic of certain psalms. The opening line of Sonnet 38: 'I am dying now because I do not die', is from a poem of St John of the Cross, whose mystical writings are partly meditations on his poetry.[17]

Though Baxter could use the techniques of prayer, he came to realize he had to look elsewhere for his material. He had hoped for forty Jerusalem sonnets, but could manage only thirty-nine:

> how can the image come
> At all to the centre where the mind is silent
>
> Without being false?
>
> (CP 474)

The centre is the point of contact between God and the soul which occurs in contemplative prayer. At that moment, the great mystics agree, 'silence is our only speech.' Baxter is not a poet of the ineffable. If prayer was to furnish material for his art it had to be nourished by the earth.

Baxter did not imagine he would find a garden of Eden at Jerusalem. He dreaded the hardships and the difficulties and the changes his plan would impose. He wrote: 'It is one thing to propose a philosophy. It is another thing to try to found a tribe.'[18] Community life was something he had thought about quite deeply: 'Care . . . is cast off for a moment . . . by . . . the Roman *fraternitas*, the Maori *aroha*, the appearance or reality of group love, a merging in the collective warmth of the tribe.'[19] And tribal love was the 'natural base of divine charity'.[20] The earthly and heavenly Jerusalems were inextricably linked.

Gradually his presence in Jerusalem became known, and the numbers built up. By May 1971 there were some forty people in residence, of whom about half were more or less permanent members of the community. On one occasion, approximately eighty people sat down to dinner. In the weekends the place was often jammed with cars. Some people would stay a month, others about a year – the floating population making it difficult for the community to cohere. Baxter said about a thousand people stayed each year.[21] He tended to exaggerate, but the numbers were certainly high. Most were between the ages of seventeen and twenty-five. Baxter would not take anyone under the age of sixteen without parental consent.

If he was content to devote his best energies to the young, it was because he believed that they were the sensitive part of society's conscience, that they felt more acutely and spoke more honestly. In the sixties they were rejecting institutionalized authority and looking for an alternative. They also wanted greater sexual freedom. Baxter championed their aspirations and helped them find a voice: 'I am glad to see the hunger for freedom that exists among the young. They want to get free of the web of bad motivation. Frequently their education at home and at school has been an education in cynical self-interest. They have to turn themselves inside out to get free of it.'[22] Because society trained the young to fight for position, for money, for kudos, any sense of community was destroyed.

Living conditions at Jerusalem were rather primitive, but residents did not have to pay any rent. Baxter slept in a dilapidated four-roomed farmhouse called 'Middle House'. Below it was 'Bottom House' and above, up a steep track, 'Top House'. When Baxter arrived 'Middle House' had blackberry growing in the windows. It slept about thirty people. Others dossed down on the verandah or by the fire, which burned all night outside the house. They slept on old coats, blankets, mattresses, or in sleeping-bags. People drifted off to bed at any hour, and there was usually someone moving around during the night. Baxter himself slept very little. He would lie down and chain-smoke while he read, or 'raved on', as a companion put it. He would often go down the hill through the long grass to the church, or to the presbytery, where Father Te Awhitu had set aside a room in which he could write. He had a good deal of correspondence from people with all sorts of problems, and he preferred to write to them rather than to his friends. Caches of his letters survive all over New Zealand.

Cooking was done on an old cast-iron stove in 'Middle House'. Most of the residents turned up for the evening meal between seven and ten, and it was often a spartan affair. An older woman considered the food was of poor quality and poorly cooked. It might include goat from the surrounding hills (predictably Baxter's portion included one testicle), eels from the river, or meat that had been bought or donated. Some local farmers believed that occasionally their sheep went into the oven. This had certainly happened once, and Baxter had to read the riot act. One young man described Jerusalem in winter as: 'Too bloody cold and not enough to eat.'

Their toilets were two deep holes dug for the purpose. Tank water was available for washing, and there was a bath-tub in the kitchen which could be filled with hot water from an old copper. In the circumstances, taking a bath required too much determination for most. In warm weather they bathed, often nude, in the river. In a Maori community Baxter had to be discreet about nudity. It was a delicate business. One day he came across a young naked woman digging the garden. After telling her she reminded him of Eve 'innocently working the clods of the first garden', he warned her that if other people came over the hill there would be trouble. She gave up gardening and spent the time inside with her boyfriend.

Living conditions were sometimes squalid. Baxter didn't like some aspects of that but he had a high tolerance for untidiness. Ten or more years earlier he had told a friend that he felt more at ease in a 'broken-down fly-specked hotel kitchen' than in a well kept suburban home.'[23] A nurse whom Baxter had invited to come and care for a girl who was pregnant and getting over the effects of drugs remained for some time. She saw that the cooking utensils were often filthy and feared an outbreak of salmonella. Her anxiety did not trouble Baxter, who dismissed it as middle-class paranoia.

Awareness of bodily functions in the crowded conditions of a community is much more acute than in an ordinary suburban home. The choice is either to ignore them, or to help people to keep them in perspective by talking or joking about them as naturally as about anything else. Often the young are much less squeamish in these matters than their elders.

Drug-taking and free love, which were said to be rife in the community, brought reporters sniffing around. Some specialized in titillating the prurience of readers while gratifying their self-righteousness. In judging the morality of the community, a distinction has to be made between the more or less permanent members and the casual visitors who sometimes misunderstood the nature of the enterprise. Many of these were young university students who dropped in at holiday times, used the place, and then moved off. Often they viewed Baxter with some cynicism. Baxter was uneasy during the university holidays when Jerusalem resembled a student holiday camp and no work was done. The students had been taught only 'to read, write and talk.' He loved them and realized they needed a great deal of help with what were often massive hang-ups. But he breathed a sigh of relief when the holidays were over. Some others who came were 'out of the trees', as a member put it. Two reporters on different occasions wrote that they saw no evidence of any general 'sleeping around'. One said: 'About three couples slept together regularly while I was there . . . I doubt whether there is more "sleeping around" than you would find in the city.'[24] Baxter himself said he had not seen promiscuity at Jerusalem, though he had observed it among university students. He thought it came from loneliness, and from a sense that they were not free to run their own lives, but were like trucks shunted about on rails laid down by others.[25]

Baxter's own behaviour was much the same as at Grafton. The man who slept beside him for two years at Jerusalem said he would have known about any sexual immorality, but saw none, though he knew that Baxter had a steady relationship with one woman and that it was probably sexual. Others have said that Baxter sometimes slept with some of the girls. And the thirty-second 'Jerusalem Sonnet' speaks of 'my two illegitimate children' (CP 470). In this sonnet, Baxter says the women 'wanted to have my children.' Fame is a powerful aphrodisiac, but that does not exonerate him. A well-balanced member of the community considered Jerusalem a very chaste place, though not a celibate one.

Some of the members had used drugs, including the highly damaging LSD. Baxter discouraged drug-taking, though he considered marijuana relatively harmless and thought it should be legalized. He saw that one important advantage of marijuana was that people could grow their own instead of having to deal with pedlars, who were often the same people who pushed hard drugs. One object of the community was to help people to get off drugs and to cope during the withdrawal stage.

Community living might appear not to have been organized but it had a structure which Baxter had chosen carefully – based on the 'five spiritual aspects of Maori communal life –

> arohanui: the love of the many;
> manuhiritanga: hospitality to the guest and stranger;
> korero: speech that begets peace and understanding;
> matewa: the night life of the soul;
> mahi: work undertaken from communal love.'[26]

One Maori writer was to say later: 'Only a few foreigners, men like James K. Baxter with the soul of a poet, can enter into the existential dimension of Maori life.'[27] When Baxter prayed for a Maori heart and changed his name to its Maori equivalent, Hemi, he was expressing a wish to see life through Maori eyes and to give a Maori response. He was also committing himself to transplanting the 'five spiritual aspects' to the Jerusalem community.

Arohanui ('the love of the many') began with an acceptance of people as they were. In Baxter's community at Jerusalem no questions were asked. People were simply accepted. It was part of his role to make explicit the science of loving well: 'To "be aroha" is simply the movement of the mother hen spreading her wings above the chickens. She may have many lice in her feathers. But the chickens come to her for shelter because they know she will die first before letting them be killed.'[28]

In practice, love meant availability: 'My limited response to whatever happens.' And he prayed: 'Make me the bread that is broken and the wine that is drunk.' Baxter took great pleasure in seeing love practised in the community. He wrote: 'These kids have heart enough to nourish the dead world.'

Sometimes morality seemed to get in the way: 'Love is crucified on the Law till the end of time. The Law is necessary; without the Law there would be no Cross.'[29] Another passage developed his mystical view of love: 'To love man leads to a broken heart. To love God leads to a dark night. To love God and man together leads to the Crucifixion. Despite various appearances that may seem contrary, I believe many of the young ones are capable of enduring broken hearts, dark nights and crucifixions.'[30]

Love became Baxter's overriding principle at Jerusalem. When I said to him: 'You are not a trained psychiatrist or counsellor, what do you think you do for these young people?' he simply replied: 'I give them my friendship and they give me theirs.' He knew it was never a one-way process: 'One has so much to learn from them, so short a time to learn it in – these idealistic, honest, curiously chaste, adult children of ours, who try to love one another, and even us as well, in the terrible social graveyard we have helped to construct for them.'[31] And he regarded 'their unrejecting tenderness' as the 'agent of my reformation'.

One public expression of aroha was the celebrated Jerusalem hug. Baxter would bear down on people and envelop them in his arms. Outside Jerusalem the hairy guru he had become caused consternation to those uncomfortable with physical contact. Hugging was part of the hippie culture.

A general ambience of freedom prevailed at Jerusalem. Everyone there had chosen to join the community. Baxter believed that God valued free choice most of all. Without it, he wrote, we would be unable to love.[32] He tried to help the doubtful clarify their minds and make their own decisions.

But he disclaimed any responsibility for their morals and he resisted any pressure to assume it himself. He would not have an electric fence

> Down the middle of the commune, separating
> He-bodies from she-bodies, and me patrolling it
>
> With a loaded shotgun
>
> (CP 503)

Manuhiritanga is the hospitality shown to the stranger or guest by the host tribe. In practice it means welcoming anyone who comes, offering them food and drink and a place to lie down. Baxter believed this open-door policy was necessary to counter the lack of hospitality he perceived so often in the towns.

In his attitude to guests and residents, Baxter's idealism was at its most transparent. He was well aware of how they were perceived by cynical outsiders: 'Everybody knows that the Jerusalem community is a band of weirdos, no-hopers, drop-outs, mad people, crimmos, thieves and junkies . . .' and 'they spend most of their time exchanging sexual partners.'[33]

He considered the community to be made up of two groups of people. First there were nga mokai, the orphans. 'In a sense the young people become orphans when their parents are unable to adjust to their motions toward independence.'[34] He was especially concerned for the Maori nga mokai, whom he wished to bring to Jerusalem to find the love of a group. In the early days this appealed to the Maori people at Jerusalem who hoped the pa could become the mother of the commune. Then there were nga raukore, those who are like trees that have had their leaves and branches stripped off by the heavy winds of the world: the junkies, the alcoholics, the young who felt ill at ease in New Zealand society.

In line with his principle, those with the greatest need were the most welcome at Jerusalem. None were turned away. Problems were solved, agreement was reached through talk ('korero: speech that begets peace and understanding').

Baxter was neither the rangatira of the Jerusalem community, nor an ethical instructor. He wanted everyone to be free to move gently and learn by their mistakes. He was 'a parent who is not a parent, a parent who has the job of responding to needs instead of making demands.' That is how he had treated his own children. As they became young adults he stood back and encouraged them to make their own decisions. Even if he did not like what they did he said he would not 'rave about it'. The approach, he thought, had 'a magical effect', and he won their confidence. He might no longer tell them what to do, but he could influence them by honest conversation.[35]

In the community, authority lay in the group meeting, which he regarded as the group conscience.[36] The values he hoped for would be learned in an ethos free from the anxiety-projecting mentality many of the community had experienced in their homes, their churches, and schools.[37] He was quite prepared for his experiment to be judged by the traditional yardstick of its fruit. On that basis he judged Jerusalem to be a good tree.[38]

Prayer ('matewa: the night life of the soul') had long been a staple of Baxter's life. At Jerusalem he attended daily Mass and often preached the homily. He was often seen saying his rosary. Yet many of the young people had very different religious backgrounds, or none at all. Baxter practised an enlightened ecumenism: 'I am a Jew because Bon is a Jew. I am a Buddhist because my son Hoani is a Buddhist. We do not only understand the essence of a religion other than our own, if we see it through the eyes of those we love, who are members of it. Mystically we do become members of it, without betrayal of any doctrine or principle of our own. That is the meaning of ecumenism.'[39] And he knew the action of the Holy Spirit was not confined to any one religion.

> Lord, Holy Spirit,
> You blow like the wind in a thousand paddocks,
> Inside and outside the fences,
> You blow where you wish to blow.
>
> (CP 572)

At the age of fifteen, Baxter had written a poem on Buddha which called him the ever-wise.[40] His interest in Buddhist thought went back at least ten years. Reviewing *Thirty Years of Buddhist Studies* in November 1968, he had said that although he was not a Buddhist scholar he had met people who had been cured of serious mental disturbances through Buddhist disciplines. Christians could not dismiss the Buddhist approach to attachment, 'since it is precisely attachment that exhausts and dismembers the souls of many in this destructively activist age.'[41]

Though he was not an expert on Christian mysticism, he was familiar with many of its key ideas, and he knew well *The Cloud of Unknowing* and the poems of St John of the Cross. A member of the community said that Baxter often read and quoted Thomas Merton's *Seeds of Contemplation*. From his own prayer Baxter knew something of the insights of the great mystics, and he was interested in their relationship with Zen.

In Christian mysticism a person enters into 'a cloud of unknowing', a state similar to that entered in Zen. That is why Baxter wrote in *Jerusalem*

Daybook: 'Through a theology of kenosis Buddhist and Catholic stand on the same ground.'[42] But the underlying commitment is quite different. Orthodox Christian mysticism is centred on the mystery of Christ, and based on the scriptures and the eucharist. Baxter was an enthusiastic reader of the scriptures. When I sent him a copy of Ronald Knox's translation of the Bible (referred to in his poem 'Letter to John Weir') he wrote that he would go through it with a fine tooth comb. Texts of his homilies at Jerusalem show how closely he had pondered the scriptural readings set down for the Masses.

In the first phase of the Jerusalem community, Baxter did not seem unduly concerned about mahi ('work undertaken from communal love'). He believed many of those who came to Jerusalem were incapable of work, or even of relating well to others. He insisted they needed time to grow and believed that this could best be achieved in a community. Occasionally there were moves to get rid of these 'bludgers', but he would have none of it: the 'bludgers and the parasites are God's gift to us, our sacred guests, jewels hidden in a ball of mud.'[43] And 'If nga raukore were pushed out, the blessing of God would go away with them, and the fountain of the community would be blocked up with stones.[44] Te Ariki 'did not despair of his friends, faulty as they were.'[45]

Tim Shadbolt and a group of his friends came to Jerusalem one day in a V8 truck and an Austin 16. They were on their way to a demonstration in Wellington. Baxter was away and they could not believe that no one was working. They moved in like an army, cleaned up the main house and dug a garden. Then they continued their journey. The novel spectacle of well-directed energy so impressed the residents that some of them wanted to go off with Shadbolt.

The community was financed by donations, and by what Baxter received for occasional articles, poems, and lectures. Some members earned a little by casual work for local farmers, and visitors sometimes brought gifts of meat and groceries. Tradespeople in Wanganui said that Baxter was punctilious in paying bills. But financially the community was no better off than the one in Grafton. A visiting journalist observed that the hippies could be divided into two kinds, the drones, who were only out for free board, and the idealists, who did the necessary work. They cleaned up, and helped around the place.

Baxter's ambivalence towards work was compounded by his attitude towards money. The appropriate attitude to money had engaged his mind for some time. Early in the previous year he had written: 'Yet for years I have felt that the way of life I have led - and that many around me lead - is hollow, burdensome in the wrong way, too analytical, too dominated by money and words.'[46] Now he felt called to live a life of poverty. Without a spirit of poverty a communal life was impossible. Poverty as a religious value is the first of Christ's beatitudes, but it is not readily understood today. For most people it suggests a lack of the material resources needed for a fully human life. In its religious context, it means a spirit of detachment that expresses itself in the sharing of material and mental possessions, something very demanding:

> Poverty, man,
>
> Is a word that skins the lips, the Prior of Taize said . . .
> (CP 498)

Baxter described poverty as the spirit of non-possession, and said that when it is lived it brings peace and freedom. That was his own experience. At the graduate service in Christchurch Cathedral in May 1970, he told the students: 'I have found that to do as far as possible without money or books has brought me to the fringes of a new universe, a universe of great beauty and powerful involvement in the lives of others. Poverty has not made me chaste or wise or humble. Yet it is a beginning. It opens up roads towards other people.'[47]

Baxter saw poverty as a 'kenosis', an emptying of the self, something learnt 'not out of a book but by tramping forty miles with sore feet in the rain.'[48] In mystical terms, 'kenosis' means an inward journey to the gap at the centre of the soul which is like the void that existed before creation. Stripped of all attachments we become a nobody before God and the world, a chaos, a void on which the Holy Spirit can rest: 'We wait to be turned into entire creatures. At the centre of the darkness we wait for the light of the spiritus to shine, the light that the disciples saw on the Mountain of Transfiguration'.[49] The journey to the centre of the soul takes a lifetime. What made it bearable for Baxter was that he always travelled in company.

He saw clearly that the link between poverty and community was a readiness to share: 'It may demand the last ounce of oneself, to go beyond oneself, to walk the waters of availability to all things and all persons.'[50] To adopt this attitude was to choose a way of life similar to that of St Francis of Assisi, who relinquished all his possessions. In that situation all that is left is God, people, the physical world and its creatures – the elements of reality. And towards them ownership can only be analogical. Franciscan attitudes to poverty, love, peace, and creation pervade the Jerusalem writings. A large piece of brown paper with Baxter's version of the 'Canticle of the Sun' was pinned on the wall of the house where he lived. He would invite those present to kneel down with him and recite it before going to bed.

Baxter's attitude towards communal work – though not to money – was later to harden. A key figure in the community said the ideal of learning from the Maori did not work out because the group was not ready for it. Most were Pakeha. Maori were slow to come. Baxter would have liked more because they were the ones hardest hit in the towns and were disproportionately represented in the jails and hospitals. He found those who did come had often retained their communal approach to life. They usually had the best rapport with the local people, and knew how to catch eels and shoot goats, make taniko bands, and play the guitar. They were 'salt in the porridge, yeast in the new bread . . .'[51] The Pakeha had their own kind of love and help to give, but they learnt a lot from the Maori.

Baxter was frequently away. One core member said he was at Jerusalem only about one week per month. In 1970 when his father was dying he went to Brighton to be with him. He made the funeral arrangements with an efficiency which delighted Millicent. He also had many speaking commitments in schools, universities, and training colleges. His speaking engagements were reasonably successful. Invited to address secondary school pupils in Palmerston North, he was greeted with loud laughter and jeering when he shambled into the assembly hall. He was not at all put out. As soon as he began to speak he won the attention of his audience. Beyond the demands made on him by lecturing, there was the restlessness that always drove him to go walkabout. In Auckland he often stayed at Newman Hall, the Catholic chaplaincy to the university. His friend the Dominican Father Eugene O'Sullivan lived there. He had first met Baxter a couple of years earlier and had become his counsellor. Baxter spent some time in the Newman Hall library deepening his knowledge of mystical writings. He often called in at the university and spent time in the staff club, or in the studies of friends like Bill Pearson, Kendrick Smithyman, and C. K. Stead.

Once, when he was away from Jerusalem, there was trouble with the County Council. After wondering if he should go back, he decided that 'if the boat could not float without me, it was better that it should sink.'[52]

On 8 February 1971 The New Zealand Herald reported a protest, at Waitangi, of a radical Maori group, Nga Tamatoa, over the non-ratification of the Treaty of Waitangi. In 1968 Baxter had heard two of their leaders, Taura Eruera and Hana Jackson, appealing to a student group in Dunedin for Pakeha understanding and support. Hana had especially impressed him: 'A Judith of Bethulia if ever there was one, standing erect as a ramrod at the centre of the pakeha world.' In 1971 he supported her protest at Waitangi. A Maori man, who was not an official member of the group, tried to burn the naval ensign as it was about to be hoisted, but only singed it. Nga Tamatoa themselves believed such militancy was premature.

When the time came for speeches, they assembled on the marae near the flag-pole. They wore green leaves round their heads, or in the lapel of their coats, as a sign of mourning for the loss of the land. While the Finance

Minister, Mr Muldoon (deputizing for the Prime Minister), held forth on the freedom of dissent, they saluted him with ironic handclapping. Men in naval uniforms pushed them back from the enclosure stamping with their boots and kicking at their shins. Baxter's daughter Hilary and several others were injured. Prudently, since he was barefoot, Baxter kept near the middle of the group. 'It was not in any case my intention to make myself prominent, since a pakeha who has the great privilege of being permitted to participate in the events of Maoritanga should remember that the Maori is the elder spiritual brother, by virtue of his sufferings and insight, and strive to follow rather than lead. For the same reasons I would not dream of speaking on the marae while in the company of Nga Tamatoa.'[53] But his reticence did not save him. A sailor shoved his boots through the legs of the others and stamped on Baxter's feet a couple of times, and kicked him in the shins with his toe-caps. Baxter felt 'grateful' to receive this minor injury on behalf of Nga Tamatoa.

His interpretation of the events at Waitangi was that 'many Maori people will not be content until there are massive reparations both in land and in money for the wholesale seizures of the Land wars. That wound has never healed in the Maori mind.' He thought that what was being seen in Nga Tamatoa was 'the back of a fish rising in the water. It is not the back of a terakihi or barracuda. It is the back of a whale. Maori militancy is here to stay.'[54]

The Jerusalem community could not succeed without the approval of the local people – the Maori, the neighbouring farmers, the nuns, and of course the authorities. The local people took an interest in it and sometimes went into the houses to see how the residents were faring. Some people in the community objected since they were revolting against authority, and the Maori owners of the marae represented an authority which made demands.

Problems with sanitation and hygiene brought the community into conflict with the Wanganui County Council. One wit remarked that hitch-hiking to Jerusalem was easy because there were so many inspectors driving up and down. At a much publicized meeting in April 1971, before television cameras and eight representatives of the media, the Council insisted that Baxter make extensive improvements to the facilities if he wanted his community to continue. He gave the assurance, though he said the work might take several months. He even welcomed the demand because it gave the community a goal. But he stuck to his philosophy: 'The state of people inside themselves is more important than whether they have two toilets or one.'[55]

What was in effect a public trial, mounted with an eye on the constituency, harmed the community. Already it had received too much attention from the media. A survey conducted by the *Wanganui Chronicle* in March found that almost all of the river residents opposed it and the types

269

it attracted into their area.[56] But a survey in July by the *Wanganui Herald* claimed there was little hostility. The venture was increasingly accepted, and farmers were prepared to employ the residents to do odd jobs.

The real feeling emerged a little later when, at a special meeting, the landowners asked Baxter and his followers to leave. They said they wanted to clean up Jerusalem and attract Maori back to the area. Baxter accepted the decision immediately and praised the plan, because the old Maori settlement provided a better community life than the Pakeha could offer. By 7 September 1971 only four of the permanent members were still at Jerusalem. The first phase of Baxter's enterprise had ended.

Jerusalem failed, not because the vision was defective, but because Baxter was unable to realize it. The commune members made much of there being no rules. The result was massive disorganization and the problems that go with that. There was no apportioning of chores. Too much was left to individuals, some of whom were disturbed. Religious orders have found by long experience that the ability to live happily in a community requires training and a good deal of discipline. Discipline was not a word much used at Jerusalem. The openness of the first community to all comers, its hand to mouth existence, the rapid turnover of members, and the lack of a shared vision, led to instability and frustration and poor relationships with the people of the river.

Baxter knew very well that the religious and social views he proclaimed at Jerusalem were at odds with those commonly espoused. While many rejected the Christian faith, Baxter sought it intensely. But he was too much a product of the twentieth century to be able to believe easily. Nor did his faith save him from anxiety and suffering, not even from the pain of falling well short of his lofty aspirations.

Baxter could live with mystery and he could live with complexity. All his life, and supremely in the Jerusalem years, his instinct drew him to the point of conflict. Like the French poet, Charles Péguy, 'he was a man posted to the frontier',[57] and like Péguy, part of his greatness as a thinker was to have known where the frontier was.[58] In his Jerusalem books he was able to register accurately many of the chief tensions of New Zealand society in the late sixties and early seventies.

The community was part of Baxter's language of gesture towards an alternative society. Going without shoes affirmed the ascetic values of austerity. The old clothes and long hair were a statement about being poor and disadvantaged. For many people the symbols never broke through the haze created by the novelty of Baxter's approach and the indignation it aroused in a conservative society. Baxter was well aware of how his message challenged people: 'He turns this man into an old coat and a broken stick. He makes him the nun's devil and a bad smell in the noses of good churchgoing people. It is not a pleasant vocation.'[59]

Baxter's spiritual journey led towards a difficult acceptance that his personal problems would never be solved in this life. He spoke of 'the wounds in my soul which God presumably means to leave open.' The alternative epitaph he suggested for himself in the twenty-ninth 'Jerusalem Sonnet' – 'He was too much troubled/By his own absurdity' – is partly a confession of failure to build the new Jerusalem, partly a recognition of his inadequacy for the task.

On 17 September, the *Auckland Star* announced that he intended to establish a community at Takapau, Central Hawkes Bay, and that he had begun to negotiate for land and a house. One attraction of Takapau was that it was near the monastery of his old friends the Cistercian monks. This time he planned a different approach. He would start with a group of 'active, idealistic people, with no particular problems, who want to help other people.' Later 'it would probably have an open-door policy – and try to establish good community relations with local people.'[60] He still believed that communal living was necessary. Accommodation was stretched in the cities, and people without shelter were liable to end up in gaol. But the new scheme came to nothing.

Late in September, Baxter returned to his family in Ngaio. He soon realized how easy it would be to settle down again at home. Love of family seemed to make it the obvious thing to do now that 'the book of Jerusalem' was closed: 'The possibility of peace tugs at the very roots of my soul. The old wooden bridge across the creek at the bottom of our bush section needs mending. There is wood to be chopped. I tuck my grand-daughter down at night, as she shouts and plays a game of raising her feet in the air. Charity begins at home.

'Precisely. This power will strangle my life as a vine chokes a tree.'

As he watched a television programme on yachting, he believed that the poor were having their heads banged on the walls of prison cells. It was not possible to open the doors of an ordinary suburban house to fifty or sixty people. Television and 'the whole echo cage and mirror house of the mass media' had been cut out of his life. Now he was again experiencing their power and he did not like it. Television could reach into every home, 'freezing the heart' and distorting values. 'My grand-daughter can grow up and find herself at fifteen in Arohata Borstal.' His conclusion was: 'For years I fought on the home front. Now I fight on the open ground. It is the same truth. I need a house that will hold at least thirty people.'[61] Whatever is to be said about Baxter's decision to leave his family once again, it was something over which he agonized. He learned of a disused house at No. 26 MacDonald Crescent, just off the Terrace in Wellington:

A three-storey mansion called Wuthering Heights
With no lighting and no water and three smashed grots
And five tons of rubbish as a playground for the rats.

(CP 531)

He moved in and a commune quickly formed around him. It lasted for six weeks.

Around the city a number of similar houses had been lying empty for long periods. Tim Shadbolt, who was living in Wellington, worked with his friends to do them up, repaired the plumbing, and dug long-drop toilets. Then they found homeless families and moved them in. Baxter knew people in authority in Wellington and used his influence to support Shadbolt. He pointed out that it was immoral to have houses lying empty while families were homeless. But the success of Shadbolt's scheme depended on anonymity, something Baxter was never allowed. His old enemy *Truth* reported on 14 December 1971 that the house in which he and his followers had been squatting illegally for two months, without paying either rent or rates, had been declared 'unfit for human habitation' by the Wellington City Council. Baxter had been told to leave immediately. His riposte is devastatingly expressed in 'Truth Song' (CP 527).

After a brief period living in McFarlane Street on Mt. Victoria, Baxter's thoughts turned to Jerusalem. By the end of February 1972 he was once again in residence with the approval of the owners of the property used by the first community. He was allowed to bring his 'family'. On 29 February 1972 he described this as friends of long-standing who regarded him as their adoptive parent. He also said the number had to be restricted to ten and that he was not free to accept any more. He assured the Maori owners that the old Jerusalem community had definitely closed and would not re-open. With smaller numbers – though it grew to about fifteen – the second community was more cohesive than the first. But problems like money, the loose organization, and the lack of a shared sense of purpose, remained. Jerusalem was undoubtedly changed by Baxter, but he was also changed by Jerusalem. The changes help to explain that final burst of creative energy which was at once a culmination of past achievements and a point of departure. In *Autumn Testament*, which came out of the second phase of the Jerusalem community, he moved back to the everyday life described in the early Jerusalem sonnets. It took on a special resonance through his awareness of that divine presence 'in which we live and move and have our being.'

Meditation in his pine grove allowed Baxter to recover something he believed New Zealand society had largely lost, a sacramental response to the universe as a vehicle for spiritual values. Because of the practice of poverty and meditation, 'the river spirit is back in the river . . . God too can return from his hiding place between the stars.'[62] A sacramental approach builds on the way poetry commonly works. Any poet could write:

> That star at the kitchen window
> Mentions your name to me
> (CP 537)

Only a poet who saw this world as the sign of another could write:

> Now at moonrise
> The glitter on the river water
> Makes every stone and plant cell grieve
> For what you lock behind the stars . . .
> (CP 587)

The actuality of the physical world throughout the Jerusalem books helps to give the poetry solidity; the sacramental view, by moving the reader on to a different level of experience, gives it depth. By sharing the experience of a world we recognize, Baxter invites an openness to the less familiar values it mediates. The method added authority to the speaking voice.

To say that Baxter's view of the world as expressed in the Jerusalem poems was sacramental, and that he thinks in metaphor, is to say that he is a poet of relationships – personal, social, and religious. Through their interaction the poetry grows. For example, his description of his house was written in an environment where people felt their ancestors in the nearby graveyard to be living presences. With equal facility he can incorporate a meeting with a kehua, a Maori spirit of the dead, or with his father on the river bed.

At times the poems give memorable expression to Baxter's relationships:

> King Jesus, after a day or a week of bitching
> I come back always to your bread and salt,
>
> Because no other man, no other God,
> Suffered our pains with us minute by minute
>
> And asked us to die with him.
> (CP 551)

Usually Baxter's values are presented in terms of what threatens them. And we are always aware of the gap between reality as modified by his imagination and the actual world. The disjunction mirrors the contending forces in his personality. On that battleground, with 'Brother thief in his rib-cage', he had to fight 'In myself what is not myself, the rind of a life-long egoism.' A pacifist father had suffered for resisting national conscription but:

> Father, is it easier to fight
> The military machine, or the maggots of one's own heart.
> (CP 547)

The strength of the poetry comes partly from its economy of form and language, and the way Baxter lets the tensions appear, whether they come from the failure of his own marriage, his religious difficulties, or the distance between the 'already' and the 'not yet'. In the best poems these tensions are not resolved, but held in equilibrium, bringing to the verse their individual pressure. The poetry communicates a sharp awareness of the complexity of the experience being set down. One thing is not left out for the sake of another. The interior struggle appears not only in single poems, but in matching or answering poems throughout the cycle. The natural world itself reminds him of his unresolved conflicts. Two wild ducks, for instance, symbolize a relationship he could not achieve in his own marriage:

> I have seen at evening
> Two ducks fly down
> To a pond together.
>
> The whirring of their wings
> Reminded me of you.
> (CP 537)

The verses are from *Autumn Testament* which, fittingly for a testament, was intended for his wife. By means of passionate utterance it expresses his deep and enduring love for her:

> At the end of our lives
> Te Atua will take pity
> On the two whom he divided.
>
> To the tribe he will give
> Much talking, te pia and a loaded hangi.
>
> To you and me he will give
> A whare by the seashore
> Where you can look for crabs and kina
> And I can watch the waves
> And from time to time see your face

With no sadness,
Te Kare o Nga Wai.

(CP 537-8)

At its close, *Autumn Testament* moves into prayer. One sonnet is addressed to Arachne, who stands at the door of the underworld:

The spider crouching on the ledge above the sink
Resembles the tantric goddess,

At least as the Stone Age people saw her
And carved her on their dolmens. Therefore I don't kill
   her,

Though indeed there is a simpler reason,
Because she is small. Kehua, vampire, eight-eyed watcher

At the gate of the dead, little Arachne, I love you,
Though you hang your cobwebs up like dirty silk in the
   hall

And scuttle under the mattress. Remember I spared your
   children
In their cage of white cloth you made as an aerial
   castle,

And you yourself, today, on the window ledge.
Fear is the only enemy. Therefore when I die,

And you wait for my soul, you hefty as a king crab
At the door of the underworld, let me pass in peace.

(CP 564)

The perspective of prayer enhanced Baxter's lifelong ability to 'move as naturally through the ageless configurations of myth as through a city street', as one of Baxter's best critics, Vincent O'Sullivan, has expressed it.[63]

It was in prayer that he encountered the mystery of God. A merely intellectual road to God could never have satisfied him:

— to wake is to lift up
Again on one's shoulder this curious world

Whose secret cannot be known by any of us
Until we enter Te Whiro's Kingdom.

(CP 544)

and he prayed in 'Song to the Father':

Father, beyond the hills and water,
Beyond the city of the stars,

275

> In a chosen overcoat of night
> You hide from me. All men find it so . . .
>
> (CP 587)

But the God he served in the darkness of faith was not a comfortable master: 'I would not advise any man to follow him. He comes like the sandstorm out of the desert, or the avalanche on a mountain village, or tons of black water from the depths of the sea.'[64] 'Christ is the winter sea whitened by whirlwinds. He is also the albatross floating at the centre of endless calm.'[65] The soul itself was 'that unknown quantity/ I stake my life on . . .' (CP 504). Baxter's vocation at Jerusalem was lived in the obscurity of faith, not in the confident light of morning:

> To go forward like a man in the dark
> Is the meaning of this dark vocation;
>
> (CP 568)

The most lasting fruit of Baxter's dark pilgrimage to and from Jerusalem is his poetry and prose. That 'dark vocation' now summoned him to undertake the last dark phase of his pilgrimage.

XIV

The Arms of Hine-nui-te-po

As a man

Grows older he does not want beer, bread, or the prancing flesh,
But the arms of the eater of life, Hine-nui-te-po,

With teeth of obsidian and hair like kelp
Flashing and glimmering at the edge of the horizon.

(CP 273)

Early in 1972 Baxter was invited to go to Dunedin to take part in Impulse
'72, an event initiated by the Union parish of West Dunedin where there was
a strong club for young men and women. They wanted to hear what was
happening in New Zealand society and to share with other young people
outside the churches what those within them were feeling. There were to be
performances by rock bands and addresses by some lively speakers.

Baxter was invited to Impulse '72 because of the impact he had made at
the preceding year's event. On 24 April he wrote from Jerusalem agreeing
to take part. He informed the organizers that he would leave Jerusalem on
23 July, stay with John Weir in Christchurch, and go on to Dunedin on the
29th. He added 'Praise the Lord. These days he is giving me springtime in
winter.'

'Praise the Lord' is a phrase commonly used in Pentecostalism — a
movement which had recently caught Baxter's interest. He believed that the
crisis then confronting the Catholic Church was one of powerlessness, not
one of authority. Since the Pentecostal movement emphasizes the power
which comes through the Holy Spirit, he concluded that it had a special
relevance for the Church.[1] He was so convinced of this that he told his friend
Father Theo to go to the Pentecostals, whether Protestant or Catholic, to
learn the difficult art of evangelizing the rich. He also told him that 'the
Pentecostals are the only ones who can make my cross break out in flower.'[2]

Another matter was also concerning him. Fleur Adcock has observed that
many of Baxter's poems are 'frosted with hints of death'.[3] 'Autumn
Testament', which he had just completed, implied that his death was near.

A prose manuscript which he compiled about this time is even more
pointed. 'Confession to the Lord Christ' responds to the question he had

277

often asked himself: 'How good does one have to be to become acceptable to God?'[4] It also gives his fullest and most personal response to death:

Lord Christ, I do not know you. My bones are taking me towards the grave. Soon I will go back to my mother, the earth. Though I do not know you, in my heart I find a small secret hope, hidden like a seed in the winter ground, that at the moment when I die, you will reveal yourself to me — shine upon me, remove by a miracle the sins I cannot remove, and take me into your holy kingdom.

Lord Christ, it is a small hope only. It is a little glowworm underneath the ferns, on the edge of the cemetery. You are like the sun in the noonday sky. You light up the whole universe. I cannot demand salvation. I cannot expect it. If at the hour of my death you say to me — 'Old liar, old sinner, you wasted whatever I gave you. You are like a pot that has melted into mud. Go into the darkness where your soul belongs' —

What could I say then, except — 'Yes, Lord, your judgement is just. I will go where you tell me to go. But —'

What is that 'But'? I think it resembles the voice of a mother speaking for her children. It says quietly and endlessly — 'but what about nga mokai, the orphans? What about nga raukore, the ones who are like trees that have had their leaves and branches stripped off by the heavy winds of the world? Lord, damnation for this man, by all means — but there was a bargain somewhere, or something like a bargain. As if I said to you — 'Let my soul and body rot, let me live and die in darkness, but give these ones light, peace, joy, the gardens of Heaven to walk in. I do not know how to say it, Lord Christ. Who can question You? But if that bargain is not kept, I will go into darkness thinking you are unjust . . . If the tribe of the poor go into Heaven, I have no complaint — the drug-users, the homosexuals, the boobheads, the porangi from the mental hospitals, and in particular the Maori ones who were crushed here on earth like iron between the hammer and the anvil. If my child Manu who had his head busted in the cells, and was filled full of drugs at Lake Alice — if he doesn't go into Heaven, Lord Christ, then you are not the Lord Christ, for whoever I failed to love, I did love Manu, and put my arms round him when the death sweat was standing on his body. There was a bargain somewhere — my life for their lives — it cannot mean nothing . . .'

My people came from the Highlands of Scotland. There they lived in houses dug out of the earth, sometimes very like caves, and walled with slate or with boulders. A man would come in from hunting. The house might be dark. He would say — 'Are you there, Dugald?' And his cousin might reply — 'Yes, I'm here, John' — and put out his hand in the dark and grip the hand of the one who had come in.

In relation to the Lord Christ, my soul is like that man who came in to a dark house. I say — 'Are you there?' And invisibly he grips my hand, and without words he says, 'I'm here . . .'

I think of Rua, the Maori prophet, who had six wives and called himself the younger brother of Christ. Perhaps I have had six wives — it is hard to know the meaning of one's life — certainly I have loved more women in my life than the Law of Moses commonly allowed, or the monogamous edict of the Lord Christ himself.

Is Rua in Heaven? I do not know. If human love carries weight with God, it
is likely. Rua certainly loved his people . . .

I think that is my destiny. I have been close to certain people — to nga mokai,
to nga raukore — closer than it is the usual fate of people to be to one another
— it has seemed as close at times as the mother is to the child she carries in her
womb. Their thoughts have been my thoughts, their pain my pain, their blood
my blood. I have held them in my arms and stroked their foreheads while they
sweated the drugs out. They have opened their deepest fears and hopes to me.
Some have called me Father. Some have even called me Mother. Some have
slept beside me when they were lonely. I cannot separate my life from theirs.

It seems I have given them the marrow of my bones to eat. Sometimes they
might be a bit greedy and careless. They might eat more of my life than they
need to eat. But who am I to worry too much about that? I am where I am meant
to be. I am doing what I am meant to do. It is not my job to reject anyone . . .

Still, I desire to see the face of that great warrior who walked on the waters
of Galilee and died on the cross. It would be light after darkness, spring after
winter, health after sickness, good kai after long hunger. What could I say to
him?

'E Ariki, taku ngakau ki a koe' — 'Lord, my heart belongs to you.' Perhaps
he will make room for me in the Maori Heaven — where the warriors and the
kuias and the strong chiefs and the tamariki who died young have gone already.

Te Kooti and Te Whiti and Rua and Ratana may take me in, men with many
sins who loved their people — the people I also love. They said: 'The man on
whom the maramatanga shines has to be the doorstep of the people . . .'

This old pakeha doorstep is nearly worn through. He knows only that God
made him, and that his body will go into the ground, and his soul to God to be
judged. And the judgement has to be left to God. No man can make it.

The 'Confession' is a sober review of Baxter's life carried out in the
presence of one before whom 'it is no good play-acting'. Words had to be
'entirely honest'. At such a time, we would expect Baxter to reveal his
deepest concerns. They prove to be the bond with his ancestors, now
enlarged to admit Maori prophets, his anxiety over his sexual relationships,
and his reliance on having loved the poor as his passport to heaven. In its
heightened rhythm and directness of spoken language — rising at times to
a lyric intensity — the 'Confession' resembles a speech by a dying Homeric
hero or an orator on the marae.

In late July Baxter began the journey south to Dunedin for Impulse '72.
During his stay in Christchurch, where friends remarked on his tranquillity,
he gave a poetry reading at the university for the Department of English. In
the course of the reading, misunderstanding a request to read 'the poem on
your father' as a reference to 'Song of the Sea-Nymphs at the Death of
Icarus', a poem he had written at the age of sixteen, he said that he did not
have a copy with him but probably had it in his head. He then declaimed,
word-perfect, its fifty-two lines.[5] Afterwards, when John Weir expressed
surprise at this remarkable feat, Baxter explained that he had worked so

hard over every word of the early poems that they were engraved on his memory.

When Professor John Garrett farewelled him after the reading, Baxter remarked: 'I don't think I am going to live very long.' Garrett remonstrated, but Baxter insisted that it was true. Something of that mood accompanied him to Dunedin.

For Impulse '72 he had proposed reading 'The Junkies and the Fuzz' and 'The Ballad of the Stonegut Sugarworks'. The organizers found him very amenable. There was nothing of the prima donna about the man whose photograph they had chosen for their poster that year, which appeared all over Dunedin. On the morning of Impulse, one of the organizers, a clergyman, visited Baxter at his mother's house in Kinsman Street, Wakari, and found him lying in bed with the Bible open at the book of Jeremiah. He spoke a good deal about the sufferings and misunderstandings the prophet had experienced. It was obvious that Baxter had immersed himself in the story and taken Jeremiah as a model. That afternoon, as Baxter stood on the stage in the Town Hall before some five thousand people, he seemed to be a modern version of the prophet, even in his manner of speaking.

In 1971 Baxter had caught the imagination of the young. He was a spokesman for all young rebels as he wittily and trenchantly exposed the weaknesses in New Zealand society. But in 1972 he disappointed the organizers. They felt he had lost his edge. He did not read the two poems he had proposed but spoke on suffering, especially that of the poor. To support his argument he quoted from the Prayer Book. This was not at all what the young were looking for. His message simply bewildered them, and some talked throughout his address. Yet one of the organizers, a man with considerable pastoral experience of bikies and V-8 boys, knew how well Baxter understood them. The informal discussion in the Concert Chamber following the address was more successful, and Baxter was surrounded by people who were anxious to speak to him.

On his way back from Dunedin, Baxter stayed briefly with his family in Wellington before returning to Jerusalem about the end of August. Those who knew him in these final months said that the life seemed to have gone out of him. His old friend Wehi, who had always understood and supported him, wondered if he had cancer because he was so thin. He realized that he no longer had the energy to administer the community. The poor food at Grafton and Jerusalem, the long journeys on foot, the fasts for various causes, had all taken their toll. Too many people had drawn too much from his personal resources and he was burnt out physically and emotionally. He was not bitter nor angry, and even though he was depressed he was also more realistic. He told a friend: 'If you're thinking of starting up a community my experience has taught me that to be successful it must be no more than eight people. They all need to be stable and they all need to have an occupation of some sort.'[6]

To be forced to abandon his original idealism seemed a kind of death. He told Greg, one of the core members of the community, that he was leaving to start something else, and asked him to take his place. His only advice was: 'Sit quietly in the space at the centre, don't be heavy, and keep good relations with the pa.'[7] His final words to Wehi were 'Look after nga mokai.' From Jerusalem he went to Auckland to a commune in Carrick Place, Mount Eden, run by a friend named Kathy, who, in fact, owned two adjoining houses, numbers 5 and 7 — the same numbers as the two houses at Boyle Crescent. Baxter interpreted the coincidence as a sign that things were falling into place. From then on, Carrick Place was his base.

Kathy saw a look of panic in his eyes, almost an appeal for help. As his health deteriorated he felt the vulnerability of a person who had given up even minimal security. He was full of self-doubt, questioning everything he had ever done. He felt defeated and wanted to start a completely new life, to settle down and receive the love and care he needed. He even wondered if he should remarry. He could not shed his 'lonely wish to be loved' (CP 593).

The same appeal for love is heard in 'The Return', one of his last poems. It is set in Grafton, which was not far from Kathy's house:

> Tell me, little one,
> That my body is strong, that my hands are clean,
> That my heart has in it a seed of light,
> Then let me come beside you and hide myself
> In the darkness of the garden of the sorrow of your face.
>   (CP 594)

His mood did not lift. For several weeks he visited a retired psychiatrist every day. He wanted to go back to his childhood and try to work things out. He was obsessed with his relationship with his mother, and believed he had not received enough love from her. These daily visits wore him out, but there was enough of his old humour left to describe them as 'going to the cleaners'. He still assisted at Mass every day and brought back to Carrick Place people he had met in the street. At Kathy's urging he smartened himself up, trimmed his beard, and took a job assembling electrical components. But he had been away from routine work too long: to his great disappointment, he was fired.

The most memorable of Baxter's early poems were about the past, the most memorable of his last poems about a present with the full pressure of the past behind them. As personal as any he had written, they reported his emotional state. 'The Tiredness of Me and Herakles' was written in early October in Kathy's commune in Carrick Place:

> I trapped the great boar,
> A Jansenist priest in his lair.
> His tusks were longer than the Auckland Harbour Bridge,
> His logic pure as the seafoam,
> 'All men are damned except myself.
> The christly do not have erections.'
> The occasion of our dispute was a teen-age chick
> To whom I had written a poem.
> Though he booted me out of his presbytery
> We parted civilly enough.
> I asked him for a conditional blessing.[8]
>
> (CP 595)

The verse refers to an incident which took place at the Wanganui Catholic presbytery where for a period in 1970 Baxter had slept on the verandah and taken his evening meals with the community. The elderly priest who 'booted him out' had no time for Baxter, and was convinced that he corrupted the morals of the young.

The priest had tangled with Baxter over sexual morality, the area of Catholic teaching Baxter always found most difficult since it did not seem to take sufficient account of human nature. Although he kept trying to find his way around the Church's moral doctrine, sometimes accepting it, sometimes rebelling against it, he was left with feelings of guilt and inadequacy which, at the same time, became central to his very real humility.

The second labour was the fight against

> Ritualism, fetichism, moralism,
> Simplicism, angelism, dualism.

Angelism — acting and judging as though people are pure spirits and not creatures with human instincts and emotions — was something Baxter always abhorred. He had invited John Weir ten years before to swear a pact with him 'never to let anyone turn us into angelists', and never to become more civilized than Christ who 'slept in the open like a hobo',[9] and Mary who carried water from the village well. This thinking lay behind the coarseness in the Jerusalem books. When the stables were cleansed of such impurities as angelism, what was left was 'one iron crucifix/And a thin medal of Our Lady' (CP 595).

The poem's fourth section describes his adversaries as 'the shield-bearing women'. The fifth refers to his battle with the Press:

> All day I ploughed with savage oxen
> That snorted and farted like runaway tractors.
> That was the labour involving the printed rubbish
> Plain men use at evening to wrap up fish and oysters.

Baxter's poem, 'Truth Song', (CP 527-8), which savages *New Zealand Truth*, shows just how fierce the struggle was.

The sixth section of 'The Tiredness of Me and Herakles' characterizes death as a Catholic policeman. The old anger against the 'fuzz' blazes out:

> The bout with Death was a hard one.
> He wore a black uniform.
> 'Why don't you cut your hair?' he asked me.
> 'Life is filth. I keep the world clean.'
> He had come with a pure heart from morning Mass
> For a work-out at the police gymnasium
> Before supervising the cleaning of a cell
> That had some blood and vomit on its wall.
> We wrestled in a fog of greyness
> Till the swastika pin fell out of his shirt.
> I was glad when the boss man called it off.

All Baxter's friends must find the final verse disturbing:

> Today I smashed a green hydrangea bush
> With a walking stick
> At the edge of somebody's private lawn.
> Every leaf was the head of a friend.

The demands of friends over many years resembled those of the horseleech's daughter of the seventh verse who keeps crying 'Give! Give!' By draining his energy they prevented him from achieving his self-imposed task.

Myth is used powerfully in the poem to bind it together, and the supple and varied language is equal to the wide range of experience it encompasses. The poem is 'a letter to Herman Gladwin', a Marxist who wanted Baxter to edit the Communist newspaper *The People's Voice*. Baxter comments mildly:

> I do not take my compass from Lenin.

Baxter sent me 'The Tiredness of Me and Herakles' for publication in *Poetry New Zealand*. That made it a public statement of where he stood in October

1972. Since he was always concerned with how he was perceived, he offered an explanation: 'My sense of humour. A bit dry and rough — use it for the *Poetry Yearbook* [sic]. It will add some pepper to the diet.' But he was clear about the grounds for his anger: 'Our heaviest weights seem always to come from the Church herself.' The poem ended:

> Five labours still to go
> I am tired already.

He knew that his chosen way of life had damaged his health irreparably, and that he was to die without accomplishing his aims. In 'The Return' he seems to deny this:

> Sister, if I tell you —
> 'I have slain a man to my hurt' —
> Do not believe it.

Yet the very act of making the statement shows that, reluctantly, he believed it to be true.

He still could not settle. He set off for a speaking tour of schools north of Auckland. After a time Kathy became worried and rang Karamu High School. When he came to the phone he sounded exhausted and said he would return soon. On Friday 13 October he visited Whangarei Presbytery. Father George McHardy, who had instructed him in the Catholic faith, thought he looked very tired and miserable. Nevertheless, in the afternoon Baxter spoke to the primary school children at St Joseph's convent school. That night a parish youth group was to begin a catechetical weekend at Marsden Bay and Baxter was invited to go with them. He fitted in easily, gave a couple of talks, and took part in learning activities. He also piggy-backed a rather plump girl along the beach, and kept running in and out of the waves. In the evening he played cards, five hundred, with great seriousness, discussing each hand after it had been played. In the course of an impromptu concert he recited 'Lament for Barney Flanagan' in a flat, expressionless voice.

At about 4.30 a.m. on the final morning, he brought a cup of coffee into the bedroom of one of the young priests in charge of the camp and announced: 'I'm going to rave on for a couple of hours, so you'll just have to listen.' He spoke negatively about his mother and her relationship with his father for a considerable time. He also quoted what the pagans had said about the first Christians: 'See how they love one another.' He added: 'Wouldn't it have been wonderful if they had said "See how they love us".'

When he returned to the presbytery in Whangarei, Father Jim Beban, a long-term friend and helper, persuaded him to write a letter making his peace with the Sisters of Compassion who had so disapproved of his administration of the Jerusalem community. He wrote the letter, admitting, characteristically, that in some respects he had been wrong. More generally, he seemed aware that the time had come for final reconciliations.

On the Monday of what would prove to be the last week of his life, Baxter was driven to Puhoi. There he spent a few days with Michael and Dene Illingworth, who were renting an old house in Tunnel Road. Baxter lay down most of the time, occasionally raising himself on his elbow to write. He seemed to have become old and slow. When he climbed into bed with them, they noticed how cold he was, and the difficulty he had in getting warm. And he kept talking. They had no doubt that he knew he was dying. Dene remarked on his concern for small domestic details as if he was trying to ease himself back into life. For example, he insisted on continuing his search in the mangrove swamp for a child's lost gumboot.

The Jerusalem community was finished. He had done all he could for it — now its members would have to look after themselves. Yet, even though he was utterly drained, he kept arguing that a vast structural change was needed if New Zealand society was to become just. The revolution he proposed would be based on a blend of Marxism and Christianity.[10] He wanted to take this new approach to the Auckland street kids, who were just beginning to appear. Many were Maori, and he hoped to persuade them to return to their maraes where they could find a caring community and work on the land. Illingworth did not think Baxter's blend of Marxist and Christian thinking meant any diminution of his Christian commitment, but rather he seemed to be working towards a more radical understanding of his faith. He also expected that what he had in mind would stir up a hornet's nest among the civic and government authorities.

On Wednesday Baxter and the Illingworths drove up Tunnel Road towards high ground commanding a magnificent view over the Kaipara. Before they reached the top Baxter got out of the car and walked a few hundred yards on his own as if he wanted to withdraw into himself. He shuffled along, stopping frequently to get his breath. That day he talked frequently about death and asked Michael to arrange for a jazz band to play at his funeral, and to put a stone on his grave. When they came to the huge kauri tree Michael had been keen to show him, he hongi-ed with it for a long time, holding it tightly as if to draw strength. That night the two men talked until dawn, though this was not unusual; in all the years Illingworth had known him, Baxter did not seem to need more than two or three hours' sleep.

On Thursday morning, 19 October, after breakfast at the Illingworth's big kauri table, Baxter pushed the dishes aside and in a period of intense concentration that lasted for about half an hour, copied out the whole of

'Ode to Auckland'. Afterwards he read it to Michael and Dene. At Michael's suggestion 'Titirangi housewife' was changed to 'Glen Eden' and one or two other words were changed. He then wrote the poem out again.

'Ode to Auckland' was Baxter's last poem. It expressed a passionate disillusionment with bourgeois Christianity, with educational and cultural institutions, and with the city itself, which the poem depicts as a loathsome place lacking in humanity.

At Newman Hall he had met followers of a bourgeois Christ, younger versions of the Pharisees already satirized in 'The Holy Neighbours' of 1971. He had glossed that poem during his reading at the University of Canterbury in July: 'It's an objection to the Pharisees, it's a joke poem but rather a grim one. If you live in a Church you're a Church member, you'll always find some of the Pharisees around, you may love them but you don't want actually to be executed by them. This is a distressing fact if you yourself are a humanist.' As the students in 'Ode to Auckland' sit down in the university cafeteria, Baxter appeals to them:

> I said, 'Excuse me a minute, there's a Maori friend of mine,
> If he doesn't get a place to crash tonight
> The cops will pick him up for the four crimes
> They dislike most in Auckland,
> Not having a job,
> Wearing old clothes,
> Having long hair,
> Above all, for being Maori.
> When they shift him to the cells in the meat wagon
> The last crime might earn him five punches in the gut.
> Could any one of you give him a night's lodging?'

Like the guests in the parable of the wedding feast, the students have their own mode of evasion. But it is Keir Volkerling, neither a Christian nor a student, who puts the Maori lad up for the night.

The city is Baxter's main target:

> The sound of the opening and shutting of bankbooks,
> The thudding of refrigerator doors,
> The ripsaw voices of Glen Eden mothers yelling at their children,
> The chugging noise of masturbation from the bedrooms of the bourgeoisie,
> The voices of dead teachers droning in dead classrooms,
> The TV voice of Mr Muldoon,
> The farting noise of the trucks that grind their way down Queen Street
> Has drowned forever the song of Tangaroa on a thousand beaches,
> The sound of the wind among the green volcanoes,

And the whisper of the human heart.

Boredom is the essence of your death,
I would take a trip to another town
Except that the other towns resemble you exactly.

How can I live in a country where the towns are made like coffins
And the rich are eating the flesh of the poor
Without even knowing it?

(CP 597-600)

The natural environment, myth with its dimension of otherness, and humanity itself, are ignored. Apathy prevails:

> The people seem to enjoy building the pyramids.
> Moses would get a mighty cold reception.
> They'd kiss the arse of Pharaoh any day of the week
>
> For a pat on the head and a dollar note.

It is to Lenin as a protector of the oppressed that Baxter appeals:

> O Father Lenin, help us in our great need!

The final lines of the poem affirm for the last time that the sources of vitality needed by twentieth century New Zealand society are to be found among the Maori people.

'Ode to Auckland' is carried on a controlled tide of anger. References to the university, for example, are restrained but devastating:

> Outside his office the wind rustled
> Dead leaves on the concrete pavement.

The anaemic Christianity espoused by the students is treated with equal severity:

> The bourgeois Christ began to blush on the Cross.
> The Holy Spirit squawked and laid an egg.

That same Thursday morning, Illingworth and Baxter left Puhoi by car for Auckland, and went to the coffee bar at the Barry Lett gallery. After a couple of hours they said goodbye and Baxter went off to keep an appointment.

Back in Carrick Place, everybody thought he looked exhausted. But he still went out to dinner on Thursday night with friends from a house in

Grafton. They knew Baxter was ill, though he responded well to the company. After the meal he and a friend walked home together, a distance of about a mile and a half. They had to stop many times so that Baxter could catch his breath. His breathlessness and frequent depression were no doubt connected with a failing heart. On the Friday night he went out to Paremoremo prison. (The practice of visiting prisoners had long been part of his life.)

On Saturday morning, 21 October, Baxter went over to Jean Tuwhare's place, 21 Tiri Tiri Road in Birkdale, and asked if he could stay for a few days. In the afternoon he helped in the garden, hoeing out onion weed with a mattock. Next morning, he complained of pains in his stomach and chest so she rang her doctor for him. Since it was Labour weekend, they knew it would be difficult to get an appointment. The doctor, who knew Baxter's poetry, said he would open the surgery especially for him at 7.30 p.m. In the meantime, they decided to go to a sauna in Takapuna with a Maori woman who was a friend of Jean's. Baxter was unusually quiet in the sauna, but when Jean's friend asked why he had left his wife, Baxter replied that, though he loved Jacquie and wanted to be buried with her, he believed his creative gifts required the freedom to move around. On the way back from the sauna they stopped to get some tablets at the chemist because they thought the stomach pains might be ulcers. They were clutching at straws. Baxter had known for some time that he had a bad heart.

That Sunday night, Jean Tuwhare drove him to the surgery in Glenfield Road. As they came to the top of the rise in Eskdale Street, Baxter's last glimpse of the sea he had so often celebrated was across the Waitemata to Rangitoto. As they turned into Glenfield Road he was cracking jokes. Jean left him at the surgery, a little white house set back from the road, believing that Baxter and the doctor would talk for some time. She planned to come and get him when he rang. The doctor wanted to arrange a thorough check-up, but Baxter said he was too busy. And since there did not appear to be any immediate danger, the doctor responded to another call. He had hardly gone when Baxter had a violent heart attack outside the surgery. He managed to cross the road and knock on the door of No. 544 Glenfield Road. The people who lived there at that time were at first reluctant to admit this wild-eyed, shaggy stranger. When they did, he asked them to ring Jean Tuwhare and she came at once. Then they rang another doctor, who thought it better to wait for the return of the doctor who had just examined Baxter. He also said the call was outside his area. In considerable pain, Baxter was lying on a sofa in the lounge at the back of the house. Jean remembered his saying 'I have a wife and children in Wellington.' When the doctor who had originally examined him returned, he applied heart massage, but to no avail. The man who said that if New Zealand society was as it should be, there would be a welcome at every door, died in the house of a stranger. It was the night of 22 October 1972. He was forty-six.

'No death I have ever known,' wrote Bruce Mason, 'has so swept the country in a huge wave of grief.' A surprising number of people can recall what they were doing when they heard the news. I had been out fishing from early morning, so I did not hear of his death until the afternoon when the NZBC rang asking me to appear on a brief programme for the television news that night. The others appearing were Peter Cullen, president of the Victoria University Students Association, and Bruce Mason.[11]

Still in shock from the news I had heard about an hour earlier, I replied 'Yes' to the question: 'Would you say he was a happy man?' That is not what I would answer today. My dominant memory is of his melancholy, even though it was often dissipated by his lively talk. Certainly he seldom looked happy. Happiness suggests contentment with life and with what one makes of its possibilities. And the contentment is tempered by the realization that one must not expect too much from oneself, nor from the world. Baxter's was a questing spirit, he had too much restless vitality to be happy in the sense in which the word is generally understood. Like Odysseus, the Greek hero he so often referred to, he was eager to move on.

When Jacquie heard of his death from the police, she rang Colin Durning in Port Chalmers at 1.30 a.m. on Monday morning and asked him to come up. That night they flew to Auckland. The body was still under the coroner's jurisdiction, but at Jacquie's insistence, she was given permission to view it in the presence of two police officers. When the family and Colin reached the morgue, some of Nga Tamatoa, whose members Baxter had befriended and with whom he had protested at Waitangi, were already there. The police went in, and after being away for some time apologized for not being able to find his body. After it was located Colin was surprised see that Baxter had earlier trimmed his beard.

Nga Tamatoa provided a van and driver to take the body to Jerusalem, and Jacquie, Hilary, John, and Colin sat in the back with the coffin. After driving round the east side of Lake Taupo and through Turangi they became lost in thick mist and ended up in Taumarunui.

Although it would usually take about six hours to drive from Auckland to Jerusalem, on this occasion it took them nearly twelve. When they finally arrived a large crowd of people was waiting. Though it was after 10 p.m. they were called on to the marae, and the coffin was placed in a special tent. The tangi was arranged by the elders of the Ngati Hau, the commune members, and the resident priest, Father Te Awhitu. Everyone who came had the chance of being welcomed on to the marae, and anyone who wished to address the body could do so. Many did.

The *Dominion* billboard for 24 October announced to the capital: 'James

K. Baxter Friend 1926-72'. His friends, Maori and Pakeha, came from all over the country; most of them were young. Baxter's mother and brother arrived on Wednesday morning. It was their first experience of a tangi. The *Dominion* estimated that some eight hundred people attended the funeral on the Wednesday. Father Te Awhitu celebrated the Requiem Mass. Colin Durning read one of the lessons. I gave the panegyric after John Weir didn't feel able to give it, but found it extremely difficult to retain self-control in such a highly charged atmosphere, where people wept openly.

At the end of Mass, residents of the Jerusalem community carried the coffin up the steep hill overlooking the marae. A plot had been dug close to the top house, which had been the centre of Baxter's community. The body was lowered into the ground at 4.30 p.m. After the crowd dispersed, it was noticed that the head of the coffin was not facing east as is normal in Maori custom, so four young men shifted it into the correct position. Baxter was buried on Maori land, and it was said that this was a special privilege for a Pakeha. In fact, he had some rights in the matter as a member of the tribal committee.

At a ceremony held upon the anniversary of Baxter's death, a large stone from the Wanganui River, incised as he had wished with the one word Hemi, was placed on his grave.

The best account of Baxter's life is the one he gave himself in his *Collected Poems*, published in 1980, for his poetry was always autobiographical, whatever else it may have been.

> . . . and from my grave at length
> A muddy spring of poems will gush out.
> (CP 460)

The *Collected Poems* established Baxter as a major poet of the twentieth century. Yet for many his poetry is less important than his life, with all its contradictions, and he remains one of the dead, who 'blaze like the sun/ between our thoughts'.

Glossary of Maori Words and Phrases*

aroha *love, respect, and compassion*
arohanui *a plentitude of aroha*
hangi *earth oven, or by common usage, a feast*
Hine-nui-te-po *Goddess of Death*
Hiruharama *Jerusalem*
Hoani *John*
hongi *greeting, by pressing noses together*
kai *food, a meal*
Te Kare o Nga Wai *'Te Kare of the Waters' — a name for Jacquie Baxter*
katipo *poisonous New Zealand spider, black with red back*
kauri *massive cone-bearing forest tree prized for its timber*
kehua *ghost*
kina *sea egg*
korero *speech*
kuia *old woman*
mahi *work*
manuhiritanga *being a guest or stranger*
Maoritanga *being Maori, Maori traditions and culture (modern)*
marae *tribal meeting-ground*
maramatanga *clarity*
matewa *'the night life of the soul' (Baxter)*
nga mokai *captives, pet birds or animals; a term applied to the youngest members of a family;*
    Baxter uses it to mean 'the fatherless ones'
pa *Maori village (originally fortified)*
Pakeha *New Zealander of European descent*
te pia *beer*
porangi *mad; madman*
rangatira *chief*
nga raukore *Baxter uses it figuratively to mean those 'trees with leaves and branches stripped*
    off by the heavy winds of the world'; down and outs
te taipo *devil*
tamariki *children*
Nga Tamatoa *Young Warriors; Protest group for Maori rights, 1970s*
tangi *Maori funeral ceremony; cry*
taniko *woven band or belt*
taniwha *spirit or demon*
terakihi *a species of fish*
whare *house*

* Phrases beginning with *nga* or *te* are listed under the second word of the phrase.

Chronology

1859	Archibald and Margaret McColl and family arrive in Dunedin on board *Alpine*.
1861	John and Mary Baxter and family arrive in Dunedin on board *Lady Egidia*.
1874	John Macmillan Brown appointed to Chair of Classics and English at Canterbury University College.
1879	Mary McColl marries John Baxter at Winton.
1881	Helen Connon graduates with First Class Honours in Latin and English.
1881	Archibald McColl Learmond Baxter born at Brighton.
1886	Helen Connon marries John Macmillan Brown.
1888	Millicent Amiel Brown born.
1897	Viola Helen Lockhart Brown born.
1903	Helen Brown dies.
1909	Millicent Brown enrols at Newnham College Cambridge.
1912	Millicent Brown passes the Tripos Part II with Second Class Honours.
1914	First World War.
1917	Archibald Baxter shanghaied into war zone.
1920	John Macmillan Brown fills in as Professor of English at Otago University.
1921	Millicent Brown marries Archibald Baxter.
1922	Terence John Baxter born.
1926	James Keir Baxter born 29 June in Dunedin.
1931	Baxter family moves to Brighton from Kuri Bush; James Baxter attends Brighton Primary.
1933	James writes his first poem.
1935	John Macmillan Brown dies; family moves to Wanganui; James attends St John's School, Wanganui.
1937	Family sails for England.
1937-38	Terence and James attend Sibford School, a Quaker boarding school.
1939	Second World War begins; *We Will Not Cease* published by Gollanz; Baxter family returns to New Zealand; James returns to St John's School, Wanganui.
1940	Baxter family moves to 15 Bedford Parade, Brighton.

1940-43	James attends King's High School, Dunedin.
1944	James enrols at Otago University College; *Beyond the Palisade* published.
1945	James working in an iron foundry, and then at Wanaka Station.
1946-47	James working around Dunedin.
1948	James in Christchurch; received into Church of England: *Blow, Wind of Fruitfulness* published; 9 December James Baxter marries Jacqueline Sturm in Napier; they move to Wellington.
1949	Hilary Anne Baxter born 18 June; family living at Belmont.
1950	Baxter family moves to 105 Messines Road, Karori.
1951	Baxter enrols at Wellington Teachers' College; New Zealand Writers' Conference, Christchurch; *Recent Trends in New Zealand Poetry* published.
1952	John McColl Baxter born 29 October; *Poems Unpleasant* published.
1953	Baxter enrols as a full-time student at Victoria University College; *The Fallen House* published.
1954	Baxter is Assistant Master at Epuni School, Lower Hutt; gives Macmillan Brown Lectures at Victoria University College; *Numbers* launched; family moves to 166 Wilton Road, Wadestown; Baxter joins Alcoholics Anonymous.
1955	*The Fire and the Anvil* published; family moves to 41 Collingwood Street, Ngaio; Baxter takes instructions to become a Catholic.
1956	Baxter joins School Publications; graduates B.A. from Victoria University College.
1957	Baxter and Jacquie separate in October; *The Iron Breadboard* and *The Night Shift* published.
1958	11 January, Baxter baptized a Catholic; *In Fires of No Return* published; *Jack Winter's Dream* broadcast by the New Zealand Broadcasting Corporation; 16 September, Baxter sets out for Asia.
1959	Baxter's leave expires 29 April, returns to New Zealand; *The Wide Open Cage* produced.
1960	Baxter becomes friends with John Weir; controversy over *Penguin Book of New Zealand Verse*.
1961	Vietnam war; *Howrah Bridge and other poems* published.
1963	March, Baxter joins New Zealand Post Office as postman; July, Soap Powder Lock-out; writes 'Pig Island Letters' sequence.
1966	*Pig Island Letters* published; Baxter made Robert Burns Fellow at Otago University.
1967	Baxter's second year as Robert Burns Fellow; *The Man on the Horse* published; *The Band Rotunda, The Sore-Footed Man, The*

Bureaucrat, The Devil and Mr Mulcahy, produced. *Aspects of Poetry in New Zealand* and *The Man on the Horse* published.

1968   Baxter working in Catholic Education Office; April, 'vision' calls him to Jerusalem.

1969   Baxter living at Boyle Crescent, Auckland; *The Rock Woman* and *The Flowering Cross* published; Baxter arrives at Jerusalem in September.

1970   *Jerusalem Sonnets* published; *The Temptations of Oedipus* produced.

1971   *Jerusalem Daybook* published; 8 February, Baxter takes part in protest at Waitangi; September, first phase of Jerusalem community is over.

1972   *Autumn Testament* published; February, Baxter back at Jerusalem with smaller group; 30 July, Impulse Festival in Dunedin; 22 October, James K. Baxter dies; 25 October, large funeral held at Jerusalem for James K. Baxter.

Select Bibliography

I. By James K. Baxter

PRINCIPAL VOLUMES OF POETRY

Beyond the Palisade. Christchurch: The Caxton Press, 1944.

Blow, Wind of Fruitfulness. Christchurch: The Caxton Press 1948.

The Fallen House. Christchurch: The Caxton Press, 1953.

The Iron Breadboard, studies in New Zealand writing. Wellington: Mermaid Press, 1957.

In Fires of No Return. London, Wellington, New York: Oxford University Press, 1958.

Howrah Bridge and other poems. London, Wellington, New York: Oxford University Press, 1961.

Pig Island Letters. London, Wellington, New York: Oxford University Press, 1966.

The Rock Woman, selected poems. London, Wellington, New York: Oxford University Press, 1969.

Jerusalem Sonnets, poems for Colin Durning. Dunedin: Bibliography Room, University of Otago, 1970.

Jerusalem Daybook (Poems and Prose). Wellington: Price Milburn, 1972.

Autumn Testament. Wellington: Price Milburn, 1972.

Runes. London, Wellington, New York: Oxford University Press, 1973.

The Labyrinth, some uncollected poems 1944-1972. (Chosen by J. E. Weir) London, Wellington, New York: Oxford University Press, 1974.

The Tree House and other poems for children. Wellington: Price Milburn, 1974.

The Bone Chanter, unpublished poems 1945-1972. (Chosen and Introduced by J. E. Weir). Wellington: Oxford University Press, 1976.

The Holy Life and Death of Concrete Grady, various uncollected and unpublished poems. (Chosen and Introduced by J. E. Weir) Wellington: Oxford University Press, 1976.

Collected Poems. (Ed. J. E. Weir) Auckland: Oxford University Press, 1980. Paperback 1988.

Selected Poems. (Ed. J. E. Weir) Auckland: Oxford University Press, 1982.

CRITICISM

Recent Trends in New Zealand Poetry. Christchurch: The Caxton Press, 1951.

The Fire and the Anvil: Notes on Modern Poetry. Wellington: New Zealand University Press, 1955.

Aspects of Poetry in New Zealand. Christchurch: The Caxton Press, 1967.

The Man on the Horse. Dunedin: University of Otago Press, 1967. (Includes 'Notes on the Education of a New Zealand Poet', pp. 121-55.)

James K. Baxter as Critic: a selection from his literary criticism. (Ed. Frank McKay) Auckland: Heinemann Educational Books, 1978.

INTERVIEWS

'An Interview with James K. Baxter'. (J. E. Weir.) *Landfall* No. 111, Vol. 28, No. 3, September 1974, pp. 241-50.

'Drama Among the Faceless.' An interview with Arthur Baysting. *N.Z. Listener,* Vol. 60, No. 1530, 7 February 1969, p. 9.

DRAMA

Two Plays: The Wide Open Cage and Jack Winter's Dream. Hastings: Capricorn Press, 1959. *Jack Winter's Dream* was reprinted in Wellington by Victoria University Press, 1979.

The Sore-Footed Man/The Temptations of Oedipus. Auckland: Heinemann Educational Books, 1971.

The Devil and Mr. Mulcahy/The Band Rotunda. Auckland: Heinemann Educational Books, 1971.

Collected Plays. (Ed. Howard McNaughton) Auckland: Oxford University Press, 1982.

PROSE

The Flowering Cross. Dunedin: New Zealand Tablet, 1969.

A Walking Stick for an Old Man. Wellington: C.M.W. Print, 1972.

The Six Faces of Love. Wellington: Futuna Press, 1973.

Horse. Auckland: Oxford University Press, 1985.

II. Studies of Baxter's Work
Listed by Date of Publication

BOOKS

Weir, J. E. *The Poetry of James K. Baxter*. Wellington: Oxford University Press, 1970.

O'Sullivan, Vincent. *James K. Baxter*. Wellington: Oxford University Press, 1976.

Doyle, Charles. *James K. Baxter*. Boston: Twayne Publishers, 1976.

Lawlor, Pat. *The Two Baxters: Diary notes with an essay by Vincent O'Sullivan*. Wellington: Millwood Press, 1979.

Parr, Christopher. *Introducing James K. Baxter*. Auckland: Longman Paul, 1983.

Oliver, W. H. *James K. Baxter: A Portrait*. Wellington: Port Nicholson Press, 1983.

ARTICLES

Bertram, James. 'The Wide Open Cage', *Landfall* 14, No. 1 (March 1960), pp. 81-4.

Smith, H. S. 'The Poet as Playwright', *Landfall* 22 (1968), p. 56.

Bertram, James. 'Poet of Extremes', *N.Z. Listener* 1724 (20 November, 1972), p. 12.

Pearson, Bill. 'Two Personal Memories of James K. Baxter: I', *Islands* 2, No. 1 (Autumn 1973), pp. 2-5.

Olds, Peter. 'Two Personal Memories of James K. Baxter: II', *Islands* 2, No. 1 (Autumn 1973), pp. 5-7.

O'Sullivan, Vincent. 'After Culloden: Remarks on the Early and Middle Poetry of James K. Baxter', *Islands* 2, No. 1 (Autumn 1973), pp. 19-30.

Stead, C. K. 'Towards Jerusalem: The Later Poetry of James K. Baxter', *Islands* 2, No. 1 (Autumn 1973), pp. 7-18.

Smith, Hal. 'Baxter's Theatre: a critical appraisal', James K. Baxter Festival: 1973 Four Plays, pp. 3-5, 12-13, 16. Wellington: Victoria University, 1973.

Davidson, John. 'James K. Baxter and the Classics', *Islands* 4, No. 4 (Summer 1975), p. 451.

Davidson, John. 'Catullus, Horace and Baxter', *Islands* 5, No. 1 (September 1976), p. 86.

Weir, J. E. and Lyon, Barbara A. (Eds). *A Preliminary Bibliography of Works by and Works about James K. Baxter*. Christchurch: University of Canterbury, 1979. (This has a full list of Baxter's writing including articles in periodicals, his reviews, and references to reviews of his own work. John Thomson has updated this bibliography in the forthcoming *The Oxford History of New Zealand Literature*, edited by Terry Sturm.)

McKay, Frank. 'Baxter's Jerusalem Poetry', *Landfall* 137, Vol. 35, No. 1 (March 1981), pp. 66-76.

James, Trevor. 'Towards the Wanganui: the poetry of James K. Baxter', *London Magazine,* New Series, Vol. 21, No. 12 (March 1982), pp. 20-34.

Proceedings of the CRNLE/SPACLALS Conference, Adelaide. 'Myth, omen, ghost and dream', *Poetry of the Pacific Region* (Ed. Paul Sharrad), 1984, pp. 9-18.

Notes

1. Baxter's notebooks are dated 1936-1967. All 28 volumes are kept at the Hocken Library in Dunedin, Manuscript numbers 704/1-28.
2. The majority of Baxter's letters to his parents, Archibald and Millicent Baxter, reside in the Hocken Library. They are listed under Manuscript number 975/184 unless otherwise stated.
3. All of Baxter's letters to Charles Brasch reside in the Hocken Library in the Brasch Papers collection, Manuscript numbers 996/7.
4. The Department of Education Records can be found in the New Zealand National Archives. They contain S.P.E. 32/2/5/[Part]III. However, S.P.E. 32/2/5/[Part]II can be found in the School Publications records.
5. All letters referred to are written by Baxter to the person(s) listed in the notes, unless otherwise stated.

Periodicals referred to in the Notes:
Arachne a literary journal, Victoria University of Wellington, published by the Literary Society, 1 (January 1950) — 3 (December 1951).
Aumla Journal of the Australasian Universities Modern Language Association, August 1953 —
Canta University of Canterbury Students' Association, Christchurch, 1 (1930) —
Canzona Composers' Association of New Zealand, Wellington 1979 —
Chronicle University of Canterbury, Christchurch 1964 —
Critic Otago University Students' Association, Dunedin, 1 (2 April 1925) —
Craccum University of Auckland Students' Association, Auckland, 1 (10 March 1927) —
Education New Zealand Department of Education, School Publications Branch, Wellington, 1 (February 1948) —
Eikon Palmerston North Teachers' College, Nonesuch society, Palmerston North, 1 (November 1964) — 2 (December 1966).
Here and Now an independent monthly review, Auckland, 1 (October 1949) — 4 no.4 (March 1954); no. 39 (April 1954) — 62 (November 1957).
Hilltop Victoria University of Wellinton, Wellington, nos. 1-3 (April-September 1949). Superseded by *Arachne*.
Image literary magazine, Auckland, 1 (January 1958) — 8 (August 1961).
Islands Dunedin, McIndoe, 1 (Spring 1972) —
Landfall a New Zealand quarterly, Christchurch 1 (March 1947) —
Manuka Auckland Teachers' College, Auckland 1909 —
New Zealand Listener New Zealand Broadcasting Corporation magazine, Wellington, 1 (30 June 1939) —
New Zealand Monthly Review, Christchurch 1 (May 1960) -
New Zealand Poetry Yearbook Wellington, 1 (1951) — 11 (1964).
New Zealand Tablet New Zealand's national Catholic weekly, Dunedin, 1 (3 May 1873) —
Numbers Wellington, 1 (July 1954) — 10 (October 1959).
Poetry New Zealand Christchurch, Pegasus Press, vol. 1 (1971) —
Spike Victoria University of Wellington Students' Association, Wellington, 1961.
Year Book of the Arts in New Zealand Wellington, no. 1 (1945) — 7 (1951).
Zealandia Auckland 1 (10 May 1934) —

Notes

I: The Ancestral Face

1. Lines of W. H. Auden, used by Baxter to open his address 'Recent Trends in New Zealand Poetry' 1951.
2. *James K. Baxter as Critic*, Frank McKay (ed.), Heinemann (Auckland, 1977), p. 100. Hereafter known as *Baxter as Critic*.
3. *Baxter as Critic*, p. 3. The distilling of whisky can easily be dismissed as an example of his fantasy. There is usually some basis in fact for what Baxter says. Two of the best known illicit stills in Otago and Southland were at Hokonui and Saddle Hill, Brighton. Cf. Erik Olssen, *A History of Otago*, John McIndoe Ltd (Dunedin 1984), p. 45.
4. *The Otago Witness*, 2 February 1861, p. 5; *The Story of the s.s. Lady Egidia* [an immigrant ship of 1860], W. H. Davidson (ed.), Lady Egidia Centenary Committee (Dunedin 1961), p. 21.
5. *The Story of the s.s. Lady Egidia*, p. 21.
6. *A History of Otago*, p. 39.
7. *The History of Otago*, A. H. McLintock, Otago Centennial Historical Publications (Dunedin 1949), pp. 244, 246. They were near the present junction of High and Rattray Streets with Dowling Street, at the foot of Church (later Bell) Hill.
8. Xerox in Hocken Library, 19 June 1859.
9. *The Memoirs of Millicent Baxter*, Millicent Baxter, Cape Catley Ltd (Whatamongo Bay, Queen Charlotte Sound, New Zealand 1981) p. 118.
10. The McColls have always claimed to know the murderer's identity and they have handed down a name as a family secret. James K. Baxter was told by his great-uncle Hugh McColl that Campbell's murderer was Hugh Roy McColl. Hugh escaped the gallows because his brother gave false evidence against James Stewart, a man from whom he had received many kindnesses. I have presented the view taken by the Baxters as represented by Millicent. A different opinion has been argued by Sir James Fergusson in *The White Hind*, (Faber and Faber, London 1963), pp. 133–79. Robert Louis Stevenson presented his own version of the mystery in *Kidnapped* and *Catriona*. James K. Baxter gave the murder an original twist and set it in Otago in his poem 'The Debt'.
11. Millicent said that Archie saw such things quite often, and speculated that it was some form of 'Highland second sight'. In *The Man on the Horse* (University of Otago, Dunedin 1967) one of James's ancestors, Chennor, appears to him in a Brighton gully at dusk. He wears a plaid over his shoulders and has in his hands the needles of shining black wood the clan used for thatching their houses.
12. Hocken MS 975/195.
13. *We Will Not Cease*, Archibald Baxter, Victor Gollanz Ltd (London 1939) p. 9.
14. Radio New Zealand, Replay Radio, 'The History of Peacemaking in New Zealand' Part 1.
15. *We Will Not Cease*, p. 9.
16. Conversation with Millicent Baxter. My first interview with Millicent Baxter was in January 1978. I spoke with her many times after that date, right up to a few months before her death in 1984.
17. *Armageddon or Calvary: The Conscientious Objectors of New Zealand and The Process of Their Conversion*, H. E. Holland, (Wellington 1919), p. 57.
18. Ibid. p. 31.
19. *We Will Not Cease*, p. 66.
20. *Armageddon or Calvary*, p. 48.
21. *We Will Not Cease*, p. 103.
22. Ibid. pp. 105–6.
23. Ibid. p. 131.
24. *Armageddon or Calvary*, p. 50.
25. Ibid. p. 164.
26. Ibid. p. 87.

27. This material has been drawn from *The Memoirs of John Macmillan Brown*, University of Canterbury (Christchurch 1974), as well as from the memories of relatives and acquaintances of Macmillan Brown.
28. *Memoirs of John Macmillan Brown*, p. 32.
29. *Scholar Errant*, R. M. Burdon, Pegasus Press (Christchurch 1956), p. 25.
30. *Memoirs of John Macmillan Brown*, p. 186.
31. *The University of New Zealand*, J. C. Beaglehole, New Zealand Council for Educational Research (Wellington 1937), p. 366.
32. *Memoirs of John Macmillan Brown*, p. 32.
33. *Memoirs of Millicent Baxter*, p. 28.
34. I was told this by a close personal friend of Millicent's.
35. *Memoirs of Millicent Baxter*, p. 29.
36. *Memoirs of John Macmillan Brown*, p. 214.
37. Conversation with Frances Mulrennan.
38. *The University of Otago: A Centennial History*, W. P. Morrell, University of Otago Press (Dunedin 1969), p. 126.
39. *Memoirs of Millicent Baxter*, p. 56.

II: The Colour of Identity

1. Published in *Armageddon or Calvary*, p. 49; and in *Memoirs of Millicent Baxter*, p. 51 - where two sentences are omitted.
2. *Memoirs of Millicent Baxter*, p. 63.
3. In a letter to Lawrence Baigent (5 May 1945), Baxter explains the origin of his second name, Keir, and Terence's first: 'my brother is named after Terence MacSwiney, the great Irish hunger striker'. Baxter misspelt MacSwiney in 'An Ode to the Reigning Monarch on the Occasion of Her Majesty's Visit to Pig Island' (CP 266-7).
4. Letter from Terence's wife, Mrs Lenore Baxter, 7 July 1985.
5. Millicent told John Weir, who became the editor of Baxter's poems, that when Hardie visited New Zealand, well before she met Archie, they both heard him speak at a meeting in Dunedin.
6. Archie was at Kuri Bush in 1931 and living in Brighton by 1932. See Stones' *Otago and Southland Directory*, Post Office Records.
7. *Memoirs of Millicent Baxter*, p. 72.
8. Looking back on the incident, his mother commented, 'At six or forty-six he had no prudence whatsoever.'
9. 'Notes on the Education of a New Zealand Poet' in *The Man on the Horse*, p. 130.
10. Ibid. p. 124. The poem contained some fifty lines, but when he began the regular practice of transcribing all his poems into small black notebooks, all he could remember were these opening lines.
11. 'Notes on the Education of a New Zealand Poet' in *The Man on the Horse*, p. 132.
12. Conversation with Terence Baxter, 8 July 1984.
13. 'Notes on the Education of a New Zealand Poet' in *The Man on the Horse*, p. 132.
14. Ibid. p. 132.
15. Ibid. pp. 130-1.
16. *Memoirs of Millicent Baxter*, p. 75.
17. *Baxter as Critic*, p. 2.
18. 'Notes on the Education of a New Zealand Poet' in *The Man on the Horse*, p. 131.
19. Conversation with Bob Craigie, May 1982.
20. Conversation with Millicent Baxter.
21. *Memoirs of Millicent Baxter*, p. 70.
22. This is what Millicent had told Frances Mulrennan.
23. *Baxter as Critic*, p. 51.

24. *Memoirs of John Macmillan Brown*, p. xxxiv. From the section of the introduction written by James K. Baxter.
25. Letter from Viola's daughter, Mrs Antonietta Baldachino.
26. The authors of *A History of the University of Canterbury 1873-1973*, felt that Canterbury College took much of its early character from Macmillan Brown. (W. J. Gardner, E. T. Beardsley, T. E. Carter, *A History of the University of Canterbury 1873-1973*, University of Canterbury, Christchurch 1973, p. 88.) Keith Sinclair regarded him as a great man. (See *A History of the University of Auckland 1883-1983*, (AUP/OUP, Auckland 1983), p. 80.) All in all he was, as Charles Brasch put it, 'one of the intellectual dynamos and steam-rollers of his time.'(See *Indirections: A Memoir 1909-1947*, OUP, Wellington 1980, p. 119.)
27. Even when he was an established writer he could not muster enough sympathy for his grandfather to complete the straightforward commission of editing his *Memoirs*. He was simply bored and threw up the task in frustration. When the book came out in 1954, edited by someone else, he contributed an introductory essay which reveals the ambiguity of his attitude. He wrote of his grandfather in Section 3 of the introduction: 'No doubt if he were alive today he would find his grandson uneasy company. As a pioneer in education, whose labour and devotion helped to shape our society, he would find it hard to understand the view of a descendant that the pioneer ideals were constricting and even destructive.' Nevertheless he conceded: 'I am haunted by this ancestral voice which insists that the intellectual and moral betterment of mankind is achievable and should be every sane man's goal and concern.'
28. 'Notes on the Education of a New Zealand Poet' in *The Man on the Horse*, pp. 132-3.
29. Most of the copies of the first edition of *We Will Not Cease* were destroyed in the blitz so its circulation was severely limited. Only with the Caxton Press reprint of 1968 did it reach a wide readership in New Zealand. Cape Catley Ltd. brought out further reprints in 1980 and 1983.
30. 'Notes on the Education of a New Zealand Poet' in *The Man on the Horse*, p. 123.
31. Letter from Mr Barrie Naylor, 16 October 1983.
32. 'Notes on the Education of a New Zealand Poet' in *The Man on the Horse*, p. 133.
33. *Memoirs of Millicent Baxter*, p. 84.
34. Ibid. p. 93.
35. Letter from Harold Pugmire, 3 September 1985.
36. 'Notes on the Education of a New Zealand Poet' in *The Man on the Horse*, p. 135.
37. Others are 'The Ice Spirit' 'The Ocean Spirit' 'The Flower Spirit' and 'The Cloud Spirit'.
38. Hocken MS 975/187.
39. Ibid.
40. 'Notes on the Education of a New Zealand Poet' in *The Man on the Horse*, p. 135.
41. Conversation with Millicent Baxter.
42. Letter from Margaret Hargreave, 17 November 1983.
43. Ibid.
44. Hocken MS 975/187.
45. A copy of this poem was sent to me by Mr Barrie Naylor.
46. 'Notes on the Education of a New Zealand Poet' in *The Man on the Horse*, pp. 133-4.
47. Ibid. pp. 134-5.
48. Letter, School Publications 32/2/5 III, 26 October 1956.
49. 'Notes on the Education of a New Zealand Poet' in *The Man on the Horse*, p. 135.
50. Hocken MS 975/187.
51. 'Notes on the Education of a New Zealand Poet' in *The Man on the Horse*, p. 136.
52. Letter to Archibald and Millicent Baxter.
53. Ibid. Baxter's letters to his parents are in this manuscript, dated 1 November, 1939.
54. 14 June 1939.
55. Ibid.

56. 'Notes on the Education of a New Zealand Poet' in *The Man on the Horse*, p. 135.
57. Ibid. p. 136.
58. Letter from Harold Pugmire, 12 November 1983.
59. Hocken MS 975/197.
60. 'I from high windows' Notebook 5, p. 72.
61. Letter to Mrs Lenore Baxter, 7 July 1985.
62. 'Notes on the Education of a New Zealand Poet' in *The Man on the Horse*, p. 121.
63. Ibid. p. 130.
64. Ibid. p. 124. Millicent Baxter writes in her *Memoirs*: 'Jim sailed happily through primary school. I don't think the frightful agonies described in his poems assailed him at that time.' She thought he had invented them because his reading told him poets were meant to have an unhappy childhood.
65. 'Notes on the Education of a New Zealand Poet' in *The Man on the Horse*, p. 122.
66. Ibid. p. 132.
67. 'On Returning to Dunedin' *Otago Daily Times*, 22 September 1966, p. 4.
68. Letter from Mrs Lenore Baxter, 17 July 1985.

III: King's High School 1940-1943

1. *The Man on the Horse*, p. 126.
2. Letter to Noel Ginn, undated, 1945.
3. *A History of Otago*, p. 160.
4. Another Burn prize that year was awarded to John McIndoe, who was to become a well-known Dunedin publisher.
5. *Islands* 2, No. 1 (Autumn 1973), pp. 2-3.
6. Notebook 5, pp. 93.
7. Letter from Millicent Baxter to Lincoln Efford, 28 September 1944. Alexander Turnbull Library, Lincoln Efford MS Papers 445 3 Millicent Baxter.
8. 'Ignorance' in Notebook 2, pp. 56-7. Cf. also 'The Tree of Life' Notebook 4, p. 135.
9. Notebook 4, pp. 37-8.
10. 'Notes on the Education of a New Zealand Poet' in *The Man on the Horse*, p. 123.
11. Letter to Noel Ginn, 28 August 1942.
12. 'Notes on the Education of a New Zealand Poet' in *The Man on the Horse*, p. 137.
13. Ibid. pp. 123–4.
14. Letter to Noel Ginn, 4 May 1943.
15. *Canta*, University of Canterbury Students' Association, 7 July 1948 (Christchurch 1948), p. 4.
16. Letter to Noel Ginn, 12 February 1943.
17. Letter in private hands.
18. 'Notes on the Education of a New Zealand Poet' in *The Man on the Horse*, p. 128.
19. Ibid. p. 137.
20. Ibid. p. 123.
21. Ibid. p. 123.
22. Ibid. p. 126.
23. Conversation with Noel Ginn, February 1987.
24. Letter to Noel Ginn, 14 March 1943.
25. *Prophets Without Honour*, Frederic V. Grunfeld, Hutchinson of London (London 1979), p. 16.
26. Letter to Noel Ginn, 29 November 1943.
27. Letter to Noel Ginn, 16 April 1943.
28. Letter to Noel Ginn, 4 May 1943.
29. Letter to Noel Ginn, 14 June 1943.
30. Letter to Noel Ginn, 11 September 1943.
31. Letter to Noel Ginn, 4 October 1943.

32. Letter to Noel Ginn, 6 November 1943.
33. Letter to Noel Ginn, 1 November 1943.
34. Letter to Noel Ginn, 29 November 1943.
35. Letter to Noel Ginn, 15 November 1943.

IV: The Making of a Poet

1. Letter to Noel Ginn, 12 January 1944.
2. Letter to Noel Ginn, 10 February 1944.
3. Letter to Noel Ginn, 19 February 1944.
4. Letter to Noel Ginn, 25 May 1944.
5. *Critic*, 4 May 1944, p. 6.
6. *Critic*, 7 September 1944, p. 4.
7. *The Spike* (1961), p. 61.
8. 'With Stubble and Overcoat' *N.Z. Listener* 1364, 26 November 1965, p. 25.
9. Letter to Noel Ginn, 25 May 1944.
10. Much later Baxter became a friend of Sargeson and a great admirer of his work. He wrote in a letter to Sargeson (1 December 1955): 'Your prose has the guts and hardness which I would like to see in New Zealand poetry including my own.' (Alexander Turnbull Library, Frank Sargeson, MS Papers 432.)
11. Letter to Noel Ginn, 3 June 1944.
12. Letter to Noel Ginn, 3 June 1944. Comma supplied after 'atheist'.
13. Ibid. Baxter misspelt 'consanguinity' as 'consanguineity'.
14. Ibid.
15. Letter to Noel Ginn, 16 July 1944.
16. Ibid.
17. Noel Ginn, pers. comm.
18. *Spring Fires: A Study in New Zealand Writing*, O. E. Burton, Pilgrim Press (Auckland 1956), p. 25.
19. Ibid.
20. Letter to Noel Ginn, 13 September 1944.
21. Letter to Margaret Hargreave, 3 February 1944.
22. Millicent wrote to Lincoln Efford on 14 August and told her that they would be there from 29-31 August.
23. *Chronicle* 20, No. 5 (4 April 1985), University of Canterbury (Christchurch 1985).
24. Conversation with Lawrence Baigent.
25. Letter to Noel Ginn, 13 September 1944.
26. Ibid.
27. Ibid.
28. Ibid.
29. 26(?) November 1944. The 6.1.1944 on the letter is clearly an error.
30. Much later the farm contributed to the atmosphere and general situation of his play *The Devil & Mr Mulcahy*, though its events are far more sensational than anything he knew at Purakanui.
31. Letter to Noel Ginn, 26 November 1944.

V: First Book, First Love

1. 'Essay on the Higher Learning' in *The Spike* (1961), p. 62.
2. Letter to Lawrence Baigent, 24 February 1945.
3. 'A Writer's Vocation' in *Manuka* (1958), p. 11.
4. 'Essay on the Higher Learning' in *The Spike* (1961), p. 62.
5. 'A Writer's Vocation' in *Manuka* (1958), p. 11.
6. Ibid.

7. Letter to Lawrence Baigent, 4 March 1945.
8. Letter to Lawrence Baigent, 10 March 1945.
9. Interview with Denis Glover, 1979.
10. Conversation with Allen Curnow, 18 May 1982.
11. *A Book of New Zealand Verse 1923-45*, Allen Curnow (ed.), The Caxton Press (Christchurch 1945), pp. 54-5.
12. Letter to Lawrence Baigent, 15 November 1944.
13. Letter to Noel Ginn, 11 August 1943.
14. *A Book of New Zealand Verse 1923-45*, p. 55.
15. Letter to Lawrence Baigent, 27 October 1944.
16. Letter to Noel Ginn, 16 January 1943.
17. Letter to Noel Ginn, 4 July 1943.
18. A clue to the poem's meaning was given at a poetry reading a few months before Baxter's death. In response to a request to read 'the poem on your father' he responded with a magnificent rendering, without any help from a text, of 'Song of the Sea-Nymphs'. Archie was one of those who did not cease to grieve.
19. Letter to Noel Ginn, undated. [I would estimate July, 1943. On 4 July 1943 Ginn had asked for his copy of *New Bearings* by F. R. Leavis back. In the undated letter, Baxter says he will send it in in about 5 days.]
20. Letter to Noel Ginn, 3 June 1944.
21. Letter to Lawrence Baigent, 5 May 1945. John Weir, the editor of Baxter's *Collected Poems*, has suggested that the habit of seeing the poems in terms other than those of their ostensible subject is apparent also from the very first of Baxter's poetry notebooks, begun when he was eleven. Each poem has beside it a letter of the alphabet. D presumably stands for death, S for sex, and L for love.
22. Letter to Noel Ginn, 16 July 1944.
23. Letter to Lawrence Baigent, 25 June 1945.
24. Letter to Noel Ginn, 1 May 1945.
25. Letter to Noel Ginn, 8 April 1945.
26. Letter to Lawrence Baigent, 24 March 1945.
27. Letter to Lawrence Baigent, 17 March 1945.
28. Letter to Lawrence Baigent, 8 April 1945.
29. Letter to Lawrence Baigent, 5 May 1945.
30. Letter to Noel Ginn, 23 June 1945.
31. Letter to Lawrence Baigent, 25 June 1945.
32. Ibid.
33. Ibid.
34. Letter to Lawrence Baigent, 12 October 1945.
35. Ibid.
36. Letter to Archibald Baxter, 23 September 1945.
37. Letter to Millicent Baxter, 1 October 1945.
38. Ibid.
39. Letter to Lawrence Baigent, 15 October 1945.
40. 'Notes on the Education of a New Zealand Poet' in *The Man on the Horse*, pp. 129-30.
41. Letter to Millicent Baxter, 15 October 1945.
42. Ibid.
43. Letter to Millicent Baxter, Labour Day, 1945.
44. Letter to Lawrence Baigent, 12 October 1945.
45. Undated but written from the sheep farm in Wanaka in 1945. Hocken MS 975/183.
46. Letter to Lawrence Baigent, 12 October 1945.
47. Ibid.
48. Letter to Millicent Baxter, 15 October 1945.
49. Interview with Canon Paul Osterreicher, April 1987.
50. Noel Ginn, pers. comm., 13 January 1983.

51. Conversation with Terence Baxter, 8 July 1984.
52. Letter to Lawrence Baigent, 26 March 1946.
53. 'Sunday: Chingford Park'. Found among Baxter's letters to Baigent. It is dedicated to his mother.
54. In later years he attributed the colour of his complexion, 'this wattled Adam' to an excess of cholesterol caused by years of drinking a great deal of milk.
55. *Reluctant Editor*, Monte Holcroft, A.H. & A.W. Reed (Wellington 1969), p. 119.
56. 'Notes on the Education of a New Zealand Poet' in *The Man on the Horse*, p. 138.
57. *Baxter as Critic*, p. 29.
58. 'Notes on the Education of a New Zealand Poet' in *The Man on the Horse*, p. 138.
59. Letter to Rae Munro, 9 July 1957.
60. Ibid.
61. 'With Stubble and Overcoat' *N.Z. Listener* 1364, 26 October 1965, p. 25.
62. 'Notes on the Education of a New Zealand Poet' in *The Man on the Horse*, pp. 140-1.

VI: A Seeding Time

1. 'Essay on the Higher Learning' in *The Spike* (1961), p. 63.
2. Ibid. p. 61.
3. Conversation with Leo Bensemann, 1979.
4. *Landfall Country*, chosen by Charles Brasch, Caxton Press (Christchurch Press 1962), p. 14.
5. *Indirections*, Charles Brasch, Oxford University Press (Wellington, 1980), p. 421.
6. Conversation with Leo Bensemann.
7. Interview with Denis Glover, 1978.
8. Letter to Millicent Baxter, June 1948.
9. Letter to Archibald and Millicent Baxter, undated 1948.
10. Ibid.
11. 'Two Personal Memories of James K. Baxter' in *Islands* 2, No. 1 (Autumn 1973), p. 3.
12. Conversation with Colin McCahon, 17 May 1982.
13. 'Art in Canterbury' in *Landfall* 2, No. 1 (March 1948), p. 50.
14. 'Beginnings' in *Landfall* 20, No. 4 (December 1966), p. 364.
15. Letter to Archibald and Millicent Baxter, undated, September 1948.
16. Letter to Millicent Baxter, [June] 1948.
17. Letter to Charles Brasch, 28 July 1948.
18. Letter to Archibald and Millicent Baxter, [September] 1948.
19. 'Notes on the Making of "The Martian" ', Weir Papers, University of Canterbury.
20. Letter to Noel Ginn, 16 January 1943.
21. Conversation with James K. Baxter, 1961.
22. Letter to Noel Ginn, 10 February 1944.
23. Conversation with Alistair Campbell, 5 May 1982.
24. *Landfall* 2, No. 3 (September 1948), p. 233.
25. *Schindler's Ark*, Thomas Keneally, Hodder and Stoughton, 3rd imprint (London 1982), p. 150.
26. Conversation with Colin McCahon, 17 May 1982.
27. Pers. comm.
28. *Canta*, 9 April 1952, pp. 1, 8.
29. Letter to Archibald and Millicent Baxter, undated 1948.
30. Ibid.
31. Letter to Archibald and Millicent Baxter, [October] 1948.
32. Letter to Millicent Baxter, undated 1948.

VII: The Young Married Man

1. 11 December 1948.
2. 30 June 1949.
3. Ibid.
4. Letter to Hella Hofmann, 30 June 1949.
5. Letter to Millicent Baxter, 14 July 1949.
6. Letter to Charles Brasch, 8 April 1949.
7. 30 June 1949.
8. 8 April 1949.
9. Conversation with Richard Campion, November 1983.
10. Letter in private hands, 18 May 1949.
11. 28 January 1955.
12. *Hilltop* 1, No. 2 (June 1949), p. 27.
13. 4 November 1949.
14. Letter to Archibald and Millicent Baxter, 30 June 1949.
15. Letter to Millicent Baxter, 7 September 1949.
16. Letter to Archibald and Millicent Baxter, 4 November 1949.
17. Letter to Archibald and Millicent Baxter, 16 July 1950.
18. Conversation with Denis Glover, 5 June 1978.
19. 'Essay on the Higher Learning' in *The Spike* (1961), p. 64.
20. Ibid. He inaccurately states he did Greek History Art and Literature extra-murally. He meant part-time.
21. Letter to Archibald and Millicent Baxter, 16 July 1950.
22. Ibid.
23. *Hilltop* 1, No. 3 (September 1949), p. 3.
24. *Arachne* 1, No. 1 (January 1950), p. 26.
25. *Baxter as Critic*, p. 4.
26. Conversation with Patrick Macaskill, 21 June 1983.
27. Johnson was the founding editor of the *New Zealand Poetry Yearbook*.
28. Conversation with Patrick Macaskill, 21 June 1983.
29. Ibid.
30. N.Z.B.C. Broadcast 2YC, 24 March 1978.
31. Ibid.
32. Wellington Teachers' College Records.
33. Letter in W. J. Scott estate, dated 7 February 1956.
34. *Poems Unpleasant*, James K. Baxter, Louis Johnson, and Anton Vogt, Pegasus Press (Christchurch 1952).
35. *Recent Trends in New Zealand Poetry*, James K. Baxter, The Caxton Press (Christchurch 1951). Text of a talk given by Baxter at Canterbury University College during the New Zealand Writers' Conference, 8-11 May 1951. Brasch wished to publish it in *Landfall* but Baxter had already promised it to Glover. He also felt that since it was a talk it would have to be polished up. He was reluctant to do that. Letter to Brasch, 27 May 1951.
36. Conversation with John Garrett, 1980.
37. *Landfall* 5, No. 3 (September 1951), p. 222.
38. *Critic*, 7 June 1951, p. 8.
39. *Recent Trends in New Zealand Poetry*, p. 9.
40. Ibid. p. 16.
41. Ibid. p. 17.
42. Ibid. p. 18.
43. *Autobiography*, Eric Gill, Jonathan Cape (London 1940), p. 282. Gill was a writer whose life parallels Baxter's own. Both became converts to Catholicism, and Gill's attempt

to achieve a fully integrated life in a Christian community at Ditchling in Sussex could be compared to Baxter's involvement in the community at Jerusalem.

44. *Recent Trends in New Zealand Poetry*, p. 19.
45. Ibid.
46. Letter to Charles Brasch, 17 October 1955.
47. 'Conversation with Frank Sargeson (II)' *Landfall* 24, No. 2 (June 1970), p. 152.
48. 6 December 1960, This could also be said of the sexually explicit letters he sometimes wrote to women friends at various times in his life. He could also write a coarse letter to disabuse people of the notion that he was a holy man. Cf. 'Letter to John Weir', 11 March 1961.
49. Notebook 22 [1961].
50. Conversation with Brian Brake, 24 July 1983. Letter from R. D. Dick, 5 September 1983.
51. 28 July 1961.
52. 1 September 1954, Epuni School Records.
53. 11 April 1954.
54. Letter to Charles Brasch, 28 September 1965.
55. *N.Z. Listener* 866, 9 March 1956, p. 12.
56. *Numbers* 5, No. 1 (May 1956), p. 29.
57. John Weir kindly drew this to my attention.
58. *We New Zealanders*, A. R. D. Fairburn, Progressive Publishing Society (Wellington, no date), p. 59.
59. *The Fire and the Anvil*, James K. Baxter, New Zealand University Press (Wellington 1955), p. 74.
60. Ibid. p. 24.
61. Ibid. p. 23.
62. Ibid. p. 48.
63. Ibid. p. 56.
64. Letter to Millicent Baxter, 7 August 1954.
65. 'the last will and testament of james q oxter', Notebook 20.
66. See *James K. Baxter*, Charles Doyle, Twayne Publishers (Boston 1976), p. 64. An illustration of the feeling for Thomas among New Zealand writers of the 1950s is that when he died in 1953, Wellington paid tribute to him with a poetry reading. Baxter, Curnow, Brasch, Johnson, and Vogt took part.
67. Letter to Rae Munro, 9 July 1957; Letter to Charles Brasch, 20 October 1955.
68. 'Elegy for an Unknown Soldier' *Collected Poems*, p. 67.
69. Letter to Charles Brasch, 20 October 1955.
70. Letter in private hands, 21 February 1958.
71. She was the widow of Hurst Seagar, an early Christchurch architect and a man with innovative ideas on domestic architecture. He tried to discover a style suitable for New Zealand conditions. He designed the Chamber of Commerce building beside the Worcester Street bridge and the first section of the Christchurch Sanatorium, including the morgue which was the subject of his nephew's poem titled 'The Morgue'.
72. Terence was under the impression at the time that his share had been left to him by his aunt, and did not learn until much later than he owed it to his brother's generosity.
73. *Alcoholics Anonymous*, 2nd revised edition, (New York 1955), p. 438.
74. Ibid. p. 59.
75. Letter in private hands, 9 July 1957.
76. *Alcoholics Anonymous*, p. 59.
77. Ibid. p. 59.
78. Ibid. p. 97.
79. Ibid. p. 564.
80. Ibid. p. 565.
81. Letter to Rae Munro, 9 July 1957.

82. Ibid.
83. Ibid.
84. Ibid.
85. Letter to Millicent Baxter, November 1962.
86. *The London Magazine* 6, No. 2 (1959), p. 69. Fuller read the poem in *In Fires of No Return* which was published in London in 1958 by Oxford University Press.
87. Letter to Millicent and Archibald Baxter, 4 November 1954.
88. *the flowering cross*, James K. Baxter, New Zealand Tablet (Dunedin 1969), p. 29.

VIII: The Path to Rome

1. 'Essay on the Higher Learning' p. 64.
2. Pers. comm., 4 December 1983.
3. 7 February 1956. Hocken MS 975/187.
4. *The New Zealand School Publications Branch* 25, Unesco (Paris 1957), p. 10. [Educational studies and documents]
5. *The New Zealand Scholar*, Margaret Condliffe Memorial Lecture, Canterbury University College, 21 April 1954, Whitcombe and Tomb's Ltd (Christchurch 1954), p. 18.
6. 10 October 1956. S.P.E. 32/2/5/III.
7. 'The Maori Motif' in *Here & Now* 3, No. 5 (December 1952), p. 51.
8. 6 March 1958. S.P.E. 32/2/5/II.
9. Letter to Ruth Dallas, 14 March 1957. S.P.E. 32/2/5/III.
10. Conversation with Malcolm Ross, October 1984. Ruth Ross's article was reprinted in 1972. See 'Tiriti o Waitangi: Texts and Translations' *New Zealand Journal of History* 6, No. 2 (1972), pp. 129-57. It marked the beginning of a new understanding of the treaty in New Zealand.
11. 30 May 1957. S.P.E. 32/2/5/III.
12. 18 October 1956. S.P.E. 32/2/5/III.
13. 9 October 1957. S.P.E. 32/2/5/III.
14. 8 October 1956. S.P.E. 32/2/5/III.
15. 23 November 1960. S.P.E. 32/2/5/II.
16. 9 October 1957. S.P.E. 32/2/5/III.
17. Cf. Letters of 11 October 1956; 10 December 1956; 20 December 1956. S.P.E. 32/2/5/III.
18. *Numbers* 9 (February 1959), p. 64.
19. Letter to Roderick Finlayson, 16 September 1957.
20. *The Fire and the Anvil*, p. 48.
21. Letter to John Weir, 10 May 1962.
22. Letter to Roderick Finlayson, 14 January 1958.
23. Letter to Charles Brasch, 21 April 1957.
24. *Numbers* 5 (May 1956), p. 10.
25. *the flowering cross*, p. 37.
26. Letter to Roderick Finlayson, 14 January 1958. The priest was Father Johnny O'Connor S.M.
27. An uncollected poem, 'For An Anglican Padre' published in *Image* 8 (August 1961), p. 35.
28. *the flowering cross*, pp. 177-8.
29. *the flowering cross*, p. 10.
30. Letter to John Weir, 29 March 1961.
31. Letter to Roderick Finlayson, 12 February 1958.
32. *The Two Baxters*, Pat Lawlor, Millwood Press (Wellington 1979), p. 23.
33. Letter to Roderick Finlayson, 20 April 1960.
34. Labre was an eighteenth century saint who lived in great poverty, devoting his time to

prayer and to the poor. Towards the end of his life he used to sleep in the ruins of the Colosseum.

35. Letter to John Weir, 20 April 1967.
36. Letter to John Weir, 12 August 1959.
37. Letter to Charles Brasch, 28 June 1961.
38. *Landfall* 10, No. 3 (September 1956), p. 180.
39. Baxter had written his play over a period of three and a half weeks while teaching at Epuni during the day. Since he resigned his job as a school-teacher on 4 May 1956, the play must have been written before then. See *N.Z. Listener* 996, 19 September 1958, p. 8.
40. *N.Z. Listener* 996, 19 September 1958, p. 8.
41. *Collected Plays*, p. 3.
42. N.Z.B.C. Interview with Bernard Kearns, July 1979.
43. Baxter said Abelstown, where the play was set, was 'somewhere near Naseby'. *N.Z. Listener* 996, 19 September 1958, p. 8.
44. *Collected Plays*, p. 2.
45. Letter from Frank Sargeson, 24 July 1955. Hocken MS 975/183.

IX: Baxter in Asia

1. Letter to Millicent Baxter, 18 February 1958. S.P.E. 32/2/5/II.
2. Letter to Betty O'Dowd, 9 September 1958.
3. See 'Tokyo 1958' in *Collected Poems*, p. 246.
4. 22 June 1961. S.P.E. 32/2/5/II.
5. 7 October 1958. S.P.E. 32/1/29/I.
6. Letter to Roderick Finlayson, 28 May 1959.
7. 'Notes From India' in *Zealandia* 25, No. 36 (24 December 1958), p. 8.
8. 6 July 1960. S.P.E. 32/2/5/II.
9. 12 May 1963. Letter in private hands.
10. Ibid.
11. Letter to Betty O'Dowd from India, no date.
12. 'Notes From India' in *Zealandia* 25, No. 36, p. 8.
13. 6 July 1960. S.P.E. 32/2/5/II.
14. 'Rabindranath Tagore: An appreciation in his centenary year' *Education* 10, No. 8 (September 1961), p. 241.
15. East Asian Journal, Hocken MS 975/106.
16. Ibid.
17. 'Rabindranath Tagore' in *Education* 10, No. 8, p. 241.
18. Ibid. p. 240.
19. Ibid. p. 240.
20. 'Notes Made in Winter' *New Zealand Poetry Yearbook* 10 (1961-2), p. 7.
21. Letter to Millicent Baxter, 5 January 1959.
22. Letter to Charles Brasch, 15 September 1959.
23. 6 July 1960. S.P.E. 32/2/5/II.
24. *Manuka* (1958), p. 11.
25. Seamus Heaney's phrase about his own work in *Preoccupations*, Faber & Faber (London 1980), p. 56.
26. Letter to Millicent Baxter, 19 May 1959. S.P.E. 32/2/5/II.
27. *N.Z. Listener* 1033, 12 June 1959, p. 11.
28. 4 August 1960. S.P.E. 32/2/5/II.
29. 'Notes From India' in *Zealandia* 25, No. 36, p. 8.
30. Ibid.
31. Letter to Charles Brasch, 28 June 1961.

32. *Recent Poetry in New Zealand*, Charles Doyle (ed.), Collins (Auckland 1965), p. 29. [Baxter's introduction pp. 29-39; poems pp. 31-45.]

X: Pig Island Letters

1. Letter to Betty O'Dowd, 6 August 1959.
2. Notebook 20. For example,

> Dear antelope, I find it hard to like
> Flat-iron, water-bottle, pins and peaches,
> The world you walk in.
>> 'The Husband's Song'

> If women show unkindness
> Should silly husbands blame them
> Who labour in their blindness
> To catch wild birds and tame them?
>> 'Song: Go Tell a Married Maid'

> Lady, your bedroom is Hell's cattle pound
> Where headless bulls go round and round and round.
>> 'To a Would-Be Hetaira'

These three poems remain unpublished.

3. *Numbers* 6 (March 1957), p. 8.
4. 19 May 1959.
5. 'Applied Music' David Farquhar, in *Canzona* 3, No. 10 (November 1981), p. 52.
6. Conversation with Richard Campion, November 1983.
7. Letter to Millicent Baxter, 7 November 1962. S.P.E. 32/2/5/II.
8. Ibid.
9. The production was a success, but the play has been judged a failure. McNaughton, for example, did not consider it worth including in the volume of *Collected Plays*. Campion himself admitted in conversation in November 1983 that 'it was a bit off Baxter's goldmine track.'
10. Pers. comm., John Weir.
11. A comparison of the inclusions in both books show that Curnow's was an anthology *à these*. The Penguin's inclusions are given first, Oxford's in brackets: Baxter 9 (21); Johnson 3 (9); Campbell 2 (7); W. H. Oliver 1 (4); Glover 18 (19); Curnow 12 (15); Mason 18 (12); Brasch 12 (9); Fairburn 15 (15). And Mary Stanley, Peter Bland, Charles Doyle, and Gordon Challis were left out altogether though Baxter and others thought they had all done first-rate work. See 'The Kiwi and Mr Curnow' in *Education* 10, No. 1 (February 1961), p. 27.
12. *The Penguin Book of New Zealand Verse*, Allen Curnow (ed.), Penguin Books (Haromondsworth 1960), p. 61.
13. Letter to Charles Brasch, 28 June 1961.
14. Baxter's phrase in 'The Kiwi and Mr Curnow' p. 29.
15. Letter to Charles Brasch, 28 June 1961.
16. 'Poetry in New Zealand' in *Year Book of the Arts in New Zealand*, vol. 2 (1946), p. 114.
17. Ibid. p. 112.
18. *Baxter as Critic*, p. 82.
19. Points made by W. H. Oliver and quoted by Baxter in 'The Kiwi and Mr Curnow' p. 27.

20. *An Anthology of New Zealand Verse*, selected by Robert Chapman and Jonathon Bennett, Oxford University Press (London 1956), p. xxxii.
21. Letter to Charles Brasch, 6 December 1960.
22. S.P.E. 32/2/5/II.
23. Letter to Noel Ginn, 11 December 1959. S.P.E. 32/2/5/III.
24. Letter from Ruth France to Baxter, 9 November 1962. S.P.E. 32/2/5/II.
25. Letter to Michael Turnbull, 23 July 1959. S.P.E. 32/2/5/III.
26. Letter to Pat Earle, 12 May 1958. S.P.E. 32/2/5/III.
27. Department of Education records.
28. *Collected Plays*, p. 164.
29. Letter to John Weir, 8 October 1962.
30. *Baxter as Critic*, p. 106.
31. *N.Z. Listener* 863, 17 February 1956, p. 16.
32. *Modern Man in Search of a Soul*, Carl Jung, Kegan Paul, Trench, Trubner & Co. Ltd. (London 1934), p. 29.
33. J. E. Weir Letters, University of Canterbury Library.
34. Department of Education records.
35. Pers. comm., 15 September 1989.
36. Published in *New Zealand Monthly Review* 140 (December 1972), p. 8.
37. *Love and Legend: Some 20th Century New Zealanders*, Maurice Shadbolt, Hodder and Stoughton (Auckland 1976), p. 173.
38. Letter in private hands, 26 July 1963.
39. The soap powder dispute lasted for six days, 17-23 July, in 1963. Copies of Baxter's ballad were cyclostyled and given to a select group of people. It was also published in *N.Z. Monthly Review* 140.
40. Letter in private hands, 26 July 1963.
41. Letter in private hands, 13 May 1963.
42. Letter to Maurice Shadbolt, 22 September 1963.
43. Ibid.
44. Letter to Maurice Shadbolt, 22 September 1963. Baxter told Shadbolt that the first Letter was 'about Dunedin, saying more or less - it's a hell of a place to be in, but perhaps we are most ourselves in the jaws of death and hell.'
45. *Baxter as Critic*, p. 107.
46. *The Man on the Horse*, pp. 82-3.
47. Letter to Archibald Baxter, 2 August 1965.
48. *The Man on the Horse*, p. 85.
49. 'Some Comments on Women's Liberation' Hocken MS 975/124, p. 4. He added: 'Once we admit that we are emotionally androgynous the Sex War is nearing its end. But it is very hard for a Kiwi to admit that he is half woman.'
50. Letter to John Weir, 25 February 1967.
51. Letter to Archibald Baxter, 2 August 1965.
52. Letter to John Weir, 25 October 1967.
53. V. S. Pritchett described T. S. Eliot as 'a company of actors inside one suit'. In *T. S. Eliot*, Peter Ackroyd, Abacus (London 1948), p. 118.
54. *Baxter as Critic*, p. 107.
55. 'Notes on the Education of a New Zealand Poet' in *The Man on the Horse*, p. 154.
56. *Baxter as Critic*, p. 28.
57. Ibid. p. 72.
58. See 'Pig Island Letter 3' (CP 278).
59. 'Notes on the Education of a New Zealand Poet, in *The Man on the Horse*, p. 125.
60. *Baxter as Critic*, p. 107.
61. Ibid.
62. Letter to Maurice Shadbolt, 23 April 1965.
63. 'Some Possibilities for New Zealand Drama' Hocken MS 975/117, p. 5.

64. 'Notes on the Education of a New Zealand Poet' in *The Man on the Horse*, p. 122.
65. *The Poetry of James K. Baxter*, J. E. Weir (ed), Oxford University Press (Wellington 1970), pp. 40-1.
66. 'An Interview with James K. Baxter' in *Landfall* 28, No. 3 (September 1974), p. 249.
67. *New Zealand Poetry*, Frank McKay, New Zealand University Press (Wellington 1970), p. 68. Baxter had this remark in mind in the imagery of 'Letter to Frank McKay I'.
68. *Collected Plays*, p. 65.
69. Ibid. p. 329.
70. *Landfall* 28, No. 3 (September 1974), p. 243.
71. Letter to Maurice Shadbolt, 22 September 1963.
72. Letter to James K. Baxter from Vincent Buckley, 12 September 1966. Hocken MS 976/183.
73. Letter to John Weir, 16 February 1967. Denis Glover awarded the Jessie MacKay award for poetry jointly; to Ruth Gilbert for *The Luthier*, and 'the rump end of the prize' to *Pig Island Letters*.
74. *Craccum*, May 1964, p. 9.
75. Letter to Archibald and Millicent Baxter, 25 August 1963. Hocken MS 975/189.
76. Letter to John Weir, 9 August 1965.
77. Letter to James K. Baxter from Millicent Baxter, 7 December 1963.
78. Letter to Millicent Baxter, 22 August 1965.
79. *The Man on the Horse*, pp. 22-3, 68-89.
80. Ibid. p. 22.
81. Letter to Charles Brasch, 8 December 1963.
82. Letter to the Secretary of the State Literary Fund Advisory Committee, 7 December 1963.
83. *N.Z. Listener* 1417, 9 December 1966, p. 13.

XI: City of Our Youth

1. *The Man on the Horse*, p. 11.
2. Letter to the Registrar, University of Otago, 27 August 1966. Hocken MS 975/183.
3. Conversation with Lawrence Jones, 1974.
4. *Landfall* 22, No. 3 (September 1968), p. 244.
5. Letter to Fellowship Committee, 27 August 1966. Hocken MS 975/183.
6. *Landfall* 22, No. 3 (September 1968), p. 245.
7. See 'Shots Around the Target'. Hocken MS 975/127, p. 7. [An Arts Festival Talk, Palmerston North, May 1966. Published in *Eikon* 2 (December 1966), p 18.]
8. Ibid. p. 24.
9. Transcript of a tape-recording provided by Mrs Sutton, Dunedin. Her husband, Peter, had been Chairman of the Dunedin Committee on Vietnam.
10. *Landfall* 22, No. 3 (September 1968), p. 245.
11. Letter to Kevin Ireland, 26 October 1965. Alexander Turnbull Library MS 2587.
12. Introduction to *the flowering cross*, p.4.
13. Letter to John Weir, 18 June 1972.
14. Letter to John Weir, 18 August 1965.
15. 'Poet Writes to Priest' in *The Sunday Times*, 30 April 1972, p. 11.
16. See 'Desert Psalm' *Collected Poems*, p. 488.
17. See 'Ourselves' *Collected Poems*, p. 184.
18. Katherine Mansfield Papers 119, Notebook 39, pp. 119-62. Alexander Turnbull Library.
19. *Recent Trends in New Zealand Poetry*, p. 7.
20. *Landfall* 22, No. 3 (September 1968), pp. 244-5.
21. Letter to Charles Brasch, 18 July 1964.
22. 'The Burns Fellowship' in *Landfall* 22, No. 3 (September 1968), p. 246.

23. Ibid.
24. Letter to John Weir, 19 April 1967.
25. 'At Naseby' (CP 389); 'To Mate With' (CP 399); 'The Chariot' (CP 423); 'Afternoon Walk' (CP 376).
26. 'The Man with the Blue Guitar' in *The Collected Poems of Wallace Stevens*, Faber & Faber (London 1955), p. 165.
27. *Landfall* 22, No. 3 (September 1968), pp. 246-7.
28. Letter to Millicent Baxter, 30 July 1965.
29. Conversation with Rosalie Carey, 1984.
30. *Rosalie and Patric Carey Present the Globe Theatre*, Rosalie Carey and Patric Carey, John McIndoe Ltd (Dunedin 1968), no pagination.
31. Ibid.
32. 'About the Globe Theatre' James K. Baxter, in *Rosalie and Patric Carey Present the Globe Theatre*.
33. Ibid.
34. Conversation with Patric Carey, 25 January 1978.
35. *Collected Plays*, p. 331.
36. Introduction to *The Sore-Footed Man* and *The Temptations of Oedipus* in *Collected Plays*, p. 334.
37. 'Philoctetes Down Under' J. F. Davidson in *Aumla* 47 (May 1977), p. 50.
38. *Baxter as Critic*, p. 220.
39. Conversation with Patric Carey, 1978.
40. *Landfall* 22, No. 3 (September 1968), p. 246.
41. *A Dramatic Appearance*, Peter Harcourt, Methuen (Wellington 1978), p. 130.
42. Three more of his plays were performed at the Globe, *Mr O'Dwyer's Dancing Party* in November 1968, *The Day Flanagan Died* in March 1969, and the seventh and last play in the cycle Baxter wrote for the Globe, *The Temptations of Oedipus*, in April 1970.
43. *A Dramatic Appearance*, p. 130.
44. Review of *The Temptations of Oedipus*, *N.Z. Listener* 1594, 11 May 1970, p. 12.
45. Ibid.
46. Conversation with Patric Carey, 1978.
47. *N.Z. Listener* 1530, 7 February 1969, p. 9.
48. *Baxter as Critic*, pp. 217-18.
49. Ibid. p. 223.
50. 'Some Possibilities for New Zealand Drama' a talk. Hocken MS 975/117, p. 2. [Excerpts published in *Baxter as Critic*, pp. 212-20.]
51. Ibid. p. 12.
52. Ibid. p. 2.
53. Ibid. p. 12.
54. Letter to William Austin, 20 December 1966. N.Z.B.C. Archives.
55. Letter to William Austin, 8 December 1967. N.Z.B.C. Archives.
56. Ibid.
57. 'Drama Among the Faceless' an interview with Arthur Baysting, in *N.Z. Listener* 1530, 7 February 1969, p. 9.
58. *N.Z. Listener* 1457, 8 September 1967, p. 19.
59. When Howard McNaughton's edition of the *Collected Plays* was published in 1982, it contained all of the 'plays which have been successfully produced, and a few shorter pieces which have been undeservedly neglected' (p. xv, *Collected Plays*). The book was well received. Philip Mann, a producer with a profound understanding of theatre, praised the breadth of Baxter's writing and the extent of his innovation. For Mann, *The Day Flanagan Died* 'in which a man's life is raked over and assessed while he lies in his coffin on stage' was the most moving of the plays. It was based on 'Lament for Barney Flanagan' at Patric Carey's suggestion that Baxter should develop something from his own work.

Mervyn Thompson, playwright and critic, considered in his *N.Z. Listener* review of the *Collected Plays* that Baxter 'had the ability to be a major playwright, perhaps this country's greatest. That he is not leaves one saddened; he emerges from the book as New Zealand drama's most spectacular lost cause' (*N.Z. Listener* 2258, 14 May 1983, p. 98). Though conceding that *The Wide Open Cage* was one of the finest works written by a New Zealander, his opinion was that Baxter's dramatic career represented promise rather than achievement.

60. Letter in possession of author.
61. *Landfall* 22, No. 3 (September 1968),p. 245.

XII: The Junkies and the Fuzz

1. *Drug Dependency and Drug Abuse in New Zealand*, Board of Health, First Report 16 February 1970, p. 128.
2. Hocken MS 975/95.
3. Letter to Millicent and Archibald Baxter, 25 June 1969.
4. 'The World of the Junkie' *Thursday Magazine*, 30 October 1969, pp. 10-13.
5. Ibid. p. 11.
6. *Waikato Times*, 15 August 1970, p. 19.
7. *Islands* 1, No. 1 (Spring 1972), p. 27.
8. Ibid. p. 26.
9. See 'Jerusalem Sonnets' No. 24 (CP 466), and 'Complaint to a Friend' (CP 583), written in 1972.
10. Conversation with Roderick Finlayson, November 1984.
11. *N.Z. Listener* 1684, 14 February 1972, p. 45.
12. Conversation with Tim Shadbolt, November 1984.
13. *James Joyce: New and Revised Edition*, Richard Ellman, Oxford University Press (New York, 1983), p. 100.
14. 'Elegy for Boyle Crescent' in *Islands* 1, No. 1, pp. 26, 31.
15. The idea had been developed earlier in England by Dr Maxwell Jones and others.
16. They have, however, been vindicated by the passage of time. In 1982, ten years after Baxter's death, a group using the name 'Narcotics Anonymous' and applying the same ideas was set up in Auckland. Its founders seemed unaware of his experiment.
17. *First Drug Report*, 7 November 1969, p. 103; *Second Drug Report*, 14 October 1971, p. 105.

XIII: The Two Jerusalems

1. *The Maori Wars*, Tom Gibson, Leo Cooper Ltd (London 1974), pp. 135-6; *A Motorist's Guide to the Wanganui River Road*, Wanganui Historical Society (Wanganui 1983), pp. 30-1.
2. Hocken MS 975/168. This is a later formulation but it expresses his original intentions accurately.
3. *Memoirs of Millicent Brown*, p. xxxvi.
4. *Jerusalem Daybook*, James K. Baxter, Price Milburn (Wellington , 1971), p. 53.
5. Ibid. p. 37.
6. 'The Maori in the Towns' *The New Zealand Tablet*, 2 August 1967, pp. 26-7.
7. *Odtaa*, p. 9. (This was a short-lived publication of Massey University, Palmerston North.)
8. Letter to John Weir, 1971.
9. Manuscript poem among the Weir papers.
10. Letter to Millicent and Archibald Baxter, 25 September 1969.
11. Ibid.
12. Letter to Millicent Baxter, 3 November 1969.
13. Letter in possession of Colin Durning. No date.

14. Ibid.
15. Vincent O'Sullivan told me that MacDonald P. Jackson had drawn this to his attention. Baxter had experimented with the form as early as 1962 in 'The Bureaucrats' and 'Easter Sunday'. He also planned to add two more poems, 'Hemi's Song' (beginning: 'My love came through the city') and 'Two Dialogues of Christ and the Church' (beginning: 'My true love and my darling'). Durning thought they would upset the balance of the sequence so they were dropped. They were eventually published in the *Collected Poems*.
16. Cf. Alan Eccleston in *A Staircase for Silence*, Darton, Longman and Todd (London 1977). His discussion of Charles Peguy suggested some useful parallels with Baxter.
17. *The Poems of St John of the Cross*, 7th impression, Roy Campbell (translator), Harvill Press (London 1963), p. 35.
18. *Jerusalem Daybook*, p. 45.
19. *The Man on the Horse*, p. 104.
20. Ibid. p. 120.
21. *Auckland Star*, 29 May 1971.
22. *Jerusalem Daybook*, p. 36.
23. S.P.E. 32/2/5/II, 23 November 1960.
24. *Auckland Star*, 29 May 1971.
25. Hocken MS 975/166.
26. *Jerusalem Daybook*, p. 54.
27. 'God, Man and Universe: A Maori View', Maori Marsden, in M. King (ed.) *Te Ao Hurihuri*, Hicks, Smith & Sons Ltd. (Wellington, 1975), p. 219.
28. *Jerusalem Daybook*, p. 28.
29. Ibid. p. 29.
30. Ibid. p. 37.
31. Ibid. pp. 36-7.
32. *thoughts about the holy spirit*, James K. Baxter, Futuna Press (Karori n.d.), p. 27.
33. *Jerusalem Daybook*, p. 42.
34. Ibid. p. 21.
35. Hocken MS 975/166.
36. 'The Jerusalem Community' Hocken MS 975/166, pp. 67-8.
37. *Jerusalem Daybook*, p. 36.
38. Ibid. p. 46.
39. Ibid. p. 27.
40. Notebook 4, p. 111.
41. *N.Z. Listener* 1520, 22 November 1968, p. 22.
42. *Jerusalem Daybook*, p. 40.
43. Ibid. p. 43.
44. Ibid. p. 22.
45. Ibid. p. 8.
46. Letter in possession of author.
47. 'Baxter at the Cathedral' *The New Zealand Tablet*, 10 June 1970, p. 21.
48. *Jerusalem Daybook*, p. 40.
49. *Autumn Testament*, p. 43.
50. Ibid.
51. 'In Praise of the Taniwha' (CP 514).
52. *Auckland Star*, 29 May 1971.
53. 'The Young Warriors' Hocken MS 975/126.
54. Ibid.
55. *The New Zealand Herald*, 7 April 1971.
56. *The New Zealand Herald*, 15 March 1971.
57. *Jerusalem Daybook*, p. 16.
58. Alan Eccleston's phrase from *A Staircase for Silence*.

59. Ibid.
60. *Auckland Star*, 17 September 1972.
61. Hocken MS 975/98.
62. *Jerusalem Daybook*, p. 37.
63. *The Two Baxters*, p. 85.
64. *Jerusalem Daybook*, p. 15.
65. Ibid. p. 16.

XIV: The Arms of Hine-nui-te-po

1. When Baxter stayed at Newman Hall in Auckland for some weeks in May, Father O'Sullivan suggested that he write some articles about the Captivity Letters of St Paul since they seemed especially relevant to support his idea. Baxter finished them in August. They first appeared in *Zealandia* and were later collected in a booklet, *thoughts about the holy spirit* (Futuna Press, Wellington, 1983).
2. Letter in private hands.
3. 'In Memoriam: James K. Baxter' in *the scenic route*, Fleur Adcock, Oxford University Press (London, 1974), pp. 16-17.
4. Manuscript in possession of author.
5. Dr Cherry Hankin of the University of Canterbury lent me her tape.
6. Conversation with Father Terry Dibble, 2 November 1984.
7. Conversation with Greg, 22 October 1982.
8. A priest faced with a case in the confessional which appears to be beyond his jurisdiction may give a conditional absolution.
9. Letters to John Weir, 10 May 1962; 19 December 1962.
10. Some years later, after hearing radio programmes about Liberation Theology, Michael Illingworth finally came to understand Baxter's proposal.
11. The clip of the programme has been assembled with other material into a film and is still in some demand from the New Zealand Film Unit.

Index

Adcock, Fleur, 277
Alcoholics Anonymous (A.A.), 145-50, 157
Angus, Rita, 85
artists in Christchurch, 100, 102
Aubert, Mother Mary, 255
Auckland, 240-54
Awhitu, Father Wiremu Te, 255, 260, 289-90
Aylmer, Jane, 95-7, 118, 200
Aylmer, Stanley, 95

Baigent, Lawrence, 75-7, 80-9 *passim*, 100, 102
Bangkok, 169
Barker, Arthur and Shirley, 120, 127
Baxter, Archibald McColl Learmond, (father),
    in army, 8-10, 20
    birth, 5
    Catholic conversion, 204-6
    as farmer, 6-8, 21-3
    marriage of, 21
    migrates, 1
    pacificism of, 8, 24-6, 34, 55
Baxter, Billie (uncle), 5
Baxter, Donald (uncle), 5
Baxter, Hilary Anne (daughter), 121, 236, 238, 269
Baxter, Hugh (uncle), 5
Baxter, Isabel (great aunt), 1
Baxter, Jacquie (née Jacquie Sturm, *q.v.*),
    academic studies of, 125
    and death of James, 288-9
    family life with James, 288-9
    in India, 170, 174-5
    Maori roots, 97, 239-40
    mother dies, 204
    separation from James, 157-9
    working in Wellington Public Library, 257-8
Baxter, James Keir,
    affair with Jane Aylmer, 95-7
    and alcoholism, 104, 144-50
    ancestry, Gaelic, 1
    Anglican confirmation, 122-3
    in Auckland, 240-54
    in Bangkok, 169
    bawdy verse of, 134-5
    birth of, 22-3

and boarding schools, 45-6
book reading by, 26
Brighton, influence of, 29-30, 46-7
and Buddhism, 265
bullied at school, 54-5
burial of, 290
at Burnside Freezing Works, 92
and cadet training, 53-4, 57
and Calvinism, 201-2
Catholic baptism, 159
at Catholic Education Office, 214-15
and Catholicism, 156-62 *passim*, 178-9, 216-19
at Canterbury University College, 100-19
caving, 29-30
and Caxton Press, 101-2
childhood, 24
in Christchurch, 100-19
Christian commitment, 123
with Columban Fathers at Choshi, 168
and communal work, 267
at commune, Mount Eden, 281
countryside, influence of, 29-30, 46-7
daughter, birth of, 121
and death, 59, 277-9
death of, 288-9
and domestic life, 181-2
as dramatist, 163-5, 182-6 *passim*, 228-35
drinking problem of, 93, 124, 128, 143-4
and drugs, 241-54
as editor, 143, 151-4
education, critical of New Zealand, 60
at Education Department, 151-4
at Epuni School, 138, 151
exhaustion of, 236
as family man, 155
at Friends School, 32-3
and girls, 71
graduates BA, 151
in Grafton, 241-54
guilt complex of, 115-16
idealism of, 264
ill health of, 175, 182
in India, 169-74
and industrial relations, 195
at iron foundry, 79, 86
in Japan, 166-9